SARAJEVO ROSES

War memoir of a peacekeeper

SARAJEVO ROSES

War memoir of a peacekeeper

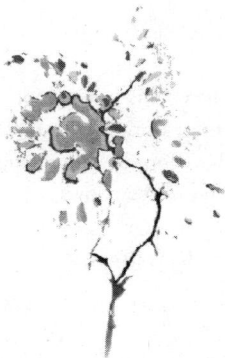

Anné Mariè du Preez Bezdrob

Oshun

Published by Oshun Books
an imprint of Struik Publishers
(a division of New Holland Publishing (South Africa) (Pty) Ltd)
PO Box 1144, Cape Town, 8000]

New Holland Publishing is a member of Johnnic Communications Ltd

First published 2004

1 3 5 7 9 10 8 6 4 2

Publication © Oshun Books 2004
Text © Anné Mariè du Preez Bezdrob

Publishing manager: Michelle Matthews
Editor: Olivia Rose-Innes
Cover design: iaminawe
Text design and typesetting: Sean Robertson
Production controller: Valerie Kommer

Set in 9.5 pt on 14 pt Sabon
Reproduction by Hirt & Carter (Cape) (Pty) Ltd
Printed and bound by Paarl Print, Oosterland Street, Paarl, South Africa

ISBN 1 77007 031 1

www.oshunbooks.co.za

Log on to our photographic website **www.imagesofafrica.co.za** for an
African experience

I dedicate this book
to my son John
and my daughter Annéne

and to Sarajevo

CONTENTS

ACKNOWLEDGEMENTS

THIS BOOK IS A TRIBUTE: to life, to the admirable qualities in human beings, and to a magical city.

Writing these acknowledgements presented me with two dilemmas. Firstly, there aren't words in the English language to describe the immense gratitude and affection I feel towards the hundreds of good people who shared my life and experiences in Sarajevo. Secondly, I couldn't mention everyone by name, partly due to lack of space and partly because I've forgotten many names. I apologise sincerely for any omissions but assure all who crossed my path that, even anonymously, they are forever etched in my heart and mind.

Dedicating this book to my daughter Annéne and son John was not a decision born out of sentiment, but out of a compelling need to recognise their pivotal place in my life, and their support while I was in Sarajevo. They sacrificed far more than their fair share and had to confront numerous difficulties on their own. Both have matured into caring and responsible adults and I am proud and fortunate to be their mother.

Trying to describe what friendship and support meant in Sarajevo warrants more than the limited space at my disposal. Anyone who has ever been in a war zone will understand. Those fortunate enough to have no experience of war might not understand – and my hope for them is that they never find out.

The dedication to Sarajevo is inclusive of everyone in Sarajevo and Bosnia who withstood four years of indescribable horror and brutality, and persevered with tenacity, hope and superhuman effort to protect the values decent people hold dear. Sarajevans have a saying: 'Sarajevo is Sarajevo.' That is because it is impossible to define the magic of this city, which is so much more than inanimate buildings and streets. Sarajevo has a soul; she is alive, timeless, revered for centuries by her inhabitants, not as a location, but as the embodiment of a philosophy that embraces our journey on earth, both the delightful and the arduous, in totality. As such, Sarajevo is everyone who has ever lived there and loved her; and the core, sum and substance of Bosnia.

Nothing we achieve is done without the support and encouragement of others. If we are also offered friendship and love, we are indeed fortunate. I had many Sarajevan friends who generously shared limited and severely tested resources: emotional, physical and spiritual. Their friendship and caring, courage and selflessness in the face of calamity sustained and inspired me to carry on when I was tempted to give up.

The original manuscript was twice the length of this book, which meant cutting out innumerable incidents and the people who shared in those experiences. As a result, some of the people listed below are not mentioned, but they all contributed to a life-altering and unforgettable journey.

I knew few of Sarajevo's defenders, who braved the frozen trenches, hunger, pain and untold suffering to protect and defend not only their families and homes, but also an ideal. I am shamed to admit that I, as a representative of the all-powerful international community, depended on them for protection, when the opposite should have been the case. To those valiant men I pledge my undying admiration and gratitude.

The people who meant most to me and offered inestimable love and support were Armin and my Bezdrob family: Hadžo, Nerma and Lana; and my friends Mima Kerken, Anja Kerken, Jasna Karaula, Gertruda Munitić and Lejla Musić.

Sarajevo's awe-inspiring artists demonstrated that inspiration and generosity of spirit can co-exist with unspeakable deprivation: Gertruda Munitić; Miro Purivatra and the creators of 'Witnesses of Existence'; Kemal Monteno; Haris Pašović; Lila Samić; the members of Sonidos Barbaros, United States of Love, the Chamber Orchestra and Sarajevo Philharmonic Orchestra; Zlatko Sarajlija; Djani Aganlić; the 'Elenes' dancers and many others.

Our interpreters belonged to a special league. Because men were regarded as combatants, it was too dangerous for them to cross the confrontation lines, and therefore most UN interpreters were women. They worked under terribly difficult circumstances, put their lives at risk accompanying us into extremely dangerous places, suffered numerous humiliations – without a murmur of complaint. My young interpreters, Jamila Milović and Ines Aščerić, awed me with their tenacity and spirit, and I also owe a great deal to Božica, Jasna, Milica, Irma, Amina, Milena and other interpreters with whom I worked.

The staff at Forward Headquarters provided a home from home and showered me with kindness: Gordana, Emina and Sabiha, Rado Djurdjić, Goran, Izet and all the others.

The dauntless broadcasters at Radio BH, Studio 99, Zid and other radio stations were an inspiration, and I am proud to have been known as their colleague.

The children in Ciglane, who laughed, sang and played and included me in their plans for concerts and parties, made my heart sing and gave me hope for humanity and the future.

The women of Sarajevo have a special place in my heart. Their grace and courage are monumental, and I hope this book will create some understanding of their fundamental role in Sarajevo's survival.

Friends in Italy showed me overwhelming kindness and provided a soft place away from the brutality of war: Franco Pitassi, Francesco Rega and Monica Garnier, Emir Bezdrob and Maja, Michele Stochino Weiss and Monica Galina.

UNPROFOR colleagues shared and understood the difficulties and frustrations of working in Bosnia. UN civilians suffered far more obstacles than the military, and I received invaluable empathy and support from Civil Affairs colleagues.

When I met Cedric Thornberry in Windhoek in 1978, I was a novice political reporter. He was instrumental in my involvement with the UN and has been a friend for twenty-five years.

With Viktor Andreev I had unique and unforgettable experiences, and he was a generous mentor and boss.

Christine MacCallum and Colum Murphy were, and still are, close friends.

Deyan Mihov and Carlos Gutierrez were the best of comrades.

Elvira Coakley generously offered her flat in Zagreb as a refuge, and Ursula Oteng, Claire Grimes, Martha Horn, Shannon Boyd and Anna Maria Corazza were true sisters.

Sergio Vieira de Mello was a kindred spirit. It is tragic that he was killed in Iraq while working to improve the lives of another beleaguered nation.

Martti Ahtisaari, former UN Under-Secretary General, the UN Secretary-General's Special Representative on the UNTAG mission to Namibia and to the former Yugoslavia (and later president of Finland), played a fundamental role in my UN career. He was a powerful role model and an example that strength of character, and defending not what is popular but what is right, will prevail.

Many of my military colleagues were sterling examples of true grit and elan. They added colour and adventure to our lives, and were bastions of support and strength. Without their generosity and friendship my life would have been unbearable.

Bill Aikman, Luuk Niessen, Patricia Purves, Kevin Mc Grath and Pat Donohue.

The Belgians at BH Forward: General Francis Briquemont, Pierre, Guido, Ides, Thierry, Vladimir, Marc and the others.

The French in Sarajevo: General Philippe Morillon, General André Soubirou, Guy de Battista, Lieutenant Colonel de Courtivron and numerous others.

The Spaniards at Forward: Pepe Gallegos, Lieutenant Colonel Julio Lopez Guarch, Fernando Lafuente, José Segura, Luis, Salvador and other colleagues.

Brigadier General Vere Hayes, Major Rob Tripp, Major Iversen and the others at Kiseljak.

The Egyptian and Danish soldiers at Forward, who were kind and helpful to a fault.

On the 'home front', I owe enormous gratitude to my friend Karen Barratt. She provided critical encouragement and support at a most difficult time and kept an eye on my children, as did former colleague Jackie Kelly.

Max du Preez and my intrepid friend Maria Wallis gave me, and all of Bosnia, a voice in South Africa.

Frans and Amelia Booysen, strangers who sent a small care parcel.

If I owe a career in journalism – and being an author – to any other person, it is to my late friend Chris van der Merwe, who encouraged me to start writing. In a sad twist of fate he died in September 2003, just weeks before my first book was published.

My family and extended family are a constant source of encouragement, gratitude, joy and pride: my mother and remarkable eighty-something uncles and aunt, my sister and brother, my children and, in particular, my granddaughters Mila, Yasmin and Leila. I know they are all happy and relieved that, eight years after I started writing it, this book is finally published.

It is not a lucky coincidence that I survived two years in Sarajevo. I narrowly escaped death and serious injury on numerous occasions. Those experiences radically changed my life and priorities – and I will be forever grateful for God's divine protection and plan with my life.

PREFACE

200 000 killed
800 prisoner camps
500 000 prisoners, of whom 200 000 were tortured
1 600 women reported rape
151 mass graves

Personal notes
Sarajevo 1993

THIS BOOK CANNOT EVEN BEGIN TO EXPLAIN the true horrors of the war in Bosnia. Nor will it explain the intricate, centuries-old history of Bosnia and Yugoslavia. But it may elucidate somewhat the dramatic news footage of events during the 1990s.

Because of limited space, I have had to present a vastly abbreviated and simplified version of the complex political machinations involved.

Having been a United Nations 'peacekeeper' for two years in Bosnia during the war, I wanted to share my experiences and create a measure of understanding of the challenges and limitations inherent to this environment. In the past few decades, 'UN peacekeeping' and 'peacekeepers' have become familiar catchphrases. However, many people have no idea what peacekeepers *do*, nor what they have to endure in order to try to bring peace – often just the notion of peace – to a country or region in conflict. The UN is not an independent establishment. It is merely an instrument, a vehicle for conveying and putting into action the decisions made by members of the Security Council, who follow the precise instructions of the governments they represent. Nevertheless, more often than not, the UN – and long-suffering peacekeepers – are at the receiving end of bitter criticism for circumstances and situations over which they have no control, and which are decided by the permanent members of the UN Security Council: the USA, the UK, France, Russia or China.

As a former political journalist with a lifetime of exposure to politics, I was appalled at the general trend of the international media's reporting on Bosnia, and the 'spin' they applied, clearly dictated by predominantly the US and UK to advance their own political interests and agendas. Insistently referring to Bosnians as 'Muslims' cast them in a specific mould in the eyes of a constituency in the West who generally typecast Muslims as suicidal terrorists with zero tolerance and little respect for the sanctity of life. We would find it absurd if the media, as a matter of course, reported on the 'American Christian government', 'American Christian Army' or 'American Christians' in reference to the US population. However, during the Bosnian war the international media routinely and consistently referred to the 'Bosnian Muslim government', 'Bosnian Muslim Army' and 'Bosnian Muslims'.

Bosnians are Europeans, as much as Austrians or Italians are. They consume vast amounts of *šlivovic* (their famous plum brandy) and eat pork – and women have total independence, equal rights and free choice. Bosnian 'Muslims' are ethnic Serbs and Croats who converted during four centuries of Turkish rule, motivated mainly by two objectives: to obtain the privileged legal status accorded to Muslims by the Ottoman Empire, and to avoid the considerable rivalry between the Catholic and Orthodox churches and clergy, which caused serious ongoing hostility between the two groups.

By perpetuating the theory that Bosnia was a 'Muslim' country, the international media provided their own leaders with an excuse for their inaction and the Serbs with an invaluable propaganda weapon. Had the truth been told, namely that the conflict was simply about Slobodan Milošević and other Serbs' aspirations to create a greater Serbia, which obligated annexing land belonging to others, the US, the UK and Europe would have been compelled to take a firm stance against the Serbs. This would have put them on a collision course with Russia and Greece, and therefore, in the interests of political unity, it was decided to sacrifice Bosnia.

Another fallacy of the Bosnian war that was exploited beyond all proportion by the international media and some political observers was that of ancient animosities between ethnic Serbs and Croats, which was cited as an inevitable cause of the conflict. But most European nations (indeed most nations) have historical animosities towards other groups and countries: centuries of strife between England and France, two World Wars that pitted Germany against the rest of the world. These would not today be accepted as reasonable causes for war. In the case of Bosnia, its history was exploited to camouflage the true basis of the conflict, which was nothing but Serb imperialism and overt aggression. The war in Bosnia was neither about religion nor about centuries-old grudges. It was founded on blatant political opportunism.

When writing about people involved in large-scale group activities, terminology and references are fraught with difficulties. As an alternative to reverting to continuous use of laborious phrase-ology such as 'Serbs who supported nationalism, a greater Serbia and the war in Bosnia', I settled for 'Serbs'. The same applies to Croats. It goes without saying that large numbers of Bosnian Serbs and Bosnian Croats – as well as Serbians and Croatians – did not support their warmongering nationalistic leaders or the war, and even actively opposed them. In this vein, the term 'Bosnian' comprises all people who lived in Bosnia and supported and upheld the philosophy of tolerance and peaceful coexistence: ethnic Muslims (Bosniaks), Croats, Serbs and people of other ethnic or national extraction. This is a universal principle, and applies similarly in reference to 'South Africans' or 'Americans', peoples of vastly different backgrounds, ethnicity and nationality.

Many people have told me that they find the war in Bosnia difficult to understand. In fact, it is quite simple:

- Milošević and other Serbs wanted a greater Serbia, which required incorporating land in Bosnia and Croatia.
- The majority of Bosnians didn't want to be part of a greater Serbia and voted for independence, which was recognised on 6 April 1992 by the UN and the European Union.
- The Serbs invaded Bosnia to take the land by force.
- The international community chose to ignore international law and precedent, decided not to intervene and stop the war, and supported the arms embargo that made it impossible for Bosnia to defend itself and drive out the Serbs.

ANNÉ MARIÈ DU PREEZ BEZDROB
Parkhurst, Johannesburg
June 2004

Nothing exists until it's told. The only question is whether anything should be told. I was conscious that I had to do whatever it took for the truth to come out. If I had not known ... my ignorance would have protected me. But now there was no longer any choice, I was condemned by the truth.

MEŠA SELIMOVIĆ,
Death and the Dervish

INTRODUCTION

THE SOCIALIST FEDERAL REPUBLIC OF YUGOSLAVIA was established after World War II under the leadership of Josip Broz, better known as Marshall Tito, and consisted of six republics: Serbia, Croatia, Bosnia, Slovenia, Macedonia and Montenegro.

Tito was a dictator who held the reigns of power tightly. No one had dared challenge him during almost half a century of rule, and he didn't mentor a successor. Consequently, when he died in 1980, Yugoslavia was left a leaderless political wilderness.

The collapse of the Berlin Wall in 1989 signalled the demise of socialism across Eastern Europe, and in many former socialist countries, including Yugoslavia, the pendulum swung towards nationalism. Tito had forbidden nationalist sentiments, but following the disintegration of the Communist Party in the six Yugoslav republics in early 1990, several parties with nationalist tendencies sprung up in its place.

The political and economic disorder after Tito's death culminated in an intense wrangle for the power to decide Yugoslavia's future. In 1987, the leader of Yugoslavia's Communist Party, Slobodan Milošević, in an unexpected and ruthless political coup, wrested power from then President Ivan Stambolić. Milošević's goal was to become a second Tito – and to realise the centuries-old Serb dream of a greater Serbia. He was determined that nothing would get in the way of this ideal. Thus, when Croatia and Slovenia declared their independence from the Federal Republic of Yugoslavia in June 1991, Milošević ordered the Yugoslav People's Army (JNA) to attack Slovenia, and then Croatia. The JNA expected to roll across Slovenia in a matter of days, but the Slovenes fought ferociously and caught the JNA – and Milošević – off guard. Since there was no ethnic Serb community in Slovenia to support Milošević's aspirations for a greater Serbia, he turned his attentions to Croatia, where some thirty percent of the population were ethnic Serbs. After only ten days the humiliated JNA was withdrawn from Slovenia, and Milošević ordered his troops into Croatia to appropriate territory for his greater Serbia. The JNA ransacked Croatia, besieged and destroyed towns and villages and murdered thousands of Croatians. Tens of thousands of refugees sought safety in the capital, Zagreb, and other cities.

Faced with escalating violence in the former Yugoslavia, the European Community held a Peace Conference on Yugoslavia in The Hague in October 1991. Germany was in favour of recognising Slovenia and Croatia's independence. Britain and the United States were not, arguing that this might lead to increased conflict. However, Germany issued an ultimatum: either the EC granted recognition to the two states, or Germany would unilaterally recognise their independence. In order to preserve European unity, the EC capitulated, and in January 1992 Slovenia and Croatia were recognised as independent states.

As one of the four remaining republics in the Yugoslav Federation, Bosnia's leaders feared Serbian control and decided to opt for independence – but the US opposed independence for Bosnia, arguing that this would complicate a potential peace process in the region. In February 1992, his hopes of independence dashed, President Alija Izetbegović agreed to sign the EC's Carrington Plan partitioning Bosnia into three 'cantons', with forty-four percent each for the Bosnians and Bosnian Serbs, and twelve percent for the Bosnian Croats. However, the US suddenly reversed its position and proposed recognition of an independent Bosnia, persuaded Izetbegović to retract his support for the Carrington Plan, and promised US support for an independent Bosnia.

On 29 February and 1 March 1992, a referendum was held in Bosnia. Bosnian Serbs were forbidden to vote by their leader, Radovan Karadžić. However, of the almost sixty-five percent of the electorate who voted – mainly Bosnians and Croats, but also a sizeable number of Serbs who supported a multi-ethnic state – more than ninety-nine percent voted in favour of independence.

The intervention of the international community in Croatia had led to a suspension of hostilities and a ceasefire. Serb forces had taken control of a third of Croatia, and the proposal that Serb and Croatian forces remain in control of areas they had acquired suited Milošević. With the situation in Croatia static, he fixed his sights on Bosnia, confident that he could repeat the exercise and take possession of a sizeable area of Bosnian territory. All the weapons provided to Croatia's Serbs during 1991 were 'withdrawn' into Bosnia to support rebel Bosnian Serbs under Karadžić's leadership. The JNA constructed heavy artillery positions around Sarajevo and other towns in Bosnia, and on 2 March 1992, Serb forces set up barricades and sniper positions around the parliament building in Sarajevo.

When the EC reconvened in Brussels in March 1992 for talks on Bosnia, the US actively lobbied European ministers, urging them to recognise Bosnia's independence – in exchange for US recognition of Slovenia and Croatia. US Secretary of State George Baker accused reluctant European leaders of supporting ethnic division in Bosnia. They capitulated, and on 6 April, Bosnia's independence was recognised by the US and the EC. On the same day, the JNA attacked Bosnia and launched air attacks on Sarajevo.

There was a crucial difference between the attacks on Slovenia and Croatia, and that on Bosnia: when Milošević turned the military might of Yugoslavia on Slovenia and Croatia, they were not yet recognised by the international community as independent states. Bosnia's independence, however, had been recognised by both the EC and the US. Yet they took a bizarre decision: to support the United Nations arms embargo against an independent state under attack from another country – which clearly constituted an act of war – effectively making it impossible for Bosnia to defend itself.

The arms embargo all but totally crippled the emerging Bosnian army. Yet throughout 1992, the ill-equipped and haphazardly assembled army defended their state in what was nothing short of a miracle. Bosnia had two tanks and two armoured personnel carriers. The Serbs had 300 tanks, 200 armoured personnel carriers, 800 artillery pieces and 40 aircraft. The Serbs had Sarajevo surrounded with the most sophisticated weaponry in the world. They never expected the Bosnians to fight back, and when they did, they thought it would be over in a week at most. But the Bosnians remained standing against all odds, even when the conflict widened and Bosnian Croats, who had fought on the side of the Bosnians, changed direction in 1993 and opened a new front in Central Bosnia aimed at securing 'independent' areas for the Croats. Milošević and Croatian president Franjo Tudjman had entered into a pact to divide Bosnia between Serbia and Croatia. The trickle of military supplies Bosnia had received through Croatia was cut off, and it seemed only a matter of time before Bosnia would be forced to capitulate. But the Bosnians increased their resistance – and improvised. They manufactured their own weapons, packing explosives into small cans and using fire extinguishers and hot water geysers as substitute grenades, artillery casings and bombs. The soldiers in the trenches shared rifles. It was hard to believe this was the army of a modern state on the eve of the twenty-first century.

The international community's reaction to the tragedy in Bosnia was perplexing. Whereas a year earlier they had jumped to the defence of Kuwait when Iraq invaded it, they made no effort to stop

Yugoslavia's military offensive in Bosnia, and continued supporting the arms embargo. Military analysts have conceded that the Bosnian government, had it been allowed to exercise its right to acquire arms to defend its country, could have driven back the Serbs and halted the war in under six months. The West's policy of appeasement resulted in a bitter, drawn-out war that lasted almost four years and ended, with the signing of the Dayton Accord, in neither victory nor defeat for any side, but a political void that is fertile ground for future conflict.

PROLOGUE

APRIL 1993

THE SERBS ATTACKED AT DAWN.

I woke early but didn't get up, luxuriating in the dreamy cosiness of half-sleep, reluctant to surrender the warmth of the narrow, lumpy hotel bed and my flannel pyjamas. The ancient city of Šibenik was quiet. Everyone was clinging hungrily to the last hours of sleep before sunrise, blissfully unaware that in the distant shadows, Serb gunners were feeding giant shells into the barrels of their massive guns. My own unsuspecting thoughts meandered, lazy as smoke, as thoughts do in the unfocused moments before the day begins – things to do, things to remember, my children far away in Africa, the strangers I'd met and would meet, the unfamiliar sounds and smells of a foreign country, a different continent. Snow.

It was my fourth day in Croatia, and I was not prepared for war. In Zagreb life had appeared normal, and the signs of war along the road to Šibenik were like cold ash: evidence of fire, but no flames or smouldering embers. I was thinking about everything but the war. Until the first shell struck.

The thundering explosion jolted me wide awake, but for moments I lay motionless, confused, rigid with fright. There was another explosion. Then another. For seconds – perhaps minutes – the town and hotel remained silent, as they had been when I woke up. Then all hell broke loose. Sirens wailed, and guests stormed into the hotel corridors, shouting and slamming doors. Explosions reverberated through the city.

As Serb shells pounded Šibenik, I lay in the narrow bed, stiff as a board, my mind wiped of coherent thought. This wasn't supposed to happen in Croatia. There was a ceasefire! No one had told me what to do in a situation such as this. No one had even mentioned that it was possible. In fact, I hadn't been told anything at all, or given briefing notes, to prepare me for the United Nations Protection Force to the former Yugoslavia (UNPROFOR) mission. Zilch. *Ništa*. Not a word. Should you try to get out when you're under fire? Stay where you were? Seek cover under a table or in a door frame in case the roof caved in? But that seemed absurd and melodramatic. So I just lay there, trying to think. Then, as my mind started working again, I realised it might be a good idea to get dressed, so that at least I wouldn't have to run in my pink pyjamas, should running become necessary. In record time I pulled on my travel clothes and stuffed my few overnight things into a bag. Other thoughts surfaced: don't get separated from Viktor; don't get left behind if everyone's fled the hotel or, worse, the town. Scenes from previous months' TV footage flashed through my mind: desperate faces of people, wrenched from friends and family, fleeing towns like this. Or picking through the smouldering debris of their destroyed homes. I thought, hopefully, that perhaps I was having a nightmare, and would wake to find the town still peacefully asleep. But the wailing sirens and frantic activity in the corridors were all too real.

Suddenly I was weirdly calm. For some reason I was thinking not about saving my life, but about my baggage in the vehicle parked at the other end of the building, and that it would be a pity to lose the supply of Easter eggs I'd brought from Johannesburg for Sarajevo's children. Curiously, once I'd got my mind around the situation, I realised I wasn't afraid. The initial shock had passed. Unknowingly, and unannounced, I'd snapped into survival mode. I wasn't exactly happy, but neither was I terrified and irrational.

The chaos in the Hotel Jadran and the rest of Šibenik didn't last long, but the tension was tangible. Viktor and I spoke to other guests in the corridor who said it hadn't been a serious attack. For me it had seemed very serious indeed. But people weren't fleeing, and Viktor didn't suggest turning round and catching the first departing aeroplane to wherever it was going. At breakfast the waiter told us that Zadar and other coastal towns had also been attacked and that the whole region was on alert. When Viktor announced matter-of-factly that we would continue our journey to Bosnia after breakfast, it gave me a bit of a jolt. True, I wasn't frightened out of my wits, but I'm a firm believer that discretion is the better part of valour, and at least we had some shelter where we were. But I didn't voice my doubts. Perhaps, with the whole country at war, it didn't make sense to hang around in one place rather than another.

It felt as if I'd stumbled into someone else's nightmare where, with every passing moment, I was tumbling deeper into darkness; like a ride through a tunnel of horrors, where the terror increases the further you go. It was hard to believe that only five days earlier I'd been aeons from Šibenik, in Johannesburg, where my most pressing daily problem was getting to the supermarket on time after work so that I could feed two teenagers.

CHAPTER I

BLOOD ORANGES

APRIL 1993

*The horrors of this war have surpassed anything which even
battle-hardened soldiers and journalists have previously experienced.
Having served in Beirut in the 80s and Sarajevo in the 90s, Sarajevo
for me has been incomparably more savage, dangerous and ...
deeply wicked in both concept and execution of strategy.*

CEDRIC THORNBERRY,
Deputy Head of Mission of UNPROFOR
Address to the Conference on Preventive Diplomacy
Stockholm, April 1993

THAT WAS BOSNIA IN APRIL 1993 – savage, dangerous and deeply
wicked. And I was on my way to the country's besieged capital,
Sarajevo.

Winter was clinging stubbornly to the Balkans when I arrived
in neighbouring Croatia on 5 April 1993. On the flight
from Frankfurt, the view of the Austrian Alps was a spectacular

vista of mountaintops blanketed in brilliant white snow; and in the Croatian capital, Zagreb, it was bitingly cold. The United Nations had recruited me to establish a radio information programme in Bosnia for UNPROFOR. My final destination was the town of Kiseljak in central Bosnia, some forty kilometres north-west of Sarajevo. But before I could proceed to Bosnia, I had to be 'processed' at the UNPROFOR headquarters in Zagreb.

My work for the UN stemmed from a career as a political journalist in Namibia. When UNTAG, the UN mission to Namibia was deployed, they offered me a position. The UNTAG job was followed by a contract at the United Nations Secretariat in New York, and subsequently I was offered a position as a 'peacekeeper' with UNPROFOR. With Bosnia in the throes of the worst war in Europe since World War II, being described as a peacekeeper seemed most inappropriate. And if 'peacekeeper' was a word riddled with irony, 'protection force' was the superlative. But I had yet to discover that.

Some of my UN colleagues and friends were deployed in Croatia and Bosnia, and I'd heard first-hand accounts of what was happening there. While I was still in Johannesburg, Cedric Thornberry called, and I unexpectedly received running commentary of an artillery attack on Sarajevo. I'd followed the tragic events in the war-torn republics of the former Yugoslavia with keen interest. Because I was still basking in the glow of optimism following the UNTAG mission's success in Namibia, I naively believed a speedy solution was also possible in Bosnia. I'd been interested in Yugoslavia's dramatic and romantic history since my schooldays, but I had little more than a basic idea of Bosnia's geographic position in central Europe. When I was told that I might be stationed in the Croatian city Split, I had to check several atlases before I found it.

Although I knew I'd be working in a country at war, I wasn't really concerned – partly because I had no experience of conventional war (my experience was limited to coverage of the guerrilla wars in Namibia and Zimbabwe), and partly because I believed I'd be protected and cared for by the UN. This couldn't have been further from the truth, but I'd only find that out once I'd more or less reached the point of no return. Not in my wildest dreams could I have imagined that in a matter of weeks I'd be based in Sarajevo, living in a flat with no food, water or electricity, in a city under constant bombardment, and that my life would be in real danger every moment of every day.

Throughout the war, the only people who could enter – or leave – Bosnia were those with UN clearance and documentation: military and civilian personnel working for UNPROFOR, employees of accredited aid agencies, approved representatives of the foreign media and the occasional diplomatic envoy. There were two routes into Bosnia. One was flying into Sarajevo in a UN aircraft, clutching your stomach as the pilot dived towards the tarmac at breakneck speed and at a death-defying angle to avoid any lethal flying metal aimed in his direction. This was a very real threat: an Italian aeroplane bringing humanitarian aid for Sarajevo was shot down close to the city by a Serb missile in September 1992, killing the entire crew; and many of the aircraft flying in and out of Sarajevo had bullet holes in the fuselage. The alternative to the UN flight was driving to Bosnia through Croatia and territory occupied and controlled by the different warring forces: the Croatian army and rebel Serbs in Croatia; and the Bosnian army, Serb rebels and Croat rebels in Bosnia. Vehicles for the UNPROFOR military in Bosnia were brought in either by military convoy or, at times, by air.

UNPROFOR civilians were, however, apparently not thought to need such assistance or protection and were, with rare exceptions, responsible for their own logistics. The chief of UNPROFOR Civil Affairs in Bosnia, Viktor Andreev, had to fetch a vehicle in Zagreb and drive it back to the UNPROFOR headquarters in Kiseljak. Viktor had been on the UNTAG mission in Namibia, and we knew each other well. I opted to drive back to Bosnia with him, looking forward to the journey and the opportunity of seeing both countries at close quarters, with the foolish enthusiasm of the uninitiated.

The journey was surreal. The countryside resembled the vacant set of a long-completed movie. But the dense silence that had seeped into the villages, the ruins of shattered buildings, the disfigured trees, abandoned gardens and tattered hedges, left no doubt as to the tragedy that had swept across the country, leaving in its wake such destruction and sorrowful emptiness. Many roads were closed as a result of the fighting, and we had to take a circuitous route to Bosnia. There was also a dusk-to-dawn curfew, and thus we had to overnight in Croatia. En route we stopped for lunch in the town of Šenj. The meal included a novelty: a glass of bright red orange juice. Viktor explained that it was 'blood oranges': although the skin is orange, the flesh is red as blood. The terrible images of war we'd encountered along the way were fresh in my mind, and I felt squeamish about drinking the red juice. It seemed symbolic of the death and suffering I was suddenly confronted with, but I couldn't think how I'd explain this to Viktor and the restaurateur who'd presented it so proudly, so I closed my eyes and gulped it down. It was sweet and delicious, and after lunch I bought a bag of these oranges from a roadside hawker.

The entrance of the rundown Hotel Jadran in Šibenik, where we would spend the night, was barricaded with piles of sandbags and gigantic slabs of concrete, and the sea-facing windows were boarded up. There was no hot water and I had my first cold bath of the war, followed by an uncomfortable night on a mattress I was certain even the Salvation Army would have refused.

At dawn the next morning, the Serbs attacked Šibenik.

The closer we got to Bosnia, the more telling the evidence of war. Many of the destroyed villages were Serb villages, testimony that they weren't escaping the scourge of the war many Serbs had so heedlessly started and supported. I was learning that nothing had changed in two thousand years of history. On the eve of the twenty-first century, and in the heart of Europe, all was still considered fair in war. In those early days there was much I didn't know or understand, and my initial pride and enthusiasm at being a member of the UN's so-called protection force would be severely tested in the months ahead. It would turn to frustration, and eventually shame. For me, living in a country where the UN's involvement was a prominent feature of political life, the world body personified freedom and fairness. My involvement in the UNTAG mission in Namibia had strengthened that notion, but my experiences in Bosnia would lead me to question seriously the worthiness of the UN institution. It had developed into little more than a giant bureaucracy, riddled with inefficiency and political and personal agendas. In the case of Bosnia, decisions were based on self-interest, most notably that of the USA. The UN had been established as an instrument to promote world peace, and its founders had vowed to safeguard the world against future catastrophes such as World War II. Alas, a mere fifty years later the UN was a sad example of the general state of the planet, where honour and integrity took second place to economic and political interests. For almost four years, children, women and men of all ages in Bosnia were subjected to abject terror, torture and cold-blooded murder because it wasn't in the interest of the major Western powers to intervene. More than 200 000 Bosnians were slaughtered as a result of the collective policy of Serb appeasement and the lack of will to interfere with the killing. The West had decided not to use force in the conflict. That was a dire mistake. By mollycoddling the Serbs and their destructive ambition for a greater Serbia, the international community set the stage for an almost inconceivable tragedy.

———————————

In Bosnia, a continent away from home, I discovered that the people of the former Yugoslavia had much in common with the people of South Africa. The Yugoslavs had been kept in the dark about alarming political undercurrents during and after Tito's reign, and were discouraged not only from involvement and interest in politics, but, especially, as in South Africa, from opposition to the status quo. For that reason they weren't sufficiently equipped to understand or challenge the dangerous trends that were developing. History has shown that people who grow up believing that opposition to authority is unacceptable are unlikely to change overnight. More likely, as has happened time after time, they will blindly follow their leaders until there can no longer be any doubt – usually later rather than sooner – that they are being lead into certain disaster. It was especially sad when this happened in Yugoslavia, because traditionally the Yugoslavs were a people with a great capacity for political and social engagement, and a temperament that questioned and opposed everything with which they weren't in total agreement. The result of the socialist experiment in Yugoslavia was sad testimony to the doctrine of communism. Contrary to its teaching, it did not bring liberation from slavery and exploitation, but scraped away independence and individuality, which is the essence of humanity, and stripped people of their spirit, until it exposed the human race at its most primitive and barbaric.

CHAPTER 2

SCORCHED EARTH

APRIL 1993

CROSSING FROM CROATIA INTO BOSNIA was like moving from cloudy weather into the ominous gloom preceding a hurricane. Bosnia wasn't just another country, it was a different world. In Croatia there had been widespread evidence of smouldering conflict, but Bosnia was unmistakably a country in the throes of a deadly war.

By April 1993, the war declared against Bosnia's new government by the Serbs a year earlier had become a three-sided campaign. The ease with which the Serbs had seized three quarters of Bosnia, and the refusal of the international community to intervene, encouraged Croatia to jump on the bandwagon and grab its share. Croatia's President Franjo Tudjman, like Yugoslavia's President Slobodan Milošević, was a communist-turned-nationalist. With the approval of Tudjman's government, Bosnian Croat rebels established the Croat Council for Defence (HVO), a militia force with civilian commanders, including a former journalist, Dario Kordić, who was later indicted for war crimes. Spurred on by the successes of the secessionist Serbs, the Croats, fired by their own nationalist aspirations, launched an armed resistance against the

Bosnian government in early 1993. Before war broke out, Tudjman and Milošević had discussed splitting Bosnia between Croatia and Serbia, leaving the Bosnians in a kind of ethnic 'homeland' surrounded by hostile neighbours. Thus, Milošević supported and supplied the Bosnian Serbs, and HVO forces were supported and supplied by Tudjman's government in newly independent Croatia.

Bosnia is breathtakingly beautiful. It is a mountainous country with large areas of dense forest, lush highlands and arid planes. And the rivers are exquisite. Bosnia's rivers aren't brown and murky like rivers in Africa, but green and clear as glass. They wind through the countryside in shades of emerald and turquoise, sparkling like strings of precious stones carelessly scattered between the hills and through the fields. It was hard to believe, in that magnificent landscape, that there were people across the next mountain or in the next village bent on destruction. Rural Bosnia was undeveloped and sparsely populated. That was still the deep country, with mountains and fields stretching to the horizon, uninterrupted by any signs of modern civilisation. At first sight the countryside seemed to exude quiet serenity, and it appeared peaceful and calm. On closer inspection, however, the country's agony was clearly visible. Apart from the many military checkpoints, the picturesque countryside was more than quiet: it was silent, devoid of life. Only the shadows and skeletons of vital rural existence remained. Everywhere were deserted and destroyed villages, the roofless houses and blackened walls all that remained of bustling communities, flourishing farms, prosperous businesses and people once content with what life had to offer. Fields and forests had been burnt to pale ashes. This was more than war: it was a systematic process to obliterate a country and its people. Scorched earth. Those dreadful words lived in my own history through the vivid stories told by my grandparents and their generation, of Britain's scorched earth policy aimed at destroying the Boers in the independent republics of the Free State and Transvaal. At the end of the Anglo-Boer War, my great-grandparents returned to farms that looked like that: roofless ruins, surrounded by blackened, twisted tree trunks, the earth dusted with white ash. When the war broke out, my maternal grandmother's father buried a dining room table and a Singer sewing machine. After the war, that was all they had. No home, no livestock, no food. My grandfather was even less fortunate. More than half his family was wiped out when his mother and sisters died in the British concentration camp at Heilbron. When his father returned from commando, he fetched his two tiny sons and took them to a burnt-down homestead on empty land. Their anguish was part of my genetic inheritance; it huddled in my soul, and I was deeply touched at the sight of the mindless destruction of the savage Serb advance, as if in some way I'd personally suffered some of the devastating loss.

I discovered the history of Yugoslavia when, in high school, I read the biography of Malcolm Fitzgerald, the British doctor who served with Tito's Partisans during World War II. I was fascinated by the fearless Partisans and, eager to know more, I found a biography about the Austrian Archduke Ferdinand and his wife Sofie, and their assassination in Sarajevo by the Serb nationalist Gavrilo Princip – the event that led to World War I. Yugoslavia's role in the two World Wars made a profound and lasting impression on me. Perhaps I was destined to share, in some small measure, the history of places that had lived in my memory since I was a young girl. What, after all, do we understand about destiny?

When I arrived in Bosnia, the mountains were covered in snow and the country was shivering in the last convulsions of winter. As I travelled through these mountains for the first time, I realised why the Partisans had managed to dust the jackets of the militarily superior Nazis. The densely forested, rugged terrain was magnificently beautiful, but totally defeating. The impenetrable woods were utterly hostile to all but those who had watched them grow, who could hear them breathe, who knew them like brothers. During the two years I spent in Bosnia, I often travelled through the mountains in the grip of mid-winter, when the lush forests of spring and summer turned into a merciless frozen fortress. During World War II, Partisans froze to death while marching through these forbidding mountains, but their awe-inspiring spirit and tenacity did not succumb: neither to the onslaught of the Nazis, nor to that of nature. That formidable spirit emerged again among Bosnia's defenders when their former countrymen turned on them in the 1990s, and the cornered Bosnians fought with the same ingenuity and fortitude against the militarily superior Serbs and Croats.

As in Croatia, the main roads in Bosnia were under the control of the various fighting forces and closed to traffic, and we had to brave forty kilometres across the mountains on a perilous dirt track. It was a frightening ordeal. In some places the snow had started melting and icy water gushed down the mountainside, turning the road into a sludgy obstacle course covered in thick liquid mud that threatened to engulf our vehicle. On one side, the mountain gave way to a deep abyss, on the other side, vertical cliffs shot up straight into the air. The mud splashed over the car and the windows, severely restricting visibility. It was clear that one dared not make a mistake here, and I was very nervous. Ahead of us was a truck, and it suddenly started sliding backwards in the mud. In a moment it had spun out of control and was headed straight for us. I braced myself for the impact, but at the last moment the truck jerked aside and careened crazily past us in reverse, rocking from side to side. It slid closer and closer to the edge of the ravine, and I could visualise it plummeting into the depths with its passengers and precious cargo, destined to save the lives of some of Bosnia's beleaguered citizens. Literally inches from the edge, it slowly shuddered to a halt. Viktor and I had escaped serious injury or death by a hair's breadth, but that the passengers in the truck had survived was a real miracle. It seemed as though calamity or terror was to be my constant companion. In half a week I'd been exposed to heavy shelling, witnessed the terrible path of devastation left by the Serb armies in Croatia and Bosnia, and almost been crushed by a truck. I felt withered and drained. For another two hours we inched along before we crossed the mountain's summit. The descent in the mud was no easier than the ascent, and we slithered down, twisting and turning from side to side. Even though we moved very slowly, it still felt too fast, and it was an altogether gruelling trip. When we finally reached the foot of the mountain I felt overwhelming relief, the kind that makes your whole body go limp. It took a while before I could start breathing normally and unclench my teeth after hours of lockjaw. For the first time in days, I felt almost cheerful.

The last stretch of the journey was mercifully on tar. The road wound through grassy plains that stretched in all directions in grey-green hues, interspersed with clumps of bright green trees and soft rolling hills. I breathed in the clear air, feasted my eyes on the countryside bathed in mild afternoon sun, and enjoyed the first soothing moments in two days. But the harsh present was ever close. At an intersection a group of children suddenly appeared and swarmed around the car, holding out grubby little hands. My sweets and blood oranges were stashed in my bags and we had nothing to give them. Viktor explained that they weren't nearly as badly off as the children in besieged Bosnian-held territory who faced starvation, and that they were probably hoping to get sweets or biscuits, but it tugged at my heart. They were the first civilians we'd seen since entering Bosnia the first signs of life in a silent, empty country that seemed to have been abandoned. And it was not a happy sight.

We arrived in Kiseljak in the late afternoon. I was trembling inside and out from strain and fatigue, but overcome with relief. That was, however, one of only two occasions on which I'd be happy to see this unappealing town. Kiseljak's claim to fame was a natural spring to which people had flocked with great enthusiasm before the war, with typical European devotion to spas. For that reason only did the small, uninspiring town boast a structure that had the potential of being revamped into a military headquarters for UNPROFOR. In happier days, the UNPROFOR headquarters in Kiseljak had been a hotel for 200 guests. With the arrival of the UN, the large, white, tiered building was converted into a military barracks for 600 soldiers from all over the world.

Civil Affairs, UNPROFOR's political contingent, consisted of a small group of six when I arrived. As the political arm of the UN Secretariat, we had to cover all political and related activities throughout Bosnia. Everything was political. Military activities were political and humanitarian assistance was political. So that meant we were involved in everything. The senior public information officer in Bosnia, my immediate superior, was Hussein Al-Alfi, a former ambassador of Yemen to the UN. He was responsible for dealing with the media and coordinating the UNPROFOR information function in Bosnia. Viktor, the Civil Affairs coordinator for Bosnia, was in overall charge of all civilian duties, including ours. The UNPROFOR radio information programme I'd been recruited to produce would inform Bosnians about the activities of UNPRO-FOR in Bosnia, and disseminate other useful information, including explanations on resolutions and decisions taken by the UN Security Council in New York. But when I arrived in Kiseljak, I found to my horror that there wasn't even a desk for me to work at – let alone

poor baby!

a radio studio or a pair of helping hands. As a result I had to embark on a murderous regime, working fourteen to eighteen hours a day, seven days a week, in order to get – and keep – a programme on the air.

By the end of 1993, UNPROFOR civilians in Bosnia still numbered fewer than twenty, including administrative personnel. Personnel of the United Nations High Commissioner for Refugees (UNHCR) weren't part of UNPROFOR, but an autonomous unit, although we cooperated on many projects and operations. The balance of UNPROFOR was made up of some 25 000 military personnel, all under the UN flag, and suitably attired in blue berets or helmets.

There was already a military Public Information office, and it was decided that I should slot in there in some undefined way. The senior officer was Lieutenant Colonel Patricia Purves, an enthusiastic and efficient Scot. Her second in command was Major Luuk Niessen from the Netherlands. The other members of the team were a Danish captain, Jes Frederikson, and two NCOs – Bill, a Canadian, and Rick, who was British. Later an American captain, also called Bill, joined the unit. Trish Purves turned out to be an undisguised blessing, and a woman after my own heart. If something had to be done, she didn't ponder, call meetings, debate and procrastinate; she just did it. My other civilian colleagues, Deyan Mihov and Carlos Gutierrez, were based at the PTT Building, HQ of the French Battalion in Sarajevo. Deyan, a bearded Bulgarian, was head of Civil Affairs in 'Sector Sarajevo' (the city and surroundings, their area of responsibility), and Carlos, a gentle Spaniard, was his deputy. The third member of the team was their interpreter, Amela. Because I represented Public Information, I wasn't strictly speaking part of Civil Affairs, but Deyan and Carlos 'adopted' me. They were loyal and supportive colleagues, a constant source of assistance and friendship, and I could call on them any time of the day or night. Nothing was too much or too insignificant to ask of them, and we weathered many crises together. They initially shared an office with the staff of UNHCR – Tony Land, Larry Hollingworth and their translator Vesna – and this small group was another source of support. While I was doing the radio programme, I had limited contact with UNHCR, but when I later took over the UNPROFOR Humanitarian Office, I worked more closely with them.

Unlike the military, who were accommodated at bases throughout Bosnia, UN civilians had to find their own accommodation. Civil Affairs and UNHCR personnel shared houses or boarded with local families. I shared a double-storey house with Viktor. The house was within walking distance of HQ, up a steep hill and down a stretch of equally steep steps. It was a relief to set down my three suitcases, labelled 'heavy bags' in Johannesburg, after lugging them to my rooms upstairs. My 'flat' was spacious but sparsely furnished, with a single bed in the bedroom, and two dining room chairs and a small table in the lounge. The blue bathroom had the smallest bath I'd ever seen and I could only just sit in it. The best feature was a balcony overlooking the rolling green hills around Kiseljak. The only kitchen was downstairs, but my living quarters were more than adequate for me, since I spent hardly any time at home. I worked long hours, seven days a week, and ate my meals in the mess hall. The wood stove in the kitchen at home was mostly used for heating water for a quick wash in the morning, or sometimes a cup of tea.

In those early days the war seemed unreal and distant, despite its physical closeness. During the day, the bustle of activity and hundreds of soldiers' boots marching around HQ drowned out everything else. But the nights were filled with the sounds of battle. Like hyenas, Croat rebels were further dissecting Bosnia's bleeding carcass after the Serbs had moved in for the kill. From Kiseljak, Croat forces fired shells into the hills to the east and south-east, where the rag-tag Bosnian army was fighting gallantly against their former allies. When the JNA attacked Bosnia, there was no Bosnian army. As one of the six former republics of Yugoslavia, Bosnia had contributed both soldiers and money to the JNA, the central defence force that invaded first Slovenia and Croatia, and then Bosnia as, one after another, they declared their independence from Yugoslavia in the early 1990s. Bosnia's only defence was a small territorial force that formed the core of a hastily assembled volunteer army. They had hardly any arms and ammunition, no uniforms and no vehicles. And once the UN arms embargo was in place, there was no legitimate way of changing their dire situation. For Bosnia the arms embargo was a death sentence. It left Serbia with the entire might of the Yugoslav army – the fourth largest in Europe – and forbade the other former republics, including the newly independent Bosnia that had been invaded, to arm and defend themselves against the Serb onslaught. But the Bosnians were sons and daughters of the Partisans, at their most resourceful with their backs against the wall. Also, they were fighting for their lives. As in Slovenia, where a few desperate men were all that stood against the attacking JNA, the Serbs expected no resistance in Bosnia. And, as in Slovenia, where those few men effectively repulsed the Serbs, they received an unpleasant surprise. So did the Croats. After being bloodied for a year by the Bosnians, the rebel Bosnian Croats, beaten and humiliated by the ferocious Bosnian defence in central Bosnia, signed an agreement in Washington on 1 March 1994 for the creation of a Bosnian–Croat Federation. The Croats then re-entered the war where they had started – as Bosnia's allies against the Serbs. But that was a year hence.

Kiseljak squatted amid rolling green hills and woods, and in the soft light of early morning or late afternoon, it was a picture of tranquillity. But scenic surroundings turned out to be the town's only redeeming feature. As soon as my relief at having made it alive across the perilous mountains had settled, I realised I felt ill at ease.

Dusty and unimpressive, Kiseljak was the 'capital' of the HVO, the seat of Croat hard-liners controlled by a fanatical Croat militia. A generic anti-everything-but-Croat sentiment prevailed. Shop-keepers who'd become wealthy overnight thanks to the large UN presence in Kiseljak and the consequent flood of international journalists and representatives of humanitarian organisations, treated us as though we were enemy invaders. A friendly and much practised *'dobro jutro'* ['good morning'] or *'hvala ljepa'* ['thank you very much'] was often met with nothing but a cold, hostile stare. They treated our patronage as though it were a physical assault. Their hostility wasn't only passive. A group of HVO soldiers attacked a Canadian officer, Major Ted Itani, while he was jogging through the town, and beat him so badly that he had to return to Canada for medical treatment. After this incident, UNPROFOR personnel were forbidden to venture into the town alone. Kiseljak's rustic grace of the past had been engulfed by the poisonous vapour of fascism and nationalism, and the stoic Bosnians in the town were existing precariously, one day at a time. No one was surprised when the Croat authorities, with total disregard for the UN on their doorstep, started 'cleansing' Kiseljak of its Bosnian inhabitants. It started with a decree that ordered fourteen Bosnian families to leave the town. Shortly after that, the house of a Bosnian family was blown up. I stood on my balcony and watched the black smoke curl slowly around the house in a morbid farewell before it drifted sadly off towards the hills. The writing was on the wall. Families who'd lived in Kiseljak for generations and were reluctant to leave were hurried along by the kind of terror tactics perfected by the Serbs. The 'ethnically cleansed' were given only enough time to grab a few valuables and essential pieces of clothing before they had to leave behind their homes and everything they owned without a murmur for an unknown, and often terrifying, destiny. One Sunday morning I saw a group of aged people gathering at the house of two elderly

Bosnian sisters who lived over the road. I'd been invited to coffee in the dusky lounge of these two kind, dignified ladies. They told me they'd been born in that house and had lived there all their lives. On that Sunday, everyone was clearly agitated, talking simultaneously, pointing and gesticulating. The women were wiping away tears. It wasn't difficult to guess what was happening. UNPROFOR lodged a formal complaint with Kiseljak's authorities and demanded that the expulsions be stopped. But in a country where even signed agreements were hardly ever honoured, UNPROFOR's feeble efforts did nothing to deter the Croat hard-liners in their pursuit of purifying their territory of other – undesirable – groups. The expulsions continued.

This was my first encounter with the UN's impotence faced with the tragedy in Bosnia. Apart from laboriously and tirelessly generating one resolution after another – totally ignored by the Serbs and the Croats – the international community took negligible steps to stop the killing and the barbaric practice of ethnic cleansing. The UN, representative of the free world, powerful international watchdog of the persecuted and repressed, campaigner for human and civil rights, with 25 000 soldiers at its disposal, witnessed and recorded chilling human rights abuses and atrocities without taking any action beyond discussing them in New York. Like an old toothless dog, its bark was half-hearted and barely audible.

I was about to learn another lesson. A lesson about courage and war. Courage doesn't mean not being afraid. Courage means indeed feeling fear – at times even blind terror – but nevertheless doing what must be done. In Bosnia, what was not only courageous but truly heroic was the mere act of living. In Srebrenica, Goražde and Žepa, in Maglaj and Doboj. In Bihać and Mostar. And in Sarajevo.

Day after day, year after year: surviving the relentless attacks, the torture in the camps, the slaughter in the besieged Bosnian enclaves. Living meant enduring the horror, nursing the wounded, burying the dead. Living meant braving the dangers, surviving without food and water, without heat in winter, without medical assistance, forgotten by the world. Watching your life slowly collapse like an imploding skyscraper filmed in slow motion. War is more than men going off to battle, the exchange of fire and weapons of mass destruction. War means that the bottom falls out of people's lives. Everything that is familiar and comfortable disappears and is replaced by terror and uncertainty. There is no water in the taps, no electricity at the flick of a switch. Not only no food in the super-market, but no supermarket. No transport, school, work, cinema, holiday. Often no home. Life becomes a living hell.

Sometimes, those who die are the fortunate ones.

CHAPTER 3

A SAVAGE WAR

APRIL 1993

The hottest places in hell are reserved for those who,
in times of great moral crisis, maintain their neutrality.

DANTE ALIGHIERI

AS PART OF MY ORIENTATION I attended meetings between the Bosnians and Serbs, the 'warring factions'. The first meeting I attended concerned the town of Srebrenica, and started a sequence of events that caused ripples within the UN and many of its member countries for years after the war in Bosnia. I had, of course, never heard of Srebrenica, and gathered what information I could find to acquaint myself with the situation. It painted a shocking, almost unbelievably gruesome picture.

Before the war about 10 000 people had lived in this bleak, ancient mining town in eastern Bosnia. ('Srebren' means 'silver'.) By March 1993 the population had swelled to over 40 000, and Srebrenica was bursting at the seams. Many of the 30 000 refugees from surrounding villages couldn't find accommodation and were living on the streets with little or no shelter in temperatures of -20°C. The siege of the town had started almost a year earlier and, as in the case of Sarajevo and other Bosnian enclaves, the Serbs were trying to starve and terrorise the population into submission. But in the eastern enclaves, especially Srebrenica, the situation was far worse even than in Sarajevo. The Serbs blocked all humanitarian aid, food and medical supplies, and the situation was becoming more desperate by the day. The ill-equipped Bosnian defenders were running out of ammunition, and clearly couldn't hold out much longer. It was a miracle that they'd managed at all to drive the Serbs out in April 1992. But the war in Bosnia was steeped in miracles and irony. One of the ironies, very painful for the Serbs, was that Naser Orić, the young commander of the small force in Srebrenica at whose hands they had suffered this humiliation, was a former bodyguard of Slobodan Milošević.

The few Bosnian enclaves in the ocean of Serb-occupied land were a military nightmare for the Serbs, and they were hell-bent on destroying them. Sarajevo, a beautiful ancient city rich in history and myth, received massive international media coverage, but the eastern enclaves were small nondescript towns that didn't inspire newspaper headlines. The world didn't register the plight of Srebrenica, despite the tales of terror and suffering told by the few people who managed to escape, until the Bosnian government declared that no more aid would be accepted in Sarajevo until Srebrenica received humanitarian assistance too. But going on a hunger strike, possibly until death, was playing into the hands of the Serbs, who simply continued their blockade. In March a World Health Organisation (WHO) doctor reported that people were dying from starvation. Many of the UN's policies and actions were unfathomable. They provided humanitarian aid to Serb areas while the Serbs were blockading aid to the Bosnians, making no attempt to introduce a quid pro quo, or use it as leverage in any other way.

UNPROFOR's military commander in Bosnia, General Philippe Morillon, incensed at the UN's refusal to take action against the Serbs and help the Bosnians, quietly went to Srebrenica under cover of night. Despite having seen reports about the situation, he was shocked at the privations suffered by people in the town. He received another unpleasant surprise: Srebrenica's desperate citizens, hoping this would force UNPROFOR into action, took him hostage. Morillon negotiated his own release by promising them UN protection – a promise he came to regret. But he also convinced the Serbs to let in an aid convoy. This, however, caused another problem. The trucks were from Tuzla, a large town to the north-west of Srebrenica under Bosnian control, and as soon as they were empty, hundreds of desperate women clambered on with their children and refused to get off. The Serbs, wanting the town evacuated so they could walk in and take over, let them go. But the trucks were so overcrowded that six people died on the way to Tuzla. Incredibly, the international media accused UNPROFOR of assisting with ethnic cleansing. I was dumbstruck. Having been a journalist in a war situation, I tried to understand their reasoning. But no matter from which angle I approached the situation, I couldn't fathom it. UNPROFOR had had nothing to do with the women's decision to escape from the unspeakable suffering in Srebrenica, and I wondered what the well-fed journalists of the world expected us to do: drag freezing, starving women and children from the trucks and refuse them this one opportunity to escape? And how would they have reported on that? They accused us of assisting with ethnic cleansing throughout the war. Why the international media wanted us to turn our backs on the few people we could help to get out of Bosnia's hell-holes, I could never understand. We could do little enough as it was. If one were a total cynic, you might believe it was because hundreds of dead civilians made for better news headlines than hundreds of saved civilians. Ironically, the journalists who were so vehement in their protestations about UNPROFOR's so-called assistance with ethnic cleansing ignored the fact that the people who so desperately wanted to escape the terrible places in which they were stuck were merely exercising freedom of choice – a basic principle in the free countries from which the media hailed. What the UN should have done was to practise the accountability and moral obligation the media advocated (when it suited them), and transport every single person in Bosnia's besieged enclaves to where they wanted to go. Not by helping them, but by refusing them assistance we were condemning them, more often than not, to torture, rape and death. Many of these journalists had never spent more than a few hours, or a few days at most, in the Bosnian enclaves before jetting back to comfortable apartments in London or New York with central heating, cupboards full of food and the doctor's rooms round the corner.

If one were to have followed the rules instituted by the UN, the Serbs and the Croats – and the international media – very little would have been done. Soon my own assessment of my work and moral obligation was that, if I felt obliged to play by all the different rule books, and to philosophise about every little thing – such as whether saving people's lives could in some abstract way be construed to be supporting ethnic cleansing by a bored journalist desperate for a story – I shouldn't be in, or anywhere near, Bosnia.

At the beginning of April 1993, the Serbs gave UNHCR's special envoy, José Maria Mendiluce, an ultimatum: either the Bosnians surrender and UNHCR evacuate all Bosnians from Srebrenica, or the Serbs step up their attack and overrun the town. Mendiluce, probably more than any other UN representative in Bosnia, knew what this would mean. In April 1992, on his way back to Sarajevo from a meeting with President Milošević in Belgrade, he had passed through the town of Zvornik on the Bosnian side of the border with Serbia (Yugoslavia). Here the Serbs had just issued the same ultimatum of surrender to the people of Zvornik. When they refused to surrender, the Serbs subjected them to heavy shelling from inside Serbia before storming the town, and then the feared 'Tigers', a paramilitary force, started 'cleansing' Zvornik. Despite the fighting, Mendiluce had insisted on being allowed to cross into Bosnia, and when the Serbs in Zvornik realised he had witnessed the atrocities, they arrested him. He was certain he was going to die. He'd seen Serb soldiers removing bodies of men, women and children before looting and burning their houses. He saw trucks loaded with bodies. Amazingly, the Serbs let Mendiluce go. They must have regretted doing that a thousand times. Mendiluce had witnessed at first hand what the Serbs were capable of, and when they told him to evacuate Srebrenica, he started organising the move of over 40 000 people, knowing the international media would accuse him of assisting with ethnic cleansing. He made a statement condemning ethnic cleansing, but said it was his responsibility and sole concern to save the lives of the thousands at risk, and he wasn't going to have a philosophical debate about the evacuation. But it never took place.

UN peacekeeping operations are structured on the basis that all parties involved in a conflict must consent to UN activities, and on UN personnel never taking sides, especially not publicly. UNPROFOR's mandate didn't allow for intervention to stop the killing, and thus the Serb offensive on Srebrenica was imminent. General Morillon, attempting to honour his promise to the people of Srebrenica, tried to reach the town, but was apprehended by the Serbs en route and forced to turn back. The UN was furious with

Morillon for breaking ranks, but was to find increasingly that it could issue orders but not always stop officials in Bosnia from speaking out, or even acting, against UN policy. Morillon had refused to ignore what was happening in Srebrenica; Mendiluce was acting contrary to UN policy and didn't mince his words about how he felt. And then another senior UNHCR field officer, Larry Hollingworth, made headlines – with an unambiguously anti-Serb statement. On 12 April, fifty-six people were killed in an artillery attack on a football field in Srebrenica, among them fourteen children. A six-year-old boy was decapitated. At a press conference in Sarajevo the following morning, Hollingworth made a formal, public statement:

> When yesterday I heard the news about the shelling, my first thought was of the army commander who had ordered the shelling. I hope that he burns in the hottest part of hell.
>
> I then thought of the soldiers who had loaded the guns and fired them. I hope that they suffer from nightmares. I hope that their sleep is broken by the screams of the children and the cries of their mothers.
>
> I then thought about Doctor of Medicine Karadžić, Professor of Literature, Koljević, Biologist Mrs Plavšić, Geologist, Dr Lukić and I wondered if today they will condemn this atrocity and punish the perpetrators or will they deny their education and condone it? I then thought about my Serb friends whom I have met on my travels. Do they wish to read in future history books that their army has chased innocent women and children from village to village, until finally they are cornered in Srebrenica, a place from which there is no escape, and where their fate is to be transported like cattle or slaughtered like lambs?
>
> – UNPROFOR Documentation

Hollingworth's words blazed around the world: over radio and television, and across the front pages of newspapers. UNPROFOR and the UN Secretariat in New York cringed and fumed. The Serbs took no notice at all. The history of the modern Serb nation would contain far more than this one bloody chapter. The fourteen dead children on that football field in Srebrenica were not the first, nor the last. There were many more attacks on football fields, and on children, all deliberate. The Serb nation was rewriting its history in the blood of the innocent: children, women, the elderly, unarmed men.

The situation in Srebrenica was critical. The town's defenders had no ammunition left and their lines of defence had collapsed. They sent a secret message to the Bosnian government announcing they would have to surrender. UNPROFOR had started talking to the Serbs about a ceasefire, and pushed ahead despite the fact that General Ratko Mladić, the infamous commander of the Bosnian Serb army, made it clear that he had no intention of halting the offensive. On 15 April, Srebrenica surrendered. After the publicity arising from Morillon's courageous but futile attempt at rescuing Srebrenica, the powerful bloc of non-aligned nations in the UN demanded action. Following a lengthy diplomatic wrangle, the UN Security Council adopted a resolution declaring Srebrenica a 'safe area' and 'requesting' the warring sides to treat it as such. It was a meaningless exercise, mere rhetoric, and carried about as much weight as the paper on which it was written. And it was disturbingly cynical: the 'safe area' of Srebrenica was one of the most dangerous places on earth.

On Saturday 17 April, I set off for Sarajevo airport with Viktor, Hussein, UNPROFOR's chief of staff Brigadier Vere Hayes, his aides and a handful of military officers to attend the meeting between representatives of the Bosnian government and the Serbs, which would seal Srebrenica's fate. This historic meeting between the notorious

General Mladić, and the commander of Bosnia's army, General Sefer Halilović, was of life and death importance to the Bosnians. Mladić's delegation consisted of Major General Milan Gvero, Colonel Zdravko Tolimir and his liaison officer, Major Milenko (Misha) Indjić, a man with the reputation of being nasty and ruthless, with whom I would work closely in the two years to come. General Halilović's delegation was a true sample of the multi-ethnic Bosnian state they were defending: Colonel Stjepan Šiber was an ethnic Croat, and Colonel Jovan Divjak an ethnic Serb. The fourth member was Colonel Fikret Muslimović. The infant Bosnian army had few generals.

The meeting was chaired by UNPROFOR. All the top guns were flown in from Zagreb to bring maximum pressure to bear on the Serbs: UNPROFOR's Norwegian Force commander, Lieutenant General Eric Wahlgren; Head of Civil Affairs, Cedric Thornberry; José Maria Mendiluce; and Jeremy Brade, special representative of European Community mediator David Owen and UN envoy Cyrus Vance. General Morillon spearheaded UNPROFOR's Bosnian delegation. Mladić was told in no uncertain terms that the Serbs would face the wrath of the international community should there be a repeat of the human rights abuses their forces had committed in other places. It was patently clear that he couldn't care less. He coldly set his conditions: Srebrenica would be spared – if the Bosnians disarmed. Then he nonchalantly went off to play table tennis with a French officer, who was no match for Mladić, and we watched as he was given a thorough thrashing by the ruthless Serb commander.

While Mladić was playing ping-pong, General Halilović retired to a private room to confer with his team and UN officials about the agonising decision he had to make. The negotiations continued throughout the day and into the night. Wahlgren, Cedric, Viktor, Morillon and Hayes went back and forth between the Bosnian and Serb camps with counter-proposals and alternative suggestions. Every word and sentence of the proposed agreement was scrutinised and rejected countless times by the Serbs. It was cold as a tomb in the concrete airport building, and those of us making up the 'support group' had little to do but stand around and wait for information to process and disseminate. There was nowhere but the cold floor to sit, and as the hours dragged on, it became difficult to support even ourselves. I found out that one of the French legionnaires, Charlie, had lived in South Africa. This small connection earned me some special consideration, and once or twice he brought me a much needed cup of hot tea. There was sporadic firing outside, and suddenly a burst of bullets hit the wall of the room where we were sitting, right next to the window. This caused a momentary flurry and we all moved to a safer corner, away from the window.

After many agonising hours, Generals Halilović and Mladić finally signed the Srebrenica agreement. The Bosnians had no choice but to accept the Serbs' demands. The result of the marathon meeting was a deceptively simple document that offered no hint of the frantic political flurry the Srebrenica crisis had caused in New York. The essence of the agreement was that the Bosnians would disarm. The Serbs agreed to allow those who wanted to, to leave Srebrenica in evacuations organised by UNHCR. A Canadian UNPROFOR contingent would be stationed in the town to monitor the disarmament and see that the Serbs honoured the agreement. However, two years later, few of the people trapped in Srebrenica had been allowed to leave, despite Mladić's signature on the agreement. With years of war in Croatia and Bosnia, and further conflict in Kosovo, the international community reaped what they had sown with their appeasement of the Serbs.

The Srebrenica meeting lasted until well after midnight, and by the time we left the airport, it was three o' clock on the morning of Sunday 18 April. The airport was deserted and wrapped in heavy darkness. In the distance the suburbs of Sarajevo were barely breathing. The slight, cold shimmer of the moon scarcely brushed the rooftops, and the ground was invisible, black as ink. We were escorted to the row of white UN vehicles by a small group of legionnaires. They flanked us like dark shadows, the sound of their heavy boots muffled by the gently swaying mist which, touched by the muted glow of a single torch, looked like milky moonlit water. It felt as unreal as a dream.

Because of the curfew, Mladić had to make special arrangements to allow us through at the Sierra 1 Serb checkpoint between Kiseljak and Sarajevo. On the way to Kiseljak, Vere Hayes radioed orders to the sleepy officer on duty. Clearly and concisely, he stipulated every point of the agreement from memory and gave the relevant orders to be put in place. The last order was: Please get some hot soup and sandwiches ready for the returning group. The officer quipped back: 'Cheese or ham sandwiches, sir?' We laughed, and it sounded odd and out of place after the sombre intensity of the Srebrenica meeting.

I slept for two hours after the meeting and worked all day on Sunday, fervently hoping Sunday night would be quiet, without the sporadic fighting in the hills all night, so I could get some sleep. But a war is not conducted within regular office hours and there was heavy fighting across the country. 'All of Bosnia is burning,' said one my military colleagues. But Srebrenica was foremost in my mind. According to unconfirmed reports, the Serbs were continuing their advance along the south-east confrontation lines and had taken several surrounding villages. This was in breach of the agreement, and the question was whether they would honour it at all. Only time would tell. In central Bosnia, too, fighting between the Bosnians and Croats was on the increase. In the north, the Croats were pounding the town of Bihać with artillery. In Sarajevo, 107 shells had hit the city the previous day, concentrated mainly in the centre around the Presidency, and a soldier from UNPROFOR's Ukrainian Battalion died from his injuries after a mortar landed in the Grahovište area.

It was true. All of Bosnia was ablaze. In Kiseljak, too, the fighting continued. There was small arms and heavy machine-gun fire, and mortar explosions. It was nerve-racking; when it was quiet, I found I was waiting tensely for the next explosion. Life was difficult on all fronts. We had an intermittent supply of electricity and water, and I made sure to have candles and a few containers with extra water ready at home. The problems extended to HQ. There were two civil affairs offices, with Hussein and I on one side of the rambling building, and Viktor on the other, a long walk and numerous flights of stairs away. Because of the electricity breaks it wasn't advisable to use the lift, and there were no internal telephone connections. Our Motorola radios were for emergencies only, and since we constantly needed to liaise with the other side, I walked many kilometres a day between the two offices, and climbed more stairs than I'd ever done in my life.

The fighting escalated when the Bosnians started shelling Kiseljak, and the Croats returned fire from inside the town. At HQ, a report was circulated about the situation in Bosnia, ending with the following: 'In light of the close proximity of the shelling to Kiseljak HQ, personnel should remain calm.' We joked about the 'official orders' to be calm. There was a surreal sense about all the high drama, but we knew how real it was. In Vitez, not far from Kiseljak, there was heavy fighting, and UNPROFOR sources reported that the Croats were going from house to house, 'cleansing' the area of Bosnians and murdering entire families, from babies to grandmothers.

Despite the problems in Kiseljak, I would soon look back on even the tensest times there as quiet and uneventful.

It was one of the ironies of Bosnia that tragedy and the banality of everyday life existed side by side. Coping with this was something I never quite mastered, but neither could I escape from it. On the Friday evening before the Srebrenica meeting, I'd invited a few colleagues, including Vere Hayes, to dinner. In Johannesburg I'd bought several packets of dehydrated vegetables, and I prepared the sweet potatoes as the Afrikaners traditionally do, with sugar, butter and orange peel. At a critical point the fire in the stove went out and the meal was delayed because I had to build another fire. While we were having dinner, Vere received a call to say that a French soldier had been killed in an attack in Sarajevo. He hastily finished his meal and rushed back to HQ. Later General Morillon called and corrected: it had been a Ukrainian soldier, the one I would read about in the next day's report. Even though none of us had known the soldier, it put a damper on spirits at the dinner.

On the Monday I received a note from Vere. It was dated 17 April, which meant he'd made time to write it before the meeting on Saturday. It read:

> Dear Anne Marie, thank you for last night. It was a pleasure to relax
> for a while away from our 'hotel' even if the phone rang too often
> and I had to leave in a hurry! Your foresight in bringing some sweet
> potatoes and other essentials with you gave us a delicious supper, not in
> the least bit spoilt by having to wait! I hope you are able to visit Dover;
> it would be a pleasure to return your hospitality and kindness.
>
> Thank you again. Happy Easter! Yours ever, Vere.

The note made me cringe with guilt. While we were having a dinner party and enjoying sweet potatoes, the starving people in Srebrenica were locked in a life-and-death struggle for survival. It took many months, and wise counsel from General Morillon, before I could even start thinking philosophically about the incongruities of life in Bosnia.

The horrors of the war had suddenly become very real. It was no longer TV footage or evidence after the fact such as I'd seen on the way from Zagreb to Kiseljak; I was in reality up to my neck. And it was getting worse. HVO units from Kiseljak and Vitez, on the offensive in central Bosnia, attacked the village of Ahmići and murdered 120 Bosnians in cold blood. They then burnt all the houses. Whole families were massacred, a stone's throw from the base of UNPROFOR's British Battalion in Vitez. When it was discovered three days later, hardened UN soldiers, who had to gather evidence at the spot, were stunned and sickened by what they found. Their reports were horrifying, and footage of the massacred showed the charred bodies of women and girls. I struggled to put my feelings into words: outrage, shock, horror, pity. But I discovered that in Bosnia mere words were totally inadequate for describing what the Serbs and Croats were doing. I always wished I didn't know the details of the terrible things that happened. I still do. It chips away at one's humanity. And these were not isolated incidents: they were the fabric of the war in Bosnia.

The morning after the discovery of the Ahmići massacre, not having the strength to make a fire to boil water for tea before going to HQ, I decided to have orange juice. I absent-mindedly cut one of the oranges I had bought in Šenj. The sudden sight of the bloody flesh was such a shock that I had to sit down. Blood oranges. I'd forgotten. After a week dominated by Srebrenica and Ahmići, endless reports and discussions of murdered and dying children and women, I found I could not squeeze the red juice from the fruit. It seemed indecent, disrespectful. I carefully put the two severed halves together and back in the basket on the table.

Reports from Srebrenica said people were insane from months of fear and stress. I'd had a very small taste of the military activity in Bosnia. Weeks of constant bombardment had to be sheer hell. Perhaps, I thought in my naivety, as result of the agreement life would improve for the more than 40 000 miserable souls trapped in Srebrenica. For those dying slowly and agonisingly, huddled in the snow on the streets that had become their homes; for the traumatised and starving children, who were reported to be eating raw horses' hooves to survive; for the exhausted doctor performing surgery and amputations without anaesthetic. What none of us knew then was that we, officials of UNPROFOR, representatives of the civilised world, had handed the Serbs the weapon with which they would carry out Srebrenica's death sentence. By preventing UNPROFOR from taking action, the international community had abandoned thousands of desperate men, women and children to the mercy of the Serbs. We had forsaken the terrified, freezing and starving people of Srebrenica, abdicated responsibility on behalf of the international community – well-fed men and women asleep in warm beds in New York, London, Paris, Toronto.

The agreement, however, was not the end, merely the beginning of the end. The Serb leadership signed numerous agreements safeguarding the lives of Bosnian civilians, including those in Srebrenica. While that agreement was being discussed, Mladić had taken a piece of blank paper, signed it and contemptuously tossed it back at the UN delegation – indicating that it didn't matter one iota to him what the UN's stipulations were. Nor, it seemed, to the rest of the Serb leadership.

For Srebrenica, two more years of unimaginable suffering lay ahead, which would end with the barbaric killing by Serb forces of 7 000 men and boys in the summer of 1995.

Little did I know when we left Sarajevo airport that cold, dark April morning in 1993, that I had witnessed the signing of their death warrant.

CHAPTER 4

WELCOME TO HELL

APRIL 1993

Welcome to Hell.

ONE OF SARAJEVO'S EMBATTLED CITIZENS had painted these bitter words of welcome for 'visitors' to Bosnia's besieged capital. The anguished greeting was sprayed in black paint in large, uneven letters on the bullet-scarred, roofless wall of what used to be a small shop. Throughout the war this caustic graffiti stood as silent testimony to Sarajevo's agony. It became the most photographed and telecast three words in the world, flashed and beamed around the globe by the international media as the catchphrase for the misery that had enveloped the people of Sarajevo and Bosnia. It was no exaggeration. Sarajevo indeed offered an uncharted experience: a glimpse of hell. This beautiful city, which had inspired poets and artists for centuries, was now in its death throes.

My first visit to Sarajevo was on 10 April 1993, two days after arriving in Bosnia. It was an acutely distressing encounter. Sarajevo was a ghostly city. Empty streets wound past the stark skeletons of burnt-out buildings and the faded beauty of Austro-Hungarian architecture, once the pride of the empire's brilliant architects.

The old city, Baščaršija, bustling for centuries with traders and craftsmen displaying their exquisite wares, was silent, devastated by thousands of Serb shells. It was bitingly cold and the luminous snow on the mountains was brighter than the bleak daylight in the city. The day before there had been heavy tank and mortar attacks, and the few people who braved the danger and cold hurried along with grim faces. The children were pale, their expressionless eyes and pinched, grim faces bespeaking privation and lost innocence. I remembered having read, 'To witness violence is to be a victim of violence.' Shattered glass carpeted the deserted pavements, reflecting fleeting flashes of sunlight. Piles of burning garbage sent clouds of foul black smoke billowing into the cold air. It was a scene from Armageddon, life at the end of the world. It was difficult to imagine how some 400 000 people could be living in this city – and that it had been like this for a year. Why was the international community doing nothing to stop this? What were we *doing* if it looked like this a year after the UN had become involved? Day after day, hundreds, sometimes thousands, of heavy artillery, mortar and tank shells rained on the city, fired from Serb cannons in the surrounding mountains. And as if that wasn't enough, Serb snipers, perched around the city, indiscriminately murdered children, women, the elderly, international peacekeepers, the media – whoever appeared in their deadly sights. The Serbs were generous: anyone who wished could share in their efforts to annihilate Bosnia, and men from Serbia and Montenegro started a tradition of travelling to Sarajevo on weekends to fire a shell or two at its beleaguered inhabitants. The fact that many Sarajevans were Serbs evidently didn't bother them. The end apparently justified the means, and the end was the end of Bosnia and Bosnians – at any cost. Many Serbs had parents and families in Sarajevo. Some were trapped; some didn't want to leave. I met a senior Serb official whose ex-wife and children were living in Sarajevo. And I met the ex-wife and daughter of a Serb soldier. One could perhaps understand ex-wives being expendable in Serb illusions of a greater Serbia. But the children?

Nothing I'd read, seen or heard could have prepared me for coming face to face with the carnage wrought by the Serbs. The graphic TV images of devastation and suffering were too compartmentalised and abstract, too far removed from the reality of average everyday life in the 1990s, to convey the actual effect. While I was in Johannesburg, I studied a pile of information about the situation, and after travelling for three days through war-torn Croatia and Bosnia, I thought I had a complete picture of the war. But what I'd seen there were merely the symptoms of the disease; entering Sarajevo was like stumbling into the heart of the cancer. It was the chilling evidence of the tidal wave of hatred that was sweeping over Bosnia. People in Sarajevo were like the walking dead. They were pale and emaciated with sunken eyes, incessantly smoking anything they could lay their hands on, and drinking the strongest coffee I'd ever tasted – those fortunate enough to have coffee. Those who weren't burnt rice to make a kind of ersatz coffee. The city's beleaguered citizens had made it through the first year of war, and the first winter. They'd survived with hardly any food, water, electricity and medical supplies. But they were starving and freezing. During winter, from early October until well into April, families huddled in a single room in their apartments, trying to keep warm. Here they cooked, lived and slept. Mercifully they didn't know then that this would be their fate for another three years, another three long, terrible winters.

———————————

Sarajevo had for centuries blended the philosophies of socialism and capitalism, the cultures of East and West, Christianity and Islam.

The old Orthodox Church, circa 1539; the Careva Mosque, built in 1560; the old Jewish Synagogue, built in 1566, two decades after Sephardic Jews expelled from Spain had found sanctuary in Bosnia; the Roman Catholic Cathedral, built in 1889 – all had kept vigil over Sarajevo through centuries of war and turmoil. They still stood side by side, mute witnesses to the inconceivable: a war, in the final decade of the twentieth century, where people were brutally killing their neighbours to get their land. For hundreds of years, Sarajevo had stood as evidence of the promise of peaceful co-existence. In 1992 the city became the dividing line between everything that was noble and courageous in man – and everything epitomising evil.

The Serbs fired the first shots in Sarajevo on 5 April 1992, claiming the war's first victim. Suada Dilberović was twenty-one, blonde, beautiful and a medical student at the University of Sarajevo. She wasn't Bosnian, but from Dubrovnik, the ancient Dalmatian city that had fallen prey to Serb barbarity in 1991 when the JNA attacked Croatia. Her parents lived there, and she joined thousands of Sarajevans in a peaceful demonstration to protest against the threat of war. The next day, 6 April, JNA aircraft dropped the first bombs on the city. It is painfully ironic that this happened forty-seven years to the day after the Partisans liberated Sarajevo from German occupation in 1945 – a day Sarajevans had celebrated as a day of liberation and joy for close to half a century. The German occupiers had left Sarajevo virtually untouched. But the Serbs were systematically destroying the city with a daily barrage of bombs, rockets, artillery and mortar shells. On 3 May, combined forces of the JNA and rebel Bosnian Serbs closed the last road into and out of Sarajevo. The city was surrounded by Serb forces, totally isolated – the way it would remain for almost four years. General Ratko Mladić stood in the mountains encircling Sarajevo, gazed out over the city, and ordered: 'Shoot at slow intervals till I order you to stop. Target the Muslim neighbourhoods, not many Serbs live there. Shell them till they're on the edge of madness.'

When I first set foot in Sarajevo, a year after Mladić's diabolical order, many of its people were indeed close to the edge of madness. This, however, had brought Mladić no closer to the satisfaction of witnessing the city's capitulation. On the contrary – the brutal Serb offensive had strengthened Sarajevans' resolve never to surrender to their murderous former neighbours. They knew from the many reports of the previous year that surrender meant certain death. Instead, they stoically endured the endless bombing and starvation – a slow strangulation.

I visited the spot from where Gavrilo Princip had triggered the bloodiest war of the century almost eighty years earlier. It was too dangerous to leave the protection of the armoured car, so I gazed through the window at the empty space on the wall of the Youth Museum, Mlada Bosna, from where the Serbs had removed for safekeeping the plaque with Princip's footprints immortalised in cement. The Serbs were so close that they could see the monument's empty pedestal from the hills around the city. From there they kept their ominous vigil over Sarajevo and shelled their neighbours, friends and family with whom – only months earlier – they'd been living, laughing, working, sharing love and sorrow.

———————

Because of the three-pronged war, the forty kilometres of road between Kiseljak and Sarajevo passed from Croat-controlled territory in and around Kiseljak, across no-man's-land, and through Serb-controlled territory between Kiseljak and Sarajevo, across another stretch of deadly no-man's-land and then into the besieged territory controlled by Bosnian government forces. The military situation in Bosnia was extremely confusing: in some areas Serbs

NOT TRUE! YOU CANNOT SEE OVER MOD bldgs.

were fighting the Croats and Bosnian forces, in other areas allied Serb and Croat forces were battling the Bosnian army, and in yet others Croats were fighting against the Serbs. UN personnel were supposed to have unhindered freedom of movement, but like much of the terminology in war-torn Bosnia, this existed on paper only. We were stopped and questioned at checkpoints, often searched, regularly refused passage, and sometimes threatened. Soldiers at checkpoints had absolute power and often didn't answer to their military high command, but to regional warlords with their own agendas and objectives.

One of the most dangerous stretches of road in Bosnia – if not the most dangerous – was the road through no-man's-land to the south [*west*] of Sarajevo that bordered the airport. Battling with difficult Bosnian names, UNPROFOR identified the Serb checkpoints as S-1, S-2 and S-3, and to facilitate radio communication the military christened them Sierra 1, 2 and 3. From 'Sierra 3', the Serb check-point on Kasindolska Road next to the airport, to the first Bosnian checkpoint on a hairpin bend in the suburb of Nedžarići, travellers were at the mercy of shells and gunfire from both sides, and I had my share of terrifying moments on this road. If you drove slowly enough to be safe on the twisting road full of large potholes and craters left by exploding shells, you were an easy target for snipers. If you drove fast enough to be a difficult target, you risked overturning the vehicle. Because this was the only way in and out of Sarajevo from Kiseljak and Pale, there was no avoiding it. Later, when I had to brave it several times a week, I started having a nightmare: that one of the graves in the small graveyard in no-man's-land was mine.

This road passed through some of the worst battlefields of Bosnia. Here the earth was drenched with the blood of fallen soldiers, the clear skies dense with the thunderous echoes of battle and, beneath, the silence of death. The confrontation lines criss-crossed the wasteland that, before the war, had been the thriving suburbs of Butmir and Nedžarići. The only traffic allowed here were UN vehicles, humanitarian agencies affiliated with UNHCR, and on the odd occasion an armoured car belonging to the BBC or CNN. Drivers dashed across at breakneck speed, and thus I first saw Butmir and Nedžarići through the windows of a vehicle hurtling down the crater-filled road. Although it was like watching a film on fast-forward, it nevertheless left me numb with shock. Craters gaped from houses' bullet-ridden walls like large empty windows. Roofs had been torn off, walls blackened by fire. The road was lined with the skeletons of tanks and other vehicles. On the other side of the airport, like a mirror image, lay the suburb Dobrinja. Here the virtually unarmed Bosnian army fought a desperate ongoing battle with the heavily armed Serbs for the precious ground on which stood the Sarajevo airport – a lifeline into the besieged city. Many of Sarajevo's thousands of dead had died in Nedžarići, Butmir and Dobrinja during the fierce fighting for control of the airport. Every inch of ground had been paid for in blood. The lives, dreams and hopes of inhabitants were buried beneath the rubble that had been their homes. I was astonished to find on my first trip that people were still living there. On one side of the road a man was standing in the garden of his half-destroyed house gazing with unseeing eyes at the surrounding hopelessness. On the opposite side was a young woman with a laughing baby on her hip. Whenever there was a moment's respite, these die-hards would be working in their gardens, hanging out laundry or just enjoying a few hours outside the confines of their cold, dark homes. Oblivious of the sadness and desperation that had engulfed her world, a dog with heavy, swinging teats was crossing the road, trailed by three tail-wagging puppies. The air was heavy with tension and it was eerily quiet – the silence before the storm. In time I came to dread this silence. It fell over the city like a heavy, suffocating blanket between the thunderous bouts of shelling, and was as bad, if not worse, than the high-pitched whining of the shells, the earth-shattering explosions and the ominous rattle of gunfire.

Throughout the centuries of her existence, Sarajevo had been depicted in the enraptured terms usually reserved for an irresistible woman: as a temptress, a seductress, bewitching and alluring. Two thousand years of enchanted tradition had seeped into the walls and trees, and whispered secret poetry to those who would listen, to enchant them for life. From underneath the debris of war, Sarajevo still breathed a silent siren song that entwined many in an embrace at once awe-inspiring and deadly. Despite the devastation, I immediately fell under this magical spell. For me, incredibly (or perhaps not, after my experiences in Kiseljak) Sarajevo was to become a kind of retreat.

By 1993, the Holiday Inn near the city centre had become one of the most famous hotels in the world, and a popular target for Serb shells. The bright yellow walls, a mocking reminder of the prosperity and cheer of the past, were blackened by soot from a year's fires, and the shattered windows were covered with black plastic bags. Incredibly, the foreign media, who flitted in and out of the city like frantic business executives, were still staying there at the exorbitant price of US$150 per night, which included cold meals in the windowless restaurant – but no electricity or hot water. A short distance from the Holiday Inn, down Maršala Tita Street and left into Djure Džaković, was UNPROFOR's 'Forward headquarters', the headquarters of military commander General Philippe Morillon. Abbreviated to 'BH Forward' or 'Forward HQ', and called 'the Residency' or 'Delegates Club' by Sarajevans, we settled in general for 'Forward'. Amid the destruction and palpable hopelessness it represented a refuge, a bastion of order and normality. The UN had decided it was too dangerous to base the main UNPROFOR headquarters in Sarajevo, and had relocated to Kiseljak. The Forward headquarters was located in the city at the insistence of Morillon, with about sixty support personnel, to facilitate access to the seat of the Bosnian government. There was one office for an UNPROFOR civilian, which had been occupied briefly by two of my predecessors. Conditions in Sarajevo were murderous and few people even considered working there. When I arrived, a fellow colleague had just returned to Zagreb after two weeks in Sarajevo because she found the conditions too daunting.

My first visit to Forward was on the Monday after the Srebrenica meeting. A follow-up meeting had been arranged at the airport to discuss the implementation of the agreement, and we went via Forward. I was feeling nauseous, probably because I'd had very little sleep for days and was drinking too much coffee, and I made the grave mistake of thinking I might feel better if I could splash my face with cold water. I asked directions to the bathroom, and the housekeeper showed me to the toilets in the lobby of the Residency. After a year without water, Sarajevo's sewage system was completely blocked, and the source of the smell that hung over the city. I was totally unprepared for my first encounter with a Sarajevo bathroom. As the door closed behind me, I was overcome by the stench and, not fast enough to make it to the reeking cubicle in the corner, vomited in the nearest receptacle – the basin. To add to the torture, I then had to clean it without running water. There was a large drum of water in the corner and a small plastic container beside it. With tears of nausea and self-pity streaming down my face, and my insides heaving, I tried to hold my breath, scooping several times from the drum to clean the basin. Then I rinsed my hands and face and dashed out, feeling worse than when

I'd arrived. The facilities at the airport also left much to be desired, but were kept in slightly better shape by French soldiers. In time I developed resistance to the stench, as well as the ability to stop breathing for minutes at a time.

Hussein had stayed behind in Kiseljak, so I represented Public Information. By the time the meeting started I was feeling really ill, and ahead lay a whole day – and perhaps night – in the freezing cold concrete building at the airport. The meeting, between the Bosnian army's Colonel Divjak and the Serb General Gvero, lasted twelve agonisingly long hours. The negotiations were difficult, and as the day dragged on, I realised that being reasonable was not a Serb characteristic. Victory hadn't made them any more susceptible to logic, and they were impossibly stubborn. Negotiating with them required dogged perseverance and almost inhuman patience. It was one thing to be actively and directly involved in the negotiations, but sitting on the sidelines, especially when one was in less than mint condition, was torture. Charlie, the kind legionnaire who'd been to South Africa, brought me a cup of hot coffee when I was on the point of collapse. At midday a battle broke out around the airport and the legionnaires immediately filed out to assess the danger and form a protective barrier if necessary. They were professional and efficient, and it was always comforting and reassuring to have them around. As the battle continued, one of the legionnaires was wounded, a grim reminder that danger constantly lurked around every corner.

In Kiseljak there were rumours that the Bosnian army had surrounded the town. Croat refugees were flooding into Kiseljak, and there were increasing rumours of atrocities committed by the retreating Croats against Bosnians. Soldiers at the Croat checkpoint outside Kiseljak threatened a Danish APC with an RPG-7 rocket launcher, and then fired on it with machine guns. The UN soldiers fired back and hit a Croat soldier. Fortunately he wasn't killed, but the tension in Kiseljak reached breaking point. The streets were deserted and UNPROFOR personnel were strictly forbidden to venture into the town. Kilsejak, too, was turning into a ghost town. As always, I found the ominous silence worse than the fighting. It really frayed one's nerves.

Easter was approaching, and Major Vince Hill, a tall African American soldier, started collecting sweets from UNPROFOR personnel for Sarajevo's children, who hadn't seen a single sweet in a year. The box of marshmallow Easter eggs I'd brought from Johannesburg was added to the big black plastic bag, and Vince drove to Sarajevo to distribute the sweets. This, as I later found out, was easier said than done. Like everything in Bosnia, even giving sweets to a group of children was fraught with difficulties. Vince and another soldier who'd accompanied him had a graphic demonstration of this. They went to a sports field where a bunch of children had gathered, and Vince simply started handing out sweets. But within minutes children were converging on them from out of nowhere, and soon Vince was swamped by a horde of desperate children, fighting and clawing to get at the sweets. He eventually had no choice but to run, trailed by the kids. When he told the story we couldn't help laughing at the image of the large soldier running from a bunch of children, but there were tears in many eyes.

I started making regular trips to Sarajevo, and made every effort to meet and speak to people in the city. It was crucial for my work to know as much as possible about the situation, and I was genuinely interested to know how Sarajevans survived and managed in this city where life was simply unthinkable but where people, incredibly, managed to carry on. Sometimes I stayed in the city for a few days, made possible when the Spanish Deputy

Chief of Staff, Lieutenant Colonel Julio Lopez Guarch, offered me the VIP guestroom at Forward. It was like a walk back into history. The slightly dilapidated villa had been a Sarajevo base ('the Residency') of the late Marshall Tito, and after his death it was turned into a private club for the city elite ('Delegates Club'). In 1993, only the exterior revealed that it was a military headquarters: the compound was swathed in barbed wire, sandbags were stacked on scaffolding outside the windows of both lower and upper storeys, and a guard post at the large gate was manned around the clock by an Egyptian soldier in bullet-proof jacket and blue helmet. But the Residency's interior looked as I imagined it had during Tito's time, resulting in the bizarre coexistence of the faded glory of a forgotten era with a modern war machine. Off the entrance hall was the main staircase to the upper floor, wide, curved and carpeted, the kind that would have formed the perfect backdrop for elegant ladies in sweeping ball gowns. General Morillon's office and living quarters were in one wing of the upper story, and the VIP guestroom was in the other. Between the two wings was a communal lounge with television, where the officers gathered to watch the news; and a large area that had probably once been a ballroom, but had been converted into Forward's military operations and communications centre. The walls were covered with maps of all sizes and descriptions, and here the pattern of attacks on Sarajevo and the rest of Bosnia formed a garish mosaic of coloured pins and thick red and black lines. Behind a partition was the communications centre, where radios and other sophisticated equipment crackled, wheezed and screeched day and night. The kitchen was downstairs, as were the foul-smelling bathroom from my earlier encounter (that I avoided at all costs), two dining rooms and a large, quiet reception area with elegant furniture and paintings. The smaller dining room for NCOs was impersonal, like a typical military mess. In the main dining room, where General

Morillon and his officers, including me, had their meals, there was only one large table, but heavy curtains and paintings on the walls gave it the homely feel of a dining room. UN civilians on missions that incorporated a military presence carried a rank comparable with military rank. I thus had the rank of a senior officer. This amused me, and I thought it an unnecessary UN bureaucratic gimmick. But I was wrong – it was absolutely crucial, as I would find out.

Travelling between Sarajevo and Kiseljak was fraught with difficulties, and we regularly got stuck at either end when the Serbs closed the checkpoints. The first time this happened to me I was stuck in Sarajevo for two days because Sierra 1 was closed. A Danish APC, known as the 'shuttle', travelled daily between Kiseljak and Sarajevo with mail and other goods, and there were also some seats for soldiers being rotated, and for other 'passengers', like me. One of the Danish soldiers refused to hand over his box of dirty laundry for the Serbs to check. For him it was a matter of principle. So, too, for the Serbs. While the convoy was stuck there – for forty-six hours – nobody could get through. The Serb checkpoints had become notorious for their 'searches' – often just an excuse to confiscate anything from personal cameras and radios to UN-owned computers and other equipment, most of which was never seen again. It all disappeared into a black hole at the police station in Ilidža, a Sarajevo suburb under Serb control.

The Chinese were right to consider it a curse to wish someone: 'May you live in interesting times.' I was living in all too interesting times. I shuttled between Sarajevo, where fierce battles were raging between the Bosnians and Serbs, and Kiseljak, surrounded by warring Bosnians and Croats. Because of the fighting around Kiseljak, UNPROFOR made contingency plans to evacuate HQ if necessary. There were drills to prepare us for such an eventuality. 'Green alert' meant that the situation was more or less under control. If 'yellow alert' was declared, meaning the possibility of an attack on HQ, everyone had to wear flak jackets and helmets when they left the building. 'Red alert' would be declared if there was an actual attack on HQ. Then everyone had to put on flak jackets and helmets and go to the shelters in designated inner areas or the basement. Danish soldiers taped all the windows so we wouldn't be injured by large pieces of flying glass in case of a direct hit or explosions close to the building. I was really upset when I found out that UNPROFOR, unlike the International Red Cross and UNHCR, would not evacuate their interpreters and other local personnel from Kiseljak. They'd be left behind to fend for themselves. If UNHCR, with more local personnel than UNPROFOR and fewer means could evacuate them, why couldn't we, I demanded to know. Everyone said they were just following orders.

CHAPTER 5

UNPROFOR RADIO

APRIL–MAY 1993

THE WEEK AFTER I ARRIVED, I started working to establish UNPRO-FOR Radio. But I didn't have a single piece of radio equipment. When I was in Zagreb, Cedric explained some of the difficulties and demands of a mission spread over two war-torn countries and said, diplomatically, that circumstances weren't always ideal. I would have formulated it a good deal less tactfully. It was clear that I'd have to be creative and do the best I could, but I had no idea that it would be months before I received so much as a tape recorder. Viktor and Hussein said I shouldn't worry, and that the equipment and other personnel would arrive soon – but I was sceptical.

UNPROFOR's mandate in Bosnia was two-pronged: the military was there to support the distribution of humanitarian assistance by UNHCR and other agencies to a population being slowly starved and frozen to death by the Serbs; and UN civilians were there to promote a peace process. The people of Bosnia – quite reasonably – had expected the UN to come to their rescue, stop the killing and put an end to the war. Their country was, after all, a member of the UN, recognised by the USA, the UK and most European countries.

But within the complex context of 1990s international politics, their expectations were hopelessly unrealistic, and it was my task to explain this to them. Of course not in so many words, although I often wished I could. I had to explain the mandate and clarify the role of the UNPROFOR mission. During the first few weeks I attended meetings, met dozens of people and read whatever I could to familiarise myself with the situation in Bosnia. Then I explained to Viktor and Hussein that I couldn't possibly sit around waiting for something to happen. It would have driven me crazy, and I was either going to work – not just maybe, and not in six months' time, but immediately – or go home. I mapped out a strategy for the radio information programme, Hussein and Viktor approved it, I faxed a copy to Cedric in Zagreb, set up meetings with the relevant Bosnian authorities and got to work.

UNPROFOR couldn't do anything without the agreement of the warring parties: the Bosnian government, the Croats and the Serbs. In particular the Serbs. Since they occupied seventy-five percent of the country and had the Bosnian government besieged, they took it for granted that they could call the shots. On Croat territory, the Croats followed suit. I found it very difficult to reconcile the fact that the UN was letting itself be prescribed to by people acting like barbarians. To my mind the Serbs and Croats had no right to be treated as legitimate political entities in the conflict, and I said so. They were armed rebels, trying to overthrow a legitimate govern- ment and member state of the UN. They were committing wide- spread atrocities, for which there was adequate proof. They showed no regard for the principles of human rights underwritten by the UN in the Geneva Convention, and revelled in the misery of the people they were mercilessly murdering, starving and shelling. Tragically, it took five years and hundreds of thousands of innocent lives before the international community understood that their policy of appeasement had no ameliorating influence but, on the contrary, fed the prevailing ideology of lawlessness and aggression. But there was no changing the ground rules, and I had to toe the line at least some of the time.

In order to demonstrate UNPROFOR's impartiality, we couldn't broadcast from Sarajevo only, as that would be construed as pro-government propaganda and unacceptable to the Serbs and Croats. Thus I had to negotiate airtime for UNPROFOR Radio with the three lots of wartime authorities, which entailed three rounds of difficult negotiations. My previous negotiating experiences stood me in good stead, including the skills I'd acquired during the UNTAG mission in Namibia, where I'd been involved in negotiations with the South African authorities on equal radio and TV airtime for SWAPO and other political parties taking part in the 1989 elections.

On 22 April I had a meeting with the Mayor of Kiseljak, Mr Boro, and his delegation. Mr Boro was also in charge of the HVO in Kiseljak, and the atmosphere was very tense. It was difficult to communicate with the stony-faced Croats through an interpreter, but gradually they relaxed. Since we were based in Kiseljak, I asked whether we could use the primitive studio facilities there for producing and copying our programmes. I stuck to my guns, politely but resolutely, and convinced them that cooperating with us would be beneficial. Eventually Mr Boro offered not only what I'd asked for, but additional radio time. The next negotiations were with representatives of the government-controlled radio station in Sarajevo, Radio BH, officially Radio and Television Bosnia-Herzegovina (RTVBH). The senior government official, Mr Memija, and personnel from the station who attended the meeting were formal and correct and kept their distance. They were totally professional: they asked for nothing, made no demands and agreed to daily broadcasts of the UNPROFOR programme. Last were negotiations with the Serbs – a complicated and frustrating process.

I had to submit a detailed memorandum, motivating the reason for the radio programmes. Even the Bosnians hadn't demanded this. The memorandum had to be sent to the chief liaison officer of the Committee for Co-operation with UNPROFOR, Colonel Zarković, which of itself was a major operation. I sent it to Deyan in Sarajevo, he handed it to the Serb liaison officer at the PTT Building, who carried it to the base at Lukavica, a suburb of Sarajevo under Serb control, and from there it went to Pale, where the Serb leadership had dug themselves in. The reply was that they were, in principle, not opposed to broadcasting the programmes and were prepared to talk about it. And so came my first trip to Pale, much publicised mountain stronghold of the Bosnian Serbs, for a meeting with Bosnian Serb 'president' Dr Radovan Karadžić, whose personal approval was needed. Because Viktor was Russian, he was fairly popular with the Serbs, who were traditional allies of the Russians. For the same reason he was moderately unpopular with the Bosnian government, and the object of much speculation as to his sympathies in the conflict. But he was an experienced diplomat and UN official, and the fact that the Serbs trusted him was to the advantage of UNPROFOR as well as the Bosnians, because he regularly obtained results where others failed. Viktor accompanied me to Pale to smooth the way, and I duly met the Serb leader. He received us warmly, and said he thought the radio programme was a good idea. He smiled throughout the meeting, and when I explained how everything would work, he said it sounded fine and would give the necessary orders for it to be set in motion. Designated Serb officials in Pale and Lukavica would be my contacts. The Croats had swung from hostile and abrasive to the other extreme. The Bosnians had been courteous and professional. The Serbs were friendly and helpful, as they generally were towards UNPROFOR personnel as individuals. However, they never passed up an opportunity to mention their distrust of the UN leadership and the international community. Why they should feel that way I never understood, with the international community bending over backwards to appease them.

The negotiations completed, UNPROFOR officially had a half-hour slot from Monday to Friday for the information programme on the three main radio stations in Bosnia: Radio BH in Sarajevo for the Bosnians, Radio Kiseljak for the Croats, and the Serb radio, SRNA, in Pale for the Serbs. In addition we had an hour on Saturdays and Sundays, which Radio Kiseljak had offered for music broadcasts. The radio net was later extended to include a number of private radio stations, mostly in Sarajevo.

I leapt into action. Carefully. This was a political minefield, and there were numerous issues to be considered and avoided. Since the content would be translated into a language that neither I nor any of my colleagues understood, I decided on a bilingual programme, broadcast in English as well as Serbo-Croatian/Bosnian. This was long-winded and tiresome, but it had to be done. The rationale was made apparent in the introduction:

This is an official UNPROFOR radio programme, produced in English by UNPROFOR personnel. For ease of understanding, programmes are translated by UNPROFOR interpreters. Should there be any ambiguity or misunderstanding, the English original shall prevail.

In two weeks I organised a modus operandi for UNPROFOR Radio, airtime, a production studio and an interpreter. Many months would pass before I received anything from Zagreb, and I borrowed a small tape recorder from Major Luuk Niessen, the Dutch military public information officer, to get started. My planning was dangerously ambitious, and my colleagues warned that I wouldn't be able to keep up broadcasting a daily radio programme from a number of radio stations on my own, and under these conditions. But I focused on the horizon and the promise that help was to arrive soon. I put an SOS message on the notice board at HQ in Kiseljak, asking for soldiers with interest or experience in radio to join the venture. The British chef in Kiseljak, Jason Eskdale, was duly appointed DJ for the Saturday programme, a music and requests slot for UNPROFOR soldiers, which we christened 'At Ease'. He had no radio experience, but took to it like a duck to water. The first of May was D-Day for 'At Ease', the first official UNPROFOR Radio programme to hit the Bosnian airwaves. However, we hadn't managed to produce a programme announcement and signature tune – and had to do it live in the studio. I was certain this hadn't been done since the 1930s, but gathered the 'actors', who lined up behind the microphone. Rick from Public Information barked the order, 'At Ease!', the 'extras' smashed their heavy boots on the studio floor, and the music was patched in. Two seconds of silence preceded the signature tune, but it could have been worse, and we all crept out of the studio and outside cheered loudly at our successful launch. A British officer, Major Rob Tripp, also responded to the SOS. He had radio experience, and became host for the Sunday programme, which he named 'Musical Interlude'. He played soothing middle-of-the-road music, some his own and some borrowed from other soldiers, beautifully presented in a smooth, rich voice. UNPROFOR military generally only stayed in Bosnia for four months. Fortunately, I didn't waste time worrying about the fact that both volunteer presenters would be rotated out of Bosnia in a few months. In Bosnia that was a long time in which much could, and did, change.

The official launch of UNPROFOR Radio's 'flagship' information programme was on 3 May. With millions of displaced people in the country, many forced to flee with little more than the clothes on their backs, it was impossible to tell how many listeners we had. The Bosnians were quite ingenious, however. Information was passed on by word of mouth, and, where possible, groups of people would meet around a single radio to hear the news or listen to their favourite programmes. Some people had solar-powered transistor radios or rechargeable batteries, which locals working for the UN recharged at UNPROFOR compounds where there was generator power. In time, feedback indicated we were reaching enough people to spread the message. Programme content varied, and included information on the UNPROFOR mandate and Security Council resolutions pertaining to Bosnia, the distribution of humanitarian aid, and UNPROFOR's role in repairing roads and electricity, and 'putting a human face' on the mission by introducing individual members of UNPROFOR to the local people. It was a logistically testing operation, covering a vast area in which movement was difficult, dangerous and time-consuming. But I embarked upon the murderous schedule with visions of a convoy of eager broadcasters making their way to Sarajevo, crawling all over Bosnia, collecting information, interviewing UNPROFOR personnel in the field and writing programmes. In my dreams. With the exception of two very short sojourns from personnel stationed in Zagreb, both of whom stayed less than three weeks, the only help I would have was my interpreter.

The purpose of 'putting a human face' on the mission was to illustrate to Bosnians that the daunting and distant figures in fatigues and blue helmets were ordinary people with families, homes, hobbies and pets, who were offering their time and doing their individual best to help. I decided to begin with Vere Hayes, chief of staff at Kiseljak. He had an interesting life to share, with a military career that included terms in Malaysia and Borneo, Germany, Canada and Northern Ireland. He spoke of his wife, four daughters and two dogs. The best part, however, was his home. He was the 205th deputy constable of Dover Castle, and one of the benefits of his civil position was living in the castle. This entitled him on occasion to dine with Queen Elizabeth, the Queen Mother. However, the feedback I received from a Bosnian friend was that some of Vere's sophisticated narrative had been misunderstood by the interpreter, and that in the vernacular Hayes appeared to be somewhat of a lunatic with strange habits. An important endorsement for bilingual programmes, especially when it came to intricate political matters.

In addition to doing the radio programme, I had a mountain of information to absorb, which included military terminology and intimidating Bosnian place names. It took practice saying Nedžarići ['Nedzharichi'], Gračanica ['Grachanitsa'] or Baščaršija ['Bashcharsjiya'], and since I was communicating with the people of the country, I had to get it right. People's names, like Karamehmedović and Hadžisalihović, were equally difficult. Not least was the need to learn the basics of the language so that I could follow what people were talking about. And then there was the confusing military situation, the names of political and military leaders, and knowing who belonged where and which armed faction was controlling what part of the country. I felt it was also important to try to understand not only *what* was happening, but *why*, so I started studying the history of Bosnia and Yugoslavia. My days were long and crammed with things to do from early morning until late at night. Bosnia took over my life. In a sense it was a lifesaver, because it left hardly any time for personal concerns, of which I had plenty. In the two months before my departure, I'd made elaborate plans for my son John and daughter Annéne's care in my absence, but as I was packing the last of my large supply of teabags, tampons and liquid soap, catastrophe struck. The person who was to stay with them while I was away became ill, and this upset all the careful arrangements. There was no time to properly remedy the situation, and I had to resign myself to a hastily made crisis plan, assisted by my friend Karen, John and Annéne, and their father.

John was at university and Annéne in her second last year at high school. Having grown up with a journalist mother who often travelled at home and abroad, they took my decision to go to Bosnia in their stride. Still, I seriously considered not going, but having already signed a contract with the UN, didn't see a way out. It was a terrible dilemma, and I was propelled forward and onto the aeroplane by the momentum of weeks of frantic preparation, with a total nervous collapse snapping at my heels like a pack of wolves. After take-off I ordered a double Scotch, which was more than I usually drank in a month, and read the letter my children had pressed into my hand as I was leaving to board the flight. The words were full of love, support and reassurance. I drank another double Scotch, cried myself to sleep under the furtive curious glances of my fellow passengers, and woke up when breakfast was served on the approach to Frankfurt, feeling as though I'd been involved in a world heavyweight boxing match.

I soon had serious misgivings about producing the programmes in Kiseljak. The conditions, albeit inspiring, were shocking. Radio Kiseljak was broadcasting from a poorly lit bunker so smoke-filled that it was almost impossible to breathe. The local personnel chain-smoked the inferior cigarette brands that were available during the war. Having never smoked, I found it unbearable. With the equipment they'd scraped together (most of which belonged to a disco club before the war), they miraculously managed regular broadcasts. In the small studio, records, cassettes and reels of tape were strewn all over the floor and table, liberally spattered with cigarette ash. My admiration for their ability to manage productive output under these circumstances was sincere, but I had a real problem with the lack of order, and the smoke. And the sound quality was not quite that of the BBC. I shuddered to think that I might have to work there for any length of time, and thought longingly of the immaculate studios in Windhoek where I'd produced programmes for the UNTAG mission.

When I delivered the first programme to Radio BH in Sarajevo, the editor-in-chief, Milenko Vočkić, took me on a guided tour of the building. Built in anticipation of the 1984 Winter Olympics in Sarajevo, it was modern and well equipped, but Serb shells had destroyed half of it, as well as much of the equipment. The only power came from a small generator, just enough to run the broadcasting equipment, and there were no lights or water. Personnel worked three-day shifts to avoid the dangerous entrance, which was a favourite target for Serb snipers and shells. The Serbs tried their utmost to destroy Bosnia's only means of communication with the country and the outside world, but despite the thousands of shells fired at the radio and TV buildings – and at the building that housed *Oslobodjenje*, the daily newspaper – broadcasting continued resolutely throughout the war. For me the pièce de résistance was the Radio BH studios, and the minute I laid eyes on them, I decided I had to produce the programmes in Sarajevo. There was order, discipline and proper broadcasting equipment. It was a heaven-sent alternative to the chaos at Radio Kiseljak. To keep up daily broadcasts, I'd have to work in Sarajevo. But there were several obstacles to overcome. Firstly, I was assigned to the UNPROFOR headquarters in Kiseljak, and UN officials didn't take kindly to any questioning of their absolute bureaucratic right to organise people's lives. Another was housing. But I decided to cross each bridge as I came to it. I scheduled a meeting with the management at Radio BH. Mr Vočkić had been pleased with my compliments of their studios, and when I requested permission to produce the programme at Radio BH, it was immediately granted. Next, I had a talk with deputy chief of staff Julio Lopez Guarch at

Forward, and asked whether I could squat there for a few weeks. He agreed. Only then, armed with what I saw as a fait accompli, did I confront Viktor and Hussein. As I'd expected, they fiercely resisted the idea, but I refused to back off and insisted that if we were to have a programme with any semblance of professionalism, it had to be done in Sarajevo. After some give and take, they agreed that I could produce the programmes in Sarajevo, but had to spend two or three days a week in Kiseljak. We all knew that nobody was going to monitor my movements, but this was their way of emerging from the battle with dignity.

As word of the radio programme spread, I was approached by private radio stations in Sarajevo that wanted to broadcast our material. I had a meeting with Adil Kulenović, director of the independent radio station, Studio 99, close to Forward. The personnel at Studio 99 were working under unspeakable conditions. It was underground – literally – and airless in the cigarette smoke-filled tunnels. Adil told me they desperately needed equipment, including a transmitter. They'd had a transmitter on loan from the Bosnian government, but it was removed because Studio 99 was critical of the government. The Voice of America had offered assistance, but when VOA demanded twelve hours of airtime per day in exchange, Studio 99 declined. Unfortunately I was in no position to help them, but promised to do so if the situation changed.

Initially I used an interpreter from the pool in Kiseljak, then started working with Božica Petković. She'd been a journalist, was experienced and efficient, not as young as many of the others, and I liked her. I did the interviews in English, transcribed the content and wrote the programmes, and Božica translated them into Serbo-Croatian. Then we went to the studio and produced the programmes. Radio BH kindly donated a sound engineer, Fuad, and the two of them were my first team. Fuad spoke no English, but Božica translated. For a while I took her to Sarajevo for recording sessions, but this meant that she, a Bosnian Croat, had to travel through territory held by one de facto enemy, the Bosnian Serbs, to the territory of another enemy, the Bosnian government. She was supposed to be safe with me, but it couldn't be guaranteed. Just four months earlier, in January, the Bosnian deputy prime minister, Hakija Turajlić, had been in an UNPROFOR APC when a Serb soldier at a checkpoint pulled out a gun, shot and killed him. It wasn't worth risking Božica's life, and we tried recording the translation in Kiseljak, but the sound quality was poor. I had to find an interpreter who lived in Sarajevo. After interviewing a number of applicants, I decided on Jamila Milović. She was young, strikingly attractive and spoke excellent English, which she'd learnt as an exchange student in the US. Jamila was a Bosnian. Her father, a Serb, a police officer and loyal Bosnian, had been killed by a sniper in 1992. Her mother was a dentist. Jamila was intelligent, reliable, hard-working and undaunted, and slipped into the routine with ease. Having worked for the Bosnian Department of Foreign Affairs, she understood the political potholes and could advise me on sensitive local issues. In no time we worked together effortlessly. It was just as well. Sarajevo was considered a hazardous location, and in keeping with UN policy, only volunteers could be sent there. In the next few months two of my male colleagues from Zagreb gave it a try, but neither were prepared to stay.

CHAPTER 6

BILALOVAC

MAY 1993

FINGERS OF FEAR GRIPPED MY THROAT. My heart was beating like a wild African drum. At the checkpoint barrier, the Croat soldier, whose stern signals to stop we had ignored, was shouting furiously. His face was crimson and distorted with anger, his fists fiercely punching the air in impotent rage.

The two boys and their great-aunt, whom we'd smuggled out of the imperilled village of Bilalovac, were crouching in the back of the vehicle, making themselves as flat as they could. I was terrified. Their safety was in my hands. Not just that of the boys and their great-aunt, but also of Božica and the two UN soldiers. The unsolicited rescue mission had been solely my idea, and was therefore my responsibility. The two soldiers didn't even know where we were going until we were halfway there. And Božica, like all UN interpreters, stoically carried out whatever tasks she was requested to perform without arguing or complaining about the danger. If we were captured, if anyone came to any harm, I would carry that burden forever. I was praying desperately that we would get back safely.

And that the people of Bilalovac might be saved.

The haunting picture of the helpless villagers was etched on my mind. As the armoured GMC wound its way through the treacherously quiet Sunday countryside, my imagination conjured up images of merciless Croat rebels advancing on the hapless village. I could almost hear the pitiless crunching of their heavy boots as they bore down on the few, virtually unarmed defenders. I thought about Ahmići, where villagers like those in Bilalovac had been shot, their throats cut, burnt to death. I felt sick to my stomach.

Sakib had said the women and children would be evacuated before the men dug in to defend Bilalovac. I wanted to weep. Most of the men were old, like him, with patient eyes and weathered faces, and had little but their bare hands to fight with. And where would the women and children go? Most of the area was already under Croat control. Would they survive? Would they escape the slaughter, which in Bosnia did not spare young, old or women?

During a recording session at Radio BH, Fuad had asked Božica to translate a request: Could we get information about his two sons? When the fighting broke out, he and his wife Vahida had sent the two boys to family in the village of Bilalovac, in the then peaceful countryside. Like almost everyone in Bosnia, they thought the attacks on Sarajevo and other towns were nothing more than a few stupid skirmishes, a sudden, short-lived madness that would be over in a matter of weeks. Even so, they decided to send their children out of Sarajevo until everything had quietened down. The boys, Omar, fourteen, and Jasmin (pronounced 'Yasmeen'), ten, went to their father's uncle Sakib in Bilalovac for the summer. Now, a year later, hostilities in central Bosnia were escalating daily, and the peaceful village of Bilalovac was at risk of being engulfed by advancing Croat forces. Because Fuad worked at Radio BH, he heard every report about the war and knew of the danger to Bilalovac. And he hadn't received news of his children for months.

Back in Kiseljak, I went to G-5, Civil Military Operations, tasked with liaising between civilians and the military. G-5 was run by two American officers, Lieutenant Colonel Greg Hightower and Captain Craig Harrington, and a British major, Justin Hayward. I asked if they could help locate the boys, but the next time I went to Sarajevo, there was still no news of them. Tears trickled down Fuad's cheeks when I told him. Then he announced that he'd decided to cross the runway at the airport to go look for them. Serb snipers had killed scores of people trying to cross the runway, and his chances of survival were slim. I convinced him to give me a few more days to see what I could do. What I thought I could accomplish in a few days I had no idea, but I felt honour-bound to try. When I told G-5 that Fuad was ready to risk his life to find his children, they faxed a 'Missing Persons Trace Request' to the British Battalion at Vitez, and the request was forwarded to the Canadian Battalion at Visoko. Two days later, the Canadians replied that the children were well and with their uncle Sakib in Bilalovac.

Fuad was ecstatic about the news. But he wanted the children out of Bilalovac. One couldn't blame him. There were rumours in Kiseljak that the Croats were planning an attack on Bilalovac, and I made Božica promise not to tell Fuad. Knowing there was imminent danger, I felt compelled to do something, although I didn't even know where to start. Nevertheless, I told Fuad to write a letter to his uncle Sakib, authorising me to take the children from Bilalovac. I didn't want to give him unnecessary hope, and explained over and over that I didn't have a plan and, even if I did, there was no guarantee it would work. All he said, with tears streaming down his face, was, 'Please, please,' one of the few English words he knew.

G-5 confirmed the rumours of an impending attack on Bilalovac. They also emphasised that there was absolutely no way of getting the boys out, since UNPROFOR was not authorised to move local people. UNHCR did family reunifications, but the procedures took weeks at best, sometimes months. The same applied to the International Committee for the Red Cross (ICRC). Moreover, neither UNHCR nor ICRC would reunite the children with their parents because there was an official policy not to return children to Sarajevo. If it were possible, they would have evacuated every single child from the city. There simply wasn't time for lengthy procedures. I'd been in Bosnia only three weeks, and hadn't yet learnt how to cut through the endless regulations and maze of UN red tape. If I attempted to fetch the children, I'd be breaching UN regulations – and I'd be on my own if anything went wrong. I received information that advancing Croat forces were apparently planning a revenge attack on Bilalovac after two Croat girls had allegedly been murdered by Bosnian forces. Thousands of Bosnian civilians had been driven out of their homes by the advancing Croats, and there were reports of brutal killings and atrocities in other villages. Bilalovac would be no exception. Omar was old enough to be considered a combatant and could end up in a prison camp, or worse. Even Jasmin might not be safe. There was proof enough to validate the bloodcurdling tales about the killing of children. I was in a panic. True, I didn't know these people, and tens of thousands of families were in the same predicament. But Fuad had pleaded with me, tears running down his face, to save his children, and I simply could not tell him to fill in a form and wait.

There was another snag. Fuad suggested that I contact his aunt in Kiseljak to ask whether the boys could stay with her if I got them out of Bilalovac. But when Božica and I went to her house it was locked, and a neighbour told us she was away visiting her son. It was impossible to take the boys to Sarajevo. If I got them out of Bilalovac, I'd have to take them to Kiseljak, which was only moderately safer, as the Croat authorities had also started expelling the Bosnians from this town. I knew I should explain the situation to Fuad, say that I was sorry but couldn't help, and get on with my work. But I also knew I wouldn't be able to shrug helplessly and mouth empty words of sympathy if the children were killed. I didn't know what to do. I thought it might be possible to hide the boys upstairs in my part of the house in Kiseljak, but it would be difficult to keep two children cooped up in an upstairs room for weeks – or months. What if they ventured out when I wasn't there, what if Viktor discovered them, what if they fell ill? It also seemed a little silly and melodramatic, like an Anne Frank fixation. I decided to cross each bridge as I came to it. If I got the boys out, I could fret about the next obstacle.

On 9 May I celebrated my birthday. It was a Sunday. Neither fact made any difference to my work routine, however. Helping Fuad's boys was uppermost in my mind, and thus, when the opportunity arose, I acted almost instinctively. On Sundays the pace usually slowed down somewhat and people were a little more relaxed. I was in Viktor's office when he told his secretary that General Morillon was in Kiseljak, and that he was on his way to a meeting with him. In an instant a plan formed in my head. I ambushed Viktor as he marched through the door and asked whether his driver could take me somewhere. I braced myself for a refusal or interrogation, but all he said was, 'Yes, but don't be long.' Viktor's car, an armoured GMC, might ensure the success of the mission. Not only because it was armoured, but because it had tinted windows. And as the only one of its kind, the GMC was recognised in the region as the Civil Affairs chief's vehicle, and didn't have problems getting through checkpoints. I raced to the reception area where Viktor's driver, a British soldier, waited when on duty. The regular driver was on leave, and I told his replacement, Danny, that Viktor had given permission for him to drive me, and that we had to leave immediately. There was considerable risk involved in the trip, and I told him this. I said he could refuse to go, but that I would take full responsibility if there were any problems. I was hoping he wouldn't refuse because I couldn't drive the GMC. It was like a submarine – you needed special training to drive it. He agreed, and I thought he seemed a touch amused. Perhaps he thought I was being melodramatic; perhaps he couldn't imagine an ordinary girl like me getting involved in anything dangerous. I rushed to my office to grab my things. Bill the American major was there and asked why I was in such a hurry. I panted that I was quickly going somewhere, and he asked if he could come along for the ride. I could think of worse problems than having an armed babysitter, so I told him what I'd told Danny about the risk and my responsibility. 'Okay,' he drawled, suitably unimpressed by my secretive explanation. 'I'll ride shotgun.' I told him to meet me at the car, and ran like the wind to fetch Božica, praying she'd be there. It would be hopeless going without her. I didn't know where the village was, and couldn't speak the language. She knew I wanted to fetch the boys, so all I needed to say, breathlessly, was, 'We're going to Bilalovac.' Her eyes widened in surprise, but she immediately jumped up, grabbed her bag, and we ran to the car, ready for take-off. Danny turned the key and we anticipated the drone of the powerful engine, but it produced nothing but a sterile click. It emerged only now that he hadn't received the necessary prior instruction on driving the vehicle. Bill walked around to the driver's side, and the two of them flicked switches and pushed knobs. I was wringing my hands. After a while Bill shook his head, indicating defeat. Danny continued fingering the panel of switches that looked like the controls of a Boeing 737, fiddling with one switch after another without success. I was getting frantic. It would be a terrible blow to lose the sudden stroke of luck in getting Viktor's car. Danny was still pressing switches, and suddenly the engine purred into action, eliciting a collective sigh of relief. We glided past the Danish guards in their military fatigues, blue helmets and heavy bullet-proof jackets at the gate, and into the HVO-controlled area. Božica navigated, but I still didn't tell Bill and Danny where we were going, or why. If things went wrong, all of us could be sent home in disgrace, lose our jobs, or both. And that would be the good news. In May 1993 in central Bosnia, where senseless violence reigned supreme, much worse was possible. UNPROFOR personnel had been killed and wounded, and we knew that physical danger was our constant companion wherever we went.

The biggest problem wasn't getting to Bilalovac, because we could make up any story while we didn't have the boys with us. But if we managed to get them out of Bilalovac, the danger would be in returning to Kiseljak. I wondered whether I should forget the whole thing and turn back. But I couldn't – not having come this far. The road from Kiseljak to Bilalovac passed through several Croat check-points, and I gave Danny strict orders not to stop at any of them. He was to drive slowly and steadily through the checkpoints, not too fast, not too slow, but no stopping. I reasoned that if we didn't stop on the way to Bilalovac and got away with it, we could attempt a repeat on the way back. If, on the other hand, the entire HVO stormed after us, shooting and firing rockets, then I'd need a different tactic. What if it worked on the way there, but not on the way back, with the boys in the car? I decided to take a leap of faith. Fortunately the Croats had not yet erected beams across the roads as the Serbs had done. HVO checkpoints consisted of a barrier across one side of the road, and another barrier a few metres further on the opposite side, and although one had to drive fairly slowly to get around the barriers, you could nevertheless keep going. We would exercise UNPROFOR's so-called freedom of movement, which in practice was non-existent, but we couldn't risk jeopardising our mission by stopping and being turned back. Soldiers at checkpoints had total power and could turn us back with any excuse. We had to keep going. Despite much smiling and waving through the windscreen, the soldiers at the checkpoints were none too pleased with us for not stopping, and looking back I could see them angrily gesticulating at the disappearing vehicle. But the fact that it was known to be Viktor's vehicle seemed to work, and we reached Bilalovac without incident.

It was a small village, indistinct from hundreds of others in the former Yugoslavia, with quiet streets, a few shops and a cluster of modest homes, all white with red roofs. We didn't have the address for Fuad's uncle Sakib, but asked a woman walking at the side of the road for directions. Sakib and his wife Emina were simple, elderly people – the salt of the earth. Božica gave them the letter from Fuad and answered their questions. In view of the impending danger to the village, they instantly agreed that the children should leave with us.

Inhabitants of small villages the world over are driven by the determination to know everyone else's business. Bilalovac was no different. Soon a large group of people had converged on the house. It was unusual to have UNPROFOR visitors in their village, and they wanted to know what we were doing there, but I'd asked Božica, Sakib and Emina to say only that I knew the boys' father in Sarajevo and had come to see them. I was in a desperate hurry to get away. The longer we were there, the better the chances that word might get out to the soldiers at the checkpoints. There were many divisions in this society, and in a war between people who had lived together all their lives, almost nothing the one side did was a secret to the other. We'd already attracted too much attention, and I was terrified our visit might be reported, prompting investigations at the checkpoints. But since there'd been no way of sending a message to Sakib and Emina, time was needed to pack the children's things. Sakib offered beer to Danny and Bill, who stayed outside to keep an eye on the GMC, and Božica and I had coffee in the lounge while Emina went to pack the boys' clothes. Danny was making his debut as an amateur entertainer, and the children in front of the house were screaming with laughter at his antics. Bill was having an intense discussion with the men, who were very interested in his rifle and our impressive vehicle. They asked questions in Serbo-Croatian, which Bill answered in his American drawl. The language barrier seemed to be no problem. I wanted Božica to explain the situation to Omar and Jasmin, and asked to see them. Only then did it appear that we were facing a major crisis. Jasmin had gone off to play with friends and Omar was sent to bring him home, but couldn't find him. This really gave me a fright, but Božica said not to worry, it was a small place and they'd find him while his aunt was packing their things. After a while Emina emerged with the first bags. She was accompanied by another woman, whom she introduced as their houseguest, Fuad's aunt Hatidža from Kiseljak. Everyone called her Tidža. This was the aunt with whom the children were supposed to stay in Kiseljak, and as divine providence would have it, she was visiting Sakib and Emina. She agreed that the children could stay with her, but of course she'd have to get back first. Considering the threat of an attack on Bilalovac, she was more than happy to return with us, despite the less than enviable situation in Kiseljak. I was relieved beyond words that we'd found her, although it meant an additional illegal passenger in the car, an extra liability. But Jasmin was still missing, and I was fast becoming a nervous wreck. It would be a catastrophe if, having come this far, we had to leave the boys – or one of them – behind. There wouldn't be another opportunity to get them out of

Bilalovac if the Croats were indeed ready to attack. What was I to do if we couldn't find the little one? Dare I separate them and take only Omar? He was, after all, in more danger. But all they had in this hostile world was each other. It was a serious dilemma and I was frantically weighing up the pros and cons. We couldn't wait much longer. I wished someone would tell me what to do, but as Fuad's official delegate the decision was clearly mine. It was a scenario from hell. I was thinking of the dozens of villages that had been destroyed, the tens of thousands of innocent people – including children – who had already been killed. What if the village was attacked the next day and everyone was massacred? Shouldn't I at least save one of the boys in case the worst happened?

Although not a word had been said to any of the bystanders, they guessed what was going on, and many joined in the search for Jasmin. While we were waiting, Sakib quietly discussed the impending attack with us. Božica translated. They were making arrangements to evacuate the women and children from the village. The men, he said, would stay and fight. He was neither confident nor defiant, just stoical and resigned. His quiet words gave me an enormous lump in my throat. These simple people's terrible predicament made me feel suddenly ill equipped to deal with the emotional onslaught of all this tragedy and suffering. I was sad, angry and frustrated about being a witness to people's fear and misery, yet forbidden to help them. Why couldn't UNPROFOR move them all to a safe place? We were supposed to be impartial, yes, but surely this couldn't mean leaving helpless, unarmed civilians, the elderly, women and children, at the mercy of advancing – and barbaric – enemy forces.

In front of Sakib's house was a cluster of little girls between six and ten years old. They were dressed up in their mothers' clothes, their small feet wobbling on high heels several sizes too big. Bright red and pink lipstick, and blue and green eyeshadow, were clumsily smeared over their faces. They were playing like little girls do all over the world, pretending to be adults. Their world was teetering on the brink of an abyss, and could disappear over the edge at any moment. I wanted to scream like a banshee. At the Serbs, the Croats, the UN Secretary-General, presidents and prime ministers and kings – at everyone who could do something to stop this terrible, terrible war, and did nothing. Božica, who'd been talking to some women, tugged at my arm and said they wanted her to translate something for me. 'They say thank you for fetching Omar and Jasmin and taking them away from the danger.' Half a dozen smiling faces were turned in my direction, their eyes fixed on me. The words were like a burning dagger in my chest. Tears filled my eyes. These women, mothers, were thanking me for rescuing the children of strangers, while their own children had to stay in this damned village and face the advancing terror. The shame of the whole world bore down on me. They would join the thousands of women in Bosnia who had to set off with the few belongings they could carry, clutching their children's hands, leaving behind unarmed men to defend their homes. How many would end up in camps, separated from their families, never to see them again? What fate was awaiting these laughing little girls with the innocent eyes I was leaving behind? I struggled to choke back the tears. It would have been easier if the women had cursed me, even attacked me, for turning my back on their children. But they smiled at me, though their eyes were full of sorrow. Not anger. Just deep sadness.

We had to leave. This meant I had to announce the awful verdict and leave behind another child – or two – in Bilalovac. I felt like an executioner, and all I could think was that I wanted to be as far away from this place as I could get; where I didn't have to turn my back on children and mothers who might be killed the next day by people who were once their friends and neighbours.

Incredibly, like a scene from a third-rate sentimental movie, Jasmin appeared at that very moment higher up the road on a friend's bicycle. A loud cheer went up, and when the little boy with the smiling, grubby face jumped off the bicycle, everyone talked at the same time, scolding him for going off, for getting dirty, for making us wait. Emina wanted him to clean up, but I refused. We had to leave. Immediately. The boys had lived with Sakib and Emina for almost a year, and their goodbyes were emotional. Omar was at the age where he had to appear tough, and although tears were brimming in his eyes, he kept his face stony and stared straight ahead. Jasmin looked a little bewildered, not having had any time to adjust to the thought of leaving. I was grateful that Tidža was going with us, and that they would be staying with her. At least she was someone they knew. The boys' faces were passive and resigned, and my heart went out to them. Like millions of Bosnians they were shunted from pillar to post, at the mercy of other people – strangers – with no say about what was happening to them. We bundled them into the back of the luxury car while the other children looked on with longing, their natural childish envy like a wordless accusation. I forced myself to look at them: the children we were leaving behind, the children who might not live beyond tomorrow. Refusing to look at them would be to disregard what was happening to them; and I pledged that I would remember. My silent promise to them was that I would keep this memory with me – and not allow the world to forget. Not Bilalovac's nightmare. Not Bosnia's nightmare.

I felt like a badly frayed piece of rag. And we still had to get back to Kiseljak. I suddenly felt blind terror. What if the Croats stopped the car and took them? What if we were attacked? What would I say to Fuad and Vahida? Admittedly, they'd begged me to fetch the children, and Tidža had come along voluntarily, happily, but that would be small consolation if they came to harm. This was why people weren't prepared to stick their necks out. It was an awesome responsibility, not to mention the risk of personal injury or capture, losing your job and having your career and professional reputation ruined. But sometimes you have to act as your conscience dictates. Whatever Bill and Danny might have thought earlier, they now fully understood the gravity of the situation. There was no need to explain it to Tidža and the boys: they were Bosnians; they knew. It also wasn't necessary to remind Danny to keep going at all costs. Getting shot at wasn't the biggest danger, because the armoured GMC was built to withstand a major attack; even its tyres were bullet-proof. Still, I was hoping it wouldn't be put to the test – and that it would live up to its reputation if disaster did strike. It was quiet in the car. Nobody spoke. We clenched our teeth and hands, and fixed our eyes on the road where the first checkpoint would soon appear. Božica relayed my instructions to our three passengers: when a checkpoint appeared in the distance, they were to make themselves as small as possible. Fortunately the tinted side windows made it virtually impossible to see them from outside. Unless we were forced to open the doors, we had a chance. We did a test run. The boys curled up tightly in the open luggage compartment, pressing themselves against the back seat. Bill and Božica covered them with the bags. Tidža curled up with her head on Božica's lap, and we covered her with my jacket. None of us, least of all me, believed we'd get away with these absurd improvisations if we were stopped. Apprehension was written all over Bill and Danny's faces. Božica was nervously chewing her lip. It was almost a relief when the first checkpoint appeared. As we approached the first barrier, a soldier jumped into the road and indicated that we had to stop. Danny's face was grim, and from the corner of my eye I could see Bill on the back seat tightening his grip on the gun.

My throat was as dry as dust. Danny slowly wove around the barriers and kept going, without accelerating, without slowing down. Again, as we had on our way to Bilalovac, we smiled and waved at the soldier, and I was hoping that the fixed grimace on my face didn't look as suspicious as it felt. It seemed as though we were hardly moving. Danny swung to the left, drove slowly past the barrier on the right, past the soldier, past the barrier on the left and on towards Kiseljak. When I looked back, the soldier was doing an impersonation of a boxer in the middle of the road. His face was contorted and his fists punched the air around him. He was clearly not impressed with us for ignoring his gesticulations to stop. As the distance between us and the performing soldier increased, I concentrated on bringing my breathing under control and forcing a calm expression onto my face. Božica gave our three 'fugitives' the all-clear, they sat up, and I gave them a tight little smile, which didn't fool Tidža. But she smiled back serenely and reassuringly, and I immediately loved her. There was clearly fibre under the soft, somewhat nervous exterior. She was signalling to me not to worry, that she was prepared for whatever may happen. Someone should erect a monument to the women of Bosnia. Throughout the war they were pillars of tenacity and grace, and I never met anyone who was not impressed by their courage and inner strength.

Our ordeal was far from over. We had no idea whether the soldiers at the checkpoints were in radio communication, and I imagined an urgent message splitting the air to the next checkpoint. We knew that at the very least there would be a repeat performance, and it might be worse. But we had crossed the point of no return. We sat in silence, straining to see when the next checkpoint would appear. As soon as it loomed in the distance, our three passengers assumed their hide-and-seek positions. When we came close enough, it seemed that my worst fears had come true. A soldier was already standing in the road. The usual slouch of boredom had given way to an air of alert expectancy. Had he received a message from his comrade down the road, or was he just trying to prevent us from ignoring him and driving on as we'd done earlier? I thrust my face as close to the windscreen as I could, told Bill to sit forward, and we smiled and waved. The soldier had fixed himself in the middle of the narrow road like someone playing chicken. He ignored our smiles and frantic waving, which was probably to be expected. Danny slowed down, trying to mislead him into thinking we were going to stop. Then he accelerated, but not too much, and swerved around the soldier to the other side of the road. The soldier realised that we weren't going to stop. Again. As I glanced back I saw his face, contorted in rage. He was outdoing his colleague at the first checkpoint in a furious dance, like a menacing character from a Chinese opera. Mesmerised, I couldn't take my eyes off him. Then, suddenly, he stopped jumping and swinging his arms. In one quick movement he swung the automatic rifle off his shoulder and into his hands. My heart stopped, and a thousand frantic thoughts raced through my mind. There was no need to say anything; Danny was watching in the rear-view mirror. He stepped hard on the accelerator and the vehicle shot ahead. A part of me refused to believe that the soldier would shoot at a UN vehicle, especially this particular vehicle. But UN vehicles were constantly getting shot at. I was still staring at the soldier behind us, unable to tear my eyes away, waiting for him to lift the rifle and aim. He didn't. As he shrank into the distance, he furiously waved his fist in the air. Why didn't he shoot? Perhaps the gun had just slipped off his shoulder, like a shoulder bag sometimes does. Perhaps we were out of range. Perhaps he just thought better of it. The silence in the car had become thick and audible. And there was yet another checkpoint to cross. Thankfully Tidža and the boys hadn't witnessed the hair-raising drama. But the tension showed clearly on the other three's faces. And no doubt on mine. It was an agonising wait until, finally, the last checkpoint appeared in the distance.

My heart stopped. There was a group of soldiers at the check-point, engaged in intense discussion, pointing and waving.

This, then, is the end of the road for us, I thought. So near, and yet so far. Danny clutched the steering wheel, his knuckles white. Were they planning to force us to stop? The tension in the car was palpable. It felt as if we were racing towards the checkpoint and the clump of soldiers at high speed. I tried to think what I could do if they wanted to take Tidža and the boys away, and knew I'd be powerless to prevent it. I'd insist that I be allowed to stay with them. And then what? My determined resolution was laughable, ridiculous. I'd already seen enough in Bosnia to know how much attention the Croat soldiers would pay me. The UN with all its lofty agreements and declarations didn't exist for these people. And I was a civilian woman. My brain was swimming in adrenaline, thoughts cascaded into my mind. I knew it would be unwise to be confrontational, but I wasn't going to quietly hand over Tidža and the boys and slink back to Kiseljak. I would demand to see a Red Cross representative. Would Viktor come to our rescue? We were now so close that I could see their eyes. They didn't move. We were at the first barrier. They hardly looked at us. One or two lifted limp hands in an unenthusiastic greeting. What was going on? Were they trying to trick us? They continued with their animated meeting, making no attempt to stop us. We passed the second barrier. Was that it? Or was there a nasty surprise waiting around the next bend? An ambush? Mines in the road? Hundreds of Bosnia's roads were mined, and we often had to stop and wait for mines to be removed before we could pass. I scanned the road ahead for a sign of the familiar triangular objects. Nothing. There were no mines, no more soldiers. As we kept going, and going, and going, it finally dawned on us: we were through. At last we could unclench our teeth and hands. I tried to feel relief, but there was nothing but empty black space. The danger was not altogether over. We could still be confronted before we got back to Kiseljak, or even once we were there. For the moment, however, it seemed the worst was behind us.

Perhaps the soldiers would report to Vere that the vehicle hadn't stopped at the checkpoints, and I would be hauled over the coals. That would be a pleasure.

At last the houses on the outskirts of town appeared. Whatever else happened, we'd made it back to Kiseljak. Never again would I be glad to see Kiseljak, but at that moment it was the most wonderful place on earth. It was late afternoon and dusk was gathering behind the horizon. Soon darkness would be falling slowly across the quiet town. Beneath the treacherous surface of tranquillity, the forces of hate and evil swirled, waiting to envelop the helpless and innocent in their deadly tentacles. But for now, in the lap of the rolling green hills, was the relative safety of UNPRO-FOR. If I had to, I could barricade Tidža and the boys at HQ and create an international incident. I was feeling boisterous, heady with relief, prepared to take on both the Croats and the Secretary-General. Tidža and the children were safe, if only for the moment.

Careful not to arouse suspicion, we dropped Tidža off around the corner from her house. She would go home, greet her neighbours – and make up her own story about how she'd got back. In the meantime we'd drop Božica and the boys at her house and return the GMC. We drove through the early evening to Božica's house with the two boys, silent since Bilalovac. At HQ, Bill, Danny and I transferred the children's baggage into my car, and they readily agreed when I asked them to keep our escapade a secret. This was in everyone's interest, especially Tidža and the boys'. I fetched them and we set off on the last lap. As we left, Božica's sister, Ružica, put her arms around me, and with tears in her eyes said, 'Thank you for saving our children.' She was a Croat, and although she knew Tidža, she didn't know the boys or their parents. But for many people in Bosnia the deliberate division of ethnic groups by their political leaders was a tragedy they neither wanted nor understood. They had lived together, been friends, married each other. These were still 'their' children.

More than anything I wanted to have a hot bath and crawl into bed. I felt as though I was bleeding on the inside at the thought of Bilalovac. But my colleagues had organised a special table for dinner to celebrate my birthday, and since I couldn't let on about anything, I had to put on a cheerful face. After dinner I was presented with a chocolate cake they had organised with the kitchen staff as a birthday surprise. It had 'Happy Birthday Anné Mariè' written on it, and we washed it down with champagne. There were even a few presents, including a huge bunch of red and yellow tulips. But I felt as though I wasn't there. In my mind the images rippled, as in a large still lake scattered with pebbles: of the little girls of Bilalovac with their brightly painted faces; of the sadness and resignation in their mothers' eyes; and of Sakib's wrinkled face when he said, 'The men will stay and fight.'

I had been in Bosnia for one month. It felt like ten years.

Bilalovac disappeared into the massive firestorm raging across Bosnia. I tried to find out what had happened, but there was heavy fighting throughout central Bosnia, and reports were conflicting and confusing. I wondered about Sakib and Emina, about the little girls and their mothers, about the village's unarmed defenders. But I wasn't sure I could deal with finding out that the village had been destroyed, and dozens of the villagers and their children murdered, as in Ahmići. I decided to be grateful for getting Omar and Jasmin out, and not to dwell on Bilalovac's fate. But the innocent faces of those little girls, clumsily painted like drawings in a nursery school scrapbook, are etched forever in my mind, as is the memory of the women gathered around our vehicle, mute with resignation and anguish.

CHAPTER 7

SARAJEVO

DURING WORLD WAR II, a legend originated about Sarajevo. Its inhabitants resisted the brutal German occupation with a tenacity of spirit that baffled and frustrated the invaders. A high-ranking Wehrmacht officer on a visit asked the officer commanding the German troops in Sarajevo about rumours that a certain mysterious 'Walter' was said to be leading the resistance against the occupation. The Sarajevo-based officer said, 'I will show you Walter.' He took his superior to a hill overlooking the city. 'That,' he said, with a sweeping gesture to include the entire city, 'is Walter.'

In 1992, Walter, the legendary spirit of Sarajevo, awoke from a long slumber. Authentic integrity and genuine beauty are impossible to destroy, and under the layers of pain and suffering, Sarajevo's true qualities remained: in the spirit of her people, their perseverance and unflinching courage. Everyone who had a weapon and could fight took up position in the narrow streets to battle the invading Serb tanks. With a collection of weapons that would have been laughable had the situation not been so deadly serious, and with extraordinary bravery and determination, the city's people forced the surprised Serbs to retreat. Sarajevo's valiant fighters then regrouped, formed the Patriotic League, started digging trenches and prepared for war.

Sarajevo's resistance consisted of more than military defence. The city's artists developed their own brand of non-violent resistance, which for me was a living miracle. What kept me sane in Sarajevo was that amazing thing we call the human spirit, and Sarajevo was the Mount Everest of the human spirit. In the words of American writer Susan Sontag: 'To make art in Sarajevo is a heroic act, an act of moral resistance to the genocide and the siege.' Many actors, artists, musicians and dancers had died or disappeared, but those still in the city set about reviving Walter. They retrieved paints and palettes, costumes and musical instruments, rounded up the city's talent and started painting, singing, dancing, rehearsing and organising theatre performances and art exhibitions. Their moral strength and defiant, creative endeavours provided vital cerebral and spiritual nourishment for their fellow citizens. Achille Oliva, director of the Venice Biennial, aptly summarised the importance of Sarajevo's artists to the city's survival:

Of course, art does not defeat war but it can produce a strong moral resistance to violence. This effect is capable of spreading, even within a short period of time, throughout a besieged population.

When a population is forced to live hidden away from mortar attacks, besieged in a way that reminds us of ferocious tribalism from the past, artists have sometimes had to conceal their creative needs as they may seem inappropriate or anachronistic. Under these conditions, they work quickly, quietly, underground, in seeming defiance of fear, determined to keep alive the expressive dignity of an entire population.

This ferocious siege has been unable to destroy the desire and need for creativity and it is obvious that the inner riches of this work result from a strong resistance to ... barbarism ...

On 24 April 1993, two weeks after my first visit to the city, I was introduced to this heroic act of moral resistance when I was invited to the opening of the art exhibition, 'Witnesses of Existence'. Then I also heard that local artists were staging a production of *Hair*. This wasn't New York or even Johannesburg; there was a war going on, Sarajevo was under constant bombardment, and you had to be very careful to stick your head out in case it got in the way of a sniper's bullet. And they were staging a musical and an art exhibition? They were indeed. I was to discover that, behind the suffering and destruction, was a world of wonder, hope and life. The 'Witnesses' exhibition was the work of six well-known Sarajevo artists: Zoran Bogdanović, Sanjin Jukić, Edo Numankadić, Nusret Pašić, Mustafa Skopljak and Petar Waldegg. Not only was this a collection of out-standing works of art; it was a moving, disturbing depiction of war. The exhibition was held in the skeleton of the Obala Gallery, which had been destroyed by Serb shells, and the building seemed to be part of the exhibit, a grotesque impressionist sculpture. It was a burnt-out shell with gaping holes in the walls and roof, blackened and twisted pipes reaching into the dark space. Water dripped from the roof, forming puddles on the floor. Where the roof used to be were pieces of twisted metal and charred beams; the walls were pitch-black. There was no electricity, and candles were placed next to the sculptures and paintings, casting a dim, eerie light on the extraordinary work. The artists had worked with whatever was available: strips of bed linen; bricks and glass from the remains of the Obala Gallery; soil from the city shaped into a mass grave, with the faces of fallen friends and colleagues, immortalised in ceramic, peering out through small windows; a collage of hundreds of small photographs from the obituary pages of the newspaper *Oslo-bodjenje*; bits of humanitarian food aid. The message, however, was not death, or grief, or despair. In every exhibit there was something symbolising hope. One of the exhibits was a video presentation juxtaposing images of Sarajevo during the 1984 Winter Olympics with images of war. The candles were blown out and the theatre cast in total darkness. First there was footage of jubilant crowds along the sparkling streets, and victorious athletes and cheering spectators in the stadiums. Then the thunder of shelling filled the black space, exploding in one's head and on the terrible, bloody images of the dead and dying on the large screen. It was so realistic that several people fainted and had to be carried from the gallery. In me it instilled a dread that remained throughout my stay in Sarajevo: a fear greater than fear for myself, but fear that I would come face to face with the aftermath of an exploded shell or sniper's bullet: mangled bodies, severed limbs and pleading, pain-filled eyes.

After the exhibition I met the director of the Obala Gallery, Miro Purivatra. We exchanged a few words, and he invited me to visit again. Neither of us could imagine the adventure that lay ahead for us, and for 'Witnesses of Existence'. My life was about to become intertwined with Sarajevo's amazing battalion of creative 'soldiers', fighting to preserve the sanity and human dignity of 400 000 people, in the largest concentration camp in history.

In May the Eurovision Song Contest took place in Dublin. The Sarajevo group Fazla had entered a song, 'Sva Bol Svijeta' ['The World's Sorrow'], but the only way out of Sarajevo was across the dangerous airport runway. Adamant that nothing was going to prevent them from taking part, they decided to risk it. One of the members of the group, Erliha, told me the story of their trip to Ireland. On their first attempt they'd hardly set foot on the tarmac when they were spotted by the ever vigilant French legionnaires in charge of the airport, intercepted and taken back to Sarajevo in an APC. Undaunted, they planned another attempt. Again the French intercepted them. They begged, pleaded, explained why they wanted to leave, and promised they were coming back. The French soldiers looked at the handsome young faces and laughed.

To Ireland? That they might buy. But back to Sarajevo? The soldiers said they didn't blame them for wanting to leave but, sorry as they were, they couldn't allow it. Again they were bundled into an APC and taken back to Sarajevo. They made a third attempt. Again they were intercepted. This time the soldiers recognised them, and scolded: 'You again! You young people are irresponsible. This has got to stop. Don't you realise how dangerous this is? You could get killed!' The ritual was the same: into an APC and back into Sarajevo. By now they were thoroughly disheartened. So many people had made it out, and some had made the trip several times. Well, Fazla decided, if others could do it, so could they. Fired by desperation and the relentless march of time, they sped across the runway and ran like the wind, not looking left or right, thinking about nothing but making it to the other side. Erliha lost her shoes, but they all made it on their fourth attempt. There was no transport waiting for them, no accommodation along the way. They were on the outskirts of Sarajevo and they had to reach Split, more than 200 kilometres away, and in between lay battlefields, minefields, the Bosnian Serb Army and the HVO.

Fazla made it to Dublin, sang 'Sva Bol Svijeta', and almost literally brought the house down. Then they returned – along the same tortuous route, the death-defying dash across the runway, back to Sarajevo. I was speechless. Why had they come back? Because they loved Sarajevo.

During my two years in Sarajevo, many of these extraordinary people became my friends. They shared companionship and time, as well as their small, precious supplies of horrendously expensive coffee and food – and entrusted me with what was most dear to them: their artistic endeavours. Most importantly, they inspired all of us in Sarajevo with their courage and hope.

I was honoured and privileged. Few people outside Sarajevo would ever know Walter.

In mid-May I moved into the VIP suite at the Residency on the condition that I'd vacate the rooms if they were needed. Fortunately visitors were few and far between, and I settled in comfortably. The room was spacious with a wide bed in one corner, and in the other a small sitting area with coffee table and chairs covered in faded gold velvet. The en-suite bathroom was a delight, even without water en-tap. Water had to be carted up the wide staircase in buckets and poured into a large plastic drum, from where I scooped it with a jug for washing and flushing the toilet. I had to shower in the main bathroom, which I shared with thirty soldiers. This was a military HQ, not a hotel, and I cherished what little privacy I had. Sandbags were stacked on scaffolding outside the room, completely covering the window closest to the bed. This became necessary after a sniper had fired a bullet through the window, hitting the wall above the bed while someone was sleeping there. But the other window was unobscured, and offered a view of the police headquarters next door and the treeless park across the road. Paintings adorned the walls and the atmosphere was one of quiet comfort and tranquillity. Under any circumstances it would have been comfortable accommodation; under the prevailing circumstances it was positively luxurious. The Residency's front entrance, a wide glass door, led onto an oval driveway encircling a rose garden, bursting with the fragrant blooms that grew effortlessly everywhere in Bosnia – in gardens, hedges, on the roadside, in the fields. One evening in summer, General Morillon picked a lovely orange rose on his way into the dining room and presented it to me. I dried and kept the impromptu gift, a reminder of a simple, gentle moment in a world gone mad. In the garden, stone steps led down into an empty swimming pool. On quiet summer nights, bathed in moonlight, or in winter when the devastation was obscured by a thick layer of snow, the Residency could have been in Italy, France or Switzerland: a comfortable, slightly battered family villa.

The Residency's staff was like a doting family. Some of them had worked there during Tito's time, and were still lovingly tending the building and grounds. Some were ethnic Croats and Serbs, but despite the war continued working together as they had in the past. Rado Djurdjić, also known as Nikola, had been the manager for years. He was always smartly dressed in a light grey suit, white shirt and grey tie, and carried a briefcase, like a successful businessman. He was quiet and dignified and everybody, from the resident general to the most junior NCO, called him 'Mr Manager'. He strongly resembled Boris Yeltsin, and blushed deeply whenever someone remarked on this. Like many of the other staff members, he walked miles to and from work, but was there from early to late, checking on the personnel and inspecting their work. The housekeeper, Gordana, was also there all hours of the day and night, carrying out her duties, which included ironing piles of military fatigues alongside starched white bed linen in a tiny room off the foyer. She had a habit of lovingly brushing the fringes of the Persian carpets on the gleaming wooden floors, and worked tirelessly from dawn well into the night, when she walked miles up the steep hills of the city to her home. The longer I was there, the thinner and more haggard she became, but her energy never seemed to sag. Mirsada, a young attractive woman with a radiant smile, doubled as cleaner and kitchen hand. Goran, the headwaiter, a former Olympic gymnast, regarded everybody as a friend. Every time he saw you, which could be several times a day, he would fling his arm around your shoulder and exclaim, 'My friend!' The other waiter, Izet, was a quiet young man with a shy smile. They became like family to me, and we depended on each other.

———————

Staking my claim to an office at BH Forward proved more difficult than I had anticipated. As I was to find out, practically everything in Sarajevo and Bosnia was fraught with a multitude of problems and personal and political agendas, and invariably required a battle. Sometimes more than one. I'd won the battle with Viktor and Hussein, but there was another one ahead to secure my squatter's rights – with General Morillon. The romantic archetype of an officer and a gentleman, Morillon had started his military career as a Foreign Legionnaire, and could have stepped out of *Lawrence of Arabia*. He smoked Davidoff cigars, had a deep, gravelly voice and the proud bearing of a professional soldier. He was much loved by the staff of 'La Residence', and worshipped by the people of Sarajevo and Bosnia for challenging the Serbs – and the UN – in an attempt to protect the people of Srebrenica in March 1993. From the get-go, my colleagues (male and military) informed me that General Morillon would never allow me to live or work at his HQ, because he didn't want women around. He promptly reassigned the only French female soldier at Forward to HQ at Kiseljak. The general, of course, had his reasons for this, and not many people chose to argue or disobey him. But I said that: 1) I had a job to do, like everyone else, and it so happened that Sarajevo was where I had to do it; 2) I did not expect to be treated any differently to anyone else at Forward; and 3) I was not leaving. They laughed knowingly. I unpacked my bags. For the first two or three days, General Morillon greeted me stiffly and then studiously ignored me. Since I wasn't in the military he couldn't reassign me, and I carried on with my work without asking for help or any favours. Gradually he started to thaw, talked a little to me at the dinner table, and asked about my work. My reply was always that I was fine and didn't need any help – even when I wanted to weep and complain about all my problems, beg him to arrest the Serbs at the checkpoints and whip the rude French soldiers at PTT. One evening, as we were entering the dining room, he invited me to sit next to him. After dinner I was informed by his military assistant that the request denoted a permanent arrangement. The seat next to the general became 'Anné Mariè's chair' and the object of much good-humoured jesting, but the simple gesture indicated that he accepted me as one of the team, and I was much relieved.

When I arrived in Sarajevo, the storm was still raging over General Morillon's defiance of UN policy in Srebrenica a few weeks earlier. His detractors accused him of acting in pursuit of personal glory, and said he lacked the necessary diplomacy and vision. What he had in fact done was put his head on the block. His critics were either people who didn't understand or know anything about the inherent shortcomings and frustrations of being on the UNPRO-FOR mission, or whose agendas were not served by his actions. Morillon was vilified because he'd had the moral courage to defy the Serbs and expose the international community's inconceivably cowardly policy in Bosnia. I came to know him as a man of integrity and moral courage. He was sincerely troubled and saddened by the dire situation in Bosnia and his impotence to alleviate it. He put on a brave face, but we who worked closely with him saw him more than once with his head in his hands, dejected and demoralised by the situation, and frustrated by his inability to act in the face of such enormous human suffering. He often voiced the hope that the Bosnian women, whom he admired for their strength and perseverance, would bring the men to their senses and force them to stop the senseless war.

———————

The Residency was a haven from the madness raging on the other side of the stately walls. The building itself was as vulnerable as any other in Sarajevo but, once inside, one was cushioned by the false sense of security provided by the substantial UN military presence, and the luxury of communication with the outside world, transport, food and medical care. There was also reassurance to be gained from the familiarity and order: formal military rules and strict routine governed life within these walls. The day started with a briefing at 07h30 in the Annex, the building next to the Residency, where I had an office. The designated officer in G-3 (Military Operations) reported on the current state of the war, illustrated by a large map of Bosnia indicating where the Bosnians, Serbs and Croats were engaged in battle; where offences were expected; where UNPROFOR was repairing roads or power lines; and where convoys with food or medical equipment were expected – or had been stopped by the Serbs or Croats. We also heard how much, or how little, humanitarian aid the airlift had brought from Italy in the previous twenty-four hours, how many incoming and outgoing shells had been fired in different areas, whether there'd been small arms fire and heavy machine-gun fire, and the number of casualties. It was not an inspiring start to the day. After the briefing, we went our separate ways.

Dinner, for which we gathered at 19h30, was our only escape from the stringency of our professional lives. It was quite a formal affair, from waiting for the general to enter, and be seated first, to the very correct service by the waiters. The officers dusted off their uniforms and combed their hair, and if I could I changed into a dress, before taking our seats around the large oval table. The simple food was prepared masterfully by the general's personal chef, and we always had French wine. It was an unspoken rule that we'd all be there – and would wait for the general. When he was in negotiations or travelling, we sometimes waited until ten o'clock or later. Some officers grumbled about this custom, but it was the only time we could interact outside of meetings or the routine of our work environment in an informal manner. It was round the dinner table that we debated issues, exchanged ideas, asked each other for advice, and discussed strategy, problems, frustrations – and small victories. We shared support and companionship, which we all needed under the circumstances. It was also an excellent way of building a cohesive team, where we all felt we had a place, despite nationality, rank, or, in my case, gender. We became more than a team: we were substitutes for friends and family. General Morillon enjoyed classical music, and every evening Major Ted Itani, back from Canada after the attack in Kiseljak, and now based at Forward, brought a portable tape recorder and tapes with violin music. Ted's son was a violin virtuoso and some of the tapes were of his performances. Some evenings after dinner, General Morillon made time to let his hair down and relax with the rest of us, and would lead the other officers in singing songs from different countries. When he found out I could play the piano, our musical evenings would commence with the growled order: 'Anmaghrie, play ze pihano!' And I played, and we sang. One of my many unforgettable memories of my time in Sarajevo is General Morillon's gruff voice leading his officers in a French rendition of the well-known Scottish song 'Sweet Ellie Rhee', which the Afrikaners adapted as 'Sarie Marais' during the Anglo-Boer War.

Once, when General Morillon was severely criticised by the media for our 'lavish living', we discussed it over dinner. We weren't eating Russian caviar and strawberries with cream. Just soup, salad, a little meat and vegetables, and a simple dessert – but an unthinkable luxury for the average Sarajevan. We understood the criticism for we were, after all, in a starving city. However, if all the food for the thirty of us were to be shared among the 400 000 hungry people in Sarajevo, it would make hardly any difference to them – whereas we then wouldn't be able to do our work. We were already tired to the bone from working eighteen hours a day, seven days a week. We'd be of no benefit to the Bosnians if we were starving too. This made sense, but I constantly struggled with the fact that we had access to food when so many people in the city were going without. At every opportunity I shared what I had, bought food for my Bosnian friends and colleagues, and gave my share of fruit from the Residency to children in the city. I gathered leftover bones and bits of meat and fed some of the many abandoned dogs in the neighbourhood. After a few days, one of them, a woolly and loveable brown creature, started waiting for me in the same spot every morning for her breakfast, wagging her tail and grinning in welcome.

In addition to the thirty officers and soldiers from France and Spain based at BH Forward, there were also three Americans: an officer and two NCOs. The Americans coordinated 'air drops', which meant humanitarian aid was dropped by parachute into places like Srebrenica, where the Serbs had blockaded the roads. It sounded like a noble idea and a practical solution to a terrible problem but, like almost everything else, it carried the curse of Bosnia, where even the best and most admirable efforts were doomed. When the large pallets were dropped, people on the ground, desperate for food, were crushed or stabbed by other, equally desperate people. Parachuting the pallets in the dead of night, changing the locations and times – nothing helped. People walked for miles, converged on all possible locations, where they waited all night if necessary. The air drop operation commenced in March, and during the first month fifteen people were killed in the wild skirmishes for food. UNPROFOR was caught between a rock and a hard place. People were starving, and we had to keep dropping the food – at the risk of more injuries and deaths.

There was also a contingent of thirty Egyptian soldiers at Forward. They were in charge of security, and all lived on the third floor of the Annex. My office was on the second floor. Ground and first floor were occupied by the Bosnian army. I never understood the decision to move into a building with the Bosnian army; this made UNPROFOR personnel the target of many Serb shells and bullets. The Egyptians, since most of them were Muslims who followed specific dietary prescriptions, cooked for themselves and had their own dining room. Their commanding officer, a captain, was handsome, well educated, spoke perfect English and French, and attended the general's briefings. The friendly faces of the Egyptian guards greeted everyone at the main gate. For the rest, they led a private existence with prayer mats on the floors of their rooms and plaintive calls to prayer. There was a guard post right below my bedroom window and my sleep was often disturbed by Egyptian guards conducting loud conversations in Arabic in the dead of night. Perhaps it was to keep each other awake, or perhaps they were feeling lonely and unsettled under the unfamiliar, threatening Bosnian skies. One of the guards, Mohammed, was a teacher by profession and became my language instructor. He taught me some basic Arabic phrases, and by the time he left I could greet him and reply to his greeting and inquiry as to my well-being.

Soon I was spending most of my time in Sarajevo. The trips to Kiseljak became fewer, as I wrestled with the various demands of my work. When the radio building had no electricity, which was more often than not, all national broadcasts had to rely on the small generator, and I had to wait my turn and live with the numerous interruptions that happened whenever the generator needed to be filled. It often took up to six hours to produce one or two thirty-minute UNPROFOR programmes. Since I had to conduct all the interviews, write the scripts and transcribe them for Jamila to translate, and then deliver the programmes to the radio stations myself, I worked sixteen to eighteen hours a day. It was madness to put in an appearance in Kiseljak if it wasn't essential, and I realised I'd have to live in Sarajevo permanently. Again I encountered strong opposition from Viktor and Hussein. They pointed out that I'd been assigned to Kiseljak, and reminded me that my accommodation arrangement at Forward was temporary and by the grace of the military. When I said I'd find a flat, everybody thought I'd lost my mind. Nobody wanted to live in Sarajevo voluntarily, under constant bombardment and unimaginably difficult conditions. But de facto I was already living there, and I wasn't prepared to spend hours travelling the forty kilometres from Kiseljak to Sarajevo and back in an APC, at an average speed of about 20 kph. Not to mention getting stuck for hours – or days – at checkpoints while UNPROFOR soldiers and Serbs wrangled over underwear! Furthermore, the way I saw it, if the 400 000 people in the city could survive there, I could too. So I transferred myself to Sarajevo.

I quickly learnt that as soon as one problem was solved, there was at least one more waiting to fill the space. In getting my work done, work which was of crucial importance according to the official UN line, I encountered another serious hindrance. To carry out interviews, produce the programme and deliver copies to the different radio stations, I had to travel to Radio BH every day, and between Sarajevo, Kiseljak and Pale several times a week. Transport was a nightmare and I had to beg for lifts from the military, or use the APC shuttle. A one-way laborious trip in the very slow Danish APCs with their caterpillar tracks took over an hour. If there were delays at the checkpoints, it took much longer. I urgently needed my own transport. It was a perfectly reasonable expectation to have transport in order to do my work, but I almost literally had to hijack a vehicle. After struggling for a few weeks without transport, I told Viktor I needed a car. Since he'd been opposed to my move, he wasn't terribly sympathetic, but said an armoured car had been ordered for me and was expected in about five weeks. But five weeks was a long time, and I'd noticed that the Nissan allocated to Hussein was hardly ever used. Viktor said it was too dangerous to drive a soft-skin vehicle (military vocabulary for an ordinary vehicle as opposed to an armoured or bullet-resistant one) in Sarajevo, and I should wait for the armoured car. I argued that any car would be safer than being stuck in the middle of heavy shelling and sniper fire when I was waiting, sometimes for an hour or more, to be fetched by soldiers who often forgot about me. When this happened I had to walk to PTT, dodging shells and bullets. Walking down the notorious Snipers' Alley during a major battle was a thoroughly unsettling experience. One felt at once very small and very, very large, as though it would be impossible for a shell or bullet to miss you. At least in a car I'd be a moving target, not a sitting duck. Viktor insisted I wait for the armoured car and wouldn't budge. But I had an immediate problem that required an immediate solution. I couldn't wait five weeks, and since I hadn't received anything I'd been promised in Zagreb almost two months earlier, I suspected it would take longer than that. Hussein was on leave, so I simply took his car key off the hook, marched to the door, and told Viktor over my shoulder that he could call the guards at the gate to stop me if he wished, but I needed a car. It was unlike me to be so aggressive, but coping in Sarajevo wasn't conducive to being patient with the UN's endless red tape. In Sarajevo that was a luxury that could cost your life. In a million years I'd never understand the UN. In Zagreb, where there were taxis, trams and buses, practically every UNPROFOR employee had a car, and in Sarajevo, where there was no public transport, we battled to get vehicles to do our work.

The Danish guards didn't try to stop me, but the young soldier at the gate said I wasn't allowed to drive alone and had to have an armed military escort. I said give me one. He opened the gate. And off I went on my first solo trip to Sarajevo, alone in my hijacked car. All my previous trips to Sarajevo had been either in the back of Viktor's GMC or in an APC with no windows, with the result that I couldn't really see where I was going. My Canadian colleague Luk Duchesne, concerned that I'd get lost on my own, had given me a map with detailed instructions. I was extremely grateful for this thoughtful gesture. Even with the map on my lap, my heart was beating in my throat. A dozen things could go wrong, and the consequences didn't bear thinking about. It was a most discomforting drive. The part of the road through the countryside was passable and reasonably safe. But once past Ilidža, a suburb of Sarajevo under Serb control, it became noticeably tense. This was a war zone. Buildings were destroyed, there were craters in the road and the Serbs were hostile. The road across the no-man's-land between the airport and Sarajevo was no better for my nerves, since I had to weigh up whether to drive slowly and get shot, or drive really fast and catapult off the road at the dangerous hairpin bend next to the small overgrown cemetery. The final stretch into Sarajevo was no easier. One did not want to get lost here, and I sighed a giant sigh of relief when I pulled into the gate at BH Forward.

When Hussein returned from leave he called and demanded that I return the car. With my newly acquired temerity, I said he was welcome to fetch it. He once told me he wouldn't under any circumstances drive to Sarajevo except in an armoured car, and I was hoping he'd meant it. Two months later he left the mission, and the Nissan stayed with me.

It was a true liberation to have my own car, but it also meant I had to brave the checkpoints on my own. Fortunately I hardly ever had problems at the Bosnian checkpoints, and for most of 1993 this also applied to the HVO checkpoint near Kiseljak. Sierra 3, the Serb checkpoint next to the airport, usually wasn't too bad either, mostly due to the fact that there was often a friendly female guard, Sanja, on duty there. The two of us always had a little chat before I drove on. Sierra 2 was at the junction of the Hadžići–Mostar road, deep in Serb territory, and wasn't guarded. But it was a different story at the Sierra 1 checkpoint at Kobiljaca, a kilometre or two from the HVO checkpoint across a stretch of no-man's-land. The Serbs suspected everyone of supporting their enemies and opposing and undermining their cause, and mostly took their checkpoint duty very seriously indeed. Sierra 1 was a large, busy checkpoint because it was on the route of UNHCR convoys to Sarajevo, which meant more traffic and more vehicles to be checked. Many Serb soldiers were decent and professional and carried out their work efficiently and courteously. But some were cold and hostile and others obnoxious and aggressive, going out of their way to make things difficult and unpleasant. One guard in particular was a nasty, trigger-happy Rambo type, with bloodshot eyes and a vicious black Alsatian dog on a leash. There was always a gun in his hand, and he seemed anxious to find an excuse to use it. He scrutinised every face and vehicle with undisguised suspicion and hostility, and insisted on searching UNPROFOR vehicles as well as personal baggage, which he wasn't supposed to do. More than once I was 'rescued' from him by the good guys who'd got to know me, and they'd intercede to let me through. I hated going through the checkpoints, feeling vulnerable and exposed and at the mercy of people like the Sierra 1 Rambo. But unless I gave up my independence and relied on the military, there was no way round it.

The armoured car I was promised in May 1993 eventually arrived, not five weeks later, not five months later, but almost a year later, in March 1994. By then, without transport, I would have been either a raving lunatic, or dead.

CHAPTER 8

MOVING TO SARAJEVO

MAY–JUNE 1993

THE MONTH OF MAY was my baptism of fire.

During April I shuttled back and forth between Sarajevo and Kiseljak, and because everything was so new and there was so much I had to learn and do, I hardly noticed where I was half the time. May was different. As I spent more time in Sarajevo, with the growing certainty that I'd soon be living there permanently, I started looking differently at the city. By the last week of the month, I woke up in Sarajevo every morning. It was becoming my home.

On 19 May, a young couple, Boško Brkić and Admira Ismić, were killed on the Vrbanja Bridge, one of the dozen bridges across the Miljacka River. The bridges linking Serb-held suburbs of Sarajevo with the besieged part of the city were mined and guarded by heavily armed soldiers on both sides. They had long ceased to carry friends and family to work, school, lazy afternoon visits with coffee and *baklava* or *kadaif*, and dinners at tables laden with *burek, čevapčići, sir, palačinci, wine* and *šlivovic*. Boško was a Serb, Admira a Bosnian, and they'd been sweethearts since high school. It was difficult for him in Sarajevo, being a Serb and a young man, potentially an enemy soldier. Thus, Admira decided to leave the city with him and go to Serbia. They obtained permission through liaison officers from both the Serbs and the Bosnian army to cross the bridge into Serb territory. But as they reached the centre of the bridge, shots rang out, and they were struck down by a hail of bullets. Boško died instantly. Admira was seriously wounded and urgently needed medical help, but the Serbs and Bosnians refused to allow anyone onto the bridge. Admira crawled to where Boško lay and put her one arm around him. Then, perhaps in an attempt to soothe herself, with the other hand she took her comb from her bag and started combing her hair. She lay there until she died three hours later, alone, still with the comb in her hand.

Their bodies lay on the bridge for six days. Neither side would allow the other to claim them. Finally, on the sixth day, UNPRO-FOR gained permission to take the bodies to the Serb side. Admira's distraught parents said they harboured no grudge, and gave permission for their daughter to be buried with her Boško in Serb territory. They were buried on 27 May. Admira's parents couldn't leave Sarajevo, and Boško's mother was the only family member at the funeral. Despite denials by the Serbs, most fingers pointed in their direction, and autopsies after the war confirmed that the shots had been fired from their side.

While the attention of the world was focused on the sad saga of Boško and Admira, twenty people died when the Serbs shelled the central market place. The markets around the city were regular targets because of the concentration of people, and the effect on morale if large numbers were killed and injured, especially when they were at their most vulnerable: exposing themselves in order to survive.

On 26 May I wrote a letter to Annéne and John. It was a farewell letter. My heart was heavy, but I tried to keep the letter light and unsentimental, just telling them how much I loved them, how proud I was of them and what they meant to me. I emphasised that

I didn't have a premonition, but just felt it would be irresponsible not to leave something behind in case the worst happened and I didn't return. I sealed the letter, wrote their names on it and put it with the rest of my documents, so it would be found and sent to them in the event of a disaster. It was true that I had no premonition, but it was impossible not to feel vulnerable and to accept that getting killed was a very real possibility.

On the night of Saturday 29 May, I went to bed with the luxurious knowledge that the next day was Sunday, and I could get up an hour later than the usual 6 a.m. I was hoping the battle-mongers would go to bed early and allow us a decent night's sleep. Battles usually started at first light with the rattle of machine-gun fire, closely followed by the boom of heavy machine guns and the ear-splitting explosions of mortars and shells. But on 30 May I awoke at four o'clock in the morning to what sounded like the soundtrack of the Battle of Britain on full volume. As if on a given signal all hell broke loose, with a barrage of light and heavy machine-gun fire, as well as mortar and artillery explosions. The heavy boom of outgoing mortar fire shattered the early morning silence, and I could tell the shells were being fired from close by. Within the moment of quiet that followed came the eerie echo of dogs howling in terror. The usual pre-dawn twittering of the birds in the large tree outside my bedroom window had given way to loud alarmed chattering, but this was drowned out by the next succession of earth-shattering explosions. It took several minutes before my sleep-dulled mind realised what was going on. I jumped out of bed and ran to the window – which was a most dangerous thing to do in view of all the flying metal in the sky, but the thought never crossed my mind. Astonished, I watched the battle unfold. Tracer bullets splashed fiery lines across the pre-dawn skies and shells exploded in large white flashes, scattering bright stars into the air. The grey of early dawn above Sarajevo was turned into an enormous, deadly fireworks display. I was mesmerised. So were the birds, perched in silent, frozen terror on the branches. Even the dogs were quiet. The poor dogs. The cacophony of exploding shells terrified them and usually they ran around aimlessly, howling and disoriented.

It was clearly a large and well-strategised battle. Bosnian forces were launching an offensive on Serb positions at Špica Špacijena in the mountains above Sarajevo, in an attempt to cut the main Serb supply route to Pale. Mortars, fired from Bosnian positions close to the Residency, ripped from the large barrels with deafening blasts, echoing moments later in the mountains where the Serbs had dug in. In some places the confrontation lines snaked through the suburbs, and machine-gun fire reverberated through the city. The Serbs had obviously been caught napping. For some time the surprise element of the pre-dawn attack provided the Bosnian army with an advantage and it was a one-sided battle, with all the outgoing fire from Sarajevo. But it wasn't long before the Serbs recovered from the surprise. They started returning fire, and soon the heavy thunder of exploding shells roared over the city like a tidal wave, sending billows of smoke and dust into the air. One explosion after another shook the Residency. I was still crouching next to the window, petrified by the ferocity of the battle yet unable to drag myself from the sight of the deadly spectacle, when Barry Frewer banged on my door and shouted at me to go to the shelter. General Morillon was in Kiseljak and Barry, a commander in the Canadian Army and UNPROFOR military spokesman, was the senior officer at Forward. I threw a thick jersey and corduroy pants over my pink winter pyjamas and, as I wriggled into my flak jacket, rehearsed the attack guidelines we'd been given in Kiseljak. This was without question a 'Red Alert' (direct attack), and required wearing the full paraphernalia – indoors as well as outdoors – until the danger had passed.

There was still snow on the mountaintops, and for extra warmth I put on my long raincoat over all my other layers. I imagined that I looked like Rupert the Bear's wife. Then I grabbed my bag and helmet, but couldn't put the helmet on because it was too big and slipped over my eyes. I'd have to wait until I was in the shelter to put it on. My bag contained money, my documents, a notebook and a few other things I thought I might need. Suddenly it struck me that I had no idea how long we'd be in the shelter, nor whether I'd ever get back to my room. One had to be prepared, so I also took the small photo album with a treasured collection of personal photos, the silver jewellery which was a family heirloom and without which I never went anywhere, my toothbrush, extra socks and underwear. Better to be safe than sorry. Before a hasty exit, and on the spur of the moment, I put Luuk's tape recorder on a chair beside the window, propped the microphone up on the windowsill, and then sprinted downstairs to the shelter. My recorded account of the battle, dubbed 'Anné Mariè's war symphony', was later copied over and over again by soldiers who wanted some tangible 'memento' of the war.

The 'shelter' was a storage area for fruit, vegetables, cheese, eggs and other such perishables. It was freezing: almost as cold, in the hours before sunrise, as the large freezers where the meat was kept. One after another, soldiers stumbled into the shelter. Most of them were still half asleep, their eyelids heavy, jowls dotted with dark stubble, faces set in a fierce scowl. Bits of uniform had been thrown hastily over pyjamas, jackets were unbuttoned, boots unlaced. They were unrecognisable as the smartly uniformed men who marched around HQ every day. They were not amused. We'd been rudely awakened, were freezing, and couldn't have coffee. In Sarajevo, coffee was as important as oxygen, and the atmosphere in the shelter was anything but cheerful. There was nowhere to sit except on the cold concrete floor, and we huddled together on our haunches to try to generate a little extra warmth. Conversation was in very short supply, and not only because of the incredible noise of constant explosions. There wasn't much to chat about. We were a sorry looking bunch, and felt foolish, squatting there with the earth literally shaking and the city being destroyed around us. It might have been funny if the situation hadn't been so grave. A deadly battle was raging around us, Sarajevo was being ravaged, dozens of the city's men were dying on the icy mountain slopes. But we, the 'peacekeepers' of the international community's so-called 'protection force', were neither keeping the peace nor protecting anyone. We were reduced to a bedraggled group with bleary eyes and chattering teeth, bedecked like clowns in fancy dress, squatting together on our haunches in a freezing storeroom, surrounded by bags of potatoes, crates of apples and piles of cabbage.

You didn't have to be a military expert to know that this was a serious battle and that the only thing to do for the moment was to stay put. Some of the soldiers were acutely unhappy and quite vocal about their forced impassivity. They'd been trained to fight, or at least fight back, and if ever there was a time and a place to put their training to use, this was it. Even I would have been prepared to take a swipe at the Serbs. When you were under attack, it became difficult to remain impartial towards the people firing the guns. And we were in the epicentre of a deadly battle. The noise was deafening, and when the sound of heavy explosions tapered off, echoes of gunfire could be heard, some of it really close, some further away. The ominous whining that preceded approaching shells hurtling through the air was a sound that made you involuntarily pull your head into your shoulders, and I had pulled my body into a tight knot. We began discussing our options in case the fighting intensified. Our 'shelter' wasn't a proper underground shelter, and vulnerable to direct attack. But if we left the building, we risked being caught in the crossfire. Some of the soldiers suggested we make our way to the designated public shelter just behind the Annex. Others wanted to stay put. We would have to run across open ground, and had never done a drill to familiarise ourselves with the terrain. Since there was no way of knowing where the next explosion would be, and considering the real possibility that snipers were training their sights on the entrance to the shelter, a mistake could be fatal. We decided to relocate only if the Residency took a direct hit or started burning. It was a fortunate decision. It was even more fortunate that we weren't forced by circumstances to relocate. We later discovered that the Bosnian army had locked the gate between the UN compound and the designated shelter, and since we didn't have a key, we'd have been stranded out in the open.

Between barrages of bombing there were pockets of dense silence. I thought about Annéne and John in Johannesburg, and why I too often seemed to find myself in dangerous places and situations. What would happen to them if I didn't go home this time? But I didn't seriously want to entertain that possibility and, anyway, I didn't feel as though I was going to die. I wondered if I'd still feel that way, still doggedly refuse to accept my mortality, even if I were mortally wounded and death were staring me in the face. I didn't particularly want to find out. We stayed in the shelter for three hours, while all-out war roared on around us. Then, with the fighting still incessant but appearing to have subsided somewhat, we filed out a little sheepishly and started our activities for the day. Mine was accompanying Viktor to a meeting in Pale with the Serb leadership. It was strange to encounter the sounds of battle 'behind Serb lines', where it was usually as quiet as a weekday in a Johannesburg suburb. The atmosphere was tense. Karadžić and his associates seemed nervous, without their customary joviality, and were vociferous in their complaints and accusations about the attack. 'This is a war, fellows,' I thought acidly. 'The other side is *expected* to fight back.' They clearly didn't like the shoe being on the other foot.

The battle for Špica Špacijena raged on for the rest of the day and into the night. It was one of the major battles of the war. Some 2 000 shells were fired at Sarajevo, and the Bosnian army suffered heavy casualties. Unfortunately their offensive was unsuccessful. In the week that followed, the Serbs took revenge. For days Sarajevo was punished with retaliatory shelling, unremittingly, day and night. The punishment extended to the rest of the country. On the Tuesday, two Danish drivers and their interpreter were killed in a calculated attack by Serb tanks on an UNHCR convoy in Maglaj. Another two drivers were seriously wounded, and several Bosnian civilians were killed. The next day, fifteen children were killed and seventy people wounded when a crowded sports ground in the Sarajevo suburb of Dobrinja was shelled. Sarajevo seethed with frustrated outrage, cold and grief. Still it was not the end. On the Thursday, three French UNPROFOR soldiers were seriously wounded in an attack on the airport. The Serbs were illustrating, in their inimitable way, that they could do whatever they wanted, not only to the Bosnians, but also to UNPROFOR and, indirectly, to the international community. The Serbs were bullies. As long as nobody challenged them, they intimidated and terrorised their powerless victims with impunity. On many occasions their much-touted bravery was exposed as nothing but empty bragging. They took to their heels when challenged by an equally equipped adversary. Yet the international community continued to refuse to call their bluff.

———————

After a month of working and 'squatting' in Sarajevo, I had few illusions about life in the city. It was brutal. There were none of the standard conveniences associated with modern life. No fuel meant no public transport, and people shuffled through the city in endless lines, their shoulders bent under the weight of buckets of water, bundles of wood and the agony of their existence. The modern, well-equipped shops were either destroyed, or closed and empty. Apart from the meagre humanitarian aid rations, the only food available had to be bought on the black market for staggering sums of foreign currency. Some food and other necessities could be bartered for with cigarettes or other foodstuffs, mostly vegetables grown in the grounds of high-rise apartment blocks or in flower boxes on balconies. There were very few jobs, and no income for those who didn't work. Schools were turned into overcrowded refugee centres, and the few that remained open taught for two to four hours a day, if and when the fighting permitted, and in certain areas only. In some areas people set up schools in the shelters so that children would receive a little education without having to risk walking to school. Many children received hardly any schooling. The overburdened sewerage system and piles of rotting garbage belched the stench of human excretion and decay into the saturated air. A cloud of fetid black smoke hung over the city, as people burnt mountains of garbage that would almost immediately reappear. People's health was in tatters. Dentists couldn't practice because of the lack of electricity and medical supplies. The only doctors were at the Koševo Hospital, and they were stretched to the limits of human endurance. There was no electricity in the operating theatres, no blood plasma, no instruments and very little medication. The hospital rarely had water, and because there was no fuel, ambulances were reserved for dire emergencies. Patients needing urgent medical attention had to find their own way to the hospital, take their own water and food and, if they needed surgery, some fuel for the generator.

Life as modern urbanised people as we knew it, even at its most difficult, seemed as unreal as a trip to the moon, like a vague memory of an almost forgotten dream. A hot bath, a quick dash to the corner cafe for something as basic as bread, or to the chemist for aspirin, had become a mission impossible. With the roads out of Sarajevo in the hands of the Serbs, and the water and electricity supply to the city cut off, the desperate inhabitants' lives centred on the quest for water, food and fuel. They were forced out of the relative safety of their homes to queue for hours for pitifully small quantities of food donated by the international community, brought into the city via the airlift from Italy, or by UNHCR convoys from Croatia. They walked for miles to the closest water source, and joined the long queues to fill as many plastic canisters as they had or could carry. The fortunate ones had wheels: baby prams, wheelbarrows, bicycles, supermarket trolleys, some little boy's converted go-cart or a home-made frame strapped to three or four wheels.

The Brewery was ~~had~~ an H₂O source

Despite the almost insurmountable difficulties, I started thinking longingly of having my own place. Life at the Residency had many advantages, but although everyone was more than hospitable, the invitation wasn't open-ended. And I longed for privacy. The only really private time I had was while sleeping. Sharing a bathroom with thirty soldiers made for amusing anecdotes, but the practicalities were extremely trying. Not for the men, who walked to and from the bathroom with towels wrapped around their waists. But with a soldier shaving or washing at the basin, I had to arrange a change of clothing within easy reach, undress in the damp, steaming cubicle, have a shower, hop around on one foot while drying the other in the cramped space, stuff a damp body into fresh clothing, and emerge feeling flustered and anything but relaxed and refreshed. I knew living in a flat would be difficult and dangerous, but I kept saying to myself, if 400 000 other people can survive in Sarajevo, so can I. Deyan and Carlos had to live in Sarajevo because they were working there, and when I mentioned to Deyan that I wanted to get a flat, he introduced me to a young lawyer with whose help I soon had an apartment in Ciglane, fairly close to HQ, in the same block where Deyan was living. I planned to move in on 1 June. My colleagues were convinced that I was crazy. Sarajevo was experiencing the heaviest shelling of the war, but I felt there really was no alternative.

On 1 June, I moved into the flat and became a resident of Sarajevo. The owners, the Karamehmedović family, were in Sweden. Like many people in Sarajevo, they'd left for a short holiday when fighting broke out, expecting to return in a couple of weeks' time. Many never returned, and most who did found their apartments occupied. Years after the war some were still battling to get their homes back. Mine was an elegant apartment, and I immediately liked it. The lounge was light and sunny and opened onto a small balcony. The black leather lounge furniture wasn't my taste, but there were lovely paintings on the walls, all originals by famous Sarajevo artists, a luxurious oriental carpet on the polished wood floor, and some pot plants. The rest of the flat comprised of a dining room, two bedrooms, a kitchen and a bathroom. There was also a guest toilet, but this small room was filled with the family's valuables and locked. After the Spartan living in Kiseljak and the constraints of the Residency, I felt elated about the luxury of privacy and space. I have never enjoyed hostel-type living – not even in luxury hotels – and cherished my own space. Even the fact that I had no water, electricity or meals laid on – luxuries I'd had at the Residency – couldn't cloud my joy. The flat was a ten-minute walk from the Residency, but this included 200 stairs, down in the morning and back up at night. I couldn't leave my car outside the building at night, as it would have either been stolen or broken into for the fuel. In view of the heavy bombardment and other difficulties awaiting me, my colleagues were kind and supportive. They organised a small house-warming party, and all pitched in to help move my things. Jack, the Dutch sergeant in Public

Information, brought two jerrycans full of water as a house-warming gift. He effortlessly carried them up the stairs (I couldn't move them an inch) and stacked them under the basin in the bathroom. Daniel Rossi, the French adjutant on General Morillon's staff, brought a large bunch of white flowers, and the heady perfume accentuated my liberation from military confines. The others brought biscuits and wine. The warm lounge was flooded with sunlight, and as we talked, laughed and sipped French wine, the war, for a while, seemed far away.

Rob Tripp was the supply officer in Kiseljak, and when he heard I'd moved into a flat, he offered me two large boxes of British rations: tinned foods, sausages, steak and kidney pudding, packets of soup, tea, coffee, a tube each of processed cheese and condensed milk, matches and paraffin blocks for cooking. The precious spread made me feel like a child at Christmas. I'd bought a small camping stove in Johannesburg, and Major Iversen, the Danish officer in charge of supplies, gave me five litres of fuel for it, worth a fortune on the black market, and some large black plastic garbage bags – a treasure in a city without refuse removal or plastic bags. At least I could lug the bags to Forward, where the refuse was removed. I'd also bought an ample supply of full-cream milk powder in Johannesburg, and a mountain of tea – the only thing in the world I truly cannot do without – and started my life of freedom confident that the small stove and suitcase full of Joko and Twinings Earl Grey would get me through the worst times.

My routine started at six in the morning. The small stove had to be kept on the balcony, otherwise the pungent smell of the fuel pervaded the whole flat. I'd light the stove, boil exactly one cup from my precious supply of drinking water stacked in the kitchen in bottles of all description, brew my tea and have it on the balcony overlooking Sarajevo in the soft light of early morning. When there was no fighting the city was silent as a farm, and I'd sip the hot tea and breathe in the peace and quiet. Then I'd take an Irish bath in a bowl of Sarajevo's icy mountain water, and recycle it by rinsing my underwear, washing the kitchen or bathroom floor and then flushing the toilet. Water for dishes was recycled in the same manner. Not a drop of this precious commodity could be wasted. It was astonishing – and alarming – how quickly a full bath of water, the reservoir in every household, became empty. Living in the flat took a little getting used to, but I wouldn't have changed it for anything. For the first few nights I slept in the main bedroom, but then realised I'd be safer in the other bedroom. The main bedroom's wall jutted out, making it vulnerable to Serb shells. Many surrounding buildings had been hit, and in the smaller bedroom I was protected by an additional wall, should the flat take a direct hit. The foldout sofa bed wasn't as comfortable as the good-quality bed in the main bedroom, but the beds were too heavy for me to move alone and I let it be. I spent many nights sleeping on the floor in the small passage. In the beginning of the war people took shelter from the shelling in the basements or stairwells of apartment blocks, which were cold and uncomfortable but safer than inside the flats. After months of shelling people became conditioned – and fatalistic – and stayed in their homes. On a typical night in Sarajevo, Serb shells continued to rock the city until well after midnight, and sometimes non-stop into the next day: wall-to-wall shelling. The Bosnians supplemented their small supply of weapons with home-made bombs made from hot water boilers or drums and used nails and other materials, which they rolled down the mountainsides. These crude devices destroyed everything in their path, and when they exploded, it sounded as though a full-blown Highveld thunderstorm were raging inside the room.

After people had relinquished fleeing to the shelters or stairwells, they simply retreated to the safest spot in their homes during heavy shelling. In most homes, as in mine, the bathroom was the safest place, since there were no windows and it was furthest back from the front of the building. But I simply could not, for hours at a time and sometimes a whole night, brave the stench of Sarajevo's blocked sewerage system. So I chose the second safest place, the small passage just outside the bathroom, where at least there was a door between me and the awful smell. I'd roll my bedding into a thick sausage and unroll it again on the floor – something that in no time I came to do almost automatically, without thought or effort. Eventually I got used to sleeping on the floor, and my body no longer ached from head to toe in the morning as it had at first. Although I closed the door as tightly as I could, the terrible smell seeped through the seams between the door and the walls. Even a rolled-up towel jammed between the door and the floor didn't help much. Although extremely unpleasant, it was the safest place in the flat, and it was no contest when it came to choosing between comfort and survival. In the passage there were two walls between me and the shells being fired from Serb Howitzers, and no windows. These small matters could make the difference between life and death, and I didn't relish the prospect of being buried in a large pile of concrete and bricks, nor that of being beheaded by a pane of flying glass. The windows in the flat were still intact, which was amazing considering how many homes were without windows, and I was much comforted by the fact that all had blinds that could be pulled down to contain flying glass. In the passage I was also a few metres closer to the front door. My personal and UN documents, some cash, my few valuables, underwear and a change of clothing were in a basket right next to the front door. Everybody in Sarajevo had such a stash ready at the door. If a shell exploded in your house, walls came crashing down and it started burning, there was no time to run around and gather things.

Many nights when I returned from Forward, I'd sit on my balcony for a while, watching the evil beauty of tracers painting neon lines across the dark sky, wondering when the shelling would resume. Once a dog in the neighbourhood was hit by a bullet or shrapnel, and I was forced to listen to its desperate howling, hearing the cries grow gradually weaker until they finally ceased. I lay in my bed stiff as a board for the rest of the night, unable to sleep, agonising over the innocent beast's undeserved and uncomprehending misery. Another time I saw a house on a hill close to the city start to burn at the end of a bright tracer line. In no time at all the house was enveloped in flames, and I could see people running, small and dark against the orange glow. Yet another family without a home, watching helplessly as everything they owned turned to ashes.

CHAPTER 9

PARADISE DAMNED

JUNE–JULY 1993

When you come to Sarajevo ... it might prove to be the most important decision you have ever made in your life. Bring: good shoes which make you walk long and run fast, pants with many pockets, pills for water, Deutsche Marks (small denomination), batteries, matches, jar with vitamins, canned food, drinks and cigarettes, [which] will be consumed or exchanged for useful information. You should know when to skip a meal, how to turn trouble into a joke and be relaxed in impossible moments. Learn not to show emotions and don't be fussy about anything. Be ready to sleep in basements, eager to walk and work surrounded by danger. Give up all your former habits. Use the telephone when it works, laugh when it doesn't. You'll laugh a lot. Despise, don't hate.

Fama Survival Guide,
Sarajevo, 1993

WHEN I MOVED INTO THE FLAT, I found out just how hard it was to survive in Sarajevo. Not only was it extremely difficult to find food, but without electricity and gas there was no way to cook it, and few options for preserving it. Another of the many obstacles was the lack of water. In Kiseljak I'd had a trial run on how to live with an intermittent supply of electricity, but there was always water, and the Residency had both commodities. Now I had to cope with no electricity and very little water. I showered at the Residency, but this was now even more cumbersome since I had to carry a change of clothes back and forth, so I often opted for an Irish bath at home. As part of my planning for Bosnia, I'd bought two camping showers in Johannesburg, perfect for Sarajevo. These comprised a large, thick plastic bag, one side clear and the other black, with a sturdy hook at one end and a small tap at the other. Fill with water, put in the sun with the black side up, and the water gets hot. In the African sun, it gets scorching hot. In the mild sun of early spring in Sarajevo, it got steaming hot. You hook it up, open the tap and voila, a shower. But I lived in a flat with no garden, and I couldn't use the bathtub, because that was my water reservoir. So I couldn't use the camping shower. It was good, though, for warming water for dishes and so on. I left it on the balcony in the morning, but soon found that it also didn't really work, because by the time I got home at night the water was cold. To keep the bath full was a challenge: when there was water in the taps, the bath and every receptacle had to be filled up. The problem was that the water arrived without warning, invariably in the middle of the day, and disappeared again after a few hours. This happened every few weeks and caused untold joy – if you were at home to fill your bath and pots. Because I was at Forward at least fourteen hours every day, and often not even in Sarajevo, I was never there when the water came on. This caused me great anxiety. The question of drinking water was even worse. Whereas UNPROFOR military personnel were supplied with a daily ration of boxed water, no such provision was made for

UNPROFOR civilians, and as with everything else, I had to depend on my own resourcefulness, which was severely tested. Water supplies to the city couldn't be sufficiently purified, and therefore drinking water had to be boiled – but this wasn't possible without electricity or gas. To make matters worse, there was a hitch in the distribution of purification tablets, with the result that practically everybody in the city, including me, fell victim to an epidemic of gastric disease. The practicalities of coping with weeks of diarrhoea, without a flushing toilet and toilet paper, is best left unexplained. In summer, when it rained, there was a temporary reprieve from the water problem. People made wonderfully inventive plans to catch rainwater, which was used for gardening, washing floors, laundry and flushing the toilet. The strangest contraptions hung from people's balconies to catch water. Even the puddles of water in the large potholes left by exploding shells were scooped out.

Electricity supply followed a similar hit-and-run pattern, except that it usually came on in the middle of the night. I was advised to leave a radio switched on so that I'd wake up if the electricity came on, and when it did I got up and, like everyone else, washed and scrubbed, ironed my clothes, vacuumed the apartment, and even washed and dried my hair. My neighbours also cooked and made bread or *uštipci* (bread dough fried in oil, like *vetkoek*). It was odd to hear the whine of vacuum cleaners and hairdryers at two or three in the morning, accompanied by the delicious aroma of fresh bread. The first time the electricity came on I got up, switched on all the lights, and then aimlessly wandered around the flat with music filling the quiet space and light glaring at me from every corner. I felt vulnerable in the brightness, having got used to muted candlelight. Even in the Residency the small lamp in my room had provided only soft light. I felt strange and lost, and too tired to decide what to do. Eventually I just made a cup of tea and went back to bed. It didn't take long to get used to the routine though, and soon I too was energetically vacuuming and ironing in the middle of the night. But there was only electricity once every few weeks, and in the interim Sarajevans had to get by. When the Serbs refused to allow candles into the city on the pretext that it was a 'strategic material', Sarajevans made candles from every scrap of leftover wax. I had yet to see a bomb made out of wax candles, but it was useless trying to argue with the Serbs. As an alternative to candles, Sarajevans made *kandilos*. A *kandilo* was a simple lamp: you poured water into a glass jar, added some oil and floated a wick in it with a piece of cork. Oil was very scarce, and extreme care was taken to preserve some of the precious humanitarian-issue cooking oil for a lamp, and use this only when absolutely necessary. Matches were also hard to come by, and thus people spent most of the night sitting in the dark, quietly talking or singing, and going to bed early.

Every effort went into preserving what little food was available. Meat was cut into thin slices, fried if possible, salted and covered with oil. Another method was washing the meat and wrapping it in vinegar-soaked cloth. As time went by, almost everyone in Sarajevo grew vegetables. Pots on balconies and window sills no longer displayed geraniums but spinach, cabbage, carrots, tomatoes, herbs and potatoes. Surplus vegetables were cooked and bottled, pickled or dried. The women of Sarajevo rose to the challenge with grace and quiet determination, and invented recipes to make the little food they had palatable. Not only flour, but rice and pasta were used for bread, cakes and other dishes. Bread dough was cut into thin strips and deep-fried to resemble potato chips. Beans – as well as old bread – were seasoned and made into paté. I discovered that most dishes requiring eggs could be made without: cakes, pancakes, even mayonnaise. Tinned humanitarian aid, often low-quality meat and fish well past the expiry date, was transformed with home-grown herbs and the few treasured spices people still had. Even garden snails appeared on the plates of hungry

Sarajevans, alongside nettle soup. Nettles and rice replaced meat and cheese as the main ingredients in *burek*, the famous mouth-watering Bosnian pie. Rice was also used to make rice wine, which, along with a crude home-made cognac, was kept for celebrations and emergency medicine.

Cooking was as difficult as finding food. People who lived in houses made fires in their backyards, but the majority lived in sprawling apartment blocks. They either cooked on a large collective fire outside the building, made small fires on their balconies, or concocted one of the many ingenious inventions they relied on during the war, such as making small stoves from empty food tins, in which they burnt cardboard and paper. For each difficulty created by the Serbs, Sarajevans found a solution. Nikola Tesla, inventor of alternating current, the alternative to Thomas Edison's system of direct current, was born in the former Yugoslavia on 9 July 1856. He is recognised as the genius who ushered in the age of electrical power, and at the time of his death in 1943, he held over 700 patents. Tesla would have been proud of the brilliant, albeit primitive, inventions of his countrymen.

Help for my water problems arrived from an unexpected source. Anja Kerken was sixteen and her parents, Mima and Seo, were my first friends in Sarajevo. News of a foreigner in the neighbourhood, and one working for UNPROFOR, travelled fast, and many of my neighbours were eager to meet someone who was, in these circumstances, seen as a lifeline. It wasn't easy: I left early and rarely got home before 11 p.m. But occasionally I dashed home during the day to pick up something, or sometimes to change. Once in a while I'd treat myself with a little quiet time, take off my shoes for half an hour, have my own freshly brewed tea on the balcony and then go back to work. This was how I met Anja. She was standing across from the entrance to my building with her friend Dženita, when I arrived. 'Hello, lady,' Anja said. I returned the greeting. 'Do you have cigarettes?' she asked. That stopped me in my tracks. I gave her what I hoped was a stern look, and said, 'No, I do not have cigarettes, because I don't smoke. And neither should you. You are much too young to be smoking.' Anja gave me a meaningful glance, and the girls laughed. Another time, when I lectured her about smoking, she said, 'If we are old enough to die, we are old enough to smoke.' We introduced ourselves and went our separate ways. A week or so later, they were there again one afternoon. Anja was pretty, with shoulder-length brown hair and the soft eyes of a doe. She also possessed a quiet self-confidence that was surprising for someone her age, and was the spokesperson for her group of friends. On our third meeting she gave me an invitation from her mother for coffee with the family. I accepted, and went to the building next door to meet Mima and Seo. They didn't speak English, and Anja had to interpret. They were surprised to learn that I was from Namibia, even more so because I was white. Seo impressed me with his considerable knowledge of Namibia. Like all the Sarajevans I came to know, they were well informed, well read and well travelled. When I lived in New York, I was astonished to find that, despite all the publicity in 1989 and 1990 generated by the UN mission and Namibia's impending independence from South Africa, most people didn't have the vaguest idea where Namibia was.

Until I met the Kerkens, the only friends I'd had in Bosnia were Božica and her family in Kiseljak. They often invited me for coffee, and I spent my only relaxing hours in Kiseljak at their home, talking to Božica and her sister Ružica, who'd lived in Sarajevo before the war. Her husband was still there. He worked at Radio BH, and while I was in Kiseljak, I sometimes took him fresh vegetables from Ružica's large vegetable garden.

The visit to the Kerkens was the first time since my few visits to Božica's family that I'd enjoyed the warmth of a home. My flat was little more than a place to sleep, keep my clothes, and have the occasional cup of tea in peace and quiet. With Anja's help we talked and laughed, and I picked up valuable information about life and circumstances in the city. The Kerkens had had their inevitable share of tragedy. Mima's brother, Nermin Tulić, a well-known actor, had lost both legs when a shell exploded close to him. He just happened to have been in the wrong place at the wrong time. In Sarajevo this could be anywhere, at any time. My time with Mima and Seo was so enjoyable that, without thinking, I reciprocated with an impulsive invitation for dinner the following Saturday. Only after they accepted did I realise with horror that I had no food to offer them. At home I ransacked my two boxes of rations, and put aside the tins of steak and kidney pie, sausages, soup powder and cheese. With some bread from the Residency, drinks and chocolates for dessert, I could improvise a passable meal. I invited two of my military colleagues so that there would be male company for Seo – an American, Major Kevin McGrath, and Justin Hayward, the British major who'd been with G-5 in Kiseljak and then transferred to BH Forward. I did the best I could to turn my meagre rations into a presentable meal, but it seemed woefully inadequate. However, for people who'd eaten nothing but boiled rice and beans for a year it was a feast, the drinks as much as the food. Mima loved the beer, and Seo closed his eyes and gave a heavenly sigh every time he took a sip of whisky. Anja enjoyed the almost forgotten luxury of a Coca-Cola, but refused a second one. 'If I drink more, I would have to go to the toilet,' she said. The reality of life in Sarajevo was never more than a breath away, and people were sensitive not to cause their neighbours any discomfort. But I had a sufficient supply of water and was fortunate enough to have bought toilet paper in Kiseljak, so I assured her it wouldn't be a problem if she had a second drink. She had her work cut out interpreting all the conversations, but it worked like a charm. Seo said Kevin and Justin should have Bosnian names, and renamed them Kemal and Jasmin. We laughed and chatted like old friends, had a lovely evening, and the *dernek* (Bosnian for 'party') forged a permanent bond between us. The Kerkens took me under their wing, and offered that Anja could fill up the bath and other receptacles in my flat when the water came on. I reciprocated by giving them one of my camping showers, about which Mima was over the moon. A few days later I was pleasantly surprised – and a little embarrassed – when I arrived home to find the flat sparkling after Anja had not only filled the bath and all the containers with precious water, but given the whole place a thorough scrub and polish. I rarely had time for more than a cursory flick with the broom and feather duster, and a quick wash of the kitchen floor.

Anja was a remarkable girl. Like many young people I met in Sarajevo, she was mature far beyond her years and carried a heavy load. Both Seo and Mima were fortunate enough to be able to continue with their jobs, although their incomes were practically nil. This meant that most of the responsibility for fetching water, food and wood fell on Anja, who took care of these chores before and after school. My skin crawled when she told me she had collected wood virtually on the confrontation line. When I said she shouldn't take unnecessary risks, she said, 'People get killed in their homes.' Anja's harsh wisdom was very disconcerting. This was the way young people in Sarajevo thought about their lives, suspended by fragile threads manipulated by the Serb puppet masters. It was saddening and infuriating that this young girl and others like her had been robbed of their youth and dreams, and were forced to take death-defying risks in order to keep alive. Which they did with grace, and without making a fuss.

Before long I was living much like a regular Sarajevan, hoarding cardboard and paper, making candles from leftover wax, and fretting over the receding water level in the bath. But I had countless blessings. Unlike my neighbours, I could drive the forty kilometres to Kiseljak, albeit across some of the most dangerous territory on earth, and buy food and other supplies. Or I could board a UN military aircraft, strapped into a flak jacket and parachute, and fly to Italy or Zagreb. However, with vehicles and aircraft continually shot at, and a more than average risk of some other serious mishap, such as having to jump out of a burning aircraft (even if you do know which string of the parachute to pull after five seconds), I never took a flight out of Sarajevo unless there was a compelling reason. Because I had meals at the Residency and bought basic necessities at the military PX shops, I bought food and other provisions for my friends and neighbours when I went to Kiseljak. At the Serb checkpoints there were always suspicious inquiries about the mountains of supplies I was carting to Sarajevo. I said it was for me and my UNPROFOR colleagues. To their credit, some guards let me through without further ado, even when they clearly didn't believe me. Some endeared themselves to me by saying they knew the food wasn't for me but that it was all right, because they knew people in the city were suffering. Like some Germans during World War II and some white South Africans during apartheid, not all Serbs supported what was happening in the former Yugoslavia. But like the Germans and white South Africans, decent Serbs will have to bear their share of judgment, albeit undeserved, for the horrific crimes their countrymen had committed in Bosnia, Croatia and Kosovo.

Since there was hardly any food in Sarajevo, it went without saying that children weren't getting sweets or other treats. I started buying soft drinks and sweets, which I'd load into my car on Friday afternoons and distribute among the children in my immediate neighbourhood. They were beside themselves with joy, but with each of these impromptu 'parties', there were more children. One afternoon I was swamped by a horde of children, including much older boys, some old enough to be in the army. When I opened the car door, these boys shoved me out of the way and grabbed the box of drinks. I was shocked and demanded they bring it back, but they ignored me and walked off. It was a very unnerving experience and forced me to change my modus operandi. I no longer distributed the treats on Fridays, but kept them in my office, put some in my carry bag every few days, and gave them to children at odd intervals. Not knowing when and where I'd produce the treats, the children in my neighbourhood became ever vigilant. They rushed up when they saw me coming, all offering to carry my bag up the stairs in case they were rewarded with a treat. This was both a joy and heart-breaking, because more often than not they were disappointed. But once I learnt how to handle the situation, I no longer had any problems. If I had four sweets and there were five children, I simply waited until I found four children on their own.

In Sarajevo the desire to help could be dangerous. Hungry children constantly swamped our white vehicles with the large black UN emblem, begging for food. And sweets – pleading '*bombon* please,' with grubby little hands outstretched, eager faces and eyes filled with the world's longing and suffering. Soldiers driving through Sarajevo in APCs would throw sweets and food to children in the streets. This caused a fair deal of debate, as some people felt it impolite to throw food at children, even hungry ones. And more than once, it resulted in tragedy. A toddler was killed when he accidentally got shoved under the wheels of an UNHCR truck, and another small boy died when, in his excitement, he fell under the wheels of an APC as Egyptian soldiers, driving down the main road, were throwing sweets to the ever present throng of children. In both cases there were ugly scenes. The UNHCR driver was pulled from the truck and beaten up. UNPROFOR issued strict orders, which were for the most part obeyed, that sweets and food were not to be thrown from moving vehicles.

The plight of the city's animals was another sad tale. All the animals in the zoo perished in the first few months of the war. Those that didn't starve to death were used for target practice by snipers, a terrible indictment of the gunmen and women who later terrorised the city's people with equal callousness. They also shot at anyone who tried to go to the aid of the miserable animals. The last to die was a bear, reduced to a pathetic skeleton and meekly waiting out his last days without food, water or company. With food in such desperately short supply, many people had no choice but to abandon their pets, and the same fate befell animals whose owners left the city. Packs of haggard pedigreed dogs roved the streets and staked out territory around the garbage dumps, where they fought viciously over every edible scrap. For a while I collected leftover bones and meat from the Residency kitchen to feed the dogs in my neighbour-hood, but this had the same disastrous consequences as the sweet distribution. After a few nasty dogfights, I was forced to admit defeat.

———————————

There was no such thing as a safe spot in Sarajevo. There was only dangerous, more dangerous and extremely dangerous, depending on where you were in relation to the confrontation lines and target area for snipers and shells. With the Serbs hugging the high ground around the city, they commanded a perfect view of the area. I was shocked when I started regularly going to Pale, and, pausing on my way up the mountains, realised how clearly everything in the city could be seen, down to people in the streets. When the Serbs shelled a school, a market, the hospital or the balcony of a senior military officer, that was what they were aiming at. When there was random shelling, it was probably because they were bored and just pointed and fired, or because there was a 'volunteer' from Belgrade on his day off behind the gun. A favourite sniper tactic was to single out a mother and child, shoot the child, and when the mother stopped to tend to her wounded child, they would shoot her too. Or vice versa. One morning, as I was leaving for HQ, I bumped into one of my neighbours at the front door of the building. I immediately saw that something was wrong. She was literally white as a sheet and there was a strange expression on her face. When I asked if something was wrong, she pointed at her trouser leg and said, 'Sniper.' There were two holes in her jeans where the bullet had ripped through the fabric, missing her ankle by millimetres. Her young son was with her, and the boy had narrowly missed seeing his mother shot while they were out getting water. The real horror lay in the fact that they had to go out again the next day, and the day after, and the day after that, to queue for water or humanitarian aid. Sarajevans became philosophical about this: they had little choice, and with no transport had to brave the dangerous streets on foot to collect food, water and bits of wood, to visit family and friends, to the hospital for treatment, to the cemetery to bury their dead, or just to get out of their cold, dark, silent homes. Many were killed because of their fatalistic attitude towards the dangers.

One evening Deyan invited a bunch of UNHCR, ICRC and UNPROFOR people to his flat for drinks and snacks. There weren't many opportunities to go out and mingle with other people. Our lives were consumed by work, and even if we could get away, there were very few places to go. We were as boisterous as children on an outing, and all crowded onto Deyan's balcony sipping drinks, talking and laughing. Suddenly, a shell whizzed over our heads and hit the Annex, just below us. There was a mighty explosion, and in an instant everyone was standing in the lounge, momentarily shocked out of our celebratory mood. Carlos had gone to the Annex to see someone, and we were very anxious about him and our colleagues at Forward. There were no private telephone lines at the time and we were reluctant to leave the building. I quietly thanked my lucky stars that I'd accepted Deyan's invitation. Initially I'd declined because of my workload, but he persuaded me to take some time off. To everyone's relief Carlos arrived a while later, shaken but uninjured. He'd had a close shave: the shell had struck as he stepped out of the building, and he was hit by pieces of shrapnel, but none large enough to do real harm. Fortunately it was a strong building and although everyone was shaken, no one was injured. Jack's room was on the side of the building where the shell had struck. He was lying on his bed and was flung onto the floor by the violence of the explosion. When we'd recovered and regrouped on the balcony, Deyan remarked drily that even though we'd 'evacuated' the balcony within seconds, it had been very orderly – and not a single drink had been left behind!

––––––––––––––

Working in Sarajevo meant I had no choice but to stick my neck out. The biggest, but not the only, dangers were getting in and out of the car and walking to the entrance at Radio BH. My work required driving around the city every day, and to surrounding areas on a regular basis. And, since the military were often reluctant to provide assistance to us civilians, I had to expose myself even more often than I would have liked. The two interpreters working for the military at Forward were fetched at home in the morning and taken back in the evening. When Jamila started working for me, I assumed they wouldn't mind including her in the arrangement, but this simple request caused such a ruckus that I decided to fetch and carry her myself. Either that or she'd have had to walk – but she lived in Pofalići with her mother and twin sister, and it was far and dangerous. When I couldn't make it, I'd ask one of my military Public Information colleagues to drive her, and because I offered my car – and also made it available for them on other occasions – this generally worked fairly well. Still, it could be unnerving. Jamila's family lived close to the confrontation line and there was often heavy shelling in the area. Moreover, because they had a Serb surname, people in the neighbourhood often hurled verbal abuse at them, even though Jamila's mother was a Bosnian. Once when I fetched her, some soldiers shouted abuse at her, became threatening and started throwing stones at the car as we drove away. But it was dangerous everywhere and all the trips were hazardous. I was often shot at, especially on Snipers' Alley and the road across the airport. Snipers' Alley was so called because of the high rate of activity, and success, of Serb snipers perched in high-rise buildings overlooking the road. I escaped bullets from machine guns and rifles, and once a tank round was fired over my car. It was on my way back from Pale, and I was amazed that I'd managed to keep the car on the road and hadn't driven straight into a tree or a ditch. My head and ears were ringing from the roar of the explosion, and I was shaking with fright, but instinctively kept going. As always, I wasn't sure whether they'd meant to miss and just wanted to scare me, or whether my guardian angel had had a hand in the outcome. There were plenty of chilling reminders of their successes: a French soldier killed on the same road two days earlier, perhaps by the same gunman; a French soldier shot in the back and paralysed; a humanitarian worker killed by a sniper bullet while driving through Sarajevo. Countless peacekeepers were evacuated with serious wounds. Many were killed. I was one of the fortunate who survived the war physically unharmed; two years in Sarajevo without a scratch was nothing short of a miracle. Many sniper bullets missed me by a hair's breadth. My car was once hit, and I came much too close to being wounded. The building in which I lived was hit by anti-aircraft missiles, and I narrowly escaped serious injury, or worse. Sparks and dust flew, but I remained miraculously unscathed.

In Sarajevo the question of one's safety could become a total preoccupation, and it was better not to dwell on it. Still, thoughts of life and survival often occupied my mind. There was no way of avoiding the danger, and soon after my arrival I sat down and took stock of the situation. The 'war exercise' in Šibenik was all the training I'd be given to equip me for Bosnia. A crash course, so to speak, but a valuable one. When I started working in Sarajevo, my entire being went into the full alert mode I'd experienced in Šibenik. It was most curious. I hardly twitched during heavy shelling, and kept my head when I was on the receiving end of sniper fire. I'd already seen that even hardened men in military uniform, certainly better prepared for war than I, sometimes became anxious and unsettled during attacks. Since I'd never been in a combat situation, I was both surprised and grateful for this survival mechanism. It wasn't that I was fearless in the face of calamity – I just remained rational and in control. I'd always been able to function during a crisis, but past crises had never involved attempts to kill me or anyone around me. However, once everything was over, I was usually shaky, sometimes tearful, and always needed a cup of hot tea to steady myself. What was certain was that I was not an adrenaline junky who thrived on terror and high drama. My approach in general was to try to control irrational fear, since it wouldn't change anything and would almost certainly cloud my judgement. I took every precaution I reasonably could, never recklessly ventured into a situation without some reconnaissance, and then relegated the danger to the back of my mind. For the most part, my rationale worked. One day I was standing in the doorway of Barry Frewer's office in the Annex, talking to him. He was sitting behind his desk with his back to the window overlooking the embankment behind the building, and the hill sloping upwards towards Ciglane. At that moment a mortar exploded right behind the office, shaking the building. Barry involuntarily lifted out of his chair. When he regained his composure, he looked at me with an incredulous expression on his face and said, 'You didn't even bat an eye!' It was true. It was as though my nerves had been petrified. The fright and shock imploded, with no outward signs. No explosion or bullet ever made me jump. I didn't try or will it, it just happened. Perhaps it was a genetic disposition; my ancestors had been warriors as far back as the Crusades and as recently as the World Wars. The moment I left Sarajevo, however, it was a different kettle of fish. If a door slammed, I jumped. If a car backfired, I ducked and pulled my head into my shoulders. On the New Year's Eve of 1995, a fireworks display in Zagreb reduced me to a quivering jelly. It was so bad that I crouched on the ground, holding my head in my lap. I've never quite recovered from being 'shell-shocked', and have a continuing aversion to fireworks or other loud noises, including Highveld thunderstorms.

Considering that UNPROFOR civilians were generally excluded from arrangements made for and by the military, one would have assumed that the civilian administration in Zagreb would do whatever it could to make life tolerable for its officers in war zones. But they apparently didn't deem it worth the trouble. Although snipers were responsible for a substantial percentage of casualties, especially in Sarajevo, the blue flack jacket issued to the handful of UNPROFOR civilians in Bosnia wasn't bullet-proof. It only provided protection against shrapnel. A kind American soldier – astounded by my inadequate safety equipment – gave me a bullet-proof kevlar helmet, and a Canadian, Major Brad Smith, lent me a spare bullet-proof jacket. Ironically, civilian personnel in Zagreb – where not a shot had been fired in two years – were issued with new, high-quality bullet-proof jackets. Civilians in Bosnia were informed that, if we wanted a proper bullet-proof jacket, we had to fetch it ourselves in Zagreb. Moreover, we couldn't take extras for colleagues, but each had to fetch our own. For the three of us working in Sarajevo, this meant a death-defying journey to and from the airport. If you survived the crazy dash down Snipers' Alley and the dangerous no-man's-land en route to the airport, you had to face a flight in an aircraft that would almost certainly be shot at – and often hit – both on take-off from, and arrival in, Sarajevo. UNPROFOR personnel were wounded inside aircraft by bullets fired from the ground. Sarajevo airport was the most dangerous in the world, and given the numbers of UNPROFOR personnel killed and wounded there, one would have thought UN personnel would be discouraged from taking unnecessary risks. Not so. The UNPROFOR officials in Zagreb obstinately refused to send new bullet-proof jackets to Bosnia in exchange for the old ones. The bizarre world of *Alice in Wonderland* pales into insignificance beside the UN.

When my 'civilian' uniform arrived in Sarajevo two months after I did, it consisted of two shirts and short tight skirts in pale khaki. The first time I had to board an APC wearing it, I found the skirt so tight that I couldn't get up the steps. I had to demonstrate elaborately to the Egyptian crew, who spoke no English, that they had to cover their eyes so I could hitch the skirt up over my hips. They hoisted me aboard with their eyes tightly shut, decently waited until I'd pulled the offending miniskirt down over my black cotton panties, and said 'Okay,' before opening their eyes. They laughed till tears streamed down their faces. It was hilarious, I had to agree, but goodness knows what they must have been thinking about Western women and their choice of clothes for battle. I then requested slacks, which only arrived two months later. The upside of having lived in Sarajevo under 'protection' of the United Nations, is that for the rest of my life, nothing on earth can or will ever again surprise or shock me.

CHAPTER 10

MIRACLES

JUNE–JULY 1993

JASNA KARAULA AND I GOT TO KNOW EACH OTHER when she started working as an interpreter for UNPROFOR. She was a quiet, extraordinary woman, a lecturer at the University of Sarajevo's Medical School. The university, like most other institutions, had closed, but final year medical students were accommodated so that they could complete their studies – not least because Sarajevo urgently needed doctors. Early in the morning, before starting a full, long day's work at BH Forward, Jasna lectured at the Medical School. She also took care of her elderly, sickly mother and younger sister, and whenever she had a minute to spare, she walked exhausting distances to distribute medicine, which she got from her medical contacts, to those in need. Her selflessness was seemingly endless, and I loved and admired her. Her life, like those of other Sarajevans, had been shaken to the core, but despite terrible and tragic experiences, she refused to be cowed. Even when she wasn't on one of her many errands, or visiting friends, she often walked around the city as she had before the war. It was dangerous, but she refused to capitulate because, she said, walking kept her sane. To me she was a shining example of Sarajevan women's tenacity. One of the many things we had in common was a love – at times a compulsion – for writing, and Jasna frequently stayed at the office late, sometimes through the night, to pour out her thoughts on her computer.

On 22 January 1993 she'd written a letter about life in Sarajevo to her friend, the American author Sandra Cisneros, in Texas:

Mi querida Sandra,

Your brief letter dated Oct 3, 1992, reached me only three days ago. Do I need to tell you how happy and grateful I was? I am hungry for any word from that other, normal world which seems so terribly remote from the now.

No need to tell you that the citizens of this sad city are deprived of simply everything. We do not have electricity for months, the water supply is cut off most of the time, telephones do not work within the city, not to speak of any kind of connection with the "outer" world. The city is heavily shelled, daily, from the surrounding hills. We still live on the humanitarian aid, which is bad and insufficient, mostly due to the bad distribution within the city.

Everything is so humiliating that I sometimes wonder how much longer I shall be able to stand all these difficulties and the terror of our everyday life, this ever-present feeling of the closeness of death, this hunger for normality, peace, freedom, civilized life. I haven't taken a proper bath for months. We haven't had a single proper normal meal since the beginning of the war. We have almost no heating in the houses, and nothing at all in our offices, schools, hospital. People are dying of cold. All the trees from the streets and city parks are gone. People have cut them in their struggle to survive, so Sarajevo may as well be called a city of fallen trees, a city of cemeteries, a city of grief and pain.

We are still alive, my mother, Zdenka, and me. My mother, however, is very sick. She weighs less than 80 pounds. Zdenka has lost some 40 pounds, and I am about 30 pounds lighter than I was. The food is terribly bad. What we eat is flour, oil, water, salt, rice, various kinds of noodles, a little bit of beans. Occasionally we get some powdered milk, but my stomach cannot take it. During these months of war, we didn't taste a single egg, not to speak of fruit or vegetables. We even tried to prepare bread from ground rice once we ran out of regular wheat flour. Almost everybody except the numerous war profiteers is undernourished. In the summertime we had some apples from the tree in my garden but they were hardly edible, full of worms and sour.

However, the food that I wrote about so much is the smallest problem. We live with some improvised lamps made of pieces of cork, aluminium foil, a shoelace, a little bit of oil in a glass. These little improvised lamps are the only source of light in the majority of Sarajevo households. The lucky ones who were able to preserve the batteries from their cars have a little bit better illumination.

My house is still in one piece, except for several windows broken by detonations. We have just a little bit of wood in my garden shed. We put on a fire in our little stove and that is how we bake bread, how we cook, how we get the house at least a little bit heated.

Maybe one day, if I survive this hell, and if I get a chance to see you again, I'll try to tell the things that I'm trying hard to forget. I still hope that one of my friends is going to leave the city soon and I'll ask him to mail this letter. I feel so miserable that I'm only complaining to you in this letter, but there is no good news here. There is no mental or emotional or physical strength left to put down something nice and comforting. We walk terrible distances just to get some water to drink and to get washed, under the mortar and sniper hits.

I only wish my mother can survive this hell and be out of here before she dies. I would like her to go to Slovenia, to my sister, but she doesn't want to leave Zdenka and me behind. At this moment Zdenka and I cannot leave the city, according to some laws invented for the circumstances of war. Therefore, it is a closed circle of difficulties. I'm lucky because I live so close to the place where I work, so, statistically my chances to survive are a little bit greater. Still, I walk around the city a lot, I move a lot and I believe that is how I am managing to remain normal.

I only wonder what is going to happen if I survive and return to the world of peace and normality. Would I be normal then, when the stress is gone? Maybe this confused and shattered letter is merely an illustration of the state of my mind. I keep thinking, why am I actually writing all this? You cannot help, so what is the point? Do I need your sympathy? It is of little or no help. I would rather write you about how I have fallen in love with a beautiful man, but all the beautiful men are already gone, or soon will be. It would be wonderful to fall in love, but there is hardly any chance for it.

Oh, Sandra, I feel so terribly, so desperately lonely. I'm even deprived of listening to music. I long for the world of peace, normality, music and normal human feelings. I feel so helpless. I have always found some kind of way out, but in a situation like this, everything, simply everything, including my love life, is out of my control. I know that the old faces can never return, what is done cannot be undone, not here, not ever again, but I wish at least that the killings, rapes, torture would be halted so we can try to go on with our ruined lives.

I'm thinking about you – it is a little bit comforting. I hug you.

Jasna

Sandra Cisneros refused to grieve silently for her suffering friend, and for Sarajevo in flames. Nor did she shrug helplessly. She started writing and speaking at every opportunity about the war in Bosnia. Newspapers such as the *New York Times* and the *Los Angeles Times* reported the speeches and spread the word.

Furthermore, Cisneros started demonstrating in front of the San Fernando Cathedral in San Antonio on Saturdays, wearing a purple ribbon, for the purple *ljiljan* [fleur-de-lis] on the Bosnian flag, and facing east with a sign in her hands: *'En Solidaridad con las mujeres de Bosnia Hercegovina'* ['In solidarity with the women of Bosnia'].

In March 1993, at an International Women's Day Rally in San Antonio, Texas, where she lives, she said:

It's embarrassing holding up a sign, sometimes alone. I must look funny to the children getting out of catechism classes, mothers in pickup trucks blaring tejano music, old women going to church, bikers who bless themselves as they roar past the door, busloads of white-haired tourists. I'm a nuisance to the wedding parties, I suppose. Who wants to be reminded of a war? Once, a woman tried to give me a dollar. Once, a man said, 'Si no hay guerra no comemos'. If there's no war, we don't eat.

After my time in Bosnia, I took a page out of Sandra Cisneros's book. I wasn't a famous author and didn't have an international audience, but I resolved to mention Bosnia at every possible opportunity. Not only at the few public appearances and interviews I gave in South Africa, but in every individual conversation, whether people would listen or not. I was mortally disappointed. People didn't understand, and clearly didn't care that much. Like Sandra, I was alone with my candle and my placard, making the wedding guests uncomfortable with my demonstration against the Serb slaughter and the international community's callousness.

In general Jasna was right: as a rule, good news couldn't be mentioned in the same breath as Sarajevo. But once in a while a small miracle happened to remind us that 'where there is life there is hope'.

Before I went to Bosnia I didn't believe in miracles. But living in Sarajevo converted me. It started with the 'coincidences' that made it possible to fetch Omar and Jasmin from Bilalovac, and continued throughout my two years in Sarajevo. One of these miracles was the 1993 World Press Photo Exhibition in Sarajevo. Miro Purivatra, director of the Obala Gallery, told me they wanted to exhibit the photos and asked if I could help. Everything had been arranged with the organisers for bringing the exhibition to Sarajevo, but the problem was, of course, getting it there from Amsterdam. As with practically everything I tried to do while I was in Sarajevo, the immediate response from the relevant military officers was, 'It's impossible.' Since the exhibition was in Amsterdam, I asked Luuk whether he had a contact at home who could help. In Sarajevo, I started believing that the mixture of Dutch, French and German blood in my family is the source of my optimism, tenacity and obstinacy. The few Dutch officers I worked with were the most undaunted by our extremely difficult situation. They also received important support from colleagues at home. Luuk put me in contact with an officer in the Netherlands, and I faxed the information to him. He was kind, helpful, prepared to do whatever he could from that end, and volunteered to liaise with the organisers. But time and again we got bogged down at the same point: no problem to get the photos out of the Netherlands, but how would they get to Sarajevo? Dozens of faxes and phone calls were made, but each time I walked into a wall at my end. I was ready to concede that it was indeed impossible, and waited for the right moment to break the bad news to Miro.

One morning a French soldier walked into my office and asked whether I knew that there was a large parcel addressed to me in the garden. It had been there for a week, he said. I thought he was mistaken, but went to have a look. And there, in the mud, stood an enormous wooden crate. It really was addressed to me, simply: *Anné Mariè du Preez, UNPROFOR Forward HQ, Sarajevo*. I had no idea what it could be. The soldier fetched some tools, pried it open and there, before my astonished eyes, was the entire World Press Photo Exhibition. Inside, on top of the photos, was a large white board, with the warning *'Keep from moisture and sunlight'*.

It would have been a better idea to fix it onto the outside of the crate, which had been standing in the rain and sun at Forward for a week! I was terrified that the photos might be ruined, and carefully lifted the top layers to check. Everything was perfect.

When I asked the Egyptian guards at the gate where the crate had come from, they said that French soldiers had brought it from the airport. The World Press Photo Exhibition had, by some incredible miracle, safely made its way to Sarajevo. Sometimes there was good news, even in Sarajevo. And sometimes all that was required for a miracle was a little temerity and a lot of faith. A determined Dutch officer had refused to take no for an answer, bit the bullet and put the crate on a train to France – and hoped for the best.

In Bosnia, miracles were often simply the result of the common decency of good people.

There were many Serbs and Croats who didn't support their leaders' diabolical cause and did what they could to uphold the ideal of a free, multi-ethnic Bosnia. In central Bosnia, a small town and a courageous doctor reminded the world that there were people opposing the madness, even when this required personal sacrifices. The town of Fojnica is twenty kilometres west of Kiseljak. In 1993, when there was heavy fighting and one village after another fell to the Bosnian army and the HVO in the area, the nondescript town became symbolic of the hope that there might after all be a future for Bosnia. The day before I visited Fojnica for the first time, a village ten kilometres from Kiseljak was taken by the HVO, who then proceeded to 'cleanse' it. The Bosnian inhabitants were fortunate: unlike people in Ahmići and many other villages they weren't murdered, just expelled. Every last one of them. Then the Croats burnt all their houses.

Fojnica's population was made up of just over fifty percent Croats and just under fifty percent Bosnians, but both groups steadfastly refused to take up arms against each other, and the Croat authorities refused to expel their Bosnian neighbours. After the local commander of the HVO repeatedly refused to cleanse the town of Bosnians, he was eventually fired. But his men continued to support him, insisted they could live together in peace and refused to give in to pressure to take up arms against the Bosnians. However, as the fighting around Fojnica intensified, along with the pressure to fight, small groups of inhabitants started leaving the town for villages that had already been cleansed of the other ethnic group. They reckoned they'd be safer than in Fojnica, which, it was feared, might be attacked by any of the sides. One couldn't blame them for being afraid. Still, everyone was fervently hoping against all odds that Fojnica might emerge from the madness as an example that reason and the desire for peace could prevail.

Perhaps there was something intangible in Fojnica that brought out the best in people. Perhaps it was just a coincidence. But it was here that Dr Zdenko Nikolajević added his voice to that of other decent people who risked their lives to oppose the mindless slaughter. Many of these people were killed. I heard first-hand accounts of how Serb men in Bosnia were shot and killed in cold blood if they refused to join the Bosnian Serb army. There was no court martial, no official procedures and sentence, no opportunity to register protest – simply a bullet in the head. Even those who weren't killed were severely dealt with by their compatriots. For this reasons such people were few and far between. And for this reason it was not to be sniffed at when someone took a public stance. Dr Nikolajević, an ethnic Croat, was called up for military service by the HVO and sent to Fojnica to establish the War Hospital. However, when he received orders not to treat Serbs or Bosnians in the hospital, he declared that he no longer regarded himself an officer of the HVO.

He told them he had taken the Hippocratic oath and would treat anyone needing medical assistance. The HVO High Command were incensed. They repeated their orders, and when that didn't work, they threatened to forcefully remove him, but he continued with his work undaunted.

Medical supplies and equipment were in critically short supply, but Dr Nikolajević made a plan. He gathered whatever broken pieces of equipment he could find in the town, and set out to improvise and build new equipment with the help of a local engineer. His hospital was as well equipped as any hospital could be under the circumstances, albeit with some very strange-looking devices. A qualified surgeon and anaesthetist, he performed both roles in Fojnica. Before the war, he had specialised in liver disease, but now he was performing everything from appendectomy to heart surgery – and the inevitable amputations. The hospital was dependent on the ICRC for ninety percent of its medicine and surgical equipment. When he needed something they didn't have, Dr Nikolajević made a plan. He proudly showed me a small pile of highly specialised equipment that was impossible to obtain during the war, and said that when he'd still been able to travel, he'd gone to one of the big hospitals and … He hesitated a moment, then candidly confessed that he'd stolen the equipment. 'They had more than they needed,' he said, 'and my hospital had none.'

He took me on a tour of the hospital and introduced his patients to me. In one room were three HVO soldiers, wounded in fighting around Fojnica. In the next were three wounded Bosnian soldiers. Curtly and matter-of-factly, as though he was on routine hospital rounds, Dr Nikolajević said they had all been wounded in the same battle. As far as he was concerned they were simply people who needed medical attention, and he was a doctor. In his improvised intensive care unit was a tiny pale boy whose appendix had ruptured, and after three operations his life was still hanging by a thread. In another room was an old Bosnian woman in her eighties with a broken arm, who scolded Dr Nikolajević every day because the cast was too heavy.

The previous week, Dr Nikolajević had received a final order from the HVO headquarters in Mostar: He was to close the hospital or all the equipment would be removed. 'Let them come,' he said, 'and let them take the equipment, even if I did work so hard to put it together.' His family and friends and everyone who supported him would help, and he'd start again. But he was adamant that the HVO wouldn't get him out of there. And, he added, he wouldn't let them touch the medical supplies. That, he said, had been donated by the ICRC to the hospital and the community – not to the military – and he'd do whatever he could to stop them.

'I take orders from no one,' he said when I left. 'I guess in a way I am a partisan: I do what I have to do.'

In that tragic country, where more than a quarter of a million people died, where hundreds of thousands were wounded and maimed, and two million became refugees, the courage of Dr Zdenko Nikolajević and the people of Fojnica was a drop in the ocean. But had there been more like them, the senseless bloodshed in Bosnia might have been stopped.

A few weeks later Fojnica was taken by the Bosnian army. Although they had hardly any weapons and ammunition, the Bosnians were driven by the sheer determination to survive the twofold attack by the Serbs and the Croats.

It wasn't possible to keep track of all the people who crossed my path, and Dr Nikolajević, like so many others, disappeared into the thick fog of the war.

CHAPTER 11

SO NEAR YET SO FAR

JULY–AUGUST 1993

THE STRING QUARTET WAS IN CONCERT. So were the Bosnian Serbs.

The relentless shelling was as certain as daylight, as inevitable as life and death. There was no respite from this never-ending storm of man-made thunder and lightning, no escape from the hurricane of destruction unleashed daily on the city by the Serbs in the hills. They'd expected Sarajevo to capitulate within a week, but a year after the barricades had gone up, Sarajevo's people were as resilient, if not more so, than in the first weeks of bitter fighting to protect their city. As he had the Germans during World War II, Sarajevo's elusive Walter was causing the Serbs a massive headache. Yet the siege was slowly choking the city, its inhabitants held in a lethal embrace from which there was no escape. Every day the shells and sniper bullets ripped away children, mothers and fathers, sisters and brothers. They were freezing and starving. But one shall live by more than bread. And the people of Sarajevo had music.

The city's artists persisted with their extraordinary programme of resistance. One would have thought coping with the Serb onslaught would require every inch of self-preservation a person could muster, but they continued to arrange art exhibitions, theatre productions and music concerts. Because there was a curfew and no electricity, concerts were held during the day. No one had money, but tickets were free and there was never an empty seat. Many disappointed patrons had to be turned away after risking their lives to get to the theatre and queuing for hours where they were easy targets for shells and sniper bullets. In July I went to a music concert at the Chamber Theatre, Kamerni Teatr 55, in central Sarajevo. The performers were the theatre's string quartet: Dževad Šabanagić, Dijana Ihas, Hrvoje Tisler and Miron Strunski. These four intrepid people, like all the other artists, walked for miles several times a week to rehearse and perform for the city's appreciative audiences, who themselves had to walk considerable distances to attend the concerts. The theatre was modern and comfortable, but, without both electricity and candles, it was pitch dark. The concert was held in a room chosen because it had large windows and needed no lighting. There'd been heavy shelling since early morning, and it was most unsettling that the windows weren't secured with adhesive tape. It was very dangerous, and didn't help my almost pathological fear of flying glass. The shelling of the city centre was increasing, and explosions echoed around the theatre. Nobody batted an eye, neither the audience nor the musicians, who didn't miss a note and serenely continued playing their well-rehearsed Mozart, Gounod and Bach, accompanied by the background thunder of exploding shells. My conspicuous blue flak jacket both reassured and embarrassed me, but shortly after my arrival in Sarajevo, a French soldier had survived an exploding shell only because he was wearing his flak jacket, and that had made a profound impression on me. Since I was all for surviving my sojourn in Sarajevo, I decided to wear my flak jacket and helmet whenever possible. As one violent explosion after another split the air, rocking the building and rattling the windowpanes, I kept furtively glancing at my helmet on the floor next to my feet, but I would've rather died than put it on. I was embarrassed enough already about my body armour, while no one else in the theatre had anything but flimsy coats and jackets for protection. I thought that perhaps I should start wearing my oversized raincoat everywhere, like the spy who came in from the cold, so that my flak jacket would be hidden. The hackneyed argument was true: unlike the residents of Sarajevo, I didn't have to be in the city and had every right to protect myself as best I could. Still, I always felt guilty and conspicuous.

Outside, the monster raged with flaming nostrils. But inside there was tranquillity. The melancholy notes of Albenoni's adagio drifted into every corner of the room, and out through the windows where they were consumed by the thunder of the explosions echoing through the city. The concert was beautiful. The musicians might have been playing in New York, Paris or Rome. Serb shells were ripping apart their city and their lives, but their souls were their own. Dijana's face was serene, her hands sure and strong on the gleaming body of the viola. On her one side was Miron, absorbed in serious concentration, on the other Hrvoje, his gentle face tinged with sadness. Beside him was Dževad, with his familiar shock of unruly grey hair, his usual mischievous smile replaced by a look of fierce and total attention. The building shuddered and the windows rattled dangerously as shell after shell exploded in the streets outside. I anxiously pulled my flak jacket closer to my chest, and noticed to my relief that I wasn't the only one feeling uncomfortable. As the explosions steadily increased, people in the audience started fidgeting. None of them had transport; they had to dash home through the deluge of shells, and there was no knowing how long it might last, or how bad it might become. One by one they started tiptoeing out. It wasn't that their homes were safer, but it's a primeval instinct to get to home and family when there's danger. As the intensity of the bombing increased, small groups started leaving. The quartet kept playing as though nothing was amiss, their faces calm and composed, their practised hands unwavering. They were in a world of their own, a world of music that enveloped the room like a giant, iridescent bubble. Even when shells exploded in the street outside, very close to the theatre, they kept playing – steadfastly, beautifully. Still more people stood up and crept out, but the string quartet were totally absorbed in their music, and I marvelled that they could be so completely unaffected by the cacophony outside. Hrvoje, who was the father of a small baby, once told me that he never knew when he left home whether he'd see his wife and child again. But that didn't keep him from attending rehearsals and playing at concerts. This stoicism was the essence of survival in Sarajevo. To complete what you'd set out to do was a victory; to give up and run for cover meant moral defeat.

After some time the audience had shrunk to a mere handful: me, and a few men with the gaunt, haggard faces characteristic of Sarajevo's warriors. Perhaps they no longer had a home and family to return to. Perhaps it just didn't seem dangerous enough to leave. For them, familiar with the horrors of Sarajevo's trenches, this probably wasn't a particularly threatening situation. For me it felt like the end of the world. The quartet kept playing: Mozart, Grieg, Schubert. I didn't hear much of the last part of the concert, partly because of the shelling and partly because I was wishing with every fibre in my body that they'd finish so we could get out of there. All of us.

My trepidation seemed to have passed unnoticed. After the last notes had faded away into the Serb firestorm and the diminished audience finished applauding, I was thanked warmly for my resolute support, and from then on I was invited to all their concerts.

On Saturday 30 July, I went to a theatre performance scheduled for eleven in the morning. The shelling wasn't unusually heavy, and I decided to walk to the theatre from the Residency. It was only about a ten-minute walk, but I left at 10h30, arrived early, and joined the other patrons in the lobby, where everyone waited until the last minute before finding their seats in the dark theatre. Eleven o'clock came and went but people stayed in the lobby, smoking and talking. Nobody was making their way into the theatre, and I took my cue from the rest of them. After a while someone came to tell me that there was a delay, because they were waiting for one of the actors. Ten minutes went by, fifteen, twenty. Then the theatre director appeared and announced that the production had been cancelled. There were groans of disappointment, then a collective gasp, and the faces around me froze into stunned masks of shock. At that stage I understood little Bosnian, and had to ask someone what the director had said. I wished I hadn't. He told me that the lead actor, Vjelko Sparavalo, on his way to the theatre, walking like everyone else, had been killed by an exploding shell. He lifted his hands in a gesture of helpless resignation. In the foyer the happy, excited chatter had become a terrible, grave silence. A number of people walked over to a man in a wheelchair in the centre of the lobby and talked to him in hushed voices. I found out afterwards that he was Nermin Tulić, the famous Sarajevo actor and my friend Mima's brother. In May 1992, he had addressed tens of thousands of Sarajevans gathered in front of the parliament building, urging them passionately, poetically, to resist being drawn into armed confrontation by their leaders. Not long after that historic occasion he was walking down a Sarajevo street when a mortar exploded just metres from him. He lost both his legs, but survived his life-threatening injuries. And, as soon as he was able, he started directing theatre productions from his wheelchair, and even acted in some. I later also met the family of Vjelko Sparavalo, the famous actor who had died on that bright July morning on his way to the theatre, in the spirit of Walter. Kira, his widow, was attractive, elegant, poised. Denis, their son, was a music student. Like his father, he was going to be a performing artist, and I heard him play at BH Forward.

I walked back to the Residency with leaden legs, expecting every step of the way that a mortar would suddenly whistle over the high buildings and explode right next to me, blasting away my legs or my life. This was life in Sarajevo, a massive game of Russian roulette where the Serbs spun the cartridge. It was nothing personal, just bad luck if you were in the wrong place at the wrong time. An exploding shell, a sniper's bullet, the end.

In the meantime, the show had to go on.

My favourite theatre production was a play titled 'Sklonište' ['Shelter']. It was a satire about the months Sarajevans had spent living underground like moles in 1992. The political and social issues of the day were woven into the lives of the characters, and every so often the play would be adapted to include new important events. A scene that brought the house down time after time was an old woman's lament about the Americans who hadn't honoured their promise to help Bosnia. The Bosnians never gave up hope that the US would come to their aid, carry out air strikes against the Serbs and force the war to end. The old woman wailed: 'Not only have they not sent air strikes, they haven't even sent a pigeon, which at least could be cooked.' The audience, all of them starving, screamed with laughter. It took me a while to become comfortable with the macabre humour that was, as much as anything else, evidence of the remarkable resilience and spirit of Sarajevo's admirable people.

I acquired a habit in Sarajevo. It came with the territory. Perhaps it was superstition, perhaps just a comforting ritual. It developed out of having to walk to Forward and back day and night, rain or shine, through heavy shelling and sniper fire. I'd learnt the hard way that it was folly to drive my car home and leave it in front of my apartment building overnight. On the single occasion that I did, it was broken into, the fuel pipes cut and the fuel drained. I was left stranded, with the added inconvenience of having to have the vehicle towed and repaired. So, I had no choice: I had to walk. Several times I was stopped late at night by the Bosnian police or soldiers on patrol and hauled over the coals for breaking the curfew. I always replied that the curfew didn't apply to UNPROFOR personnel, and even if they didn't agree, they couldn't do more than give me a warning and let me go.

The symbol of my superstition was the symbol of Sarajevo's terror: the crater left by an exploded mortar or artillery shell. Sarajevans, with their unique sense of the ironic, named these craters 'Sarajevo roses'. The impact resembled a giant flower with scattered petals – or the monstrous footprint of a giant predator. Where the shell hit the ground, it left a large indentation like the centre of a flower or the cushion of a paw; with smaller indentations, like petals or toes, from the deadly spray of shrapnel. In the first two years of the war, the Serbs fired some 500 000 shells into Sarajevo, and thus hundreds of thousands of 'roses' were scattered throughout the city. There was one just outside the entrance to my apartment building, and another on the small pedestrian bridge I crossed daily on my way to Forward. I studiously made a point of treading on each of them, both on my way to work and back, wanting to believe this would protect me from the deadly path of a shell or a sniper bullet for the rest of the day or night. If I unthinkingly missed stepping on the imprint, I went back and walked over it. I relished this small, slightly bizarre ritual – I felt I was entitled to it.

Although I am religious, had no need for superstition and always thought myself far too sober-minded for such silliness, I decided to allow myself this small indulgence. My circumstances didn't allow me to show much weakness. At work I was one woman among thousands of men, and I was a privileged inhabitant of a city that was being slowly strangled to death, which meant I couldn't complain to my Sarajevan friends. Certain experiences – if they don't destroy you – can be very valuable in setting your priorities in life. As the saying goes, they make you stronger. But I had no desire to be a moral Hercules, and so I quietly indulged this frailty of spirit.

———————

The first anniversary of the siege of Sarajevo had come and gone. The international community made statements, organised conferences, voted for or against UN resolutions. None of this relieved the suffering of Bosnia's people. For the few fortunate enough to work, an entire month's salary in Bosnian dinar was the equivalent of one US dollar – just enough to buy a loaf of bread. There was no distinction between 'basics' and 'luxuries': hunger made all food simultaneously a basic necessity and the greatest luxury. Even a tiny cup of coffee or a pot of boiled rice often came at a heartbreaking price. Many homes in Sarajevo had hardly any furniture, very few books, and no old shoes and clothes cluttering up closets. With no fuel or wood since the Serbs sealed off the city in the summer of 1992, and winter temperatures dropping to -20°C, Sarajevans had to use what means they could to survive. After almost all the trees in the city had been chopped down for firewood, the government declared it illegal, so people started burning books, clothes, shoes and furniture. Miraculously, incredibly, they sustained a sense of humour. If they visited someone who'd somehow managed to preserve a fair amount of furniture and books, they'd say, 'Well, you could easily survive two more winters.' And they would laugh heartily.

My own problems, although frustrating and difficult, were insignificant compared to those of my friends and neighbours. But I certainly didn't need life to become more difficult, as it did when my flat was burgled. The burglars stole paintings, carpets and other valuables belonging to the owners, a bottle of Scotch belonging to me – and my small camping stove with all the fuel I'd received from Major Iversen. This meant stumbling down the 200 stairs in the morning without tea or coffee. But at least I always knew there was some at Forward. Most Sarajevans hadn't had the luxury of a cup of morning coffee for many months. Of course this didn't stop me from self-pity and complaining, even if only to myself. However, I couldn't be angry about the burglary. Despondent, but not angry. Not when I knew how bitterly hard life was in Sarajevo. I hoped the goods were in the hands of some desperate refugee family and not on the black market or in the home of some racketeer. All the same, it didn't make things any easier for me, and little by little, my life was becoming more like that of my neighbours.

Some of the experiences I had in Sarajevo disappeared behind the grey curtain of forgetting. Others, such as the summer night in 1993 that followed the day of the theft, I could never forget. Serb shells rocked the city until well after midnight. After only about ten minutes in bed I got up, unrolled my bedding sausage on the passage floor, and jammed a rolled-up towel against the bathroom door. As usual, I didn't sleep well. A decent night's sleep was a rare treat in Sarajevo, a luxury from a previous life. In any case, I never really let down my guard, and even when I was asleep, my sub-conscious registered everything that happened in and around the city. My military colleagues found it intriguing that I could walk in and give an account of the night's battles: the time and intensity of the fighting at Stup, the exact time the firing started from Hum or

Žuć, sometimes even the count of outgoing shells from Sarajevo. Men can sleep through anything: crying babies, a burglary, war. This is why mothers are women and soldiers are men. If it were the other way around, babies would never get warm milk or a nappy change or gripe water at night. The upside would be a total absence of war, because after one week the majority of sleep-deprived female soldiers would be too exhausted to curl a finger round a trigger.

After a virtually sleepless night I was exhausted, and needed coffee to kick-start my weary mind and limbs before I tackled the 200 stairs. My brain went into search mode. Then, through the fog in my head, flashed: candles. Surely I could boil a little water on a candle or two! One small cup of water was all I needed. There were six candles left in the box. They meant the difference between seeing my way around the apartment and shuffling around in the dark for many weeks. But I was desperate. Anyway, I might not even be alive in a few weeks, and I needed coffee now. I tied four of the precious candles together with an elastic band, dripped wax onto a saucer, stuck down the candles, poured a cup of water into the small *džezva* pot and went out onto the balcony to brew my morning coffee. It was a tricky operation. I had to hold the pot with one hand and use the other to shield my face from the putrid black smoke of the candle flames. The hand that clutched the *džezva* tired quickly, and I had to change hands several times before the water boiled. It seemed to take ages, but was worth every bit of discomfort. As I sipped the strong, hot coffee, I wondered whether anyone at home would believe me if I told them this. No. This was another world, galaxies away from places where people switched on kettles or coffee machines for morning tea or coffee. This was Sarajevo, where being able to make a tiny cup of coffee was a personal triumph – and equivalent to emerging victorious from a battle against the Serbs.

CHAPTER 12

TOO LITTLE TOO LATE

JUNE–JULY 1993

ALTHOUGH **UNPROFOR** RADIO WAS MY OFFICIAL JOB, the force majeure of my life in Sarajevo became to provide whatever assistance I could to Bosnians caught between the barbarity of the Serbs and the disregard of the international community. At the top of this list was the matter of Fuad's sons, Omar and Jasmin. The letters I carried to and from Kiseljak were the first direct contact they'd had with their parents for a year. The children, especially Omar, seemed sad and lost. I tried my best, with Božica's help, to explain the constraints of getting them to Sarajevo, and that they had to be patient and brave. But Omar sensed the tension in Kiseljak, and the tall, gangly boy was clearly worried. Jasmin settled with relative ease. He was a happy child, and because he was younger, he wasn't as aware of the danger. Omar wrote despondent letters to his parents, which deeply distressed Fuad and Vahida. Fuad spoke of little else but their concern for the children, especially in the wake of the ethnic cleansing and expulsions of Bosnians in Kiseljak. The signs were ominous. After racking my brain, I decided on a course of action that would at least temporarily lift their spirits: Fuad would go to Kiseljak with me, ostensibly on official business, to see his children. This was extremely dangerous, because men of military age were for all intents and purposes regarded as soldiers, and were taken prisoner if found on enemy territory. With what everyone knew about the Serb camps, this could be equivalent to a death sentence. However, there was no other way for Fuad to see his children. He understood the danger only too well, but was prepared to take the risk. I applied to the UNPROFOR personnel office at PTT to officially employ Fuad as my (unpaid) assistant. My justification was that, as my sound engineer, I sometimes needed him to accompany me. A small white lie. I couldn't pass him off as an interpreter because he spoke no English. And of course I didn't mention that I was even thinking of taking him out of Sarajevo. The personnel officer agreed. The only – but crucial – difference between the ID cards for international UNPROFOR staff and local staff was that the international one was white, and the local one yellow. When we went to have Fuad's card made up they'd run out of yellow paper, and suggested giving him a white one temporarily. Thus Fuad became the proud owner of an international UNPRO-FOR ID card, and a few days later we set off for Kiseljak. Because we were driving through a dangerous area in Sarajevo and across the airport, Fuad needed a helmet and flak jacket. I borrowed a helmet for him from the Danish contingent at Forward, and a flak jacket from the administrative office at PTT. My well-meaning conniving to allow Fuad to see his children would later cause me more than one headache, but even if I'd known that, I wouldn't have changed my mind. Fuad was understandably nervous, and I promised I'd do absolutely everything in my power to see that no harm came to him. It was no small miracle that none of the numerous people (including a senior government official) I drove across Serb lines – unarmed and in my soft-skin car – ever came to harm. UNPROFOR personnel were often detained by the Serbs, and some of them had frightening experiences, but I miraculously emerged from my many hair-raising ventures unscathed and without the blood of an innocent Sarajevan on my conscience. My guardian angels had their work cut out.

The Sierra 3 checkpoint was our first test, and to my relief Sanja was the guard on duty. Because I was virtually the only woman she had contact with while on duty, she was always happy to see me. Pretty and friendly, she was everybody's favourite checkpoint guard, and many UNPROFOR soldiers took chocolates and cookies along as gifts for her. There were other female guards, but none of them had found the right balance between the required efficiency and good public relations. After Sanja and I had exchanged our usual pleasantries, she turned her attention to Fuad. She'd assumed he was a foreigner, and was surprised when she saw his name on the ID card. During the war people's names had become a question of life or death. Your name identified you as a Bosnian Muslim, Croat or Serb, and you were treated accordingly. If you were found to have a Muslim name in Serb territory, your situation could be dire indeed. The irony was that with the many mixed families in Bosnia, people sometimes had a Serb first name and a Muslim surname, or other combinations. But as in Jamila's case, no concessions were made for the fact that you might be the product of a mixed marriage. If you had political sympathies that were incompatible with your name, you had to go to great pains to prove yourself. The most fortunate were those whose parents had given them 'foreign' first names, and whose surnames weren't discernible as belonging to any group. Fuad didn't fall into this category. His surname, like many in Bosnia, wasn't specific to any of the ethnic groups, but his first name was. With all the possible complications in mind, we'd decided not to put his first name on the ID, just his initial. But Sanja asked his first name. He held out the card to her, stared straight ahead and said, 'F'. Sanja smiled pleasantly. 'I can see that,' she said, 'but I want to know your *name*, not your initial.' I was feeling more than a little nervous, and realised that I actually didn't know her at all. Would she call her male colleagues in the guardhouse if she found him to be a Muslim? Fuad looked decidedly wretched. He was pale. His voice croaked when he said his name. Sanja smiled her familiar bright smile and started chattering away in Bosnian. Then she waved us through, and as we drove off, she called, 'Goodbye Mr "F"!'

The real test was getting through Sierra 1. On the way, I told Fuad to say his name was Federico (many Bosnians had Italian names, thanks to historical connections) and that he was half-Serb, were he asked again. He nodded, looking most unhappy, but the question of honour and duty would have to take a back seat for the time being. His life might depend on that lie. Fortunately he didn't speak English, so we couldn't debate it. Because all the checkpoint soldiers between Sarajevo and Kiseljak knew me by then, I had no problems when I was alone – except when the Serb Rambo was on duty. He made my flesh crawl, and whenever I heard of atrocities committed by Serbs during the war, his face appeared in my mind's eye. I was praying he wouldn't be on duty. As usual, I started thinking too late about all the risks of my impulsive plan to take Fuad to Kiseljak. What an idiot I was. What was I going to do if Fuad were captured by the Serbs? Never again, I vowed, not for the first time (nor the last). My heart was pounding and my hands felt shaky, but I forced a smile and a cheerful note into my voice when I greeted the young soldier at the checkpoint. He was friendly enough with me, but the expression on his face was wary when he asked Fuad where he was going. We'd rehearsed this part, and he replied that we were going to Kiseljak for a few hours to record interviews for an UNPROFOR Radio programme, and would be returning in the afternoon. I nodded and smiled while the soldier seemed to be digesting this information. It was so inconceivable that any Bosnian man would appear at a Serb checkpoint like this that the guard didn't even ask his first name. After what seemed like ages the guard turned and waved at another soldier to lift the barrier. We were through. The Croat checkpoint would mercifully not be a problem, but I was worried about the return journey. After lunch, and a few glasses of *šlivovic*, the Serbs tended to become obstreperous.

We drove straight to Tidža's house, and I was hoping that the boys would be there. Without telephones in Sarajevo and Kiseljak, there was no way of letting them know that Fuad was coming. But they were there. Fuad embraced the sons he hadn't seen for over a year. Tears ran down his face and his shoulders shook with sobs. I, too, wiped away a few happy tears, but I was also thinking about Vahida who still couldn't see her children, and that Fuad would have to leave them behind in this increasingly dangerous place. We'd arranged that I'd pick Fuad up at three. The earlier the better, to avoid having to deal with inebriated Serb soldiers at the checkpoints. When I arrived around the corner from Tidža's house, Fuad and the boys were waiting. Jasmin was wearing the blue UNPRO-FOR helmet and Omar was holding the flak jacket. For the first time the sad look had lifted from his young face and he looked relaxed and carefree, smiling happily. It was excruciating for Fuad to leave them behind, but he promised they'd soon be together, and told them not to worry. He was armed with letters and drawings for Vahida, but we were both nervous about the return journey, which put a damper on his joy at having seen his sons. We were fortunate. At Sierra 1 we were waved through unceremoniously, and at Sierra 3 Sanja teased him: 'Ah, Mr "F", how was your trip?' He laughed, and they talked while we waited for an endless humanitarian aid convoy ahead of us to move. Sanja confirmed what I'd guessed – that it would take hours for the guards to complete their inspection of the long line of vehicles. This was too risky. We simply could not sit at a Serb checkpoint for hours with Fuad in the car.

There was no other way into Sarajevo and the road was very narrow, most of it obscured by the large trucks. But I'd have to give it a try. When I asked Sanja whether we could push ahead she nodded, but said I'd never be able to squeeze past the trucks. Fuad agreed. I said, watch me. In several places it seemed as though we couldn't possibly get through, but I was determined to get Fuad back to Sarajevo as soon as possible, and kept going, inching past the trucks and scraping past shrubs and trees.

Half an hour later we were back in Sarajevo, flushed with victory. Fuad said I was an excellent driver. The superintendent at the UNPROFOR vehicle workshop didn't think so. The car was covered in dents and scratches, and I'd lost a side mirror as well as my blue UN flag, snatched off by overhanging branches. I listened to his stern reprimand without a word.

The Serbs exploited the misery of hundreds of thousands of Bosnians in every conceivable way, and controlled and manipulated everything, big and small. It wasn't much different when it came to situations under control of the equally ruthless Croats. As I'd feared, Omar and Jasmin weren't safe for long in Kiseljak. More than a month after I'd smuggled them out of Bilalovac, the boys were again in danger. The Croats were systematically cleansing Kiseljak of Bosnians, and Fuad and Vahida were terribly concerned about their children. Shortly after taking the boys to Kiseljak, I approached Philippe Lazzarini, head of the ICRC's Sarajevo office, and asked whether they could bring the boys to Sarajevo. He said it was ICRC's policy not to return children to the city. I emphasised that they were in dire danger in central Bosnia, and would be with their parents in Sarajevo. He said under no circumstances could children be brought back to the city. When it was clear that this avenue was definitely not an option I retreated, but told Philippe I thought ICRC's policy was seriously flawed. I could understand not bringing children back to Sarajevo from Croatia, Italy or England. But they were already in a dangerous place; surely it would be better to be in danger with their parents to take care of them. What was to become of them if they were expelled from Kiseljak? Where would they end up? Whose responsibility would it be? He sympathised, but that was ICRC's policy and there was nothing he could do. UNHCR, similarly, would not consider bringing the children back to Sarajevo.

I turned to Deyan and Carlos. Was there anything at all that could be done? Was there a loophole anywhere? I'd briefly thought about trying to smuggle them in the way I had from Bilalovac, but immediately discarded the idea. I'd have to get them through a Croat checkpoint and two Serb checkpoints, and although I was rarely stopped at any of them, it was just too big a risk. Deyan and Carlos promised to try to help. Every other day I called, checking whether they'd come up with a solution, making a nuisance of myself. Finally there was good news. The Serbs had asked permission for an elderly Serb, Mr Bozalo, who'd been wounded during shelling on the city by his own people, to leave Sarajevo so that his family on the Serb side could take care of him. There was a possibility of arranging an exchange with the two boys. For about two weeks, Deyan and Carlos negotiated the details with the Serbs and the Bosnian government. Finally the two sides agreed. Carlos suggested that we immediately jump into action as the situation, as we well knew, could change from one day to the next and the deal be called off. The Serbs wanted a conventional exchange, made simultaneously in a neutral place. But that would take more time to arrange, time we didn't have. Carlos convinced them to allow us to bring the children to Sarajevo immediately, and to hand over Mr Bozalo afterwards. They were reluctant and said they didn't trust the Bosnians, but we gave our scouts' honour that their Mr Bozalo would be with his family by the end of the week. We never dreamt the Bosnians would stab us in the back – and cause a heartbreaking tragedy.

Early on the morning of 30 June, Luuk Niessen arrived at my flat with a message: Carlos had called and asked whether I could go and fetch the boys in Kiseljak. Save the end of the world, nothing could stop me. Luuk and I took off for the PTT Building, where Carlos was busy organising transport. I said we could use my car, but because we were going through Serb territory, Carlos had arranged for a Serb liaison officer to accompany us to smooth out any potential problems, and the Serbs said we had to have an APC to protect him on Bosnian and Croat territory. We asked the French for an APC, but there was a high-level meeting at the airport and they didn't have any available. The Egyptians couldn't venture onto Serb territory because they were Muslims, and this was a sensitive mission. The Ukrainians had an APC, but it wouldn't be available until noon. We informed the Serb liaison officer, Siniša Iser, and waited. By ten to twelve we received word that the APC had arrived and we prepared to leave, only to find that Siniša had gone to Lukavica and was stuck there. We had to go and fetch him.

When we got to the APC, the commander, a young Ukrainian captain, was pouring something into the engine. He said he was having a small problem with his vehicle and had to top up the cooling liquid because it was leaking, but not to worry, we'd be off in just a few minutes. I was armed with the relevant paperwork and confident everything would be fine. As we were about to board the APC, the French officer who'd helped Carlos arrange the logistics asked whether we were certain all the paperwork was in order. Carlos said yes. 'And arrangements with the checkpoints?' Yes. 'Also with the HVO?' Carlos's reply was lost in the bustle, but I saw in his face that the answer was no. Too late. We had to go, and hope there wouldn't be problems with the Croats. Luuk and I clambered aboard – and I had to blink to be sure I wasn't seeing things. I'd never been in a Ukrainian APC before, but had heard from others how dilapidated their equipment was. The interiors of the French, Danish and Egyptian APCs were clean and well maintained, the equipment neatly in place. This APC looked like it had been retrieved from the scrap heap. It was filthy, bits and pieces of equipment were hanging from the roof of the cabin and the upholstered seats were in tatters. But the crew was friendly and helpful, and we set off for Lukavica. I was both nervous and excited. Things were very different from when I'd fetched the boys from Bilalovac: I had an entire Ukrainian military crew and a run-down APC for protection, as well as – officially – a Dutch UNPROFOR officer and a Serb liaison officer for back-up. I had little fear that things would be okay with the Serbs, since they wanted Mr Bozalo and we had a liaison officer with us, but we were snatching the boys from under the noses of the Croats, and that could be a problem. Both the Serbs and Croats wanted to be rid of the Bosnians, but they wanted to do it in their own barbaric way.

When we arrived at the French checkpoint at the airport after a tortuously slow ride, there was bad news. The guard had a message for us: we had to return to PTT because there was a problem with the documentation. My heart sank. And before we could turn back, the captain again had to pour cooling liquid into the APC's engine. We'd been on the road barely fifteen minutes. Back at PTT, we found that the problem was that our papers said we were going from PTT to Kiseljak, and there was drama because we'd gone to Lukavica – which hadn't been arranged and reported. We promptly arranged and reported our new 'flight plan', and clambered aboard to return to Lukavica, but first the cooling liquid had to be topped up again. Only after the whole expedition was over, Carlos told me the French officer in charge had ordered the whole mission to be cancelled because our changed 'travel plans' hadn't been cleared well ahead of time. Fortunately we had arrived, and departed, before he communicated this to the downstairs office, and this small miracle, a solitary flaw in the otherwise excellent French efficiency, enabled us to escape. This time we made it to Lukavica, and I jumped out to fetch Siniša, but he was still busy. I then ran into Mladen Krsmanović of Radio SRNA, who wanted to talk to me about the radio programmes. It took ages before we could leave, and it was getting late. Again the cooling liquid had to be topped up. By now I was just a little anxious. It was only a few kilometres from PTT to Lukavica, but much further to Kiseljak, and I was wondering whether the APC would make it there and back. Just after we crossed the Kasindolska checkpoint, on the road to Ilidža, we had to stop again for cooling liquid. This set the pattern for the rest of the journey: stopping every fifteen minutes to add cooling liquid. My excitement was evaporating like mist in the sun. I wasn't worried so much that the many stops were slowing us down, but that we'd have to make at least two stops on Croat territory to refill the cooling liquid once the children were on board. The engine sounded like a severe asthmatic cough, and I refused to think about the possibilities of the APC giving up the ghost on Croat territory. We left Siniša with his comrades at Sierra 1, where we'd pick him up on the way back to Sarajevo, hopefully with the two boys on board.

Again, and against my better judgement, I'd assumed momentous responsibility for the lives of others. Fuad and Vahida knew nothing of the venture. I hadn't told them because I didn't want to get their hopes up, and with everything being so helter-skelter, I wasn't sure we'd pull it off. I'd called from PTT to ask Božica to let Tidža know we were coming, but she wasn't there. The French female soldier who used to be at Forward was just leaving for Kiseljak, and I asked her to relay a message to Tidža. I daren't let the cat out of the bag, and said I'd be there around one o'clock and needed to see both boys. But I didn't know whether the message would reach Tidža. Also, with all the delays and frequent stops, it would be much later by the time we got there, and they might think I wasn't coming. If we ever reached Kiseljak, the boys might be out with friends and would have to be found. I cringed thinking about a repeat of the nerve-racking search for Jasmin in Bilalovac, and kept telling myself to be positive – but I was getting more worried with every passing minute.

At last we chugged into Kiseljak in a cloud of black smoke. I hadn't told anyone at HQ about our mission because I was afraid they'd stop me. They had to maintain cordial relations with the Croats, and it wouldn't help if UNPROFOR was found smuggling Bosnians out for exchanges with Serbs. As it was, the Croats were accusing UNPROFOR of only helping the Bosnians. Because we had to get in and out unnoticed, we couldn't take the APC into the UNPROFOR compound. To avoid causing a stir, which we would if we arrived on Tidža's doorstep in an APC, I told the commander to park on the open ground across HQ and wait while I ran and fetched the boys. It was more than a kilometre to Tidža's house and boiling hot. I ran as fast as I could, walking here and there to catch my breath, trying not to think about the oppressive heat and the fact that the boys might not be there. When I arrived at Tidža's house huffing and puffing she was there, and so was Jasmin. Omar was missing. I groaned, 'Oh no!' but Jasmin said he knew where his brother was and would fetch him. I didn't tell him why I was there, because he might blurt it out while there were other children around. I simply said I had a message from their parents, had to see them both, and was in a tearing hurry. While he hurried off to fetch Omar, hobbling a little because he'd cut his foot a few days earlier, I explained to Tidža I was there to take them back to Sarajevo. She wanted to pack their clothes, but we couldn't run back with bags of baggage, and there was no time. I could fetch their clothes in a day or two. Fortunately Jasmin was right, and was soon back with his brother. When I said I'd come to take them home, their faces lit up like the sky over Manhattan on the fourth of July. They hugged and kissed Tidža goodbye. She hadn't had time to get used to the idea that they were going, and it wrenched at my heart to leave her there alone and vulnerable, amid all the rumours of Bosnians being 'cleansed' from Kilsejak.

The boys had grown wings and were running ahead. Since it was already the second leg of the race for me, I struggled to keep up with them. As we rounded the final corner, the last bit of wind was knocked from my chest. On the open ground stood the APC, its engine cap wide open and its insides hanging out like the intestines of a slaughtered animal. What was worse was that a group of Kiseljak's bloody-minded Croats had congregated around it to see what was going on. Without breaking stride I bundled the children into the APC and pulled the door shut. The heavy steel had been baking in the sun for an hour and it was like a furnace inside. I was in a panic, and summoned the young captain to find out what was happening. He was unruffled, kept saying I shouldn't worry, and promised to have the APC roadworthy in no time. But as the minutes dragged on, it became clear it was going to take longer than he'd thought. In the meantime the boys and I were wilting fast in the heat, and I asked Luuk to go and buy some cold drinks at the PX shop. We were all getting hotter and more bothered by the minute – and more people were joining the small crowd to watch the Ukrainian commander's efforts to get his APC back on the road. My anxiety was turning to dread. Because of the heat I was forced to open the door, and although I'd moved the boys as far forward in the APC as possible, they could still be seen. Anyway, the people who'd been there when we arrived had seen them, and of course had told others that we had two children in the APC. A few came closer, asked who the children were and where we were taking them. I'd ordered everyone to say nothing and refer inquiries to me, and I just shook my head and shrugged, acting stupid. But I was ready to have a total collapse. There were only two roads out of Kiseljak, and it was the easiest thing for someone to alert the checkpoints. I was also terrified that some UNPROFOR official would get wind of what was going on and stop the whole operation. People acted strangely about their territory and powers, and anything was possible.

After a very long time the APC was ready to leave, or so the captain said. But now there was another problem. Luuk, who'd gone to buy the drinks, wasn't back. I wasn't so worried about him because he could hitch another ride back to Sarajevo, but it would be a while before we reached Sierra 1, and the children needed something to drink. I was furious with Luuk for staying away so long. Couldn't he think we might be ready to leave any minute? Of course I was being unreasonable because I didn't know the reason for the delay, but I was so afraid something would go wrong. I asked the captain to look after the boys, and sprinted up the hill to HQ. I met Luuk halfway. He'd had to go to the bar to buy drinks, as the PX shop was closed. We raced back, jumped in, the APC was sealed and we were ready to go. I asked the commander not to open the door at the Croat checkpoint under any circumstances. It was becoming too much like the return journey from Bilalovac, and I was having a bad case of déjà vu. He grinned happily, and I could imagine how much he'd enjoy a scuffle with the Croats. But some other day, not this day; I just wanted to make it through as soon as possible. When we reached the checkpoint, the Croat soldier checked the military personnel's IDs, then asked the commander who was in the APC. He said a Dutch UNPROFOR officer and an UNPROFOR civilian, who were going back to Sarajevo. The Croat soldier wanted to see us and our IDs. First Luuk stuck his head through the hatch and held out his ID. I followed. The Croat soldier knew me, and nodded without even checking my ID. For a few moments it seemed as though he was contemplating whether he should ask for the door to be opened for a proper inspection, and I held my breath. But he also wanted to get out of the blazing heat, and turned and lifted the beam for us to pass. We were through! I'd never thought I'd be so happy to be on the dangerous patch of no-man's-land or on my way to Serb territory. Now we had to hope the Serbs wouldn't cause some unexpected problem. Never, not for a moment, could one relax and trust things would go well, no matter what the circumstances. The trump card was Mr Bozalo, who was still in Sarajevo, and his freedom depended on the safe arrival of the children. Thanks to Siniša there were no problems and we continued to Sarajevo. Whatever the captain had done to his APC in Kiseljak, its performance was greatly improved. We didn't need to stop once on the way back. But as we left the town of Blažuj behind and headed for Ilidža, my stomach muscles went into a nervous spasm. The most dangerous part of the journey lay ahead: the last leg into Sarajevo. The shells and armour-piercing bullets that were constantly fired at Sarajevo and at UNPROFOR vehicles were a real, deadly danger, and I had little confidence in the rickety APC. We passed through Ilidža, passed the Kasindolska checkpoint, and slowly chugged towards Sarajevo and Snipers' Alley. I was holding my breath, trying to appear unconcerned for the boys' sake (more déjà vu), and pointed out bits of the road to them through the small portholes. When I told them we were in Sarajevo, the excitement was clearly etched on their young faces, but also some anxiety. After all, they had no idea what they would find. They'd heard about the attacks on the city, hadn't seen their mother for over a year, and their father only once on the brief visit to Kiseljak a few weeks earlier. They knew their parents had had to flee their home in Grbavica, and had found a temporary place in another suburb. They were returning to a strange home, and a city they'd hardly recognise.

I would have liked to have taken the boys straight home in the APC, but that wasn't part of the arranged route, and the APC had to return to the PTT Building. That meant I had to take them home in my car, and that the last stretch of the ordeal still lay ahead. The fact that I'd been shot at numerous times and hadn't yet been hit did nothing to set my mind at ease. Each time I had a narrow escape, the law of averages tilted further against me, and the chances increased that the next bullet would hit the target. As soon as the boys were in the back of the car, I sped off as fast as I possibly could without further endangering their lives. When we stopped in front of the building where Fuad and Vahida lived, I asked the boys to wait in the car and raced up the five flights of stairs, hoping at least one parent would be home. They didn't have a telephone, so I couldn't check from PTT. I knew I would possibly find Fuad at the radio station, but that meant more driving around with the boys in the car, not to mention negotiating the radio building's dangerous entrance. But both of them were home, and very surprised to see me. I wished I had an interpreter with me. But I had to do the best I could with my meagre Bosnian language skills – and their scant knowledge of English. I asked them to sit down; I had something to tell them. I decided to draw the news out to cushion the shock, because the last thing we needed was for one of them to have a heart attack if I appeared suddenly and unannounced with the children. I told them an opportunity had arisen to bring the children back to Sarajevo as part of an exchange. Their faces lit up. Yes, yes, that would be wonderful. When, when? I said it had gone a lot quicker than we'd thought it would: *danas* [today]. They thought I meant I was on my way to Kiseljak to fetch their children. Their joy and excitement made my eyes misty. When would we be back? Still today? Tomorrow? As calmly and gently as possible I said I'd already been, and that the children were in Sarajevo. They just stared at me. Then Vahida asked, where? I said downstairs, in my car. I could see they had difficulty absorbing the information; it wasn't quite sinking in. I said they could wait while I went down to fetch the boys, but Vahida suddenly sprang to her feet and flew down the stairs. Fuad still couldn't believe his ears and kept looking at me as though he didn't understand what I'd said. When he started slowly moving towards the stairs, I said I had to get back to the Residency. He wanted me to stay, but I just shook my head. This was a moment for them as a family to be alone. The next moment Vahida screamed. The sound echoed up the stairwell, cutting through my bones. It was a raw primeval cry of intermingled joy and agony; a year's agony, and the indescribable relief and joy of seeing her children. Fuad was still riveted at the top of the stairs. Perhaps he'd decided to give her a few moments alone with the boys. I met them at the bottom of the stairs. She was clinging to her sons, sobbing uncontrollably. Tears were running down Omar and Jasmin's faces. And down mine.

Fuad's family was reunited. But this was not yet the end of the saga, and its end would be a tragic one.

———————

Fuad underwent a metamorphosis when his children returned to Sarajevo. The day after they returned, he told Jamila with great excitement in the studio what a joy it was having the boys home. His eyes were bright, his shoulders square and a happy grin was permanently plastered on his face. He told her Jasmin said he loved me because I knew how to keep a secret. The secret was that he'd cut his foot and made me promise not to tell his parents, so they wouldn't worry. He was a sweet little boy, they both were, and I was so happy that they were all back together again. Jamila explained to Fuad why I hadn't brought their clothes and that I was returning to Kiseljak the next day to fetch them. When I went to Kiseljak, I took Jamila with me so we could stay a while, have coffee with Tidža, and thank her properly for the loving care she'd taken of Omar and Jasmin. I'd helped her with food and money while the boys were there, but she'd treated them with real warmth and affection and they'd been happy with her. As anyone would have been, in her welcoming little house, basking in her kindness and quiet efficiency. But when Jamila and I arrived at her home it was locked and the windows were shuttered. It was never locked, even when she wasn't there, and the shuttered windows looked strange. The only other time her home had been locked was when Božica and I'd gone looking for her while she was away visiting her son, and she hadn't said anything about going away when I'd arranged to fetch the boys' clothes. Perhaps she was ill, Jamila said. We knocked and knocked, and called to her. After a while a neighbour quietly called to us through her window. Tidža wasn't there, she whispered nervously. She'd been arrested that morning by the Croat police and taken away. My legs just gave way. While I sat on the ground crying, Jamila spoke to the neighbour, but nobody knew where they'd taken Tidža or why. They found out about the children, I wailed. In this society it wasn't possible to keep anything a secret. I was relieved beyond expression that the boys were in Sarajevo, but that didn't alleviate my distress about Tidža's arrest. When UNRPOFOR inquired, we found out that many other Bosnians had been taken from their homes that morning. By divine intervention it had happened merely hours after I'd taken the boys. I asked G-5 to demand immediate information from the Croats as to her whereabouts. Then I went to see Božica, and asked her to use her connections to find out where Tidža was. She promised to try.

I called G-5 from Sarajevo every day for any news of Tidža. They found out that a group of Bosnians were being held in a Kiseljak school, but couldn't obtain permission to enter it, and the Croats wouldn't give information about individuals. The Bosnians in Kiseljak – the few who remained – said the people at the school were being beaten and tortured. While the boys had been with Tidža, a warm relationship had developed between us. I'd grown very fond of her, and was half out of my mind with worry. I went to Kiseljak and again asked Božica to make some inquiries, but she was summoned to the office of the Croat commander, who wanted to know why she was asking about Tidža. She told the truth: that I'd asked her to find out. The commander said it was none of her business or mine, and told her to back off. G-5 continued trying, but without success. The days became weeks, and there was no news. It felt as though there was a hole in my heart. This sweet, gentle woman did not deserve to be dragged from her home. Nobody in Bosnia did. Why couldn't I help her? Why couldn't I march to the commander's office and demand as an officer of the UN that she be set free and allowed to return to her small, neat house? I felt fury at the Croats and the whole world, who were allowing these things to happen and doing nothing to stop them.

The saga was not yet at an end. When Carlos went to finalise Mr Bozalo's release from Sarajevo, he was told that the Bosnians had changed their minds and would no longer let him go. The Serbs were furious, and said: 'We told you so.' Carlos and I, too, were furious, humiliated, shamed. We'd given our word that things wouldn't go wrong. Carlos tried everything, but the Bosnians were adamant. They would not let Mr Bozalo go. Of course, compared to the terrible things the Serbs had done and were doing, this was a minor blow. But every time Carlos or I went to Lukavica, we were accosted by Serb officials about their Mr Bozalo. The Bosnians would live to regret their treachery. So would I. Tidža's disappearance and my constant anxiety for her was about to be displaced in my mind by the most appalling tragedy. Two weeks after Omar and Jasmin's return to Sarajevo, a four-year-old girl in the city was wounded. Her wounds were critical, and the only hope was to evacuate her to a place with proper medical facilities. UNPROFOR agreed to an evacuation by helicopter. The Serbs refused. Without their approval, UNPROFOR couldn't bring a helicopter into Sarajevo, nor take it out. UNPROFOR pleaded. The Serbs refused. This was retribution for Mr Bozalo.

Early on Sunday 18 July, Carlos called me at the office. He said he had very bad news. Bad news was the norm, hardly worth mentioning. But his words stunned me. The little girl had died. My mind simply stopped working. I couldn't, just could not, absorb this dreadful information. I walked out of my office like a sleepwalker, past the soldiers in the long corridor, past the people in the street, climbed the 200 stairs to my apartment in a daze, paced backward and forward in the lounge, not knowing what to do. When the awful truth finally sank in, I crumpled like an empty sack, and sat on the black leather couch crying the whole morning. For a tiny girl whose name I hadn't even known, but to whom I was now linked as if with an umbilical cord. I decided that I didn't want to know her name. If I didn't know anything about her, as long as she remained nameless and faceless, maybe I could hang on to my sanity. Was I responsible for this? Had I traded her life for that of the two boys? Of course I could never have guessed that such a terrible thing would happen, but now her fate was on my conscience. And Tidža's fate. And the fate of the little girls in Bilalovac, and of their mothers and grandparents. Because I should have been able to help them and couldn't. Hatred of the Serbs simmered just under my skin. They had caused her mortal wounds, then refused her medical treatment. These monsters in the mountains were eating roast lamb and drinking *šlivovic*, and boasting about their unspeakable deeds. And now they'd made me their accomplice.

I also felt blind anger at the Bosnian government, who'd stooped to the level of the Serbs, refusing to let one old man leave Sarajevo and sacrificing a little toddler to make some point. I couldn't care less what their point was, nothing was worth her life. Nothing.

I was coming to understand why most UNPROFOR personnel just went about their work and didn't want to become involved in the terror and tragedy around them. My punishment for ignoring these rules was harsh. The little girl would be alive if I hadn't pushed so hard to get Fuad's boys back to Sarajevo. Yes, I pleaded with my conscience, but then the boys would now be missing with Tidža, maybe even be dead. How could I have foreseen it would end like this?

In Sarajevo one got nothing without paying. But the price, the price.

There was a bitterly ironic twist to the whole catastrophe. Within weeks of Omar and Jasmin arriving in Sarajevo, Philippe Lazzarini went to Geneva for an ICRC conference. When he returned, he called to tell me he had good news. He'd employed all the arguments I'd used when appealing for Omar and Jasmin's return, and on those grounds the ICRC had reviewed their policy and would consider, on a case-by-case basis, uniting children with parents in Sarajevo if the circumstances warranted it. But it was too little, too late. Now my anger and resentment was also directed at the ICRC. If they'd been sensible and practical about this issue earlier, we wouldn't have needed to make a deal with the Serbs. And a little girl in Sarajevo would not have died of her wounds.

Would I have done what I did if I'd had all the information and known the cost? I tried very hard not to confront this question head-on. What good would it have done anyway?

CHAPTER 13

A BLEAK SUMMER

JULY 1993

SUMMER AND WINTER, day and night, blended into a grey mass of struggle and painful effort. It was July, summer, there ought to have been lightness and joy everywhere. But this was Sarajevo, bedrock of a thousand grim and desolate tales. The situation in the city was desperate, and it felt absurd to be producing radio programmes on Security Council resolutions and reports by the Secretary-General. The anger I harboured towards the Serbs extended to disillusion-ment with the UN and the entire outside world that could, but refused, to intervene and bring an end to Bosnia's suffering.

Intellectually I understood the constraints of the situation, but I was consumed with frustration. This fuelled my motivation to do everything I could to make people's lives easier. And if that meant having to bend – or discard – UN rules, then so be it. By now I knew this could come at a heavy price, but there was no other way. Fortunately there were some happy endings. One day I saw boxes and boxes of fruit being delivered at Kiseljak as supplies for UNPROFOR soldiers. By shamelessly exploiting his good heart, I convinced Major Iversen that the children of Sarajevo were far more in need of the fruit than healthy UN soldiers who were well fed enough as it was. He gave me two boxes of oranges, which I decided to take to the school in the building next to my flat. Luuk was always ready to help with just about anything, from rescuing children to dropping off copies of the radio programme. Long after he left Sarajevo, I still received care packages from him and his wife with delicious Dutch biscuits, chocolates, and messages of encouragement and support. I went looking for him to help me take the oranges to the school, but he was at a press briefing. Not wanting to delay, I went in search of someone else to help.

The Americans were rotated every three to four weeks, and Major Kevin McGrath was the current air drop liaison officer. He was in his office, and I asked him to help me deliver the oranges to the school. It was an experience neither of us were likely to forget. When we appeared with the fruit and said it was for the children, the teachers started weeping. Neither they nor the children had had – or even seen – fruit in over a year. Each child clutched a single orange as though it were the greatest of treasures. It brought a painful lump to my throat, and I had to grit my teeth not to sit down and weep with the teachers. The almost hysterical excitement caused by this smallest of gifts made it impossible to continue with classes for the day, and the kids were sent home. Not a single one of them had eaten the fruit – they were taking it home. I will always remember the picture of tiny Aida, who lived down the road: she stormed home, shouting with wild, ecstatic joy, holding the orange out for her mother to see. Late in the afternoon when I passed their house, she was still holding the orange in her tiny hand. It was hard to believe that life could be reduced to such basics. That night, in the dark on my balcony, I sat thinking about Aida with the precious orange in her small hand, and the little girl who'd died, murdered by the Serbs who had not only wounded her, but also refused her the medical attention that might have saved her life. Did she look like Aida, too small for her age, large brown eyes filled with unanswered questions, in a pinched, pale face?

I slept fitfully, and had nightmares about little girls and blood oranges.

A few days later, one of the teachers stopped me on my way to Forward and asked me to visit the school, since the children had a gift for me. I was reluctant, because I found it difficult and embarrassing to accept gifts from people who had so little, but I couldn't refuse. The gift was a pile of drawings by the children. Most were of flowers: single flowers, pots of flowers, flowers enclosing little hearts. One was covered in butterflies, with the words 'peace' and *'mir'*, Bosnian for 'peace', written all over it. I was tremendously relieved that they hadn't tried to give me a precious painting or some jewellery, as other people had offered. Under no circumstances would I accept a family's valuable possessions or heirlooms as payment, or in gratitude, for a bag of food. I always refused, using the excuse that UN personnel weren't allowed to receive gifts. It was a lie, but should have been the truth. Some UNPROFOR personnel accepted or bought, for next to nothing, valuable items they didn't deserve. I gave some of the pictures to Kevin, and those I kept joined my other cherished Bosnia mementoes.

The fighting escalated, and, as it did, the situation in Sarajevo became bleaker. On 17 July one of the military interpreters, Amina, arrived at Forward shocked and covered in dust. She'd been waiting for transport to work when a shell hit the building behind her, and she was showered with small pieces of shrapnel. Fortunately she wasn't injured. Later, when I walked into her office, she was writing a letter to her fiancé, just in case something should happen to her. That afternoon a shell exploded opposite Radio BH, wounding scores of people. The next morning, as I was leaving my flat, I stopped at the front door where I kept my 'escape' basket of valuables and necessities, and pondered a long while on whether to carry it with me. What would happen if the flat got struck while I was at Forward? I couldn't decide, so I didn't take it. But I felt so vulnerable, so mortal. I had an overwhelming need to go to church, to lose myself in the silence and divine atmosphere, to be with other people who felt as fragile as I did, for reassurance that there was a purpose to life. If there was ever a place on earth where one needed God, it was Sarajevo. But once at the office I got busy and didn't have a break until it was too late.

The fighting intensified, and Sarajevo was rocked by heavy shelling. A dreadful fatigue took hold of me. Russia's special envoy, Ambassador Vitaly Churkin, visited Sarajevo and had lunch with us, but I was preoccupied with my own black thoughts. I felt no excitement at the opportunity of listening to his views and talking about the situation. My melancholy mood was lifted briefly by a letter from an old radio colleague and friend, Fanie Lategan, in Windhoek. (I'd forgotten that I'd written to some friends months earlier, just after I arrived, to say where I was.) 'Good Lord my Angel,' he wrote, 'I almost keeled over onto my back when I got your letter! What on earth are you doing in Bosnia?' Good question. I imagined his reaction if I were to tell him that it had taken me seven hours the previous day to put together a half-hour programme of an interview with Madam Sadako Ogata, the UN High Commissioner for Refugees. Producing the radio programmes was excruciatingly difficult. Everything was. Radio BH was virtually out of fuel, and the engineer was feeding the small generator on one litre of precious fuel at a time from a Coca-Cola bottle, like an orphaned lamb. Only two studios were operational, and all the programmes had to be done there, switching power from one studio to the other. Every fifteen to thirty minutes there was a rotation to give someone else a chance to do some work. The fuel was used for the equipment only, and we worked by the light of my torch. When the power went off, we had to sit in the dark and wait.

There was no air conditioning, and it was not pleasant in the airtight, soundproof studios. Everyone smoked the foul cigarettes made of anything from the very worst tobacco to ground quince leaves, and even tea. During the rotations I sat in the semi-dark corridor where – thanks to large holes punched in the walls and windows by Serb shells – there was fresh air, and awaited my next turn. In desperation I asked Larry Hollingworth of UNHCR for fuel for the generator. He obliged, but could spare only a small amount, and in no time it was finished again. Everything threatened to drag me deeper into the dark spiral of despondency. A man at Radio BH asked me if I could mail something to his children in Austria. It was a letter and two small packages, one with T-shirts for them and the other a book of Greek mythology. The book was all that was left of their possessions. He wanted the children to have it, because he didn't know whether he and his wife would survive, and he wanted them to have something from Sarajevo. He opened the book, smelt the pages with a longing expression on his face, and said it would remind them of their home. I was in tears, and I thought: *I can't do this any more. How can any human being witness all this pain and suffering and keep going?* I felt as though I simply couldn't keep putting one foot in front of the other. He later brought me a gift to thank me for mailing the parcel. It was a beautiful coffee-table book of Medjugorje, the Bosnian town where the Virgin Mary was said to appear every so often. The book was in English, illustrated with colour photographs, packaged in a matching box: a collector's item. I couldn't imagine what it must have cost him and didn't want to accept it, but he insisted. He had inscribed it: 'For showing sympathy.' Sympathy was just about all I had left. I was dejected and exhausted and felt like going home, curling up in bed and sleeping for the rest of my life. But I was too proud to show it and kept a stiff upper lip.

The studio at Radio BH was on the sixth floor, and counting mezzanine and other in-between floors, it was ten flights of stairs from the ground – and no electricity meant no lift. Thus I had to grit my teeth and climb ten flights of stairs twice a day, wearing my heavy bullet-proof jacket and helmet (and heavy military boots in winter), carrying a bag with papers and programme material, cassettes, sandwiches and flask of coffee. At the end of the day I had to carefully retrace my steps, often inching down hundreds of stairs in the dark when I had no batteries for my torch. It was hard, especially when I was exhausted after sleepless nights filled with continual bombing and fighting. While I was suffering from a protracted bout of gastro-enteritis, I was sure that, if the snipers didn't get me first, having to climb the hundreds of steps every day would. Sometimes I was so ill I had to take a break and sit down on the stairs for a while before I could carry on climbing. A few times I had to repeat the climb because I'd forgotten to bring something, but the stiff punishment for my forgetfulness helped jog my memory for weeks afterwards. Gradually I grew used to the forced workout and eventually became very fit, albeit not voluntarily.

Everyone in the city was pessimistic and dejected. The depressive atmosphere hung over Sarajevo like the stinking black cloud of burning garbage. I missed my children, my home, a normal life. But I soldiered on, trying not to think too much about it. On my way back from radio late one afternoon, I noticed there were no children playing outside. That was unusual, and it underscored the atmosphere in the city. Close to Forward I saw some young men playing with a ball. One had only one arm, the stump that remained of the other arm was heavily bandaged; another had only one leg, and was hobbling around with the help of crutches, which he also used, like a bat, to hit the ball. The city was full of mutilated young men.

Other people's problems have always helped me forget about mine, and when six of the Residency employees were called up for military duty, including Gordana, I dived headlong into obtaining an exemption for them, venting all my pent-up frustration on arguments with the Bosnian government.

A few days after I received the oranges from Major Iversen, he sent another two boxes with the Danish shuttle. I took these to the children's ward at the hospital. Lola, one of the interpreters who was a medical student, went with me. I didn't want to see the children – I found it too disturbing – so I just spoke to the sister in charge. She was extremely grateful. And it was so pitifully little. We had so much food, we ought to have given more, but not everyone shared my sentiments, not even when it involved food for the starving children of Sarajevo.

Sadly, Major Iversen's tour of duty ended shortly afterwards, and when he returned to Denmark, the source of fruit for the children was cut off. Sometimes I bitterly regretted the military rotation. Often there just wasn't the time or opportunity to build a new relationship that would allow for this kind of thing. And sometimes, regrettably, the replacements were people with different attitudes and philosophies, such as unquestioning obedience to regulations that left no space for exceptions or a little creative bending of the rules.

The small part of my life that could be described as my own would have gone by almost unnoticed if it weren't for the odd highlight or disruption. One day Anja arrived at my office with eyes as big as saucers. 'Come quickly,' she said. 'There are soldiers in your flat.' She'd been busy filling the bath when there was a knock at the door, and when she opened it, two Bosnian soldiers pushed her aside, inspected the flat, made themselves at home in the dining room and started smoking. She ran like the wind to fetch me. Jack was in the office, heard the story and said he'd come along. On the way out, he slung a machine gun over his shoulder.

When we arrived at the flat, the two soldiers were still sitting at the dining room table. They'd taken off their shoes, and were smoking and talking as though nothing was out of place. I politely said good afternoon, introduced myself and asked if I could help them. Jack took up position beside the door, the gun hanging conspicuously over his shoulder. One of the soldiers spoke some English, and explained that they were going to move into the flat. This was quite common and I'd expected it, so I kept my cool and very politely said, 'No, I'm sorry, you can't. I live here.' He said the two of them and their wives and four children were refugees and had nowhere to live. I said I was really sorry, but in a way I was in the same boat, and if they moved in here, I wouldn't have anywhere to live, so they'd have to find another place. He said all of us could live there. I said we definitely could not. He said I had no right to be there, and they'd been given permission to move in by the company that owned the flat. I said I was very happy for him, and as soon as he brought me the documentation to prove that I indeed had no right to be there and they did, I'd move out. In the meantime, would they please put their shoes on, empty the ashtray and leave. He said they'd bring the documentation, emptied the ashtray, and they put on their shoes. I walked them to the front door, said it was nice to have met them and wished them a nice day. They left. Jack hadn't said a word, but his imposing physique and the very large gun on his shoulder definitely tipped the scales in my favour. For the moment.

This was part of the insane way of life in Sarajevo. Often, people who left their flats for a few hours to fetch water or humanitarian food aid returned to find that a refugee family had broken into their home and moved in. Carlos had had a similar experience, with the difference that the whole family was there and had already unpacked their bags when he arrived at the flat one night after work. Poor Anja had had a nasty fright, but it was very fortunate for me that she'd been there. If she hadn't, I might have returned in the dead of night, ready to fall into bed, to find someone else already curled up under my blankets.

The soldiers never turned up with the documentation, and I later found out that one of my neighbours had been responsible. He'd complained somewhere about the flat being sublet in the absence of the legitimate landlord. The snake: he'd invited me for coffee with his family and been ever so friendly. But he had also asked a lot of questions about my arrangement with the absentee landlord, which I foolishly answered. There was terrible envy of people who were receiving money (foreign currency at that) from UN employees, and often the sentiment seemed to be: 'If I can't get it, why should he?' My needs were none of his concern; he just wanted to prevent his former neighbour from getting the money.

In July, Milenko Vočkić announced that Fuad had been assigned to do outside broadcasts and that another engineer would work with me. Armin's arrival was a godsend. He spoke English, took charge, organised the studio shifts, accelerated the pace and took over control of the broadcast material for Radio BH. Everything improved immeasurably, and I depended on him for far more than support for the programme. He had a reputation of being Radio BH's stalwart, and he was. If I needed help with anything, he obliged. We became close friends. As part of the Serbs' strategy to isolate Bosnia from the world, the radio building was shelled constantly, and when heavy artillery and mortar blasts shook the building, we were often trapped inside for most of the day. There was nothing to eat or drink, which was why I'd started taking coffee and sandwiches, prepared by the kitchen staff at the Residency. The coffee, especially, was a big attraction. We shared it with whomever was around and there was never a drop left. After a year without water, in a building that still housed about 300 people, the condition of the toilets was unbearable. Out of fear I might have to go to the toilet, I never had more than a few sips of coffee, and had the utmost respect for the local broadcast personnel who had no choice but to brave the onslaught on all their senses. Some of them, those who'd fled their homes in the Serb-occupied part of the city, like Armin, or whose homes had been destroyed, lived in the radio building. Often they had nothing to eat but nettle soup. When they received care packages from humanitarian organisations, Armin made snacks in the building's kitchen, which he insisted on sharing with Jamila and me. He'd also discovered a tiny stove, and we could boil water for coffee in the studio when there was electricity.

The private radio stations in Sarajevo continued to pursue me with offers of broadcasting the UNPROFOR programme, often in the hope of receiving assistance for their stations. Vrh Bosna, an organisation promoting Croatian culture, was also interested. They wanted to start a radio station, and invited me to visit them to discuss the possibility of broadcasting the UNPROFOR programme. It was impossible for me to make the programme available to any more radio stations because I was alone, working like a lunatic and just didn't have the time, but I agreed to go and talk to them. When I arrived for the meeting, I found the offices open but deserted. I decided to wait a few minutes and sat down in the reception area. After a while a breathless receptionist arrived, apologised profusely and said they'd been to a funeral, and that her colleagues were on their way. They arrived anon, and we went into the main office to have our meeting. When we sat down they apologised again, and I expressed my sympathy, fully expecting to hear the same tragic story repeated dozens of times a day in Sarajevo: that he or she had been shot by a sniper or killed in a mortar explosion. The director said their late friend had died a strange death for Sarajevo, and I braced myself for a horror story. He'd died of natural causes, he said seriously, and they all burst out laughing.

———————

Sarajevo needed good news. When it arrived at the end of July, however, it couldn't be announced from the rooftops, but had to be spread in careful whispers. As battles continued to rage around the city, it became clear that the Bosnian army would need weapons and ammunition to defend Sarajevo from the encroaching Serbs. By January 1993 the authorities realised that something had to be done, and in desperation the plan was hatched to build a tunnel under the airport, from Dobrinja to Butmir, suburbs under Bosnian control.

It was a dangerously ambitious plan, because if it wasn't properly constructed, the tunnel could collapse and damage the airport runways. Engineers were brought in, and work began on what was to become a Sarajevo legend and a monument to the resourcefulness and tenacity of Sarajevans. The Bosnian army and volunteers, working eight-hour shifts and using only picks and shovels, worked for six months to complete the 800-metre tunnel. The mountains of sand they unearthed were removed in wheelbarrows under cover of dark. At some places the tunnel was five metres under the airport, and underground water that constantly seeped into the tunnel had to be pumped out to keep the water level down. Heavy rains and melting snow compounded the problem, and twice the tunnel was completely flooded and work had to be suspended.

By the end of July, Sarajevo was finally reconnected to the rest of the country. It was a triumph beyond description. Initially soldiers carried everything through the tunnel, mostly arms and ammunition. They also brought in food, cigarettes, fuel and medicine, and carried out the injured. But in time the ingenious engineers constructed a mini-railway, and small carts started running through the tunnel, carrying supplies. People, however, including thousands of soldiers, had to walk through the dark, narrow, shallow passage waist-high in dirty, freezing water. Even President Alija Izetbegović used the tunnel to get in and out of Sarajevo. People who couldn't walk had to be carried. It wasn't only uncomfortable, it was extremely dangerous. Pipes and high-voltage electric cables dangled everywhere. In some places there was water underfoot, an electric cable on one side and a fuel pipe on the other. Up to 5 000 people a day passed through the tunnel, and it was an absolute miracle that none of the hundreds of thousands of people who waded through water with electric cables overhead were electrocuted. Improvements were constantly made. Cables were laid to reconnect the telephone service to the city, and an improvised oil pipeline was threaded through the tunnel, making it even more deadly. Oil was pumped into the pipeline from a fuel truck in Butmir. If the truck had been hit by a shell or even sniper fire, it would have ignited the fuel and the tunnel would have gone up in flames.

The location of the tunnel remained a closely guarded secret, but everyone, including the Serbs, knew of its existence. Most people in Sarajevo never saw the tunnel, but its presence had an important psychological impact. It provided people with the relief of knowing they weren't totally at the mercy of the Serbs, and the pride of knowing they didn't have to rely solely on the UN for assistance. It was a symbol of their spirit and courage. Serb shells twice hit people at the tunnel's entrance, and heavy shelling was regularly concentrated on Dobrinja and Butmir, hoping to put the tunnel out of commission, but this never succeeded.

The tunnel saved Sarajevo from military defeat. Without it, the city would almost certainly have fallen to the Serbs.

CHAPTER 14

BEHIND SERB LINES

JULY–SEPTEMBER 1993

THE PHRASE 'BEHIND SERB LINES' WAS THE FAVOURITE, almost romanticised, catchphrase of the international media. For the people of Bosnia, however, the line that divided them from their families, former friends and colleagues signified the utmost in danger and evil.

The pride and joy of the Bosnian Serbs, their self-proclaimed Republika Srpska, was largely shielded from the misery of war, and many of its inhabitants swaggered and gloated about the glory of their abominable 'victory' over the virtually defenceless Bosnians. The Bosnian Serbs received everything they needed from Yugoslavia, and because the territory they occupied was for the most part untouched by military action, they experienced little discomfort as a result of the war. However, although one could buy everything in Srpska, and I regularly travelled to Pale and Lukavica, I never bought so much as a slice of bread from them. Nor did I bear gifts of good Scotch and cigarettes. Some UNPROFOR personnel used these as bribes for Serb cooperation, but my stubborn streak simply wouldn't permit it, and as far as I was concerned they deserved their own inferior Scotch and cigarettes.

The feared 'Serb territory' was astonishingly unimpressive. Pale, stronghold of the Serb leadership, had been a popular ski resort. It wasn't a bustling city like Sarajevo, nor a busy town. It was a village, popular only for spectacular scenery and good skiing. Pale did, however, have one claim to fame: the Panorama Hotel, which housed the Serb seat of 'government', was where Nazi Germany's representatives had signed a capitulation agreement after Tito's Partisans liberated Sarajevo, and then most of Bosnia, at the end of World War II. Some Serb officials were already smacking their lips at the thought of repeating the exercise – with the Bosnians at the losing end. In winter, covered in snow, Pale was picturesque, and the mountain air fresh and invigorating. But in summer it was as dusty and unimpressive as Kiseljak, down to the poisonous atmosphere. It reminded me of similar towns in the South African countryside, breeding ground of narrow-minded political hate-mongers. For Serbs who didn't support the rabid nationalism of their ethnic leaders, it was very uncomfortable in the 'Serb Republic'. This was something else with which I, as a white South African, could identify. One day on my way to Radio SRNA, I offered a lift to a woman walking to Pale. She told me she'd been a lawyer in Sarajevo, but, unfortunately for her, had been visiting family near Pale when the barricades went up. She'd been stuck there ever since, and hated everything about the place and the so-called government. There were tears in her eyes when she said, 'I want to go back to Sarajevo, to my home, my friends and my life. But it's all gone now.'

As part of my work I regularly travelled 'behind Serb lines' and found it increasingly unappealing. For one, it was dangerous. The road across the airport runway was as deadly as Snipers' Alley, and the French military erected a memorial at the airport for the many French soldiers who had died there. To make things worse, the UNPROFOR military were sometimes as difficult as the Serbs, and had a penchant to turn a manageable situation into a hazardous one. They were soldiers, not diplomats, with a different approach to our situation. They issued an instruction that UNPROFOR personnel weren't allowed to travel alone to Serb territory. This was impossible for Deyan, Carlos and I, and Civil Affairs officers elsewhere in Bosnia. The sheer volume of our work meant we couldn't accompany each other, and the military, despite having made the rule, didn't see it as their responsibility to provide civilians with an escort. The only exception was Viktor, who had both a military assistant and a driver. Another instruction was not to open vehicle windows or doors at Serb checkpoints. It is very difficult to communicate with people through a closed window, especially mouthing words in a language they wouldn't understand even if they could hear you. Foreseeing that this would irritate checkpoint guards, and guided by inherent good manners and common sense, I ignored it. My formula stood me in good stead. I opened the window, was polite, and could pass almost unhindered through most Serb checkpoints. The UNPROFOR military who observed their non-compliance rule and butted heads with the Serbs ended up with guns pointing at their heads. I couldn't see the point in placing myself in a ridiculous position where I was alone, outnumbered, outgunned and out-resourced in every way that counted – and in any case they could simply force the door open or smash a window. Not to mention the Serb coup de grâce of placing mines around the vehicle. Then what? Was I to recite the Geneva Conventions to them through the closed window?

Foreign civilian women didn't travel alone in Bosnia, and I was therefore somewhat of a novelty for the Bosnian, Serb and Croat soldiers at the checkpoints. This mostly worked in my favour. ICRC and UNHCR personnel (male or female) never travelled alone, and the teams had armoured vehicles. It intrigued the tough soldiers of Bosnia that a woman would brave the dangers on her own, and they probably couldn't figure out whether I was incredibly brave or incredibly stupid. Neither, actually, but I had no choice. Of course it was a risk travelling on my own. Things could – and did – go wrong. I had plenty of uncomfortable experiences with the Serbs, some with the Croats – and only two with the Bosnians. However, tussles with the Croats and Bosnians were distinctly different from those with the Serbs. The large UNPROFOR presence on Bosnian and Croat territory provided a measure of security, and I never felt quite as vulnerable as when I was in a difficult situation on Serb territory. Having intimate knowledge of the terrible things they'd done to helpless people didn't help. And alone and unarmed on Serb territory was about as helpless as one could be. However, my assessment of the Serbs was that they were bullies, so I decided never to show fear, which brought out the worst in bullies. I was also careful not to show bravado, nor to be aggressive. I had another advantage. Our nationalities were printed on our UNPROFOR ID cards. Later, when relations between the Serbs and several Western countries, especially the USA, became strained, this was omitted. However, my Namibian nationality was a definite plus, and when I was offered the opportunity to be issued with a new ID sans nationality, I declined. It was also novel to be white and from Africa, which often broke the ice in potentially difficult spots.

But despite good intentions and conscious effort, I had some unpleasant encounters. On my first few trips to Pale to organise the broadcasting of the radio programme, I was met, either at Lukavica or at the checkpoint between Lukavica and Pale, by M, who was my contact. He was pleasant and the meetings were conducted in a cordial atmosphere. On a subsequent trip, Kevin McGrath asked whether he could come along for the drive. This time M behaved entirely differently, and kept trying to separate me from Kevin. He invited me to lunch, and said my 'American friend' could eat at the radio station. I sweetly said no, that would be rude, and what if he got lost or something. After lunch, M said he wanted to listen to the news in his room and insisted I went along – alone. I, still sweetly, insisted Kevin should go too. The atmosphere became disagreeable and I couldn't wait to leave. I was tremendously relieved that Kevin was there, and decided I wasn't going on my own again if I could help it. Fortunately I didn't need to. For some weeks I didn't have time to go to Pale, and arranged to leave the programmes at Lukavica with the liaison officers, Brane Luledžija and Major Indjić. I liked Brane and always suspected he'd ended up on the wrong side by accident. Even Misha Indjić, who was aggressive and belligerent at the best of times, always behaved courteously towards me. During the summer months tensions escalated markedly, and I was specifically advised by the UNPROFOR military not even to go to Lukavica for the time being. I arranged to have the programmes delivered by the UNMOs (United Nations Military Observers), and once that routine was established, I saw no reason to change it. My energy and time were critically taxed and I had to spare myself, which was as good an excuse as any to limit trips to Serb territory.

There were also problems at Radio Kiseljak. A Dutch soldier delivering a radio programme was stopped by an HVO soldier, who pointed a gun at him. I wrote a caustic letter to the authorities in Kiseljak, registering outrage at the incident, and informed them we were forthwith discontinuing broadcasts from Radio Kiseljak, and would only resume once they'd taken steps to prevent a recurrence and could assure us it would never happen again.

Whenever the fighting escalated there was a proportional increase in sniper activity, and getting shot at became a regular occurrence. The first time a sniper shot at me I'd been in Bosnia for only a week. It was at the back of the PTT Building in Sarajevo, and I was taking a photograph of my military colleagues against the backdrop of rows of white UN vehicles and the scenic mountains undulating to the horizon in ever softening shades of lime green and grey. I was peering through the lens when the shot rang out – very loud and much too close. The bullet whistled over our heads and crashed into the wall next to us. I'd never been shot at before and stood riveted. Rick grabbed my arm and dragged me to cover behind an APC. 'They must have thought you were a journalist,' he said. 'The Serbs don't like journalists.' That was a masterful understatement. More journalists were killed in Bosnia than in any other war, most of them by Serb snipers. I had many encounters with Sarajevo's snipers. At first I counted the 'near-misses'. (Funny word, near-miss. Shouldn't it be a near-hit? I asked my military colleagues.) When the count reached twelve after the first few months, I decided it was morbid and stopped counting. Eventually I had no idea how many times I'd been shot at by the infamous men and women – among them members of the former Yugoslavia's Olympic sharp-shooting team – whose occupation it had become to assassinate unarmed civilians. I was shocked when I heard that some snipers were female; there was a rumour that the record for most kills was held by a woman. It was evil incarnate.

There was nothing worse than being at the mercy of a sniper, in a place from where there was no escape. One night I left my office close to midnight, limp with exhaustion. As usual, I'd been on the go since six in the morning and worked until half past eleven. As I crossed the open ground on my way to the small arched pedestrian bridge that spanned the road in front of the ICRC offices and Radio Zid, one of the private radio stations, the hair on the back of my neck suddenly prickled, and the skin of my back rippled uneasily. The proverbial cat was walking on my grave. In Sarajevo, that wasn't a joke. And I'd been there long enough to know that I never felt threatened or uncomfortable unless there was good reason. I instinctively knew there was danger lurking in the dark shadows.

But where? And who? Or what? It suddenly struck me that I was framed in bright moonlight, but I realised almost instantaneously that light wasn't a factor for a sniper; they had sophisticated night vision equipment and could 'work' in pitch darkness. I shuddered involuntarily, imagining a sniper's eyes behind the powerful scope of the rifle, scanning my body, selecting a vulnerable spot. By now I knew very well that my blue flak jacket would provide no protection from a well-placed high velocity bullet. And, the jacket covered only my chest and back. The many UNPROFOR soldiers who'd been killed and wounded in Sarajevo were ample proof that even the best body armour was no match for the deadly bullets fired by marksmen with Olympic medals to their credit. The kevlar helmet, securely strapped around my chin, would deflect a direct hit to the head, but the impact could break my neck. Cheerful thought. Paralysing fatigue and stubborn pride wouldn't allow me to turn around and slink back to the safety of Forward. Nor to run. Anyway, I was too tired to run, and it probably wouldn't help. I took a deep breath and kept walking, a clear, slow target, past the protection of the last buildings and towards the small bridge. I hadn't switched on my torch. I didn't need to. The moonlight was bright and I knew the path well enough to walk it with my eyes closed. I told myself that, if I could make it over the top of the bridge to the 'Sarajevo rose' on the other side, I'd be fine. But my little pagan ritual brought me no comfort. I was acutely aware of the absolute silence. Nothing was moving. It seemed as though my rubber footsteps, even my own breathing, bounced loudly off the walls around me. A sniper had shot a woman on the small bridge a few weeks earlier. A shiver ran down my spine.

I crossed the bridge, walked towards the steps and started climbing: 200 stairs to the level of Ciglane, where I lived. I imagined cold, hostile eyes on my back, and the top of the stairs seemed to reach halfway to the sky. My chest felt tight, my knees shaky.

On the stairs I was totally exposed: no protection, no hiding places. I detested the satanic sniping bastards: cowards, who hid behind high walls and murdered children and women in cold blood. It was a long way home, and I tried to think about the comfort of my bed, the relief of shedding the heavy helmet and uncomfortable flak jacket. As I started up the third flight of stairs, a single shot shattered the dense silence. It ripped through the still night like a bolt of thunder. I flinched as though I'd been punched, and instinctively pulled my head into my shoulders, trying to make myself as small as possible. Momentum kept me going, up, up, my legs moving automatically. Since I was already almost halfway up the stairs, it was too late to do anything else. Too late. I didn't like the ring of that. Which made me think: didn't these monsters ever sleep? My mind worked like an engine coughing back into life, in fits and starts. Look on the bright side, I thought: at least I knew I wasn't being stalked by a rapist, or a rabid dog. Was he in front or behind me? I tried to remember where the sound had come from, but couldn't. It had just seemed to explode from somewhere in the dark. I also didn't hear the bullet hit anything, but I was quite high and it could have hit something much further away. The thick silence was suffocating me and I suddenly felt blind panic. I was suspended halfway between heaven and earth, with nowhere to hide. Up or down would make no difference. Should I fall down, make myself as flat as possible? No, he'd still see me, and then he could play cat and mouse with me all night, keep me lying there, firing every time I lifted my head. If he was worth anything as a marksman, he could kill me even lying flat on the ground. Deyan had spent hours crouching at the bottom of the stairs one night when a sniper pinned him down, firing every time he moved. I wasn't going to give him (or her, I reminded myself) the satisfaction of cowering or crawling. I kept climbing. If they wanted to kill me, they'd do so sooner or later, and I couldn't live like a mole, hiding away. I remembered the Mexican saying,

'It's better to die standing up than to live on your knees.' That was how everyone in Sarajevo felt. They refused to hide or cower, and they took a morbid, fatalistic pride in the fact that they didn't allow these demons to take this freedom from them.

I was halfway. Just another hundred stairs. My legs felt strange, as though there was nothing between my hips and my feet. In anticipation of the next shot, my back was involuntarily arched, and it was aching. I realised my legs were shaking, but it still felt curiously as though I were floating above the ground. Thoughts flashed through my head. Will I feel it when the bullet hits me? They say you initially don't feel anything. Will he shoot me in the leg? In the face? Will he find the small square of my neck that isn't covered by the flak jacket, even with my neck pulled so far into my shoulders? If I don't die instantly, will I be able to crawl up the rest of the steps?

Then all the thoughts crystallised into one: *Am I going to die alone on these stairs above this tragic, doomed city?*

The sniper didn't even fire another shot. It was probably enough fun to imagine me climbing the rest of the stairs in a state of mortal fear.

The next morning an unexpected meeting was called and, dressed in only slacks and a shirt, I went to my flat to fetch a jacket. There'd been heavy shelling around Forward, Ciglane and Koševo Hospital since early morning, and I drove as fast as I could. Explosions were thundering through the city. On my way back, as I rounded a bend in the road, I almost hit an old man on crutches, hobbling down the hill. Against my better judgement, I stopped and asked where he was going. To Koševo Hospital. My heart sank. I offered to take him home, but he insisted he had to go to hospital, and pointed to his broken leg. I couldn't leave him there, and instead of spending ten minutes arguing with him out in the open, I might as well take him to the hospital, I thought. Praying we wouldn't be hit by a shell, I helped him into the car, and while he sat back with a satisfied grin on his crinkled face, I darted across Djure Džaković and charged toward the hospital like the light brigade. As we drove up the hill, a shell exploded in the road ahead of us. Koševo Hospital was a regular target for Serb shells, sometimes because Bosnian forces placed their mortars next to the hospital and fired on the Serbs from there, obviously hoping the Serbs would be loath to fire at a hospital. But the Serbs had proved they had no compunction about firing at hospitals, children's homes or old-age homes – the more vulnerable, the better. The area between the gate and the hospital buildings was the most dangerous. Many people had been killed there, and I couldn't leave the old man there on foot. When we arrived at the gate I hooted and waited for the guard to lift the boom, impatiently holding my breath. When there was shelling they crouched inside their guard post. It felt like ages before a guard darted out to lift the boom. His jaw dropped when he saw my car. I said I'd be back in a minute, and asked him to leave the boom up. He nodded and ducked back into the hut. When I helped the old gentleman into the lobby of the casualty unit, the orderlies were as surprised as the guard had been. I felt foolish. I was totally opposed to the concept of playing hero. But I couldn't explain to them that I'd found the old dear halfway to the hospital on his crutches. He was sure to tell them, though. He thanked me profusely, invited me to have coffee with him and his wife, wrote down his address and explained where he lived. I nodded and smiled but registered nothing. All I could think was that I had to drive down that hill through a curtain of deadly shells, and I wanted to get back to Forward. I dived into the car, pulled my head into my shoulders and hurtled down the hill to the Residency. At the entrance I was furiously scolded by the Egyptian guard for being out when it was so dangerous.

He rambled on in Arabic. I didn't understand him but knew what he was saying: that women were really stupid, should be at home cooking lunch for their husbands and children, and had no business frolicking around in a war in a faraway country. Some of my colleagues were having coffee in the foyer when I stumbled in and collapsed on the nearest chair. 'Where have you been?' they asked. I said, 'At Koševo Hospital.' They just looked at me, speechless. I didn't even bother to explain.

Thanks to my radio programme, I was reminded that a sane, normal world still existed. I wanted to interview one of the airlift crews, and had to go to Ancona in Italy, because they didn't disembark in Sarajevo. They sat in the aircraft with the engine running while it was unloaded, and then immediately took off again. I wouldn't have wanted their job for anything in the world. Flights were only stopped in cases of exceptionally heavy fighting around the airport, and they braved the permanent danger to bring in Sarajevo's lifeline. I took an early flight from Sarajevo to Ancona. Mike Aitchison, the UNHCR chief in Ancona, was very helpful, and introduced me to the UNHCR staff, and to the crew of the next flight to Sarajevo. I interviewed them and was ready to fly back to Sarajevo in the afternoon. I'd checked with Civpol, the UN civilian police, whether I'd need a visa for going to Ancona and the answer was no, since I wasn't planning on leaving the airport. Because I wasn't on a permanent contract with the UN, I didn't have the UN laissez-passer [travel permit], which automatically gave UN employees entrance to most countries.

Then disaster struck. Falconara Airport in Ancona received word that Sarajevo airport had been closed, and no further flights would be allowed to land. I was marooned in Italy – and without a visa.

The Italian policeman in charge at Falconara Airport, Franco Pitassi, offered to see what he could do, contacted someone in Rome and explained the situation, and returned with the good news that I'd been granted a special visa to stay in Italy until the next day. It wasn't the last time Franco would dash to my rescue.

UNHCR employees in Ancona often spent weekends in Senigallia, the picturesque coastal village a few miles from the airport, and Mike suggested I stay there. It was summer and all of Italy was on holiday. It felt like a wonderful dream. For months I'd seen no streetlights and shops, no relaxed, carefree people. Mike took me to a large supermarket to do some shopping, but after wandering around aimlessly for about fifteen minutes, I asked whether we could go and have a coffee and come back later. I was overwhelmed. There was so much, and because I hadn't expected to go shopping, I needed time to make a list of the most important things to take back. Mike obliged. That night he and two of his colleagues took me to dinner at an excellent Italian restaurant. Afterwards we walked along the boulevard next to the beach. During summer the Italian Adriatic coast is crowded to bursting point, and Senigallia was swarming with thousands of tourists, talking and laughing. There were lights everywhere. At eleven o'clock I went into a shoe store and bought two pairs of Italian shoes. My companions teased and said I shouldn't lose them at midnight like Cinderella. Long after midnight everyone was still out on the streets and at the outdoor cafes. Like Eliza Doolittle in *My Fair Lady*, I didn't want to go to bed. At three o'clock in the morning I was still standing on the balcony overlooking the small piazza in front of the hotel, while the frantic merrymaking faded slowly with the last hours of darkness.

Mike fetched me straight after breakfast the next morning and we headed for the airport. I thanked him and Franco from the bottom of my heart for making the magical experience possible, and boarded the aeroplane for Sarajevo. I recorded the sounds of take-off and the preparations for landing in Sarajevo, then clung to the metal railings behind the pilot's seat as he dived to the tarmac. My stomach was in my throat, my lungs somewhere outside my head. I had to hang on for dear life or fly through the windscreen. Senigallia seemed like a beautiful, ethereal dream.

———————

At the end of July, General Morillon left the mission. His unsanctioned action in Goražde had embarrassed the UN, and because he'd stepped out of line they wanted him out. A Belgian general, Francis Briquemont, was his successor. I'd enjoyed working with General Morillon and grown fond of him. He was a colourful character, and though he seemed to enjoy the image of being somewhat of a rogue, that belied his true nature. He cared deeply about the Bosnians, and the country's terrible fate haunted him. I was sad to see him go, and on the day of his departure cried a little on his shoulder. He patted my back and growled, 'Don't worry, General Briquemont is a fine man.' He was right.

General Briquemont was quiet and diplomatic, a stark contrast to Morillon's flamboyance. But he, too, was a man of integrity. The atmosphere around HQ softened and became slightly more relaxed, but was equally efficient. We continued in much the same way with briefings, work and discussions around the dinner table. Briquemont, too, preferred that we wait for him for dinner. Like Morillon, he managed to draw together people from different cultures and backgrounds with different outlooks into a cohesive and successful team. I would have walked through fire for him.

I'd come to know many of Sarajevo's artists, and patronised concerts and exhibitions as often as I could. Because I was the 'old hand' at Forward, Briquemont asked me about life in Sarajevo, information about this and that, the pronunciation of difficult names – little things to help flesh out the basic skeleton. When I mentioned the artists, he was immediately interested. And when I proposed inviting them to perform concerts at the Residency, he agreed at once. He appreciated good music and art, and understood that it would be beneficial for the soldiers who were cooped up with nowhere to go. And so started the season of music at Forward.

For our first concert I organised the group United States of Love, who were famous far beyond their besieged city for their adaptation of the musical *Hair*. It wasn't possible for them to stage the whole musical for us, but they performed well-known music from the show, as well as some other evergreen and local songs. For me the most beautiful was a gypsy song, sung passionately and movingly by Srdjan Jevdjević, on his knees with his eyes closed. Undisputedly the most popular with the practically all-male audience, however, were the solo performances by the tall, lithe, beautiful Dragana Ilić, sung in a sweet, clear voice. The evening was a big success. Our entertainers were invited to have dinner with us and received a small food parcel each. These were great luxuries and they left in a haze of contentment.

Because of the intricate logistics, including a curfew that meant we needed special permission from the Bosnian military to trans-port the musicians to and from the Residency, and the fact that UNPROFOR worked seven days a week, we couldn't have regular concerts. But roughly every four to six weeks we had some enter-tainment. The supply of entertainers far outweighed the demand, and it took some fancy footwork to decide whom to invite. Fortunately the final word always rested with the general. I pro-posed ideas and he decided. One he rejected, to my disappointment, was three-year-old Arijana. She was Sarajevo's darling, the dearest little girl, and very bright. She knew by heart all the lyrics of the songs she performed with natural star quality. But Briquemont said he didn't approve of child performers. Although it was a relief to be able to pass the buck when I had to explain to her father why we couldn't invite her, I regretted it.

I made another friend during this time. Gertruda Munitić was Sarajevo's prima donna, another of the city's remarkable women. With a sister in the US, a daughter in Israel, family in Croatia and many friends around the world, she could have left on several occasions but, like many Sarajevans, chose to stay. She spent her time either entertaining the people of Sarajevo in concert or running the office of the local children's organisation, Naša Djeca [Our Children]. In recognition of her work with the children, she was nominated as a UNICEF goodwill ambassador. Gertruda was indomitable: never dejected, never complaining, always bubbling with enthusiasm and always perfectly groomed. Her flat was in the suburb Breka, high on a hill behind Koševo Hospital. It was a dangerous area, but with total disregard for the peril, she walked up and down the steep hill and to the city and back to rehearse or perform or to work at her office. She continued even when she injured her leg in a fall. When I found out she was limping around, I offered to fetch her whenever I could, and we became friends. I spent many enjoyable hours in her modest flat, surrounded by memories of her interesting past.

In mid-August there was suddenly high drama. Barry Frewer was declared persona non grata by the Bosnian government, after stating at a press conference that Sarajevo was not under siege. He'd said the Serbs were in a 'tactically advantageous position', but that didn't mean Sarajevo was under siege. The Bosnian government and besieged Sarajevans were incensed, interpreting the statement as just another way of appeasing the Serbs and absolving the international community of the need to take action to save Bosnia. UNPROFOR feared Barry's life might be in danger, and he was whisked out of Sarajevo under cover of darkness.

My six-month contract with UNPROFOR was running out, but I decided to stay on. The radio information project was just gathering momentum and I had ambitious plans for it. Moreover, I'd been lured by Sarajevo into her magical, deadly tango with life and death. Like the hundreds who ran across the airport runway and crawled back into Sarajevo through the suffocating tunnel, I was hopelessly under her spell.

It was difficult having to tell John and Annéne. They weren't happy, but took it in their stride. Since I wasn't leaving the mission, I decided to have a holiday with them in October. After six months without a break, I was physically and mentally exhausted. There simply wasn't time to recover from the numerous onslaughts on one's resources, and I was straining to keep the programme going. On 21 September we celebrated the broadcast of the hundredth UNPROFOR radio programme. I bought drinks and snacks, and invited everyone who had anything to do with the programme. For the people at Radio BH the party was a really big event, and a large number showed up. They didn't often get a treat, and tucked into the snacks and drinks with great enthusiasm. I thanked everyone for their support and assistance, promised an even better celebration when we reached 200 programmes – which was met with laughter and encouraging whoops and whistles – and we cracked open a few bottles of champagne. Someone said, 'Let's eat, drink and be merry,' and since all of us knew the unspoken rest of the saying was only too true, we got stuck in until not one crumb or drop was left.

For Studio 99, the absence of a transmitter was a serious problem. Then Adil called and told me they'd received a transmitter, but that it was in Zagreb. He asked if I could help them transport it to Sarajevo. There was no way of doing this legally. The Serbs would refuse, so I had to make careful inquiries to see if it would be at all possible, without giving away pertinent information, in case anyone might object to smuggling the transmitter in. I just said I needed a large parcel to be brought from Zagreb. I confided in only two UNPROFOR people whom I knew I could trust implicitly. One was Deyan, the other a Civpol contact at the airport. His role would be to take the 'large parcel' through the checks, which he could do with little risk. Once I was certain the plan was feasible, I told Adil to go ahead, have the people in Zagreb address it to my contact, and have it put on the flight. Our fallback position, in the unlikely event of a problem, was to say that the transmitter was for UNPROFOR Radio, and that it had been an oversight on my side not to have gone through the right channels to bring it to Sarajevo. The highly secretive mission almost died a sudden death. Adil had told some trusted staff members about it, in confidence, and one of them in a moment of utter idiocy loudly said to me at a press conference, 'I hear you're helping us to get our transmitter.' I almost had a heart attack, and it was touch and go whether I would cancel the whole thing. I made Adil promise to take care of any potential wagging tongues, and he did. Nobody spoke another word about it. A few days later the coveted transmitter was in Sarajevo. I made Adil repeat the oath of eternal silence about how it had got there, and packed my bags to go on holiday.

CHAPTER 15

HEAVEN AND HELL

OCTOBER 1993

JUST DAYS BEFORE I'd hop onto an aeroplane out of Sarajevo for my holiday, Cedric called personally to say my leave had been cancelled. Because, he said, the Bosnians and Serbs were expected to sign a peace agreement any day, and that meant every pair of hands would be needed. My task would be to beam the happy news across Bosnia via UNPROFOR Radio. But I had set my heart on spending time with John and Annéne, whom I was missing terribly. Also, I'd been in Sarajevo for a solid six months and had to have a break. Moreover, I didn't believe for a minute that a peace agreement was actually going to be signed. I stood my ground, promised to buy a newspaper first thing every morning while in Italy and France, and head straight back to Sarajevo on the first flight if there was any change in the situation. I also told him I'd eat my shoes if there was a peace agreement. He approved my leave.

My doubts about the peace agreement were correct, and for three weeks I enjoyed the almost forgotten, wonderful luxuries of life that most people take for granted. It was heaven. Rome, Venice, Paris, Toulouse, the French Riviera, back to Rome. Three weeks of bliss with Annéne and John, food everywhere, a daily hot bath, electricity at the touch of a switch. The first ten days went by in a blur. I was overwhelmed and weary. But once I'd had a few nights' sound sleep, relaxing days and good solid meals, I started feeling more myself. It rained every day, but the deluge couldn't dampen our spirits. We visited the Colosseum and the dungeon where St Paul had been incarcerated, and explored as much of Rome as time and energy allowed. On the first day I divided our spending money into three equal parts and gave John and Annéne their share, with stern instructions to spend circumspectly. Disaster struck when John's moonbag was stolen in the jostling on the subway. Fortunately his passport was with me, but we now had much less money and had to cancel some of our plans. Having John around was a blessing. He was strong and energetic, carried his own bags and mine, and each time we got off the train, Annéne and I would get a cup of tea and chat while John went off, looked around for suitable accommodation and then fetched us. When we arrived in Venice, he was in his element. He found it fascinating and wanted to see every building, climb each set of stairs. After a while Annéne and I had had enough and went window-shopping, but the prices were prohibitive and we didn't buy anything. Instead, we went to a coffee shop and each had a liberal helping of decadent Venice cake and coffee, caught up with each other's experiences, talked about our holiday and laughed a lot. Every minute with them was precious to me. We had Eurail tickets, and in the train en route from one place to the next there was time to talk, or just sit quietly together, drinking in the spectacular landscapes. In Menton on the French Riviera the children went exploring with some friends they'd met on the train. I walked to the ocean, feeling ready to burst into song and smiling to myself like an idiot. An elderly gentleman stopped me, and said he just had to ask why I seemed so happy. I told him it was because life was incredibly beautiful where the sun was shining and people were going about their normal lives, working, shopping, making plans. His name was Edmond Fradin, and when he heard I was working in Sarajevo, he wanted to hear more. He invited me to have tea at a cafe overlooking the ocean. The service was perfect, the tea and pastries delicious. I expected to wake up any moment in a barrage of exploding shells. Edmond was a gentleman farmer who owned an estate that produced calvados, and I spent a memorable two hours with him talking about Sarajevo and calvados. After I returned to Sarajevo, I received a postcard from him, saying he was thinking of us all in the city and hoping I was safe.

The constant rain caused floods in some places, which brought all transport to a halt. Having lived in Namibia, we hadn't seen so much rain in years. We bought umbrellas in Rome, but still got wet all the time, and some days the damp clothes and shoes got too much for us and we'd just sit in a cafe for hours, talking and eating. In Paris we rented a small apartment, and the first morning I rose early and went out to buy eggs, bacon and fresh bread to make breakfast. It ended in disaster, with dried-out bacon, eggs stuck to the pan and burnt toast, and the kids laughed and teased about how my cooking skills had so quickly deteriorated. It was better after the first day, but I really had lost the touch. We walked around Paris, had lunch on the Champs Elysées, went to the Eiffel Tower and other tourist sights, but also ventured off the beaten track to look at the real Paris. Annéne needed clothes, and we bought her a few trendy pieces on sale, and also had her hair cut in the latest style. She was quite excited about showing off her 'Paris look' to her friends in Johannesburg.

The last few days were bittersweet. I had a tight knot in my stomach at the thought of having to say goodbye. John was staying on in Europe for a few more weeks, and was heading back to Venice. After emotional goodbyes we parted ways, and Annéne and I went to Rome, from where she'd catch a flight to Johannesburg and I'd take a train to Ancona and then a flight to Sarajevo. The last day was extremely painful. I tried to hang on to each minute, and it took every last scrap of self-discipline not to just forget about Bosnia and Sarajevo, board the aircraft with my daughter and go home. When she'd gone, I sat in a corner at the airport and wept for a long time. Then I went to the station, bought a ticket to Ancona and boarded the train. I sat staring through the window in a stupor, numb with sadness at the thought that it would be months before I saw them again. When the conductor made his rounds to check the tickets, I handed him mine, expecting nothing more than a click as he punched it. But he launched into an angry tirade in Italian, pointing and waving the ticket around. I didn't know what was going on until another passenger explained that my ticket was for a regular train, and I was on the fast train. If I wanted to stay on the train, I would have to pay an additional amount – but I'd spent my last lire and only had a few cents left. The conductor was a mean man with no compassion, and at the next station he threw me off. As I disembarked, the passenger who'd translated earlier helped me with my bags. He said the conductor could have let me stay on the train and apologised for his bad behaviour. There was nobody else in sight, and I bit back the tears as I sat on the deserted railway platform at Orte and watched the train speed off into the distance. Hysteria threatened to overwhelm me. I thought of just running off into the countryside, leaving everything behind me, all responsibilities, all cares, and running to the edge of the planet. Then, thankfully, my sense of humour emerged and I thought, 'With my luck, I'll run straight into Sarajevo.' I started laughing, all by myself, and thought, 'No, you mean little Italian, it'll take more than you to finish me off – the entire Bosnian Serb army couldn't accomplish that in six months.' I waited for the slow train and arrived in Ancona as darkness was falling. This meant I'd missed the last flight to Sarajevo. I had no money for a hotel, but I was beyond caring. I started walking to the airport, which was way out of town, intent on sitting outside the building until the next morning and catching the first flight back to Sarajevo. After a long time I saw a pedestrian subway, which would have provided a short cut, but when I got there I found it had been closed. By now it was dark. As I turned around to walk back, a car with two young men stopped and asked whether I needed a lift. I just shook my head and started walking, feeling quite nervous. There were no people around, and nobody would see if I needed help. They turned the car, stopped next to me again and one of the men got out. I was really frightened, and wondered whether I could outrun them. He put his hand in his pocket and I expected him to pull out a gun, but it was an ID card. He was a policeman. They gave me a lift to the airport, and to my delight I found that Franco was on duty. We had a coffee and I told him what had happened. But he wouldn't hear of my staying at the airport alone the whole night. He took me to a small hotel in Falconara, paid for a room and gave me money for a taxi. As if he owed me anything after all he'd done for me over the months, he apologised for not taking me to stay at his house, but they had guests. He made me promise I'd let him know when I was coming again, which I did, and the next time I did stay with him and his wife and children.

The next morning, after three weeks of sleeping peacefully in a decent bed, and enjoying hot showers, lights, warmth and eating whatever my heart desired, I was in a French military aircraft on my way back to Sarajevo. Having experienced the heavenly luxury of normal life on the other side of the divide, I had to brace myself for the city's privations and horrors. During my holiday I'd thought a lot about life and death, heaven and hell. It was really quite simple. Heaven meant a leisurely Sunday drive or a carefree walk in the street, instead of crazily dashing from one building to another for shelter with bullets ricocheting around you, or hurtling down

Snipers' Alley with your heart in your mouth. Heaven was turning on a tap to find hot running water, a corner shop with bread and cheese, fruit and sweets. Hell was Sarajevo, as the welcome sign said.

'We maybe have to go back,' the French military equivalent of a flight attendant said in his heavy accent. 'Zere is very much fighting around ze airport and zey are stopping all ze flights. But if posseeble, zey will let us to land.' I was one of five passengers, and he helped us into parachutes and instructed us on what to do if we had to jump – most importantly, which cord to pull after counting to five. My throat was tight and I wondered whether I should be wishing to get back to Sarajevo, or to turn around. In Rome I'd only just managed to over-come the overwhelming desire to jump onto the flight with Annéne. If we didn't return to Sarajevo, I might really change my mind and run, back to Johannesburg and my own life. And it was a really ter-rifying thought that we might have to jump from a burning aeroplane into Bosnia's impenetrable forests, where Serb gunners lurked. But we made it safely to Sarajevo, and were allowed to land, despite the fierce battle raging around the airport. When the giant tail flap opened to disgorge us, slowly unveiling the mountains in their heavy green camouflage, the sight of the heart-rending beauty surrounding Sarajevo caused an excited flutter in my chest, as one has when see-ing a place or person you love. My elation was short-lived, however. Shells were raining down on the airport, and we had to run like frightened rabbits for the shelter of the heavily sandbagged building. From the trenches encircling the airport came the constant – and close – rattle of machine-gun fire. My heart went out to the Bosnian soldiers in the trenches, the UNPROFOR soldiers unloading the humanitarian aid, and the crew sitting in the cockpit, waiting to take off the minute the last pallet was unloaded. We received a danger allowance for working in Sarajevo and heaven knows, we deserved it. If, of course, one survived to enjoy it. Many UNPROFOR personnel did not, and returned home in coffins, wrapped in their national flags.

Shells exploded in giant swells of dust and smoke. The earth was shaking and growling as though an angry dinosaur was stomping across it. Bullets whined and whizzed overhead, and hit the scarred walls with loud popping sounds. This was Sarajevo at its worst, and I could feel all my defences automatically springing back into action. In an instant, the restorative value of my holiday, which already seemed distant and unreal, was swept away. Inside the airport building I bumped into Tony Land, head of UNHCR in Sarajevo. While we were talking, a soldier announced that the shuttle to the city had been cancelled, as UNPROFOR commanders had forbidden all traffic because of the heavy fighting in and around the city. That meant I could be stuck at the airport the whole night, and perhaps even the following day, and I complained loudly. Tony asked whether I wanted a lift. He'd brought someone to the airport and his armoured car was parked outside. I'd often braved similar conditions in my 'soft-skin', and could certainly risk it in an armoured vehicle. I grabbed my baggage and we headed for the door, pointedly ignoring the French soldier's warnings. Whether the count for the day was to be 300 shells or 3 000 – or just one – there was always the risk that you might be hit.

The roads were utterly deserted. Nothing moved. There were no people on the streets, no UN vehicles. Not even a single APC or a stray dog. The city was tightly wrapped in the dark thunder of Serb shells. The heavy explosions reverberated through the city as we hurtled down the empty road. Death and destruction was pouring from the skies, and I was praying seriously that my guardian angels were back on twenty-four-hour duty.

At Forward I received a warm welcome from my colleagues. My arrival caused quite a stir. Some of my military colleagues admitted they hadn't expected me to return, and certainly not when it was barely possible to enter the city. The DCOS, Lieutenant Colonel Fernando Lafuente, was on his way down the stairs when I arrived.

He beamed a wide smile at me, called, 'Ah, happiness has come back to Sarajevo!' and gave me a warm hug. Behind him on the stairs was Gordana, thinner and more haggard than when I'd left, but laughing and blowing me a kiss. I felt like the prodigal daughter.

––––––––––––

Jasna and I had much in common: we both loved music and reading, and enjoyed cooking, sewing and home-making. She often stayed late at the Residency or spent the night in her office to write, read and listen to music. Sometimes, late at night, we'd make tea, talk about dreams and disappointments, share our secrets and hopes. I also enjoyed going to her home, which was a true haven. On the few occasions I could slip away, I enjoyed her mother's delicious home-cooked meals, tea and quiet discussions. In the lounge, on the wall opposite the window, was a mark where a sniper's bullet had smashed through the window one evening as Jasna and her mother sat talking. The bullet passed between them and lodged in the wall. There were reminders everywhere, constantly, of how precarious life was in Sarajevo.

––––––––––––

As if 1993 hadn't been bad enough in every respect, weather forecasts predicted a harsh, early winter. And with this came a message from the Serbs that, if they had anything to do with it, it was going to be hell on earth. On 19 October, the day I returned from leave, a thousand shells exploded in the city. Sarajevo was as empty, grey and cold as when I'd first arrived. But now there was no promise of the reprieve of spring and summer. The second winter of the war was looming, with its cold, hunger and unspeakable misery. The only bright spot amid the struggle of trying to keep the radio programme on the air and my head from becoming a sniper's target was organising the concerts at the Residency. Until Mipić appeared in my life.

On my first day back at work I checked in at the Communications Centre as usual to pick up my correspondence. One of the soldiers showed me a litter of kittens born while I'd been away. Their mother was 'the Commcen cat', and now there was a whole family, wobbling around on spindly legs and creating havoc. The soldiers on duty fed them, but if anyone came too close, they scattered. All except the little black kitten. She was the proverbial curious cat and always up to some mischief. When I heard they were making plans to get rid of the cats, I adopted her. She'd been christened Miep by Vladimir, a Flemish-speaking Belgian soldier, but since she was a Bosnian cat, I renamed her Mipić. She spent most of her time in the Annex, and everyone loved her. She slept on the chairs, played with papers on the desks, and generally provided hours of amusement. She took turns sleeping in the Belgian soldiers' rooms and was always in the lounge when they were watching television or partying. Mipić became a legend at BH Forward.

The military rotation sometimes had distinct advantages, and the new intake of soldiers that arrived with General Briquemont was a welcome change. The Belgians had no problems asking for assistance and happily reciprocated. They were more friendly and relaxed than their French predecessors. And compassionate. Thanks to a sudden cold spell, I caught the flu. I had no medicine and became really sick. Instead of dragging myself home to a freezing flat, I slept in my office. At two o' clock one morning, on my way back from the bathroom, and on the verge of collapse, I bumped into Marc from the Commcen, who was just coming off duty. He gave me one look, and asked 'You have medicine?' I shook my head. 'I bring you Scotch,' he said, and a few moments later arrived at my office with a bottle and glass. He poured me a stiff dose of neat Scotch, sat down while I dra k it and then poured another. On his way out, he said, 'Now sleep. Tomorrow, see doctor at PTT.' This small kindness brought tears to my eyes.

———————

Thanks to living in Sarajevo, I learnt valuable lessons about survival, and realised I needed to broadcast information that would be helpful to people: practical tips on preserving food, recipes to make the most of meagre rations, how to make a simple water purification device, basic first aid, etc. I'd heard there were problems with finding water purification tablets, and wanted to start with information on dates and places of distribution. It was a chaotic maze. UNHCR brought in tens of thousands of tablets, but distribution was done by local agencies and they were almost impossible to track down. When I finally did, they couldn't provide me with a schedule of dates and places of distribution. I asked UNHCR to get me the necessary information, but it never materialised. I asked the WHO representative for their 'survival guidelines', and was astonished by the reply: they didn't have a copy in Sarajevo (where people needed all the help they could get to survive) and had to obtain one from Geneva. I asked for some other information in the meantime – whatever they had available. They had nothing. I went from one agency to another, but they had no information on how to make life easier for Sarajevo's besieged population. It was very disheartening, and I bemoaned my lot to Trish Purves. She offered to help – and two weeks later I had a pile of books and material she had received from Britain, with everything from simple first aid to directions for building a basic water purifier. I never received an iota of survival information from any of the UN agencies.

———————

October was a bad month, and I had no regrets about having missed the first half of it while on holiday. There was constant shelling, day and night, and heavy fighting everywhere. On 30 September the UNPROFOR casualty figure stood at 58 dead, 689 wounded. And attacks on UNPROFOR were escalating. Even General Briquemont came under fire when snipers hit both his car and the vehicles accompanying him. In the same week, there was a serious attack in the town Novi Travnik on an UNHCR convoy, and UNPROFOR's Dutch–Belgian transport battalion that accompanied the convoys in central Bosnia. The Canadian driver was killed, and nine UNPRO-FOR soldiers and two Bosnians were wounded. The impact of this was palpable at HQ, as Briquemont and many of the soldiers were Belgian. As a result of the attack, the UN Secretary-General announced that humanitarian assistance to central Bosnia would be suspended until assurances were received from the Bosnian army and the HVO that there would be no further attacks on human-itarian convoys. This would of course hurt the civilians, who desperately needed the food and medical provisions. But since much of the humanitarian assistance ended up in the hands of the warring factions, it was hoped the ban would have the necessary effect. It was a shock to learn the Bosnian army had been responsible for the attack, but the investigation proved that they were attacking the HVO, and the convoy was unfortunately caught in the crossfire. By the second half of October, the situation was more tense and unstable than it had been for some time. There was intense fighting in central and southern Bosnia, and in Sarajevo the shelling increased dramatic-ally. This was ascribed to an increase in the number of men from Serbia who dedicated their free time over weekends to firing on the hapless civilians trapped in the Bosnian enclaves. They wanted to get in a few shots before winter. The Serbs were proud of the fact that civilian men from Serbia and Montenegro were patriotic enough to spend their weekends firing on the besieged Bosnians.

Taking everything into account, UN estimates were that the two million people in Bosnia who depended on aid would receive only half of what they needed. And with the suspension of aid in central Bosnia, even this was in the balance. The Bosnians were weak and exhausted, and wouldn't survive without food and other winter supplies. It was getting colder fast and the highest priority was to bring in as much humanitarian aid as possible before winter arrived in earnest. UNPROFOR's 'Operation Lifeline' was declared the highest priority, and every available pair of hands was used for repairing bridges and roads, escorting the aid convoys, and negotiating them through in difficult places.

The intense fighting in central Bosnia was exacting a heavy toll. The HVO, unable from the beginning to hold their own against the Bosnian army, managed to take the town of Vareš in central Bosnia, but almost immediately realised they couldn't hold it and started planning to evacuate. The Bosnian village of Stupni Do, just a mile from Vareš, unfortunately stood in the way of the retreating Croats. On 23 October they started shelling the village, and when night fell they stormed it and set all the houses alight. Fleeing villagers were shot, and those who couldn't get out fast enough had their throats slit. Soldiers of UNPROFOR's Nordic Battalion were sent to investigate, but battled for days to obtain access to the village. When they finally did, the entire village had been burnt to the ground. They found the bodies of twenty-five people. People had been thrown into the fires, and some bodies were never found. The Croats were taking a page from the Serb book of ethnic cleansing by subjecting civilians to such unspeakable horror that those in other villages fled in terror to escape the same fate.

UNPROFOR started repairing Sarajevo's tramway, the oldest in the world. The mere thought that there would be trams in the city caused enormous excitement. But Serb snipers wounded and killed several people inside the trams, and the project had to be abandoned. The most important missions, however, were repairs to electricity supply lines. This was as endless as cleaning dishes in a restaurant. Almost as soon as a line was repaired, it was damaged again as a result of military activity. There'd been no electricity for weeks. And no electricity also meant no water, because the pumps needed power and the main pump, which provided eighty percent of Sarajevo's water, wasn't working. Often it wasn't possible to do repair work because of the fighting. Sometimes UNPROFOR engineers would work for two weeks to repair an electricity line, but it'd hardly be operational when it would be damaged again, once more leaving Sarajevo without electricity and water.

My son John had decided not to hike around Europe, but to stay in Venice for the rest of his holiday. He found a room, called Annéne and asked her to give me his telephone number when I called her, which I did every Sunday. When I called, he said he'd 'spent more money than he'd meant to' and was broke. There was no way of sending him money from Sarajevo, so early the next morning I rushed to the airport, boarded a flight to Ancona, hitched a lift into town, telegraphed the money from the post office and rushed back to the airport for the flight back to Sarajevo. It was absurd having to fly to another country to get to a post office, but normality has no place in the madness of war. One of the Civpol officers in Sarajevo sent his laundry to Ancona every week.

Absolutely everything was mired in endless difficulties and problems. Although I had little time for anything besides the radio programme, I welcomed other projects, even if it meant more work and a mere variation on the usual problems. The Obala Gallery received an invitation to exhibit 'Witnesses of Existence' in New York, and Miro asked if I could help get the exhibition to the US. It would be very difficult, but I promised to help if I could, and started putting out feelers. The minute I mentioned it, everyone said it was impossible. That really irritated me, and the more people said 'impossible', the more resolute I became that they should be proved wrong. I had an idea. The aircraft that brought humanitarian supplies to Sarajevo went back to Italy empty, and I asked Mike Aitchison whether we could take the exhibition out in an empty aircraft. He conceded that it was a remote possibility, but said it would set a precedent, and that in the very unlikely event of it happening, we had to be sure never, ever to ask them to bring the exhibition back to Sarajevo. I agreed. He added that he'd need letters from generals, prime ministers, NATO, the Kunsthalle Gallery in New York and endless other documentation to secure a specific country's aircraft for the purpose. He suggested, since the exhibition had to go to the US, that it might be easier for me to directly approach the US Defense Force. That made sense, and I started writing letters and making phone calls, thinking all the invaluable contacts I'd made would help. But after a lot of paperwork and wasted time, it became clear that we'd get nowhere with the Americans. One of the most difficult things was making people outside Sarajevo understand that you could not simply get up and leave or put people, not to mention a very large art exhibition, on an aeroplane. From the safety and sanity of New York or Rome it was incomprehensible that we had so many problems, and I repeatedly had to explain the difficulties, such as the fact that we were totally dependent on the military and their governments. The Kunsthalle people had already made plans to transport the exhibition from Frankfurt to New York, and it was difficult to explain to them that the American military refused to fly the material to Germany. The concept was so simple, the execution so fraught with complications.

I had another disappointing encounter with American official-dom. United States of Love was invited to take their show to the USA, and I was asked to help them. I started working, armed with a formal invitation from the US House of Representatives and a letter to Prime Minister Haris Silajdžić, requesting permission for

USL to visit the US. This was necessary because the male members were of military age and doing military duty. But there was an official reply from the Bosnian Ministry of Foreign Affairs granting permission for the group to go. The invitation was signed by fifty-three congressmen and senators, and said, inter alia, 'At this moment when President Clinton and the American people are faced with difficult choices about how best to support peace and democracy in the former republics of Yugoslavia, we feel it would be enlightening for Americans to see the human face of the drama in the Balkans, and to hear the personal stories of those involved.'

There was a letter from the Director of the US Information Agency, Joseph P Duffey, to General Briquemont, asking for assistance to transport the group from the city to Sarajevo airport, from where AmeriCares would provide air transport for them. Mr Duffey wrote that he advised '... The President, the National Security Advisor and the Secretary of State on public diplomacy issues'. It was a great pity that he wasn't also advising the Secretary for Home Affairs on 'public diplomacy issues'. The group was refused visas to enter the USA. It was incomprehensible. The mighty USA was afraid that thirty young, talented people might be too terrified to return to Sarajevo, and seek refuge in the land of the free and the brave. I wish they'd asked me. I could have told them how many times I'd helped people to leave Sarajevo, and how, almost without fail, they returned. I could have told them about the members of Fazla who hadn't had the luxury of flying in and out of the city and had risked their lives to run back to Sarajevo across the airport runway. I could have told them about Jamila and Jasna and Ines and Gertruda, and dozens of others who made their own arrangements to return after I'd helped them leave.

United States of Love continued singing their songs in Sarajevo, and at the Residency.

CHAPTER 16

BAD TO WORSE

IT SEEMED IMPOSSIBLE THAT LIFE IN SARAJEVO could get any more difficult. But it did, and for UNPROFOR, too. We were running out of fuel and were down to one food ration per day – tinned military rations, eaten cold. The expected agreement between the Bosnians and the Serbs, which had almost sabotaged my leave plans, now seemed more remote than ever. The international community was disappointed, even angry at the Bosnians for rejecting the peace plan, which suggested dividing Bosnia into three separate ethnic states. In its efforts to get the plan back on track, the UN sent its deputy special representative, Sergio Vieira de Mello, to Sarajevo. Sergio was in his forties, a brilliant negotiator, and people were already saying he was a future Secretary-General, earmarked for a promising future in the UN. Despite his position he was a likeable, hard-working man with no arrogance or airs. For me, his arrival in Sarajevo brought relief in more ways than one. I was overjoyed to find he'd brought a female assistant, Annique, and secretary, Martha Horne. Annique was only there for a few weeks, but Martha stayed on after Sergio returned to Zagreb, and provided welcome female company. Also, Sergio was quite unlike the majority of UN career diplomats, who usually had burning ambition and would do nothing to jeopardise their rise to the top. He had a passion for making a difference in the lives of individuals and didn't allow anything, including the UN's uncompromising regulations, to get in the way. Although he wasn't at Forward for long, we established an immediate rapport and often collaborated on 'unofficial' initiatives. In Sarajevo he had his work cut out. The media reported that President Izetbegović had told a visiting delegation of ten parliamentarians from the US that the only means of averting the partition of the country was by continuing the war. He was, of course, right, and there was proof enough of this when Bosnia was forced to sign the December 1995 Dayton Agreement, which divided Bosnia into two sections along ethnic lines: an autonomous Bosnian Serb entity, and a federation of Bosnians and Croats. The only way Bosnia could have remained a viable, undivided country would have been for the Bosnians to win the war. But the Bosnians had neither weapons nor international support. Military operations in central and southern Bosnia escalated, and in one month the situation went from relative calm to heavy, widespread fighting.

Our greatest fears were the effects of the fighting and instability on humanitarian operations just prior to winter. Bosnians were painfully thin and their health was deteriorating. The children especially were in bad shape, and if they were to receive even less food, they would have no resources for braving the growing cold. During summer the humanitarian relief operation had achieved only approximately sixty percent of its delivery targets, mostly because indirect routes had to be used due to poor roads, and because of delays caused by fighting and turn-backs at checkpoints. The target for winter was approximately sixty-five percent, but free convoy access was crucial for improving the flow of aid. Meeting the target seemed increasingly unlikely. UNHCR's 'Winterisation

Programme' had to provide not only food, but also shelter to hundreds of thousands of people who were already starving and freezing. It was their only hope of surviving the winter. But despite UNPROFOR's stringent efforts, meetings and appeals, the Serbs and Croats erected ever more checkpoints and frustrated every effort to step up the distribution of aid.

Since the beginning of the war, Bosnia and Sarajevo had reached several infamous milestones, including the worst war in Europe since World War II, the longest siege in modern history, and the worst human rights abuses since Hitler's camps. Another was added in October, when the Sarajevo airlift operation reached 467 days, overtaking the Berlin airlift of 1948/49, which had lasted 462 days. The Sarajevo airlift was already the longest-running air relief operation in history, and there was more than two years of war ahead.

What the country didn't need was a record number of people starving and freezing to death.

When I returned from holiday, the situation at Radio BH was dire, and Milenko Vočkić asked me if I could get them some fuel for broadcasting. I called Tony Land and scheduled a meeting with him. However, on Tuesday morning, 26 October, as I was about to drive to PTT to meet Tony, we were informed that no UNPROFOR vehicles would be allowed to leave HQ, because 'the city was closed', and no traffic would be allowed in or near the city centre. This had never happened before. We were marooned at Forward. The whole situation was curious. Usually, if there was a problem, it was because there was heavy shelling or an otherwise specified reason, but 'the city was closed'? Rumours started circulating that the Serbs had advanced into Sarajevo and fierce battles were raging in the city. This caused immediate panic, but we soon received information about the actual state of affairs. It had nothing to do with the Serbs. The Bosnian authorities had been having problems with criminal elements within the military, and this had come to a head. Two well-known criminals and gang leaders, Caco and Čelo, who had become the leaders of the Ninth and Tenth brigades respectively, had been fired, and the police swooped on their operations. Two hundred of their men were arrested. Caco, especially, was feared by the people of Sarajevo. During the war he rounded up anybody and everybody and dumped them on the confrontation lines to dig trenches. He was also in charge of many black market activities, and the army could no longer control him. Since these men had played a major role in saving Sarajevo when the JNA attacked the city, they'd been given a lot of leeway – but the limit had been reached. It was generally accepted that the action against the criminals followed the election of Haris Silajdžić, one of the more conservative Bosnian leaders, as prime minister.

Sarajevo was like a ghost city after the swoop. All the radio stations continued making announcements warning people to stay indoors. It took some time before we found out why. The supporters of Caco and Čelo refused to take what had happened in their stride, and were hitting back. There were clashes with the police in different parts of the city, and amid fears that it could become really ugly, people were warned to stay off the streets. The city was quiet and tense and, by the end of the day, in mourning. For once, not because of the Serbs. The police had secretly planned to arrest Caco, but he got wind of this, and his henchmen ambushed the half-dozen young police officers sent to arrest him, brutally tortured them and gouged their eyes out before killing them. The father of one of the officers, himself a policeman, reportedly went in and shot Caco. Jamila's friend Anita, a quiet young woman who was an interpreter at PTT Building, had been engaged to one of the murdered policemen. I'd met Anita and couldn't imagine what she and the families of the men were going through. It would have been bad enough if their sons had died fighting the Serbs, but to know that they'd been killed by someone who was supposed to be a comrade in arms was almost unbearable.

On the same day, one of the members of United States of Love, Lejzi, was wounded by an exploding shell. Because so few people had access to telephones, I didn't find out until a few days later, when another member of the group, Srdjan, arrived at Forward to tell me. Lejzi was in a serious condition. Shrapnel had penetrated his skull. I couldn't face going to the hospital, but every other day I called Boris, one of the band members whose aunt, Lejla, had a phone, to check how Lejzi was doing. The best neurosurgeon had operated on him and removed the shrapnel, but fluid from a severed muscle was continually leaking through his nose. An optical nerve had been damaged, and doctors didn't know yet whether he'd lose his eye. His condition eventually stabilised, but he needed the kind of medical attention that was impossible to obtain in Bosnia.

To survive in Sarajevo, two things were especially important: a unique, even macabre, sense of humour; and reconciling oneself to the fact that, no matter what happened, life went on. If you didn't have these attributes, you were finished. One had to bury the dead, turn away from the terror and tragedy and try to survive. It helped for me that I was working so hard and was surrounded by so many people in such great need. This meant I couldn't dwell on any one thing for too long. I took Jamila to see Anita, offered my condolences, and promised to do everything within my power to help Lejzi. Then I went in pursuit of Tony to see if I could get some fuel to keep the radio programme on the air. He never refused when it was possible to help, and agreed to give us some fuel. It was an incredible amount – and at the same time pathetically little for the needs of a national radio station. But the hospital didn't have fuel, and nor did the bakery, the Bosnian army and families with small children and weakened elderly family members. In this context, it was an enormous amount.

The situation in the city became increasingly tense. On Saturday 6 November, the HVO brigade in the city staged a revolt. It was one of the many strange anomalies that there was an HVO brigade in Sarajevo. They were the enemy and engaged in vicious battles against the Bosnian forces in central Bosnia, so it was probably to be expected that there'd be problems sooner or later with them in Sarajevo. Again there was shooting in the city centre, and again the city was closed. And again I was about to meet Tony about fuel for Radio BH. There was nothing for it; the fuel would have to wait. Sarajevo's famous balladeer, Kemal Monteno, had been invited to perform at the Residency that night, and we were hoping the situation would clear up sufficiently for the concert, which everyone was looking forward to eagerly. Fortunately the rebellious Croats were brought under control, and we had an enjoyable evening in the company of Kemal and his wife Branka. He was a quiet, shy man with a beautiful voice, and was known as Sarajevo's Jacques Brel. One of my favourite songs, 'Jedne Noći u Decembru' ['One Night in December'], a song he'd written for Branka when they were young lovers, was part of his repertoire that cold November night.

In Sarajevo it was as though some negative force had been unleashed. The situation deteriorated daily. On the Monday and Tuesday after the concert, a sniper trained his sights on the Residency, and fired every time anyone moved. This caused great irritation, especially because it coincided with a visit on the Tuesday to Sarajevo by Thorvald Stoltenberg, Cyrus Vance's successor as UN envoy. We were ordered to stay inside the buildings at all times, and I was informed that I would under no circumstances be allowed to leave the compound. This was one of only two occasions when I missed a broadcast of the UNPROFOR Radio programme. By Tuesday afternoon General Briquemont had organised a French anti-sniper team, who dug in at the Residency's garden, and after they fired back at the sniper, he disappeared. Unfortunately the sniper team hit the windows of a nearby school, and a very embarrassed and apologetic UNPROFOR had to arrange to have them repaired.

We were constantly reminded of how fragile our status really was. On the Monday, the Serbs forcibly abducted two Bosnian security officers who were in an UNPROFOR APC, under our protection. They were accompanying a group of clergy from Sarajevo to Vareš to encourage Croat refugees to return to their homes, following the offensive in which the Bosnian army had taken control of the town. Because of the Stupni Do massacre, Croats were frightened of revenge by the Bosnians and reluctant to return. But although the Bosnian army was at times involved in retaliatory incidents, and committed some atrocities, they didn't practise ethnic cleansing, and Serbs and Croats were generally safe on Bosnian territory. The abduction took place at Rajlovac, a Serb-occupied suburb where the Serbs were more obnoxious and obstructionist than almost anywhere else in the country. As the three French APCs crossed into Serb-held territory, they were stopped by Serb tanks. The Serbs demanded that the two Bosnian officers, Andjić and Dejanović, be handed over, claiming one of them was a war criminal. When the French UNPROFOR convoy leader refused, the Serb soldiers pried open the hatches of the APCs with crowbars and dragged them out. UNPROFOR was severely criticised for not preventing this, but if the French soldiers had fired even one shot, everyone could have been killed. Viktor immediately started negotiating for the release of the two men, and the negotiations continued for three tense days.

For once the Bosnians had some leverage. The government had agreed to allow two busloads of Serb civilians, mostly elderly people, to leave Sarajevo on the Tuesday. But as a result of the Rajlovac incident, they were refused permission to leave. By

Wednesday the Serbs had agreed to release Andjić and Dejanović. At Forward we all had our ears glued to our Motorola radios, following every second of the intense, nerve-racking operation. Among the media, who had to follow everything from a distance, there was a rumour a minute, including one that the two men were no longer alive. But at noon on Thursday, Viktor radioed that they'd been released, and word could be given for the buses with the Serbs to leave. The Bosnians, as with Mr Bozalo, suddenly did an about-face and refused to let the buses go. Viktor rushed to the Presidency, and it was extremely tense until, finally, shortly before two o' clock, the first bus was allowed to leave and the drama was over.

While Viktor was negotiating the release of Andjić and Dejanović, the Serbs carried out two mortar attacks on the Sarajevo suburb of Alipašino Polje. On the Tuesday they attacked a school. Five children and their teacher were killed, and another twenty-two children were wounded. The rage and grief were always worse when children were killed, especially in deliberate attacks on schools and sports areas. On the Wednesday, another mortar landed in the same area, right across from Radio BH, where I was working. Ten people were wounded, half of them children. Three died. The situation seemed to be spiralling out of control. Not only because of the increased attacks, but because the Serbs were blockading all humanitarian aid convoys, including those with supplies for UNPROFOR. The critical fuel shortage meant we had to cut down on using our vehicles, and I was faced with having to cut back on broadcasts, as it was difficult both to travel and to record the programme. We were also marooned at Forward more and more regularly because of heavy shelling or sniper fire. After considering all my options, I had no choice but to cut back the broadcasts from five programmes a week to three.

The general deterioration in conditions continued. The Serbs did their best to frustrate efforts aimed at improving the situation, and the Croats followed suit. After behaving quite civilly at the checkpoint between Sarajevo and Kiseljak, they now decided it was time to start harassing us. My fairly regular trips to Kiseljak to buy food and other provisions became very difficult. The HVO soldiers at the checkpoint started demanding that I open the car, and then rummaged through the goods I'd bought, asking why I needed this or that. It was totally unnecessary. Why did they think one needed rice, or soap, or toilet paper? On one trip a soldier decided to 'confiscate' two bottles of whisky I'd bought at the UNPROFOR PX shop. This, of course, was just a ploy to encourage me to offer a bribe; many UN and agency personnel gave them liquor in order to be let through unhindered. He'd miscalculated his chances with me. I said no, he had no right to confiscate anything I'd rightfully bought; I had the receipts to prove it, and would sit there until doomsday unless he allowed me through with all my things. He shrugged and went back to his hut while I sat there in the snow and freezing cold, gritting my teeth. After a while he came out and paced around, then said all I had to do was leave behind the whisky. I said, absolutely not. He went back into the hut. After about forty minutes a vehicle approached from Kiseljak with some UNPROFOR soldiers. By this time my teeth were chattering and my hands were blue. When they stopped, the Croat soldier came to me and said I should give him the whisky because I was blocking the checkpoint. I said that wasn't my problem and we could all sit there till kingdom come, but he wasn't getting anything from me. The driver in the vehicle behind started hooting impatiently, and it looked as though the soldier was reconsidering his stance. I said, 'Call Mayor Boro and ask him to come here so that we can get this sorted out.' Now he was clearly uncomfortable. He didn't know what to do with me. It was cold. He had snowflakes in his beard, and would rather be in the hut where he had a fire going. And now I'd mentioned Mayor Boro. What if we were friends? That was the final straw. He walked around the car and lifted the boom.

Sometimes I doubted I could carry on and seriously considered throwing in the towel. But then I thought about the thousands of people who would have no hope if everyone like me decided to go home. Even if our work and assistance were a drop in the ocean, it still might mean the difference between life and death.

Winter arrived in full force, and as the weather deteriorated, I was faced with a simple choice: to move into the Annex, or freeze to death. After the first snow, the 200 steps to my flat turned into a mass of solid ice, like a glacier. The average temperature in my apartment seemed to be -20°C, and it was so cold my bedding burnt like dry ice. Having to face the dark, frozen tomb of my flat when I arrived home around midnight after almost literally crawling up the frozen stairs was too much for flesh and blood. And then there was the sniper. Since our first encounter, it had, seemingly, become a battle of wits between us, and he continued playing cat and mouse with me. I never knew when he'd be there, and on my long, slow ascents up the endless flight of stairs into the dark sky, I often thought about him: Who was he (or she)? What did he think while he trained his sights on a defenceless woman or child – or peace-keeper? Did he have a family? Did he go home after a day's 'work' and cuddle his children, read them bedtime stories, make love to his wife? Sometimes days passed without him firing the odd shot to remind me he was still there; at one time more than two weeks went by. Perhaps he was on leave. Perhaps some French legionnaires had found his hideout and broken his arms, as they'd done to other snipers. I always wore my flak jacket and helmet, identifying me as UNPROFOR, and perhaps he was intrigued by me, wondering why on earth I – a civilian – was still there. Perhaps he wanted to see how long I'd last. Perhaps he was just waiting for the right moment.

Perhaps my working relationship with the Serbs kept me alive, and there was a special directive from Major Indjić to all snipers in the Sarajevo area not to kill me. The thought made me smile. Still, if I moved into the Annex, I might survive a little longer. I didn't want to give up my freedom, but after clawing my way up and down the frozen stairs a few more times I admitted defeat and moved, telling myself I spent almost all my time there anyway, and a break would be as good as a holiday.

CHAPTER 17

A NEW YEAR OF WAR

DECEMBER 1993

IN EARLY DECEMBER I visited a French base on Mount Igman, south-west of Sarajevo, to do a radio story. Communities in the mountains had been cut off by the fighting and were risking death by starvation. The terrain was extremely inhospitable: there were no roads, and the only way the French could reach these people and distribute humanitarian aid was by using skis. It was reminiscent of scenes from World War II: soldiers in snowsuits on skis rescuing people in isolated hamlets trapped by the vicious fighting. It was very cold, and I'd dressed in as many layers of clothes as I could accommodate: thermal underwear, thick wool socks, gloves. But it was freezing in the APC, and in no time I was shaking with cold. We were taken on a tour of the base and surrounding area, walking through the snow and climbing a hill to get a better view. Soon my teeth were chattering and my feet and legs aching with cold. I'd never been so cold in my life and felt like bursting into tears, but soldiered on, asking questions and taking notes. By the time we got back to the camp I had no feeling left in my legs, and couldn't speak or bend my fingers. I was in agony. The commanding officer ushered us into a large tent. The sides were stacked high with bottles of wine, and in the centre steam was rising from a large iron pot over a fire. He gave us each a mug of steaming red wine. It wasn't Glühwein, with sugar and spices, just plain red wine, but within moments the life started returning to my frozen limbs and face, and soon I was filled with a warm glow. I returned to Sarajevo counting my blessings.

Christmas was approaching and I was determined it would be a time of celebration at Forward. I'd used up my leave, couldn't go home, and decided I'd rather stay in Sarajevo than go somewhere for Christmas where I didn't know anyone and was a lonesome tourist. Christmas was a time to be with family and friends, and although my family was far away, I had many friends in Sarajevo. I proposed a whole week of performances between Christmas and New Year, and when General Briquemont agreed, I lined up the artists. Then I planned a trip to Senigallia to buy Christmas gifts, and invited Jamila along. She was as excited as a little girl at the prospect of her first trip out of Sarajevo in almost two years – to go shopping in Italy. I'd booked us a room at the Palace Hotel, and although the purpose of the trip was shopping, what we probably enjoyed more than anything were the long, leisurely hot showers we took twice a day. My grandparents were farmers in the Free State, and I grew up with a healthy respect for the importance of conserving water. Years of living in Namibia had reinforced the habit, and in Sarajevo I never used a drop more than I had to, but on this trip to Senigallia I shamelessly indulged myself, morning and night. Then we went shopping. For two days we ransacked Senigallia, spending every cent on gifts for friends and colleagues, and for Jamila's family. Most of the gifts were foodstuffs: biscuits, cheese, smoked sausages, dried fruit, chocolates and other sweets. Since I'd initially planned to stay on the UNPROFOR mission for only six months, I didn't have adequate winter clothes, and had to stock up. So did Jamila who, like everyone in Sarajevo, hadn't had the opportunity to buy any clothes for two years. We tried on jerseys, scarves, gloves and boots. Back at the hotel, we triumphantly piled everything onto the beds and took photographs of each other and all our purchases. It was a mountain of things. We were as happy as could be. In the evenings we went out to dinner and took long walks along the brightly lit streets. When we headed back to Sarajevo, we had to brave the inevitable checking at Ancona airport. Everything was fine, except that we had more alcohol than was allowed, as we'd each bought a few bottles of Scotch as presents for the men on our lists. We asked one of the agency employees who was flying back to take it in for us, and he agreed. We never saw it again. When we reached Sarajevo, we missed him in the jostling at the airport, but I wasn't worried as they had offices in the Annex. However, every time I went to his office to fetch our Scotch, he had some excuse: it was at home, he'd forgotten to bring it, he couldn't go and fetch it. Eventually he admitted he'd 'borrowed' it for an impromptu party, but promised to replace it. He never did.

When word got out about our Christmas programme at Forward, I was inundated with proposals from local entertainers. I tried to put together a varied programme and included the Elenes Dance Club. One of the members of the troupe, Djani Aganlić, came to see me to discuss the details. He was young, enterprising and very pleasant. Before the war he and his wife, who was also his dance partner, had run a florist and gift shop in Grbavica. Like all the other Bosnians who lived there, they had to abandon their home and business when the Serbs invaded the area. When he told me he was in the process of starting a coffee shop, I was intrigued. It was incredible to think that people were planning a future while this terrible war was going on. He related his plans, which were inspired, and the problems he was encountering. I offered to make copies of music for him to play in the shop, and to reciprocate he invited me for coffee. On the day of our appointment there was heavy shelling. Djani arrived at the Residency on his bicycle. I said we could take my car to go into the city, but he said it would be better to walk, since there wasn't parking where we were going. But it was impossible to walk. It almost seemed as though the Serbs knew where we were heading, and shells exploded all along our route. We had to run most of the way, sprinting across empty streets to reach the relative safety provided by buildings. It was an incredible relief to reach the elegant cafe. The people of Sarajevo continued to amaze me. The cafe was lovely, but I was very nervous because it had large windows, all still intact – and untaped. The shelling was intensifying, and I could think of few things worse than being in there with all that glass if it were hit by a shell. But everyone else seemed relaxed and unconcerned, talking and laughing as though nothing was out of place. The atmosphere was infectious, and even though the cafe was filled with the obligatory cigarette smoke, there was good music, coffee and cakes, and soon I was enjoying the outing. Djani was doing his military duty as a member of the police force and told me about a recent case he'd had to deal with. He was on patrol when he noticed a small group of people shouting and gesticulating. A sniper was firing continually in the area, and he went to investigate. A man was lying on the opposite side of the street, his face in the snow. The bystanders told Djani he'd gone to fetch water, and been shot by the sniper. Djani started calling to him, and after a while the man answered. Djani asked whether he'd been hit. He said he wasn't sure. That wasn't as strange as it sounded. When in shock, your body cloaks the pain in adrenaline and it sometimes takes time to establish whether you are okay. Djani called to him to crawl, but as soon as he moved, the sniper fired another shot. Because snipers had night vision equipment, it wasn't a solution to wait for dark, and if the man lay half-buried in the snow for too long, he might die of exposure. Djani racked his brain and came up with a plan. Because it had been snowing the ground was slippery as soap where people had walked on it, and it appeared to be solid enough. He explained his plan to the man and, satisfied that he'd understood and was ready, went into action. While the bystanders held their breath, Djani walked a few paces back, then turned and sprinted forward. When he reached the spot from where he thought the sniper could see him, he jumped, flew through the air and hit the man with enough force to propel him to safety. The sniper fired a shot, but because they were moving so fast, it hit nothing but vacant air. The man was winded but safe. For a while they both lay quite still, gathering their wits. Then, suddenly, the man jumped up and starting screaming insults at Djani, calling him a bloody idiot. Djani was stunned. 'Hey,' he said, 'I just saved your life.' ' Yes,' the man screamed, 'but you didn't bring my water!'

On 21 December I attended the Chamber Orchestra's winter concert in the State Theatre. There wasn't an empty seat in the house. The music was beautiful, and there were also performances by solo artists and the Sarajevo Philharmonic Orchestra. But the theatre was dark and cold as a tomb, and I sat through the entire concert with my teeth chattering. To make things worse, heavy shelling was rocking the city and the explosions echoed through the large theatre with its excellent acoustics. The Serbs clearly weren't taking time off for Christmas shopping.

Our festivities at Forward were met with real pleasure and enthusiasm. On Christmas Eve, Gertruda Munitić and the Chamber Orchestra performed at the Residency. Their programme was. perfect for the occasion: Albenoni's lovely, melancholy adagio, which became one of my favourites in Sarajevo, because it perfectly captured my emotions there most of the time; and some Grieg, Mozart and Bach. But the highlight of the evening was when Gertruda performed her solos. When she sang Hasse's 'Majka' ['Mother'] there were quite a few tears in the audience. But it was Gounod's 'Ave Maria' that brought about a distinct change in the atmosphere. She captured the ambience of sacredness and prayer, and brought home the realisation that it was Christmas and we were far from home and our families, not knowing for sure whether we'd see them again. The climax was Gertruda's version of 'Silent Night', sung in Serbo-Croatian. It was the most moving version of the age-old song I'd ever heard. We all joined in for probably the most unusual performance ever of 'Silent Night', sung simultaneously in Serbo-Croatian, Russian, Spanish, French, English, Dutch, Flemish and Afrikaans. This time everyone wiped away a tear or two.

The atmosphere on Christmas Day was still tinged with the nostalgia and emotion of the previous night. We were missing our families and friends at home. I'd spent many hours wrapping Christmas gifts for the Residency staff and my friends, and there were peals of joy when they opened their small parcels of food and sweets. Some of the local staff were ethnic Muslims who didn't celebrate Christmas and hadn't expected any gifts, but everyone received one. Us UNPROFOR lot also shared small gifts among ourselves. We all had breakfast and lunch together, and it was unusual to spend a whole day in each other's company, talking and having three leisurely meals. That alone was enough to make it a special day for us. We'd invited Kemal Monteno and his wife Branka for Christmas dinner, and after a delicious meal and a programme of his lovely songs, we sat around the tables, talking and singing until late.

Apart from Christmas Day on Saturday, we had no respite from our work, but the concerts and performances created an atmosphere of excited anticipation and gave us a little spring in our step.

On the Monday night everybody's favourite group, Sonidos Barbaros, came to entertain us. But there was a big disappointment. Dragana, the group's beauty with the lovely voice, was seriously ill in hospital and couldn't be there. Nevertheless, the group treated us to their repertoire of Bosnian and Spanish songs, and we had a lovely evening. For the majority of the soldiers, however, the Wednesday night's performance was undoubtedly the highlight of the week. The Elenes Dance Company, who were well known in Sarajevo and regularly appeared in the city's theatres, performed at Forward, and the attractive, scantily dressed girls were wildly popular. The applause and whistles just about brought down the roof.

With all the activity at Forward, time was flying, and before we knew it, it was New Year's Eve. The Serbs had agreed to a ceasefire to allow Sarajevo a few quiet days between Christmas and New Year. But as usual this was meaningless, and they continued their bombardment throughout the festive season. This made us even more determined to enjoy every minute of our leisure time, and to start the New Year on a happy, positive note. USL had been invited to provide the music at our New Year's celebration, and they had a surprise for me. Lejzi had just been released from hospital, and although he wasn't able to play, they brought him along. The shock of seeing him stopped me in my tracks, and it took all my self-control not to show how upset I was. I swallowed hard not to cry and gave him a careful hug, because his emaciated frame looked so fragile I was frightened I might hurt him. We put a chair for him next to the stage area, and launched ourselves into an evening of music, dancing and celebration.

Shortly before midnight, Sergio arrived with Barbara Hendricks, the American opera star. We hadn't known she'd be there and were delighted. Of course everyone wanted her to sing. It was an unreal experience: Barbara Hendricks, standing in the packed dining room of Forward Headquarters, singing 'Summertime'. In Sarajevo. In winter. The familiar music fluttered off the piano's keys, conjuring up a nostalgic blues mood. The expression on her face reflected an undefined longing, and the passion in her voice evoked a place far from the snow and ice and suffering of war and winter, where the night air was warm and a full moon shone on dark, glistening bodies moving slowly and voluptuously to the sensual rhythm.

The last note from her exquisite voice hovered in the crowded, smoky room, embraced by a comfortable silence. We clung to our brief escape from reality, an imagined journey to a place of warmth and life. The next moment a loud explosion shattered the dreamy atmosphere, and a wave of thunder flooded the room. A shell had landed right outside Forward, and for long moments we all stood absolutely quiet, the reflection of another, faraway world frozen on a hundred faces. Another shell exploded, and another. Still nobody moved, but the silence had become uneasy, heavy with underlying tension. Then Lejzi picked up a guitar and started strumming, and there was a happy buzz of approval. And we carried on as if nothing had happened.

We celebrated until well after midnight. When the festivities fizzled out at around one o' clock in the morning, Lejzi was clearly exhausted. As a rule the Egyptians provided transport for our entertainers in an APC. But because we knew the festivities would carry on for most of the night, and the Egyptians weren't participating, a Danish driver was designated to take the members of USL home – in an ordinary vehicle. As he was leaving, I asked whether he had a radio. He said no, and I insisted he take one. Almost everyone had gone to bed, and the few of us still in the dining room were reflecting on the evening when the French officer on duty stormed in and shouted, 'The vehicle with USL is under fire, they need help!' We all ran up to the operations room. There was chaos. Unbelievably, the Danish soldier didn't know – or in panic had forgotten – how to operate the radio. His finger was on the transmit button and he kept shouting 'Help, help, they are shooting at us!' They were pinned down and couldn't move. At least one tyre had been blown, and they were sitting ducks. My first thought was for Lejzi, wounded, looking like a ghost, and now in the first hours of the New Year in danger of being killed. Finally the terrified Danish soldier took his finger off the button and could be asked where they were. He didn't know. I asked the duty officer for his radio, told the Danish soldier to give the radio to one of the musicians, and asked him to explain where they were. I showed the officer on the map. Someone in the ops room fetched a Danish APC crew from their beds and sent them on a rescue mission. They were dispatched, but radioed after a while that they couldn't find the vehicle. These weren't the best circumstances for a rescue mission. A fairly large quantity of alcohol had been consumed in the course of the night, and I was one of the few sober people at Forward. None of the officers in the ops room could find the APC or the other vehicle on the map, and again I navigated for them. It helped that I'd been in the city for almost a year and criss-crossed it daily, whereas most of my military colleagues were confined to Forward. We pinpointed the APC and they, after some time, found the other vehicle. Everyone was transferred to the APC, and, because of the danger, the members of USL were brought back to the Residency. There was no choice but to wait until daybreak to take them home, and we made them as comfortable as possible in the entrance hall.

Whenever there were guests at the Residency, some of the kitchen staff had to stay to assist with serving meals and cleaning up. Gordana and Mr Manager also usually stayed to see that everything went smoothly, and were always the last to leave. They both lived beyond the suburb Bjelave, high in the hills and very far from the

Residency. Because they were local staff, they weren't entitled to transport home, and if nobody volunteered to take them, they had to walk. I simply couldn't bear to see them walking home, uphill and for miles in the dark and danger, and often ended up driving them, also on New Year's Eve. They were always touchingly grateful, but it was a hell of a trip for me because there were no street lights, I didn't know the area and Gordana lived very close to the confrontation line. After twisting and turning dozens of times, following their directions, I had no idea where I was, and on my way back didn't know whether I was stumbling towards the confrontation lines. Once an UNPROFOR soldier who accidentally drove across the confrontation lines in the dark was killed. Fortunately I had a good sense of direction, but I was always terrified until I could see the lights at Forward, which wasn't difficult since they were the only lights in the pitch-dark city. Once the lights were visible, it was fairly easy to wind my way towards them, but I was always a nervous wreck by the time I got back. The early hours of New Year 1994 were no different, and I was tremendously relieved to join USL in the foyer, waiting for first light.

It was a bedraggled and exhausted little group that welcomed the first day of 1994. We ruefully wished each other a happy year, then they went home and I prepared myself for the day's work.

CHAPTER 18

A MASSIVE HEADACHE

JANUARY 1994

THE NEW YEAR BROUGHT MANY CHANGES, both good and bad. After running UNPROFOR Radio on my own for a year, I was physically and mentally worn out, so I seized the opportunity for a transfer to Civil Affairs when Viktor announced that he needed a personal assistant. It would bring a welcome change to the frustrations of running the radio programme, and I'd have some support in carrying out my duties. But until there was a replacement for me at UNPROFOR Radio, I also had to keep the programme going.

General Briquemont suddenly announced that he was leaving the mission. In a strongly worded statement, he accused the UN of tying his hands behind his back. He said he couldn't in good conscience stay in Bosnia, since he was unable to do his job to the best of his ability, and felt that what was happening was immoral. He found the constraints of the international community's modus operandi as frustrating as General Morillon had. This was a disaster. For Sarajevo, for Bosnia – and for me. I was terribly dejected. I'd worked effortlessly and happily with him and his team, and everybody at Forward was content, as much as that was possible in Sarajevo: the Residency staff, the interpreters, the military. After the extreme difficulties of the past months I felt I didn't have the resources to adjust to the impending change. I was somewhat consoled by the fact that the new general, Sir Michael Rose, was British. I'd always liked the British, and had often worked with them. Also, coming from a former British colony, there was comfort in the familiarity of their culture that was part of my heritage, and I was looking forward to the tea, peanut butter and Worcester sauce they were bound to bring along.

On 11 January we celebrated the broadcast of 200 UNPROFOR Radio programmes. For a number of reasons, though, I couldn't keep my promise to outdo the 100 celebration. A few of my military colleagues and I clubbed together, and Jamila and Armin joined us for drinks and a modest meal.

Amid the dozens of setbacks, disappointments and failures, the joy of success, when it did happen, was almost overwhelming. But it never came without a battle. One morning the guard called from the gate and said someone wanted to see me urgently. It was Srdjan. Lejzi was back in hospital, and doctors said if he didn't receive immediate specialist attention he would lose his eye – 'immediate' meaning within days. I said I'd try my best, my standard reply. I called Erna Ribar, who worked with medical evacuations at UNHCR, explained the situation, and asked if they could organise an urgent evacuation. She said they'd try to fit Lejzi in – in two weeks' time. I put on an air of authority beyond that which I possessed, and said, 'No, I think you didn't understand me; he needs urgent medical treatment and must be out of here not in two weeks, but in two days.' I'd never been involved in anything to do with medical evacuations and had no idea whether what I was asking was at all possible. All I knew was that it was a complex procedure because a hospital had to be found in another country, willing to take the patient, before the evacuation could be carried out.

Furthermore, I had no right to be making the request, and was trading on the fact that many people didn't know exactly how the UNPROFOR chains of command worked. Medevac requests had to go through numerous convoluted channels, and I was simply taking a chance with little hope of success. Erna said she'd get back to me, and I thought: That's it, the usual cul-de-sac. To my surprise she called back almost immediately, and said they could indeed get Lejzi onto an aeroplane in two days' time. An opening had been found for him in Denmark. It was quite unbelievable and I was ecstatic, while hoping it wasn't some kind of mistake. But I called Boris, gave him a message for Srdjan, and two days later Lejzi was on his way to Denmark. Or so we thought. Poor Lejzi had not yet endured his last ordeal of the war. The paperwork got mixed up, and the minute the aircraft touched down in Italy, he was marched to a refugee camp with the other Bosnians. He protested and tried to explain his situation, but the officials simply ignored him. It was a few days before he was fortunate enough to attract the attention of Mike Aitchison, to whom he showed his documentation. He was immediately put on the next flight to Denmark. Lejzi's eye was saved, and the other members of USL kept me up to date on his recovery and life in Denmark.

I will always remember what he told me of the day he was wounded. When the shrapnel hit him, he was flung against a building and sat there with blood pouring over his face from the head wound. A woman kneeled next to him and asked whether he could hear her. He replied that he could hear but couldn't see a thing, had a blinding headache, and asked if she'd fetch him some aspirin.

———————

There weren't enough hours in the day, what with my two full-time jobs and 'extra-curricular' activities, and one day flowed into the next. Often I didn't know which day of the week it was, but since we worked all seven it didn't really matter. I was still struggling to organise the travel arrangements for the 'Witnesses' exhibition to New York. Since aircraft involved in the UNHCR airlift to Sarajevo were under the direct command of their respective countries, I approached the French. General André Soubirou, the French commander of Sector Sarajevo, was a refined man with an appreciation of the arts, and a good person through and through. He immediately agreed to support the mission. Armed with this invaluable weapon, we could go ahead with the planning. Having Sergio de Mello around made a lot of things easier as well, since he was also in favour of supporting the city's artists. Sergio's name and title on a letter smoothed the way tremendously. He signed formal letters of request, and Lieutenant Colonel Guy de Battista, a French officer who'd been in Sarajevo and was now based in Zagreb, endeavoured to obtain the necessary permission from the French government. The arrangements to get 'Witnesses' out of Sarajevo began to resemble the strategic planning for a major battle. A score of people in New York, Italy, Zagreb and Sarajevo were enlisted, each with a specific focus area. It took several weeks of hard work and constant communication with Miro, Sergio, General Soubirou, Guy de Battista and New York, but one by one we overcame the many obstacles. The exhibition had to leave Sarajevo in early February to arrive in New York on time for the opening on 24 February. All we still needed was a final date for the shipment. Lieutenant Colonel Joncheray, the officer charged with the 'Witnesses' operation at Sector Sarajevo, confirmed that it would be in early February, and it was all systems go.

My job as Viktor's PA required accompanying him virtually everywhere for meetings and negotiations, and standing in for him at Forward when he wasn't there. It also meant spending more time than I cared to face to face with the Serb leadership, but I decided to give it time and see how it went. It didn't go well. I gritted my teeth and tried to maintain a professional distance from the acute loathing I felt for them, but it became increasingly difficult. In mid-January we went to Pale for negotiations with Karadžić and other Serb leaders. When we paused for lunch, they invited us to join them. Dr Radovan Karadžić, President of Republika Srbska, sat diagonally opposite me on the other side of the long lunch table in the Panorama Hotel. He was flanked by his deputies: Nikola Koljević, Momčilo Krajišnik, Jovan Zametica (their Bosnian spokesman) and other senior Serbs. Karadžić was laughing at one of Koljević's anecdotes, with his famous trademark mop of tousled hair spilling over his forehead. It was a nostalgic account of their student days, their daring youthful involvement in politics, the risks they'd taken, the lifelong friendship they shared. It was surreal. These were educated, sophisticated men: a flamboyant, charismatic psychiatrist and poet, and a soft-spoken Shakespearean scholar. Watching them talk, laugh and sip their wine, it was hard to believe that they were engineering the demise of Bosnia, the systematic murder, rape, torture and expulsion of people with whom they'd shared the same youthful dreams about which they were reminiscing. From their behaviour it might have been an everyday business lunch at the country club. In Pale, high in the mountains above Sarajevo, the skies were clear and the air smelt of pine. There were no exploding shells, no echoes of gunfire, no choking odour of burning garbage, no wine-coloured stains where blood had dried on the roads and pavements. The white-jacketed waiters served a fruity white wine from Dalmatia, a starter of smoked meat, white cheese and fresh, wholesome bread, followed by steaming lamb, roast potatoes and vegetables. It was a sumptuous meal, but the food felt like cement in my mouth and stuck in my throat. I was thinking about the children in Sarajevo begging for food. And of the aching misery in Anja's young eyes when she said, 'I'm always hungry.'

On the morning of 27 January, I took a few quiet moments to think about my sister Erna on her birthday, and spent the day working through the multitude of tasks that demanded attention, including UNPROFOR Radio. Dusk crept over the city as I drove Jamila home. We were chatting about the day's broadcast, family, friends and colleagues. As we approached the yellow frame of the Energo Invest building where ICRC now had their offices, I slowed down to turn right out of Snipers' Alley. Suddenly the car jerked sideways with such force, I thought for a moment that we'd been hit by another vehicle. Had a tyre blown? No, the vehicle was steering perfectly well. Then I realised: we'd been hit by a sniper's bullet. But with such force? I remembered the fear and panic in the Danish driver's voice when their vehicle was hit as he was driving USL back at New Year. 'Are you okay?' I asked Jamila. She was fine. Was I? With the rush of adrenaline, I almost couldn't be sure. It was not a pleasant feeling. We were driving down a wide, open road with the sniper somewhere behind us. Would he shoot again? I'd had the vague feeling of being watched since I'd given a lift to a man with one leg a few days earlier. He lived right on the confrontation line – directly behind us, and from where the bullet had come. Had the sniper had me in his sights since then, or was my imagination playing games with me? It was strictly against UN regulations – not to mention Serb sentiment – to transport the local population, but I didn't care. I simply could not drive past someone struggling to get home on one leg, or an exhausted woman with heavy water canisters in one hand and a baby, blue with cold, on the other arm.

It took only moments to reach the turnoff to the road where Jamila's aunt lived, but it felt as though time was standing still. I swerved right at hair-raising speed, out of the sniper's sight behind the high-rise buildings of Čengić Vila. Overwhelming relief flooded my body. I got out to look for a bullet hole, tried to reconstruct the moment of impact, and deduced the car must have been hit on the driver's side, towards the back. The sniper had either been aiming at me, and was slightly slow to find the mark, or at the tyre. It was common sniper procedure to shoot the tyres; then, with the vehicle immobilised, to continue shooting, forcing the passengers to abandon the safety of the vehicle. Once out in the open, they were easy targets. That was exactly the modus operandi with USL at New Year, and the same had recently happened to a foreign journalist. The sniper hit a tyre, he was forced to stop, and he crawled out of his vehicle into a ditch at the side of the road, hoping and praying it wasn't mined. It wasn't, but the sniper could still see him, and shot him in the leg. He had to stay there, in the direct line of fire, until he was rescued much later. I was at the Holiday Inn with Bill Aikman, Canadian military spokesman for UNPROFOR, and a group of journalists when someone rushed in with the news. We were all horrified at the thought, because we knew how easily each of us could be the one lying helplessly in a ditch in Sarajevo with a shattered leg.

Jamila and I looked the car over, but we couldn't see anything. There was no bullet hole, not even a scratch. Well, we definitely hadn't imagined it; not both of us. Perhaps the bullet was in the tyre after all. Usually Jamila was calm and unruffled, but she fretted about my going back, and wanted me to wait. But wait for what? Snipers had shot at me early in the morning, at midday, late at night. The threat was ever present, and there was no escaping it. I promised to call her when I got back to Forward, and to return via the back road. But I had no intention of doing that. A cold fury was rising in my body, slowly from the bottom up, like liquid filling an empty bottle. Seething, I headed back to the main road even though I knew the thug might be waiting for me. It was irrational, reckless and dumb, but I was livid and beyond caring. At the junction to the main road I stopped, staring ahead at the spot where I imagined him to be. I lifted my head, signalled with my hands and said, in a shaky voice, 'Come on, shoot! But shoot me while looking me straight in the eye, you cowardly bastard.' Hysteria was threatening to choke me. It felt as though I was watching myself from a high place, and part of me was feeling slightly embarrassed at my melodramatic performance. But the other half was overcome by a frozen fury.

Then, as suddenly as it had struck, the fury and bravado vanished. Icy fear clutched at my heart, and I remembered Bill, sobbing, when he'd returned after going to the rescue of a man who'd been shot in the head by a sniper. I slowly turned left, and waited with resignation for the bullet to smash through the window. Nothing. I made it back to the Residency safely, but shaken. Not for the first time, I understood the urge to kill. I was ready to go and find that sniper and deal with him in a way he'd understand. If I'd had a weapon, I would have blasted him from the face of the earth. They were the lowest form of life, killing indiscriminately: women, children, the elderly. And not by some form of remote control like the gunners who fired shells at the city, but while they could see the colour of their victim's eyes.

That particular bullet, as the saying goes, didn't have my name on it. Thankfully, the deadly metal had lodged in the car's body and seat upholstery. Captain Richard Macrae, the Canadian Operations officer, found the bullet and reckoned the sniper had been aiming at the right rear tyre and had shot slightly high. While I watched him extract the jagged pieces of metal I shuddered, and thanked my lucky stars they didn't need to be dug from my body. I wished I could go home, have coffee with Mima and pour my heart out to her about the day's trauma, but as always there was urgent work to be done. And on my desk was a cable with terribly sad news.

In 1993 I'd met a humanitarian worker, Paul Goodall, who was working for ODA, the British government's Overseas Development Administration. We had a brief talk and, always on the lookout for radio material, I suggested perhaps doing an interview with him. He said he'd call me. The cable on my desk reported that he had been killed in the town of Zenica. He and two of his colleagues were forced from their vehicle at gunpoint by foreign Muslims and told they were being taken hostage in exchange for prisoners. However, their captors took them out of town, made them kneel at the edge of the Bosna River, and shot Paul twice in the back of the head. The other two men leapt into the dark, freezing river while the gunmen shot at them. One was hit in the arm and leg, the other shot in the chest. They were lucky to survive.

I was expecting that the next time I heard from Paul it would be about interviewing him on the delivery of humanitarian aid. Now I had to process the fact that he'd been murdered. As a young girl in Sarajevo had said to me, if you arrange to meet someone for coffee and they don't come, there's at least a fifty percent chance they are no longer alive.

The incident shocked us all to the core. We knew there was risk involved in our work, even recognised that the risk was increasing – but Paul had been executed; there was no other way of looking at it. Humanitarian agencies instructed workers not to travel alone or venture out at night. UNHCR considered pulling out of Bosnia, but were assured by the authorities that the 'terrorists' would be dealt with. Zenica, an important Bosnian stronghold, harboured a guilty secret. Bosnia, hardly in a position to reject any offer of assistance, had allowed volunteer fighters from Muslim countries and mujahidin from Afghanistan to rush to its aid, and given them a base in Zenica. The fanatical foreign Muslims, a few hundred in total, had bred fear into the lives of Bosnians in Zenica, smashing restaurants that served alcohol and insisting women should observe Islamic dress customs. I'd received a number of complaints from Bosnians in Zenica about the situation, but there was nothing UNPROFOR could do about it. The Bosnian army wanted to get rid of them, not least because they were a law unto themselves and refused to integrate into the Bosnian chain of command. But the Bosnian government was afraid this would jeopardise the assistance they were receiving from Turkey and countries in the Middle East. The Serbs exploited the situation as 'evidence' that Bosnia was 'collaborating' with Muslim countries. This misinformation was used to convince ordinary Serbs that the war was unavoidable, since President Izetbegović was planning to convert Bosnia into a Muslim state. The fact that the Bosnians feared and detested the foreign Muslims was never mentioned, not by the Bosnian government, and definitely not by the Serbs. Two days after Paul Goodall was murdered, three men were arrested near Zenica. One of them, a Saudi citizen, Abdul Hadi al Gahtani, was identified by the two survivors of the attack. Two days later, three Arabs and an Iranian, who were driving the stolen ODA Land Rover, were shot dead by Bosnian forces near Sarajevo. Al Gahtani mysteriously vanished when the police transferred him from Zenica to Sarajevo. It was rumoured that the government, afraid that a trial would damage relations with Saudi Arabia and other Muslim states, had had a hand in his disappearance.

This was not the first disturbing incident involving foreign nationals in apparent terrorist activities. In July 1993, Civpol at Sarajevo airport intercepted two Turkish 'journalists' whose passports had expired. On closer investigation, their baggage was found to contain documents with detailed instructions on the use of explosives, and maps marking areas around Kiseljak. When questioned, their answers were contradictory. UNPROFOR didn't have jurisdiction to take any action, and the Bosnian government had more serious problems on their hands, and thus the two were eventually allowed to leave.

There were a number of farewell functions for General Briquemont in the weeks before he left, the most memorable being a dinner at a restaurant near the Residency, where we were the guests of Kemal Monteno; and General Soubirou's formal military farewell dinner at the PTT Building, which might have been at an elegant Paris restaurant. The table was set with silver on a blindingly white starched tablecloth. I was the only woman in the company of a dozen senior officers, all in dress uniform. French soldiers served dinner. The food and wine were excellent, the atmosphere relaxed but refined. All the guests received two pins that had been specially made for French soldiers in Bosnia: one for the Fourth Infantry Battalion and a very attractive one for those who'd served under General Soubirou's command at Sector Sarajevo.

I also arranged a farewell function for General Briquemont at the Residency, and invited Sonidos Barbaros to perform. The general, like everybody else, loved Dragana Ilić's beautiful voice, and had been very disappointed when she wasn't at the concert in December. Dragana was still in hospital. Selen Balić, her partner and leader of the group, said she urgently needed Vitamin C. I smuggled a box of lemons from the storeroom and gave it to him, hoping this would help to get Dragana well in time for the concert. The day before the function Selen called and said Dragana had been discharged, and the full complement of Sonidos Barbaros gave General Briquemont a rousing send-off.

The last few weeks before General Briquemont's departure at the end of January were sad and difficult, and the day of his departure was simply awful. The bitter circumstances in Sarajevo forged close relationships, and saying goodbye to the general and his contingent was like bidding farewell to close friends. His parting words to me were, 'We will never forget you.' I would never forget them either: we'd been through too much together.

CHAPTER 19

WITNESSES OF EXISTENCE

FEBRUARY–MARCH 1994

IN EARLY FEBRUARY we received the good news that the 'Witnesses' exhibition would leave Sarajevo on a French aeroplane on Wednesday 9 February. A truck, courtesy of the French military, would pick up the cargo at Obala Gallery and take it to the airport. Miro had obtained all the necessary documentation from the government, duly signed and rubber-stamped. To ensure that no valuable art or contraband was being smuggled out, it would be inspected by Civpol. The precious cargo would then go to Ancona, and from there representatives of the Kunsthalle had organised transport to Rome, and then New York. We were all very happy and excited and counting the days.

On Friday 4 February, a function took place at the Residency. I spoke a few words to Prime Minister Haris Silajdžić, who thought, as always when I met him, that I was a Sarajevan. A former Yugoslav ambassador to somewhere in Africa had enthusiastically sampled the available whisky and French wine, and was telling his small bemused audience that he'd had no real interest in Yugoslavia's foreign policy, but had loved the hunting. Sarajevo's

Mayor, Hamdija Kreševljaković, elicited peals of laughter with his explanation of why he was still in the city after having been appointed Bosnian consul to Italy: because the government had forgotten to appoint an ambassador. According to protocol he couldn't arrive before the ambassador, and was waiting for that formality to be taken care of. The pleasant function belonged to another life. At times, for a short while, submerged in the tranquillity of art, music, poetry and togetherness, one could almost forget about the slaughter in Bosnia.

On 5 February, Kamerni Teatr 55 gave its 100th concert of the war in the Svečana Hall of the Presidency. The occasion was the unveiling of a portrait of Sarajevo's first victim of the war, Suada Dilberović, the student from Dubrovnik shot during the protest march in March 1992. It was cold, the razor-edged cold that cuts mercilessly through flesh and bone, and I dressed in thermal underwear and several layers of other warm clothing. The concert was in the afternoon, and I spent the morning at the office. Because the Presidency was only five minutes from Forward, I decided to walk, but the Egyptian guards refused to let me out on foot. Non-stop sniper fire had been concentrated around Forward and along the route to the Presidency all morning, and they insisted I use my car. As though to prove the point, the snipers fired a few rounds in our direction, and the few civilians on the pavement dashed for cover in the guards' hut. I went back and fetched the car. Gertruda and I had agreed to meet at the side entrance, and while I was parking the car, sniper bullets crashed into the walls of the Presidency. People cowering in the entrance shouted at me: *'Pazi, snijper!'* ['Careful, sniper!']. It was a somewhat superfluous warning, but characteristic of the way in which Sarajevans looked out for each other. Every few seconds a bullet whizzed across the small park overlooking the entrance, and I walked very fast from the car to the safety of the lobby, which was secured by rows of sandbags on all sides.

Everyone in the small audience was swathed in coats, hats and gloves. Even in the Presidency, official seat of the Bosnian government, there was no escape from the bitter cold. The elegant, imposing building that housed Bosnia's besieged rulers, like all Sarajevo's homes, was without heating. Attempts to warm up the room for the occasion offered little comfort. The atmosphere was sombre. Suada's eyes seemed to be smiling sadly from the canvas at the select company of the country's leadership, dignitaries, famous and well-known Sarajevans – and a solitary UN representative. There were the inevitable speeches. The string quartet played Mozart, Grieg and Schubert, and Gertruda sang one of my favourites – Hasse's poignant 'Majka'. Her voice flowed through the room and lingered, drifting on the cold air. In his beautifully trained actor's voice, Dragan Jovićić recited words chosen with great care for the occasion, Abdulah Sidran's intense poetry, 'Planet Sarajevo'. I didn't understand all the words, but I'd come to understand the music of the Bosnian language and the tone of Sarajevo's voices: sad, beseeching, angry, frustrated and, above all, uncomprehending.

The violence of the massive explosion ripped through the room, its thunder invading the hushed serenity. It was very close. The Presidency was a favourite target of the Serbs, and many of the solid walls and majestic rooms carried the scars of heavy artillery, missiles and bullets, and the attacks had claimed numerous casualties. Earlier I'd counted sixteen holes on the wall in front of me, pockmarked by the shrapnel of shells that had blasted out windows, now covered with plastic sheeting supplied by UNHCR.

A heavy silence descended on Sarajevo in anticipation of the next explosion. But the silence dragged on uninterrupted. A single mortar explosion: that rarely happened. An immediate, tangible tension had filled the room. My Motorola suddenly crackled, loud in the silence. Embarrassed, I struggled to muffle it with my gloved hands, but heard enough to know the message wasn't for me.

Then ambulance sirens wailed past the Presidency. Just moments earlier we'd been lost in music and poetry, but the enormous explosion had jolted everyone back into the present, into the stark reality of Sarajevo. People were used to the shelling and generally simply carried on with their activities, hardly noticing the explosions. Oddly, this time a single explosion brought everything to a standstill. It was as though we all instinctively knew there was something different, something sinister, about that explosion. When Prime Minister Silajdžić walked to the front of the room nobody moved, nobody breathed. In a grave voice he announced the terrible tragedy that would shake the world. He had just received word of an attack on the central marketplace, 200 metres from the Presidency. First reports indicated that as many as fifty people might have died in the single blast. Everyone was stunned. Tears silently crept down some faces. In Sarajevo death was ever present, as one's own shadow. People died in the city every day. But fifty people in a single gigantic explosion shocked even the toughest Sarajevans. As always, life and death, agony and ecstasy were separated by a hair's breadth. While we were listening to Grieg, people lay dying in agony in the debris of a cheerful Saturday afternoon.

As soon as the programme ended, everyone quietly filed out of the room. In the corridor Gertruda and I wordlessly hugged each other. What was there to say? She asked if we could go to her office, as she was concerned about her co-workers. On our way out, we bumped into Armin. He was clearly shaken. He'd been assisting with a live broadcast of the event and had slipped out to deliver a parcel to his aunt's home. He had just passed the market on his way back when the shell exploded. Knowing there was a strong possibility that some of my friends might have been at the market, I was tremendously relieved to see him.

The silence of death hung over Sarajevo. The streets and pavements were deserted; it was a ghost city. At Gertruda's office, everyone was weeping. One of the young women was hysterical. She'd walked past the market on the opposite side of the street when the shell exploded, and seen bodies flung through the air; mangled bodies in pools of blood; heard the screams of the wounded and dying. I started shaking and my teeth were chattering, and I knew it wasn't from the cold. We had coffee and Gertruda bustled around, comforting, organising and asking staff members to check on other colleagues and friends. When she was ready I took her home and returned to Forward. The atmosphere was one of acute crisis. Our interpreters and the other local staff were beside themselves with shock and worry, and were frantically calling family and friends who had phones to check whether they were alive. Whenever there was heavy bombardment, people did the terrible 'body count'.

All the local staff at Forward were weeping. The death toll was steadily rising: from the initial fifty to sixty. One hundred and fifty wounded. By Saturday evening it was announced: sixty-eight dead, almost 200 wounded.

For once, it seemed as though the effects of their actions had shocked even the Serbs. After the single explosion in the marketplace there was no further shelling or fighting. Not one single shot was fired. An eerie, breathless silence hung over the city. Radio stations played melancholy music, interspersed with appeals for blood donors. Some of our interpreters went to donate blood, and reported that hundreds had responded to the call. The government was bringing soldiers from the front lines to donate blood. Sarajevo's people might have been freezing and starving, but they still had blood to give. I made a list of my friends in the city, terrified of what I might find if I lifted the receiver and called those who could be reached. Initially I didn't call anyone, in order to give people the opportunity to call relatives and friends closer to them than I was. Late in the afternoon I gathered all my courage and started calling: Jamila and her family were safe. Then the musicians, artists, dancers, radio personnel and other people in the city who had become my friends. Selen, Dragana and everyone else from Sonidos Barbaros were safe. Selen said they'd seen me on the TV broadcast of the concert. A few days later it was also noted, rather ominously, by a Serb official in Lukavica, that I'd been seen at 'the Bosnian government's concert'. Lejla, who was my contact with Boris and the other members of United States of Love, was safe. So were the others. Miro had checked with a large number of artists and they were all safe. The Residency staff and my radio colleagues were all safe. I couldn't call Mima, Seo and Anja, because they didn't have a telephone, so I drove to their house with my heart in my throat. They were safe, as were my neighbours. It was a miracle. Not a single person I knew had lost a family member or loved one in the terrible tragedy. But they all knew people who had. In a moment, 400 000 people had been plunged into the deepest despair.

On the Sunday, Sarajevo awoke soundlessly, as though even the birds were silent out of respect for the city's loss. The government had declared a day of mourning. Heavy sadness lay draped over the city like a dark veil. Some of the local staff came to work, but they moved around slowly, as though in a thick fog, their speech muted. Even though none of them had lost family or close friends, they had known some of those killed, knew some of the wounded and all knew someone who'd lost a loved one. A friend of Jasna's had been wounded and there was little hope he might survive. Shrapnel had torn open his abdomen and chest. Both he and his wife were doctors and they knew, given the inadequate medical facilities, that his chances were slim.

Despair had set in. If almost 300 people could be maimed and killed in a single explosion, the city could be wiped out in a matter of weeks. The market bomb casualties were so high because of the concentration of people, but everyone in Sarajevo was vulnerable.

Most people lived in high-rise buildings in densely populated suburbs. They queued for food and water with hundreds of others. Almost everywhere were concentrations of people. Sarajevans were saying they'd survived two years of hell for nothing, that the Serbs would slaughter every one of them. Knowing of the international community's shameful indifference and appeasement of the Serbs, I couldn't even try to convince them otherwise.

Urgent arrangements were made to evacuate the wounded. The Serbs offered no resistance. I couldn't help thinking, bitterly, about the little girl for whom they'd refused to allow an evacuation. Ironically, people seriously wounded in the market explosion were more fortunate than the thousands of others wounded in Sarajevo and elsewhere in Bosnia. For them, there'd been no frantic arrangements for evacuations to decent hospitals or the MASH in Zagreb, simply because they hadn't been part of such a noteworthy slaughter. Their tragedies, as individuals or small groups, didn't make big enough headlines to warrant intervention. Like the little girl who haunted me, many of them died of their wounds while endless negotiations and bartering about their fate went on between the UN and the Serbs.

The Serbs made a feeble attempt to blame the Bosnians for the explosion, but it was justifiably ignored. The Bosnian government demanded air strikes against the Serbs. This had been threatened often enough, and it finally seemed as though the writing might be on the wall. UNPROFOR's military commander, General Jean Cot, and Civilian chief Yasushi Akashi flew in from Zagreb, visited the marketplace and then tried to arrange a ceasefire – but failed. The international community, however, knew that some action had to be taken, and diplomats converged on Belgrade and Brussels to discuss their options and decide on a plan of action.

Gospodin Sakib Bezić !

Otac Omara i Jasmina Penjavaca, gospodin
Fuad Penjavac, zamolio je mene Anne Marie
Dupreez, da dovedem djecu iz Bilalovca u
Kiseljak.

Naime, gospodin Fuad vam je izuzetno
zahvalan za ovu preuzetu brigu dva djece, ali
smatra da je za njih trenutno mnogo
bezbjednije u Kiseljaku.

The note from Fuad to his uncle Sakib in Bilalovac,
authorising me to take Omar and Jasmin to Kiseljak

With Annéne and John the week before
leaving for Bosnia

A mournful birthday celebration – after Bilalovac

A photo taken through the windscreen while I was driving, of the no-man's-land between Sarajevo airport
and the city, destroyed tanks lining the road

My own Sarajevo rose, on the bridge in Ciglane

Playing the piano for an evening of song at Forward

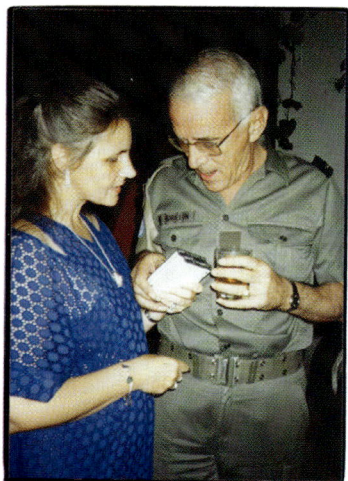

For General Morillon: a gift of UNPROFOR
Radio programmes about him at his farewell

Cover of *Vrye Weekblad* with a story
I wrote about the war in Bosnia

One of the sketches by the children
to thank me for the fruit

In the studio at Radio BH with Jamila and Armin

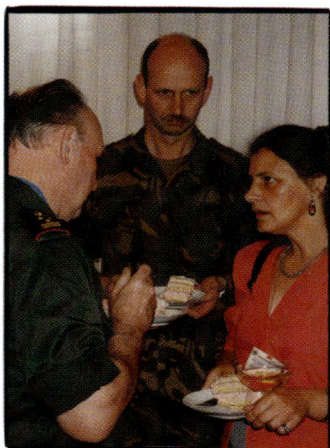

Discussing work at General Briquemont's birthday party, Luuk Niessen looking on

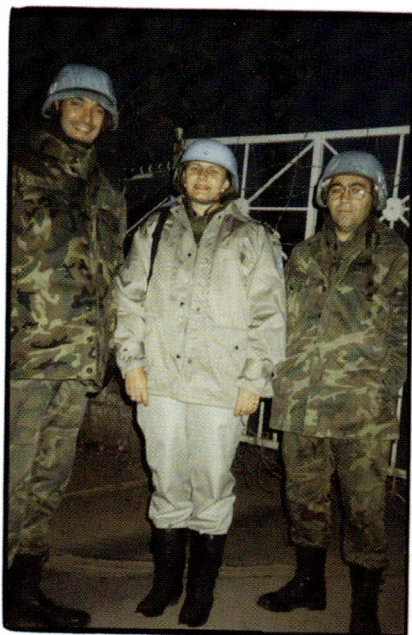

In front of BH Forward with my Spanish Public Information colleagues Luis (left) and Manolo

In my UNPROFOR uniform

Invitation to the 100th concert of the Chamber Orchestra at the Presidency on 5 February 1994 – the fateful day of the market bomb

Gertruda and the Chamber Orchestra at the Residency

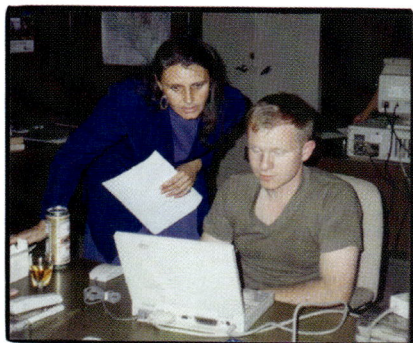

At work in the Public Information office with Major Brad Smith

Singing Kemal's famous song 'Sarajevo Ljubavi Moja' with him and Branka (right)

ai gospodine

Marie

štovanjem
am
al n o s
ste n
ciji
oncert
prinije.

55

United States of Love. Lejzi seated, Srdjan in black behind him, Sergio de Mello on the right

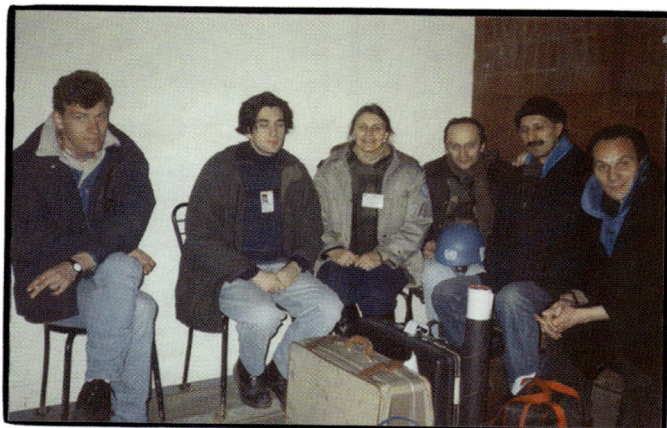
With Miro (helmet on lap) and the artists at Sarajevo airport on their way to New York

Invitation for the 'Witnesses' exhibition
at the Kunsthalle in New York

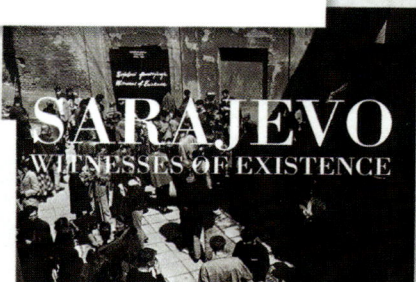
SARAJEVO
WITNESSES OF EXISTENCE

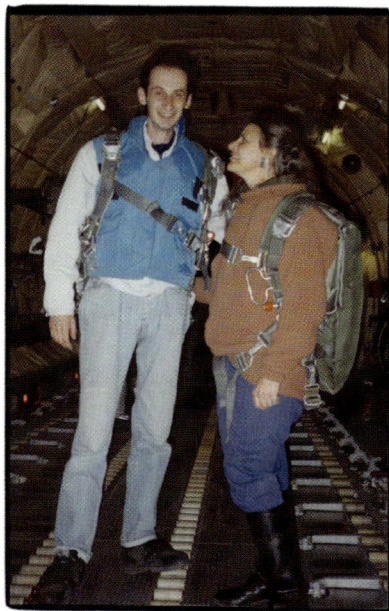
Armin and I en route to Italy, dressed in
bullet-proof jackets and parachutes

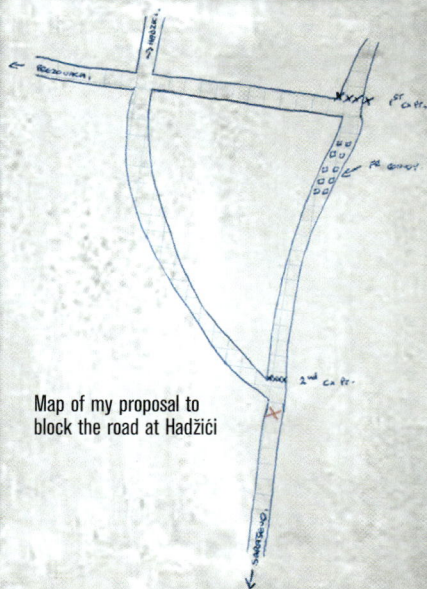
Map of my proposal to
block the road at Hadžići

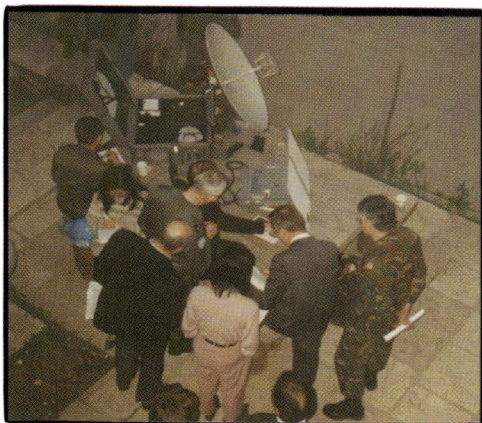

Hastily erected 'communications centre' in the garden at BH Forward, for negotiations with the Serbs during the Goražde crisis

Letter from Prof Dr Nikola Koljević guaranteeing safe passage for Sarajevo children who were offered a holiday in Croatia

MONDAY WAS JUST ANOTHER DAY!

A sigh of relief, signed by Viktor (left) and General Rose on the Monday after the Goražde crisis

Ines (left) and Jamila at Kiseljak HQ

Card signed signed by the members of the
Sarajevo Philharmonic Orchestra, December 1994

Mima at the little round table where we spent
hours together

Meeting in Kiseljak with my Civil Affairs colleagues from all over Bosnia, clockwise
from bottom left: Viktor, Ed, my friend Christine, John, David, me, Carlos, Andrea,
Jay, Luuk, Paavo, Ken (back to camera)

In Zagreb, having a brief peaceful respite,
December 1994

In the black days after the market bomb, the promise that the exhibition would be seen by the outside world was like a thin ray of sunshine. Everyone involved had arranged to meet at Obala at seven on the Wednesday morning. But as I was about to leave the office, Miro called. I could hear from his tone of voice that something was seriously wrong. He said that a French officer, Captain Brucker, had just been to Obala to say that 'Witnesses' wouldn't be leaving after all, because all non-essential missions in the city had been cancelled. I made a frantic call to Brucker, and was told that all available UNPROFOR personnel, transport and logistical back-up were needed for monitoring artillery positions and to support the high-level meeting at the airport scheduled for later that morning. There was nothing we could do, and I called Miro to tell him not to worry – we'd reschedule. I tried to sound positive, but it was a serious blow and I knew rescheduling wouldn't be easy – if we managed at all. I was disappointed beyond words, and wanted to hide somewhere and weep. Months of back-breaking work, and opportunities that might not arise again – especially since I'd been told that Akashi wanted trips out of Sarajevo by Bosnians stopped because both the government and the Serbs were complaining about it. I dragged myself to the dining room for a coffee. One of the British officers had his Motorola on, and we all listened to a conversation between General Rose and Nicholas, his interpreter. Rose had taken over command of UNPROFOR Forces in Bosnia two weeks earlier.

As soon as General Sir Michael Rose had arrived it was clear that life at BH Forward would change – and not for the better. Rose was nothing like his two predecessors; in my opinion he was undiplomatic, high-handed and lacked the essential qualities needed to run such an operation. In a very short time the atmosphere of quiet, contented efficiency at BH Forward became one of disharmony and discontent.

After his appointment, Andrew Hogg of the *Sunday Times* wrote that Rose wasn't a man who accepted defeat gracefully, and his military career had shown a ferocious will to succeed. Also, that Rose stood out as one of the 'few remaining warriors, a man who enjoys the challenge of war'. On the Tuesday after the market bomb he seized the moment and forced the Bosnian government and Serb leadership into agreeing to a ceasefire.

When Rose arrived at the airport for the meeting, General Divjak, deputy commander of the Bosnian army, wasn't there. Rose sent Nicholas to fetch him. Nicholas reported that Divjak refused to attend the meeting because he hadn't received written notice. What had in fact happened was that President Izetbegović had ordered him not to attend. The next moment, Rose's voice barked over the Motorola, telling Nick to wait there, he was on his way. Reportedly, Rose sped to Divjak's HQ and ordered him to get into the car. Divjak protested, but Rose insisted and then went straight to the Presidency to see President Izetbegović, who was giving an interview to CNN. When Rose was told he couldn't see the president, he delivered an ultimatum. If President Izetbegović didn't agree that Divjak could attend the meeting at the airport, he, Rose would tell the world via the available CNN crew that the Bosnian government refused to negotiate and would be responsible if the conflict continued. Izetbegović relented, and Divjak meekly attended the meeting. The two sides agreed to a ceasefire, and Rose emerged as the man of the moment. But it was a hollow victory, one that plunged Bosnia deeper into war, resulted in another two years of misery, and cost the lives of tens of thousands of Bosnians.

The international community's response to the gruesome catastrophe of the market bomb was to threaten the Serbs with NATO air strikes if they didn't move their heavy weapons beyond a stipulated twenty-kilometre zone around Sarajevo, or hand them over to UNPROFOR forces. The ultimatum was extended to the Bosnian government. In their case, since they were besieged by the Serbs and couldn't move anything out of Sarajevo, weapons would have to be handed over to UNPROFOR. The Bosnians protested, but the reasoning was that the ultimatum wouldn't work if it was directed at the Serbs only. Addressing it to both sides was meant to illustrate the international community's resolve.

The aftermath of the market bombing was the closest Bosnia had come to international intervention by force, but the British were opposed to NATO involvement. One of the flaws of a UN operation involving military from a number of countries was that commanders, such as General Rose, followed orders from their governments that were often in conflict with the wider interest. There were many political and military views on the reasons for, and implications of, intervention or non-intervention. Both the USA and France were in favour of NATO intervention, but Rose was under pressure from his government to prove that the mere threat of NATO air strikes was enough to produce a ceasefire. It was understandable that President Izetbegović didn't want a ceasefire – he knew Bosnia's only chance of survival was by winning the war. And if timely and sizeable air strikes had been carried out against the Serbs, Bosnia could have been spared two more years of war.

As I was leaving the Residency after my coffee, I ran into General Soubirou. As UNPROFOR commander for Sarajevo, he was in charge of the practical implementation of the urgent operation to immobilise the Serbs, and even though there wasn't yet a formal agreement, planning went ahead as though there would be. He was clearly preoccupied and in a hurry, but ever courteous and attentive, he stopped and asked how the moving of 'Witnesses' was going. I told him it had been cancelled, along with other 'non-essential' missions. 'No,' he said sternly and emphatically, 'not that mission. That mission must go ahead.' He told me not to worry, at once turned to his chief of staff and told him to relay his personal order that the 'Witnesses' mission was to be carried out as planned. Immediately. It was nothing if not divine intervention. And not a moment too soon. We were home, but not dry. Too much time had been lost, and we might not get our precious cargo to the airport on time. Because of all the politics involved in the mission, it had to be a French flight, so we couldn't just put the cargo on the next flight to Ancona. And it had to arrive on time to connect with the other intricate transport arrangements from Italy to the US. If we missed that flight, everything would still have to be reorganised from scratch. To add to our problems, it started to pour with rain. This turned out to be a blessing in disguise, but didn't help with getting the exhibition material loaded. The French truck arrived with four soldiers, and they started loading the crates. Having been told these contained material for an art exhibition, they hadn't expected them to be filled with bricks, earth, furniture and other heavy objects, and it was a major battle to load the heavy crates onto the truck. It was freezing cold, everything was wet, and we were racing against time. But Miro and the artists pitched in, and eventually everything was loaded. We sped off to the airport. Miro, in a borrowed flak jacket and helmet, was making his first trip since the beginning of the war out of Sarajevo – into Serb territory. Understandably, he was nervous. So was I. I had to get the cargo as well as Miro, a well-known Sarajevan, past the Serb checkpoint.

Thanks to the pouring rain, the checkpoint guards paid no attention to us. General Soubirou's personal orders, relayed by the soldiers in the truck, smoothed the way past the UNPROFOR checkpoint at the airport. We arrived at the airport at 11h00, and the flight was scheduled to leave at 11h30. I told the French soldiers to take the truck through the Civpol check while I sorted out the paperwork with the Norwegian soldiers at 'Movement Control', including for Miro who had authorisation to accompany the cargo to Italy. That was highly irregular because everything – passengers and cargo – had to be checked in two hours before a flight. But General Soubirou's name swept aside all objections. I ran to the UNHCR office to tell them we were there, and to clear the papers for the cargo, then ran back to where Civpol officers were half-heartedly inspecting the crates. The rain was coming down in buckets, and this persuaded them to approve everything very quickly. Only minutes before departure, the last of the crates were hoisted onto the aircraft, and at 11h30 Miro and 'Witnesses' were airborne and on their way to Ancona. That was the real victory of the day, one that would give Sarajevo a voice in the outside world, and without adding in any way to Bosnia's suffering.

On Thursday 10 February, UNPROFOR took over the first military positions. It was the first peaceful day in Sarajevo since the beginning of the war. UN military observers reported only four shells, which in Sarajevo amounted to nothing. The city started breathing again after holding its breath for five days. It was Mima's birthday and we were all badly in need of a celebration. I went to her apartment with a small present, a precious bottle of whisky and a few beers, and carefully climbed the stairs in the dark. Mima, another friend of hers, Anja and I sat around the tiny table in the dining room, next to the small stove. We toasted Mima's good fortune and the possibility of peace, and ate improvised 'war pizza' and 'war cake', made with whatever ingredients could be scraped together.

Saturday 12 February marked the first day in almost two years that nobody was killed in Sarajevo.

On Sunday 13 February, we embarked on the last leg of the 'Witnesses' mission. Miro had returned after overseeing the safe delivery of the exhibition to Ancona, and he and three of the artists, Srdjan, Nusret and Sanjin, were now on their way back to Ancona and from there to New York for the opening at the Kunsthalle. I fetched them at Obala and took them to the airport. We laughed and joked and took pictures of them and of the sign 'Maybe Airlines' at the airport, a standing joke because no flight was ever certain. Everything went off without a hitch, and within days they were in New York, a world away from Sarajevo and the war. Miro had invited me to go along but I couldn't, and he promised I'd be there in their hearts. But he went further than that, honouring me in a way that truly humbled me. In his address at the opening on 22 February he said:

> After the two-year long Sarajevo experience marked with big losses and deep disappointments, the only thing left is a hope in the victory of individuals. Because of them and thanks to them, this exhibition makes sense in New York and in any other city in any other corner of the world. Therefore, 'Witnesses of Existence' is dedicated to them: Guy de Battista, Maria Blacque-Belair, Paula Gordon, Marusa Kresen, Paul Lowe, Anne Marie du Preez, Jean Rolin, Susan Sontag, Stefano Tealdi, Marc Vachon and to the numerous defenders and citizens of Sarajevo who cannot be mentioned by name.

Susan Sontag's fitting tribute to Miro and the artists was a tribute to everyone in Sarajevo:

> I wish it were no big deal to see art made in Sarajevo now here in New York. But of course it required heroic efforts for this exhibition to happen. Miro and these young Sarajevan artists have been unable to leave their native city for twenty-two months, since the Serb aggression started. (Don't let anyone tell you the siege isn't still on!) That they are among us briefly – after opening 'Witnesses of Existence' here, they will return to Sarajevo – is a kind of miracle. They bring their irony, their gallantry, their refusal to be pitiful, their dignity; and, above all, their talent. Their appearance at the New York Kunsthalle is a great gift to us. May we be worthy of it.

After the market bomb, the international community leapt into action, and UNPROFOR was ordered to strike while the iron was hot. I accompanied Viktor to numerous meetings and negotiations, and sometimes our superiors from Zagreb travelled to Sarajevo to add pressure. While we shuttled between Pale and Sarajevo to obtain agreement on elements of the plan, NATO ambassadors finalised the ultimatum, which called for the withdrawal of all heavy weapons twenty kilometres from the centre of Sarajevo, and placing the weapons under UNPROFOR control – within ten days. On 10 February the clock started ticking: if the Serbs didn't comply, they would be subject to NATO air strikes. Any heavy weapons found within the exclusion zone would be targeted. The ultimatum expired at midnight on Sunday 20 February. If the Serbs hadn't complied by then, NATO would start with its bombardment on the Monday. Ambassador Churkin went to Pale and urged the Serbs to comply. They started moving their guns – but only some, and not totally out of the twenty-kilometre zone. By midday on 20 February, the heavy weapons were still within the exclusion zone. It was up to UNPROFOR to make a last-ditch effort to press home the gravity of the situation to the Serbs. I honestly didn't know where to put my vote. Part of me very badly wanted every single Serb gun blasted off the face of the earth, but I also didn't want any more misery for Sarajevo, and unfortunately at the time we still thought the Serbs might put up a real fight if NATO took action against them. Akashi, Viktor and a small group of support staff, including me, set out to Pale to convince the Serbs to move the weapons. The mountains were covered in ice and snow and the vehicles struggled to get up the steep, slippery tracks. Halfway to Pale, we all had to get out of the GMC because it couldn't ascend a particularly steep incline. It was quite a picture. Akashi and Viktor pitched in to push, and even once the GMC was mobile we had to walk for quite a distance until the road levelled out and we could clamber into the vehicle again. The trip had taken on the atmosphere of an epic polar journey.

The meeting with Karadžić and Mladić was long and utterly exhausting. Hour after hour dragged by as Akashi and Viktor negotiated hither and thither, explaining, begging, pleading and threatening. The Serbs used every trick in the book: the weapons were dummies; they were stuck in the snow; they didn't have enough fuel to move them and UNPROFOR should give them fuel. Finally, with the shadow of midnight creeping closer, the Serbs agreed at last to withdraw all the heavy weapons, all the way. We left Pale after midnight, in the early hours of Monday 21 February. We still didn't know what the day would bring. But on our way down the treacherous mountain track the most incredible sight met us. Through the curtain of frozen mist, a dim glow appeared in the distance. As it came closer, we could see it was headlights. At first just one set, then more and more, like the eyes of a pack of predators in the dark. As they came closer, it became possible to identify the vehicles behind them – the Serbs were pulling in the heavy weapons. It was a truly awesome spectacle. An endless row of cannons and gigantic guns of all descriptions were laboriously struggling up the mountain. Some were on the back of enormous military vehicles, others were being towed and crawled along on their own wheels. The lights illuminated hundreds of luminous sprays as snow swirled from under the heavy wheels. It was eerily beautiful. The track was too narrow for two-way traffic, and we had to pull off and wait on the edge of the mountain road for the iron monsters to pass. The soldiers on the first trucks stared at us in silence, but as more and more crept past, they started waving and shouting. Perhaps they, too, were hoping this would signal an end to the war. In a never-ending line the huge guns crawled up the mountain. These were the lethal weapons that had wrought such carnage in Sarajevo, and I wished every person in the city could see that sight, could see how the monstrosities that had terrorised them for two years were going home, like a large herd of gigantic prehistoric animals. But I also wondered how long it would be before they started moving them into place again. True, UNPROFOR would be monitoring the weapons, but that somehow didn't instil much confidence in me.

Rose had been confident all along that air strikes would be averted, and said that the Monday after the deadline for the NATO ultimatum would be 'just another day'. It was touch and go, but once it was clear that the Serbs had met the deadline, his officers printed copies of an A4-size notice saying: 'Monday *was* just another day!' It was signed by Rose and Viktor, and put up on the notice board.

Nobody had yet arrived to take over UNPROFOR Radio, but I'd reached saturation point and made my own ultimatum: I was stopping all radio work at the end of February, whether there was someone to take over or not. In general things weren't going well for me. I hated my new job, because I was constantly exposed to the malevolence and arrogance of the Serbs. Then an escape route opened up. Viktor announced that an UNPROFOR Political/Humanitarian office would be opened in Sarajevo. I convinced him to let me take over the new office, and was overjoyed when he agreed.

On 7 March I attended my last negotiations with the Serb leadership on the agreements after the market bomb. Akashi, Sergio de Mello and General Rose were there too. The international community was convinced that the end of the war was within its grasp, and UNPROFOR had drawn up what was called a 'War to Peace' agenda. I didn't share in the optimism. Neither the Bosnians nor the Serbs were ready for an end to the war: the Bosnians because they were fighting for their lives and a viable future, the Serbs because they believed they'd get their Serb homeland. Karadžić might have been a psychiatrist, but he obviously hadn't read *How to Make Friends and Influence People*. He embarked on a tirade, accused the UN of 'violent diplomacy', and warned that a military alliance between the Bosnians and Croats (which was a fait accompli following the Washington Agreement negotiated in February) against the Serbs would be 'a terrible mistake'. His threats had no effect on Akashi, who this time had clear instructions not to pacify the Serbs, but to push home the message that the international community had had enough. He simply ignored Karadžić and turned to other matters on the agenda.

There were two things about which the Serbs were paranoid. They had an almost pathological fear of losing men in action, something they had in common with the Americans. The other paranoia was losing Sarajevo. They wanted half of the city: it was an international capital of historical significance, and was recognised as a civilised place. Even a piece of it would lend some legitimacy to the bastard country the Serbs were trying to conceive. Karadžić said the Serbs were prepared to give up sizeable territory in exchange for part of Sarajevo. But negotiations on Sarajevo were strictly outside our mandate. And we knew nothing on earth would persuade the Bosnians to give up even an inch of Sarajevo to the Serbs.

CHAPTER 20

THE HADŽIĆI WOMEN

MARCH–APRIL 1994

THE POLITICAL/HUMANITARIAN OFFICE dealt with all things of a humanitarian nature and most things of a political nature, and since just about everything in Bosnia was either or both political and humanitarian, my new job was multifaceted. There was never an idle moment, nor a dull one.

My first assignment as Political/Humanitarian officer sounded like an April fool's joke. An UNPROFOR convoy that was being brought to Sarajevo by the French military had been taken hostage by a group of civilian Serb women in the town of Hadžići. It wasn't the first time the Hadžići women had made headlines. They'd already become notorious for 'kidnapping' UNPROFOR soldiers, including General Morillon. He charmed himself out of captivity, and then sent them hot soup to have while they were keeping their vigil over the strategic road from Croatia to Kiseljak and Sarajevo. Because of the risk of falling into the Hadžići women's hands, the UNPROFOR military had issued strict orders that no convoys were to use that route. The French soldiers said they had ended up on the road by accident because they had got lost, but it was generally accepted that they'd decided to take a short cut and so had ended up in the hands of these tough ladies. It was my job to negotiate their release.

It was to be my first such negotiations, my only other solo negotiations in Bosnia having been for the radio programme, and I naively thought if I spoke to the Hadžići women seriously and reasonably, woman to women, they'd let the French soldiers go. It was to be another phase of my invaluable education in the ways of man (and woman) at war. When I arrived, all the women were at their posts at the roadblock they'd erected months earlier. Rain or shine, they were there to ensnare any hapless vehicle belonging to the UN, foolish enough to cross this path. The reason for their blockade was to get their hands on hostages in order to negotiate the release of Serb prisoners held by the Bosnian army at the Silos Prison in Tarćin. I had no idea how complicated the negotiations would be, nor how long I'd be involved in this very difficult issue. First I asked to speak to the French convoy commander to see how they were holding up under the pressure of the unconventional hostage situation, and to find out how they were being treated. They'd been allowed to remain with their vehicles, and assured me they were being well treated and had no specific problems, except that they'd like to return to Sarajevo. As dozens of times before and after, I promised to do the best I could.

All the women were assembled in a shed at the side of the road for the meeting. It was cold and they'd made a fire in a drum to heat the place. Their leader was Borka Krstić, known as Beba. She welcomed me, I introduced myself and said I'd come to solve the problem. I said that I was sure that as women we'd find we could do that. Although I knew the background, I asked them to explain why they'd taken the soldiers hostage. I hadn't yet had time to organise my own interpreter and had borrowed a young Serb from PTT Building. Beba explained that they'd taken the UNPROFOR soldiers hostage to secure the release of their people held in Tarćin. She said ICRC was not forthcoming with information, and it had been too long since they'd heard from the prisoners. I said I couldn't imagine in my wildest dreams how terrible it must be to know that your loved ones were imprisoned, that it had to be excruciating not hearing from them, and that I'd be happy to make inquiries with ICRC about the issue. Then I tried to explain that we could not, however, link the release of Serb prisoners held by the Bosnian army to the release of UNPROFOR soldiers, because we weren't the ones holding their people and had no leverage with the Bosnians – or Serbs – on such issues. She said that was a pity, because until we did, they would keep the soldiers. I promised that if they let the soldiers go, I'd initiate new negotiations to try to secure the release of the prisoners in Tarćin. That seemed to interest several of the women. They hadn't had an UNPROFOR person lobbying for them before, and there was a visible change in their attitude. One stood up and said she wanted to talk, but before the interpreter could translate her first sentence, Beba angrily interrupted her and a fairly heated discussion followed in Serbo-Croatian. The interpreter quietly translated. I'd guessed correctly. Some felt they had an opportunity of securing an UNPROFOR lobbyist for their cause. But Beba wanted it done her way, and that meant keeping the French soldiers. She convinced them that they would lose their last trump card if they released the soldiers. In that she was probably right. It was the first convoy for months to have used the road, and after what had happened to the French soldiers, it was unlikely anyone would get 'lost' there again. After a marathon four-hour meeting, the soldiers were still hostages. I had to return to Sarajevo to rethink my strategy.

When I'd arrived in Hadžići for my first meeting with Beba and her ladies, I had no idea to what extent Hadžići and Tarćin would invade my life in the months to come. What had started out as a seemingly simple matter, securing the release of some French soldiers, became a complex situation with many different offshoots. I reported to General Soubirou, as commander of the French soldiers, that his men were healthy and safe, but not likely to be back soon. He asked what the chances were of getting the men out if we left the vehicles as 'surety'. The next day I returned to Hadžići. As I'd promised, I'd immediately made inquiries about the Tarčin prisoners with ICRC, and when they expected to be visiting them again. It wasn't encouraging. The Bosnians had refused to allow ICRC access to the prison for two scheduled visits and their hands were tied, but they, too, would keep trying their best. I relayed the information to Beba and her ladies, and promised to draw up a formal UNPROFOR appeal to the Bosnian government that very day, requesting that ICRC be allowed to visit the prisoners. If ICRC as well as UNPROFOR approached the government, it brought twice the weight to bear. But please give us back our soldiers. I didn't immediately offer the vehicles as surety. When it was clear we weren't going to move beyond the stalemate, I asked to speak to the French convoy commander. I told him I'd been given a mandate to try to secure their release in exchange for the vehicles. Surprisingly, he wouldn't hear of it. No, they were going nowhere without their vehicles. Strange, I thought. Those weren't personal vehicles; they belonged to the French army. If General Soubirou was prepared to part with the vehicles, why wouldn't they? A misguided sense of duty and honour, perhaps. I asked to speak to the other soldiers. They all agreed: they weren't leaving without their vehicles. The commander reiterated that they were in no personal danger and were being well treated. Nevertheless, I returned to the negotiations to offer Beba and her ladies the vehicles as General Soubirou had ordered. They, too, were not interested.

During the coffee break, I took the opportunity to talk one on one with some of the women. Many were quite friendly towards me after I'd so promptly brought feedback about the situation regarding the Tarčin prisoners. They reassured me that the French soldiers would be safe, and that they went out of their way to see they were given good food – and after dinner in the evenings they made music and danced a little around the fire. A few of the soldiers, they said, winking, were looking at some of the young ladies with more than just casual interest. Aha! That explained why the French soldiers were reluctant to leave. They were enjoying the company of their captors, and obviously found the situation preferable to life at PTT. It was most interesting.

I continued talks with Beba and another representative for the group of women. We discussed everything at length, and I reiterated that UNPROFOR was being unfairly penalised, since it wasn't in our power to have the Tarčin prisoners released, and that we were pursuing the matter with the Bosnian government to prove our goodwill. When politicians and senior UNPROFOR officials came away empty-handed from difficult negotiations, they would say they'd had 'fruitful discussions'. I'd had fruitful discussions with the Hadžići women.

I went to Hadžići often to give feedback on the situation and to convince the headstrong women to let the French soldiers go. Pressure from UNPROFOR on the Bosnian government was paying off, and ICRC were allowed to resume visits to the Silos Prison. I used every opportunity to point this out to the women. On 16 March, ICRC returned from a visit with 1 385 messages from the prisoners, many for the women in Hadžići. On 23 March, ICRC again visited the prison and distributed food – including canned meat – directly to the prisoners. The fact that ICRC had access to their loved ones made a big difference in the women's attitude towards me. But they still wouldn't let the soldiers go.

I needed an interpreter. I had helped a young girl, Ines Aščerić, to get a position at the Civil Affairs office in Vitez, but after nine months in an area of heavy fighting, and working long hours, she was worn out, missed her parents and friends, and wanted to return to Sarajevo. I employed her.

On a visit to Lukavica, Major Indjić asked me whether I'd take a letter to Sarajevo for a friend of his, a woman. I took the letter, Ines called the number on the envelope and we offered to drop off the letter, but she said she'd fetch it. A few days later she returned with a letter for Indjić and a gift for me – a book she'd written. She was an author and her name was Radmila. She looked at me imploringly and said, 'I … leave. You help me?' It was a shock. I approached a friend in Sarajevo, someone I trusted implicitly, to act as go-between, and found out Radmila wanted to go to the Serb side. Trying to get someone on an aeroplane out of Sarajevo was one thing. But to the Serb side? My friend warned sternly that it would be folly even to consider it. But Radmila was clearly distressed and wanted to leave. I let her know I needed time to think about it, and started considering ways of getting her to Lukavica.

———

Having gone straight from doing two jobs – producing the UNPROFOR Radio programmes and working as Viktor's assistant – to the strenuous task of opening the Political/Humanitarian office, I felt I was going to collapse if I didn't take a break soon. In more than a year I'd had only one break, my other two trips out of the city having been to collect material for the radio programme. I started planning a short trip to Italy.

The fact that Italy was so easily accessible was a blessing. The two overnight trips to Senigallia in 1993, albeit brief, had been so restorative that I couldn't wait to go. I spent a few days in Senigallia, walking on the beach, having leisurely meals, and sitting for hours over steaming coffee thinking about life. Then I boarded a train, which I love, and took a long trip south to Bari, where I stayed in the flat of Monica and Francesco Rega, friends of friends. Francesco's late father had been a well-known artist, and every wall in the elegant flat was covered in paintings. I went shopping, cooked, sipped wine and listened to lovely music – and lay in the bath for hours. It was heaven. On my way back to Sarajevo, I spent another few days in Senigallia. In August the lovely coastal resort brimmed with life and carefree holiday-goers. But in April it was a quiet, dreamy town. Peace and tranquillity enfolded it like a soft shawl, and I had to brace myself to return to Sarajevo. Because every day of the week was a working day there, I hadn't thought for a moment that it might be a problem to return to Sarajevo on the Saturday. But when I arrived at the airport, it was closed! The Italians were celebrating *Pasqua* [Easter], and out of reverence closed even their airports. That meant that UN flights were grounded because there was no air traffic control, and the airport would remain closed until Easter Monday. Since Falconara was closer to the airport I stayed there, and revelled in the extra few days off. It wasn't possible to book a seat on UNHCR flights to and from Sarajevo, you just put your name on a list upon arrival at the airport. Having had no problems getting onto previous flights, I expected to be in Sarajevo by lunchtime. But there was pandemonium at the airport. Because there'd been no flights for four days, scores of UNPROFOR soldiers, civilians, UNHCR personnel and journalists were already queuing for flights. In terms of pecking order, the UNPROFOR military and UNHCR personnel had priority, then UNPROFOR civilians, then local Bosnian UNPROFOR personnel, and lastly the media. The problem was that there was a rotation of the military and dozens of soldiers had to get to Sarajevo. With no hope of getting onto an aircraft, I returned to the hotel in Falconara and tried again on the Wednesday. I immediately went to the British sergeant in charge and put my name on the list. Previously, French soldiers had been in control of the checking in. They were thorough and precise, but polite. I expected no different from the British, who had taken over. There were still many people desperate to get back to Sarajevo, all wanting to know what their chances were of being given a seat. But instead of simply telling people how many flights there were, and how many seats, the British sergeant started screaming at the astonished UN employees and international media to sit down and be quiet, as though they were a bunch of idiotic kindergarten children. There were regular passengers in the airport building, waiting for scheduled airline flights. They all turned and stared.

Finally I was called to report for the next flight. There was always a routine luggage search, mainly to discourage people from taking large quantities of coffee, cigarettes and liquor into Sarajevo and selling it on the black market. Those commodities were as good as gold during the war. However, the search mechanism was a farce. Only the bags of UNPROFOR civilians, Bosnians and the media were searched. The bags of the military, known to be culprits in black market activities, were not searched, and they could take in whatever they wanted whenever they wished. Even the most junior soldier was exempt from such a search, while even the most senior UNPROFOR civilian had to submit to it. The soldier put on gloves and methodically started taking every individual item of clothing from my bag. At first I was stunned. We were in an open waiting area, in full view of other passengers, and he was lifting out my clothes and underwear, piece by piece, dangling it in the air, then dropping it on the counter. When I complained, he called his senior – the rude sergeant in the departure lounge. He barked at me that they had orders. I insisted he call Mike Aitchison. Mike told them a surface search would do for UNPROFOR civilians. But the minute he left, they carried on with their intensive search.

The soldier fished around in the small box with my tampons, opened jars of face cream, leafed through photographs I'd taken. He rummaged through my handbag, and found my Swiss army knife, which I took everywhere because it came in so handy. He said it was a dangerous weapon and I couldn't keep it in my bag. By now I was livid and it was on the tip of my tongue to tell him that I'd be happy to demonstrate just exactly how dangerous by slitting his throat with it. But I just demanded in an icy voice that he take his hands out of my bag and leave my things alone. The sergeant turned on me like a rabid animal, screaming that if he heard another word from me, I would not get on any aeroplane back to Sarajevo.

At that instant all the pent-up frustration and stress of a year in Sarajevo came to a head. I'd been living through sheer hell, and it was only the second time I'd afforded myself the luxury of a proper break. Not only did I have to fight my way out of Sarajevo, but now I had to fight my way back in. I had just about had enough. I screamed at him like a shrew: I couldn't care about their rules, which applied only to civilians. And why wasn't he scrutinising the men's underwear? I had a senior rank on the mission but was being treated like a criminal by some young punk in uniform. Franco, who was on duty, tried to intervene. He told the soldier he was being unfair and should behave himself, but he also received a brush-off. He looked like a dog that had been kicked. Then the sergeant turned to me and said my baggage was one kilogram overweight and I wouldn't be allowed to take overweight baggage. I was dangerously close to losing all self-control. I grabbed an armful of clothes and my boots, threw them on the floor and hissed, 'There! I will not take one more ounce than I'm entitled to.' He just turned and walked away. Franco picked up the bundle of clothes and brought it to me, holding it out like a peace offering. I refused to take it. He looked as though he wanted to cry. He was a decent human being, and just by watching TV he understood how difficult life was in Sarajevo. But the British sadist was some mutation of humanity, and obviously enjoyed harassing us as much as he possibly could. (Franco kept the clothes until the next time I was in Ancona, months later.)

Back in Sarajevo I wrote a scathing letter to Akashi. I discussed the situation with my colleagues, who were all complaining about the same treatment. A few of us agreed to draw up a petition, demanding that the situation be explained to the British military. But then someone said: What if we lost our privilege of using UNHCR flights if we raised this issue? It was, after all, not a right. We all agreed that we didn't want to forfeit being able to go to Italy, and thus we had to shut up and endure the indignities.

It seemed to me as though Rose's arrival had signified a declaration of war on UNPROFOR civilians. We were informed that we had to take our meals at Želježničar, a restaurant in the city centre that was opened just to cater for us. Dealing with the many and varied issues of the Humanitarian office – and on my own – meant I was often too busy and exhausted to make the trip, find parking and go to the restaurant. It was also just a block away from the Presidency, a constant target for Serb shells and sniper fire. The worst was entering and emerging from the restaurant, and having to face the hollow-cheeked Sarajevans on the street outside. I almost never went there, and lost a lot of weight. The administrative personnel at Forward complained bitterly. They didn't have their own transport and often, when there was heavy shelling and they couldn't get a lift, they had to go without meals. Sometimes the shelling was so heavy it was madness to even consider going, transport or not. A restaurant was also set up for the increasing numbers of soldiers based at Forward, but closer to HQ, and in a much safer area.

It took every ounce of my resolve to continue. Rose decided that the bulk of personnel from Kiseljak had to be moved to Sarajevo, and more and more people were crammed into the limited space at Forward. The garden was bulldozed and turned into a parking area, causing outrage in Sarajevo. Other UNPROFOR commanders had arranged their HQ with respect for the surroundings. Yes, there was a war on, but was it necessary for UNPROFOR to destroy what the Serbs had not?

———————————

The French soldiers were still hostages of the Hadžići women, and my first meeting after I returned from Italy was with Beba. After a female UNPROFOR officer was detained by the Serbs for several days, I decided to no longer take Ines out of Sarajevo, and instead took Viktor's interpreter, Darko, along to interpret. Events in Tarćin had taken a turn for the worse. Many inhabitants of the town had disappeared in the first months of the war, and there'd been no news of them in almost two years, despite ICRC's efforts at extracting information from the Serbs. This fuelled fears that they had been killed. Bosnian officials, using this as a tool, incited the frantic families of the missing, and they stormed the prison and took three Serb hostages. As a result of the tension in the town, ICRC was again refused access to the prison. This situation made it impossible to obtain any concessions from Beba. The prisoners in Tarćin were kept hostage for more than two weeks, during which time they were badly beaten. My meetings with Beba became little more than a routine of reiterating our respective views, and again I had to leave empty-handed.

On the way back from a meeting with Beba, we drove past the Vlakovo Cemetery, which was in Serb-occupied territory. There had been rumours that the Serbs had desecrated the graves of Bosnian Muslims and Croats in the cemetery, and both Jasna's mother and Armin's father were terribly distressed by the thought that their spouses' graves had been dishonoured. On the spur of the moment I decided to make a quick detour to the cemetery to check. The gate was open and there was nobody there, so we drove in. Darko had been to the cemetery before the war and knew where the sections for Muslims and Croats were. The graves hadn't been touched. I pulled out my camera and took pictures of the different sections to give to Jasna and Armin. Just then there was a loud shout, and we looked up to see a Serb soldier run to the gate and close it. He shouted at us and motioned us to the gate. I hid the camera and asked Darko to say that he'd just wanted to see the grave of an old friend, and since there was no one at the gate, we thought it would be all right to enter. The soldier angrily shouted that this was Serb territory, we had no right to be there and that UNPROFOR had to have special permission to leave the road. Darko told his story, but the soldier said he had to talk to his superior officer on the radio, which he proceeded to do. He listened, then asked who we were and why we were there. When his superior heard that we'd been to see Beba in Hadžići, he decided our bona fides were acceptable and told the soldier to let us go with the stern warning *never* to do something like that again.

It was an altogether eventful trip. At one of the Serb checkpoints, a long line of local trucks were waiting to pass. As I tried to squeeze past them, I touched a very broad blue truck. My mistake was stopping to check whether I'd caused any damage; I should simply have driven on. But I stopped and we got out. Within seconds we were surrounded by a dozen belligerent Serbs. There was no damage to either vehicle, but the driver of the truck immediately pointed out a non-existent scratch and demanded that UNPROFOR pay for the damage. I said there wasn't any damage and he shouldn't be silly. Although Darko interpreted a more diplomatic version of my reply, the driver, obviously fuelled by Dutch courage, became more and more agitated, and his friends started making lewd remarks. And then one gave my chin a little tweak, as one does with a small child. I hit his arm out of the way hard, and hissed: 'Don't you touch me!' Suddenly everybody was absolutely quiet, watching their comrade to see what he was going to do next. Intensely aware that the atmosphere had turned ugly, I knew that Darko and I were in a very undesirable position. My mind went into overdrive, and I told Darko to advise the driver that he could lodge an official complaint with UNPROFOR. I wrote my car's registration number on one of my cards and said, 'There are my particulars.' Then we left. On the way back, Darko lectured me: I shouldn't have stopped, and I shouldn't have confronted the man. I thought my reaction had perhaps been the right thing. Any sign of weakness might have invited more trouble. But I agreed I shouldn't have stopped.

All the way back to Sarajevo, I racked my brain to find a way of securing the French soldiers' release. Suddenly I had a brilliant idea. I went straight to the PTT Building and asked to see General Soubirou. I explained my plan to him, and drew a map to illustrate. Since Hadžići was on a strategic road used extensively by the Serb military, my plan was as follows: Given that we'd done everything humanly possible and still couldn't secure the soldiers' release, we would tell the Serbs that we at least had to be sure our men were safe and well protected, and therefore had to take all possible measures and precautions to guarantee their well-being. I proposed that we take a large mobile kitchen, an ambulance and some other vehicles for 'protection', and park them on the main road, next to the offshoot where the French were parked. By blocking the main road, we'd immobilise the Serb military and have a trump card: we wouldn't move the vehicles until they let the soldiers go. General Soubirou was both impressed and excited with the plan, and said he'd immediately give orders for it to be set in motion. However, before my brilliant plan could be executed, the Hadžići problem was overtaken by far more serious events.

CHAPTER 21

GORAŽDE

MARCH–APRIL 1994

In the eastern Bosnian enclaves Srebrenica, Goražde and Žepa, the situation was deteriorating. The intervention of NATO after the market bomb had brought a temporary reprieve from the relentless shelling in Sarajevo, but shelling of the other enclaves continued. Knowing that the international community would try to avoid confronting them almost at all costs, the Serbs turned their full attention on Goražde as soon as they were forced to silence their heavy weapons around Sarajevo. They also blockaded convoys with humanitarian food aid and medical supplies. The situation was dire. People were starving, the hospitals were overcrowded and the few exhausted doctors were carrying out critical surgery without electricity, anaesthetic or even adequate water supplies for scrubbing. NATO had made a token effort at convincing the Serbs that a line had been drawn in the sand. On 28 February they shot down four of six Serb Galeb aircraft over Banja Luka in north-eastern Bosnia in accordance with Security Council Resolution 816, which banned unauthorised flights by all aircraft in Bosnia's air space. The pilots of NATO's Flying Falcons, F-16s of the US Air Force, issued two 'land or be engaged' orders to the six Galebs, who pointedly ignored them, secure in the knowledge that nothing had happened to them before. But this time there was no ambivalence about the anger of the international community, and the Flying Falcons 'engaged' the Galebs. I'd long run out of excuses to try to explain to my Sarajevan friends why the UN and NATO kept giving the Serbs one more chance, yet another ultimatum. There seemed to be ultimatums, final ultimatums, final-final ultimatums, and so on. Nobody knew how many final, final, finals there were to be before real and significant action would be taken against the Serbs. When the Galebs were shot down, I could look people in the eye again.

Goražde, Srebrenica and Žepa were of major strategic importance to both the Bosnian government and the Serbs. For the Serbs, de-populating the entire eastern border with Serbia of Bosnians would facilitate linking up those territories into a greater Serbia – which was exactly why it was crucial for the government to hang onto them.

Early in March, my office received a request from the highest office of the Bosnian government, via the Minister for Cooperation with UNPROFOR, Hasan Muratović: Would UNPROFOR petition the Serbs to allow a Bosnian government delegation to visit Goražde? Initially there was the expected point-blank refusal from the Serbs. But the international outrage after the market bomb was still working in our favour, and we advised that they should allow the visit to show good faith. They agreed, under stringent conditions, which I relayed to Minister Muratović. Organising the trip involved not only exhaustive negotiations with the Serbs, but extensive coordinating with the UNPROFOR military, who would provide transport and other logistical support. In a country at war you don't just go where you please, and in Bosnia every inch of territory was under one of the armies' control. For the journey across Serb-occupied territory to Goražde, every step of the way had to be cleared with the Serbs. UNPROFOR put a helicopter at the disposal of the government delegation, who would be flown to the Serb control point in the town of Sokolac for 'routine checks' before continuing to Goražde – if they received the go-ahead from the Serbs. Armed to the teeth with charts, schedules and other relevant information, I coordinated the 'high-level visit' with G-3 Ops.

The trip started off on a bad note. Immediately after General Rose's morning briefing, the British officer in charge of G-3 informed me that they could no longer provide a helicopter, since it was needed elsewhere. I almost had heart failure. This was a high-level government delegation, it was a miracle that the Serbs had agreed to the trip, and I'd worked like a maniac for weeks to organise it. And the delegation was already at the Presidency getting ready to go to the airport. It would be ludicrous if the trip was cancelled by UNPROFOR, and the Bosnian government would be furious. I firmly informed the courteous British officer that the chopper had been booked to go to Goražde and that the arrangement couldn't be changed. He insisted that the chopper was needed elsewhere. I had no choice but to request an audience with Rose and state my case, which was that the minister and his delegation were already waiting at the Presidency, and if the helicopter was indeed no longer available, he, General Rose, should be the person to tell them. He agreed that it 'wasn't cricket', and ordered G-3 to have the helicopter ready at the airport at the scheduled time. Relieved, I drove to the Presidency ahead of the Egyptian APC that was to transport the delegation to the airport. My elation lasted exactly five minutes. The small group of men, including Minister Muratović, were waiting at the main entrance to the Presidency. But standing proudly in the centre was a military officer dressed in the full regalia of the Bosnian army, complete with an impressive row of medals resting below his left shoulder. One of the explicit conditions of the Serbs, understandably, had been that no Bosnian military officials would be allowed into Goražde. I took a deep breath, and said: 'Mr Minister, I thought we'd agreed about the conditions.' He looked a little uneasy, but said that I shouldn't worry, it wouldn't be a problem. Of course it would be a problem: they knew it and I knew it. I also knew that they had a reason for taking along an officer dressed up for a military parade. No effort at camouflaging him as Santa Claus or the UN Secretary-General. I also knew they weren't going to tell me what the reason was. I warned that, at the very least, they should expect the officer to be kept at Sokolac until the helicopter returned from Goražde. If he were lucky: he might be captured. That wasn't the only problem. There was a mountain of luggage, enough for an opera company going on tour. For half a dozen people on a fact-finding mission, returning to Sarajevo the same day, they seemed to need an inordinate number of changes of clothing, I said. Muratović smiled. No, he said, it wasn't clothing, it was medicine. And 600 letters. My heart sank. The Serbs weren't refusing the provision of food and medical supplies to Goražde in the hope that the Bosnian government would deliver it themselves. And the mail was sheer madness. But the delegation was adamant: they wanted to give it a try. The mail almost certainly included military information they were trying to sneak in among the hundreds of letters to grandparents, wives and cousins. I suggested leaving at least the mail behind, as I was sure it would be confiscated at Sokolac. No, they wanted to try to get it through. Of course I knew something was going on, and it made me fear that this mission could turn out very badly indeed. The Bosnians knew better than I that the Serbs would never allow them to take a senior military officer, medicine and hundreds of letters into Goražde. But I had only two options. Either I refused to let them go unless they complied with the conditions, or I passed the buck and the responsibility to them. I decided on the latter, and they reiterated that they wanted to go. UNPROFOR knew the Bosnians and Serbs were striking secret deals all the time. Money, food, weapons, prisoners and even bodies (of soldiers fallen in battle) regularly and quietly changed hands between the two sides. This could be part of a secret deal.

We set off for the airport. The members of the delegation were all in the APCs, and I led the way in my white car. When we arrived, the helicopter, courtesy of Rose's orders, was ready on the tarmac, with blades whirring in a high-pitched cacophony, whipping up clouds of dust, and I was grateful that I didn't have to brave the small hurricane. I bid the delegation farewell inside the building, handed them over to the Norwegian soldier who would escort them to the waiting aircraft, wished them a good trip and assured the minister that there'd be transport awaiting them on their return. As I was about to turn on my heel and leave, a member of the delegation put his hand on my arm and asked if he could have a word with me. There was something he needed to mention, he said. He held out a briefcase. Could we make a plan to try to get it past the Serbs? It was full of money. He opened it a crack to show me. It was, indeed, full of money. I was stunned, and just stood there gaping like a fish. For a minute I felt like doing something aggressive. Of course they'd waited until the last moment, because that would give me no time to argue. For the cash-strapped Bosnian Serbs, there were few things more important than money. Especially foreign currency. They would confiscate it at Sokolac and it'd never be seen again. Unless this was part of a pay-off. By now I knew with absolute certainty that this trip was more than just a visit to boost the morale of Goražde's traumatised population and outgunned fighters. I knew there was no money in Goražde. A colleague of mine who'd been there reported back that you could buy half the town with a packet of Marlboro cigarettes. If the Bosnians in Goražde had money, they might have some leverage with the Serbs. Perhaps they'd use it to buy weapons. That was not nearly as insane as it sounded. It wasn't a secret that there were Serbs who sold weapons to the Bosnians, on a small scale of course, and not in any measure that would affect the war. This in turn helped the Serbs get their hands on some money.

After a year in Sarajevo, and knowing what I did about the war, my conscience would never allow me to thwart an opportunity for the Bosnians to turn matters to their advantage. Especially not if it could help the desperate people in Goražde or any of the other enclaves. I grabbed the briefcase, dashed out into the tornado on the tarmac and dragged the Norwegian pilot aside. Screaming into his ear at the top of my voice and hanging onto him so as not to be blown across the airport, I explained as briefly as I could, and asked whether he'd be prepared to take the briefcase and try to hide it from the Serbs during the check at Sokolac. It would seriously compromise him if it were found, so it had to be his decision. For a few long moments he just looked at me. Then he nodded, took the briefcase, and walked over to welcome the delegation.

My heart was in my throat. There was every chance that things could go horribly wrong – and if they did, the scapegoat would be me. If the Serbs found the money hidden under the pilot's seat, implying that UNPROFOR was in cahoots with the government in smuggling money into Goražde, I'd be in serious trouble. There'd be an official inquiry, and I'd have to admit that I'd known about the money and asked the pilot to hide it. A situation such as this made it difficult afterwards to approach the Serbs with other requests. And I didn't want to think about the mess it would create if the Serbs captured a Bosnian minister. But there was nothing to do but wait and see, so I returned to the Residency.

At midday, G-3 called. The delegation had been turned back at Sokolac. Fully anticipating to hear that the Serbs had turned them back because they had a senior military officer and 600 letters on board, or because they'd found the money, I drove to the airport to wait for them. I was stunned. It had nothing to do with the Serbs. The delegation itself had decided to turn back. They'd arrived in Sokolac, the Serbs searched the chopper and its crew, didn't find the money, miraculously didn't take the senior Bosnian officer prisoner, but insisted on reading each of the letters before allowing the delegation to continue. Instead of leaving the letters and continuing to Goražde, the delegation said, 'If we can't take the mail we're going home,' and told the pilot to take them back to Sarajevo. The weeks of negotiating, arguing and grovelling before the Serbs, the intervention by Rose – all for nothing. The UNPROFOR military foamed at the mouth. Viktor, purple with rage, said I should never have allowed them to go. During the negotiations, one of the Serbs had said to me: 'We know them, they are definitely up to something, you'll see.'

Much later I was told that the objective of the trip had indeed been to convey crucial military information to Goražde's defenders. But not by the ministerial delegation. While the delegation had been occupying the Serbs' attention, a small group of Bosnian soldiers slipped from Sarajevo across Serb lines to Goražde with orders for a last-ditch Bosnian offensive to try to save the city.

The battle for Goražde was one of the most serious crises of the war, and again prompted military intervention by NATO. In the beginning of April the Serbs started a new campaign of heavy sustained shelling on the city.

Reports from the UNMOs and UNHCR in Goražde were alarming. Confirmation of the situation was received from a small group of Rose's Special Air Service (SAS) men he'd dispatched to Goražde disguised as UNMOs, and he was receiving direct communications from them. But Rose didn't release this information, because again the question of air strikes was raised, and it was his job to prevent them. He told the media that the situation wasn't serious, and had stabilised. The UNMOs and representatives of humanitarian organisations in Goražde reacted sharply to Rose's comments, and between the lines of their reports one could sense their frustration and agitation. But given enough time the media can uncover most things, and with the help of a leaked report, it became clear that the situation in Goražde was anything but under control. When this emerged, Rose became the object of sharp criticism by the international media, including the British. The book *The Death of Yugoslavia* by Allan Little and Laura Silber, which accompanied the BBC series with the same title, describes the situation as follows:

Rose played down the seriousness of the Serb attack on Goražde: 'Our own judgement was that the Bosnian Serbs were putting pressure at the tactical level and had no serious intention of taking the pocket,' he said. His spokesmen, in early April, gave daily press briefings designed to take the alarm out of Bosnian government claims of dozens dead and an imminent humanitarian disaster. Rose did not want what he considered a little local difficulty derailing a peace plan which he believed was closer than ever to achieving a lasting solution.

But his own UN military observers in Goražde, together with their UNHCR colleagues, revolted. On April 7, a leaked document revealed that the accounts they had been sending to Rose's headquarters were sharply at odds with the account Rose was presenting to the public. US Chief-of-Staff, General John Shalikashvili, had publicly ruled out a repeat of a Sarajevo-style ultimatum, arguing that the weaponry around Goražde could not be located with sufficient accuracy to make air-strikes practical.

General Mladic behaved as though this were the green light he had been waiting for. The Serb bombardment and advance sharply escalated. The UN monitors sent an urgent appeal to Sarajevo. 'The death toll continues to rise and serious losses of territory are occurring. If this is "not serious", as UNPROFOR seems to say in radio reports, I hope I don't see a serious situation develop,' one monitor reported. 'The situation today is again very serious. We have repeated that our assessment of the situation is serious and that the continued potential for loss of civilian life is very high,' the report went on.

It is very disquieting to hear radio reports from the international media that the situation is not serious. From the BBC World Service news of April 5 we heard 'An UNPROFOR assessment said that it was a minor attack into a limited area.' We again do not concur with that position. It is a grave situation. It needs to be realized that the city center of Goražde is just over 3 km from the Bosnian Serb army front line. Looking at a small land mass on the southeast corner and saying it is a minor attack into a limited area is a bad assessment, incorrect and shows absolutely no understanding of what is going on here.

The UNHCR, who also had representatives in the town, reported that a ten-day Serb assault had killed sixty-seven people and wounded 325, most of them civilians.

So unconcerned was Rose about the consequences of the Goražde assault that, on April 10, he was on his way to Brussels to address a NATO meeting.

The Serbs, of course, knew exactly what the situation was, and playing it down encouraged them to escalate the bombardment on Goražde. The situation deteriorated rapidly, and a major crisis loomed. I had an intense feeling of déjà vu. Everything that happened, down to the date, was a carbon copy of the crisis in Srebrenica a year earlier. As the shelling worsened, Rose finally had no choice but to ask Akashi for permission to launch air strikes. On the afternoon of Sunday 10 April, NATO dropped three bombs on a Serb bunker outside Goražde. But the Serb attacks on the town continued. On the Monday, another order was given for air strikes and another three bombs were dropped, this time on two Serb APCs and a tank firing at Goražde. The Serbs stopped the attacks just long enough to take a deep breath, then continued. And just to prove to the world the Serbs' contempt for its insignificant attempt to stop them, Mladić took all UNPROFOR personnel on Serb-occupied territory hostage. Among them were the French soldiers I'd tried to extricate from the Hadžići women.

The Serbs carried on with their attacks on Goražde. At Forward the atmosphere of impending crisis was steadily increasing. The stage seemed set for an all-out confrontation with the Serbs – but this would place NATO in direct confrontation with the Russians, traditional allies of the Serbs. It appeared that the crisis in Bosnia was threatening to widen into an international conflict.

On 15 April the Serbs further escalated the attacks on Goražde in a final thrust to take the town. The Bosnians couldn't hold their defensive positions, and the lines collapsed so suddenly that even two of Rose's SAS men found themselves suddenly on the new front line. Both were wounded, one critically. When Rose was informed, he called for 'Close Air Support', another term for threatened air strikes, to carry out an urgent medical evacuation. It was bitterly ironic that Rose, who was reluctant to call for international action to save 65 000 people in Goražde, would do so to save the lives of two British soldiers. Akashi, who was in Pale meeting Karadžić, refused to give permission for Close Air Support.

On 16 April we received reports that the Serbs had captured all the strategic high ground around Goražde, and that the Bosnian Army was no longer resisting. As the crisis deepened, there was a frenzy of activity and meetings. Akashi and Churkin were on their way to Pale when they were informed that Goražde was again being shelled, and Akashi returned to Sarajevo. Churkin continued to Pale to negotiate with the Serbs.

Karadžić claimed UN personnel in Goražde were under pressure from the Bosnians to report false information. What he didn't know was that Rose's SAS men were reporting from Goražde, and that Rose knew the truth. Tanks continued moving in on Goražde, and Viktor delivered an ultimatum via Churkin in Pale: If the attacks hadn't stopped by five minutes to four, there would be air strikes at four o'clock. We were all assembled in Rose's office, which had taken on the look of a crisis operations centre. Akashi was there, Rose, Viktor and I, a few UN civilians and about a dozen military officers of every description. One officer was called out of the shower, and arrived with nothing but a towel wrapped around his waist. Every minute a report came in from somewhere. Communications flew in and out, reports were deciphered, heads bent together in grave discussion. To be able to talk to Churkin in Pale, a radio receiver was installed outside, since there wasn't proper reception inside the building. Viktor sat on the bench outside with the communications system on the table in front of him, talking to Churkin in Russian. Information from Viktor to Rose in his office and vice versa was relayed by a kind of conveyor belt of soldiers lining the wooden stairs that led down into the garden from the main office. There was frenzied activity at BH Forward.

By four, the deadline for the ultimatum, the shelling hadn't ceased, and 'Blue Sword' orders were given to attack the tanks. But the weather deteriorated and the aircraft couldn't find them. To everyone's extreme frustration, the tanks then moved into the surrounding woods, where they couldn't be seen. The crisis became acute when it was reported that the Serbs had shot down a NATO aircraft, a British Sea Harrier. Fortunately the pilot ejected safely and landed in Bosnian territory, and it was later confirmed that he was in Goražde in a bunker with the UNMOs. Suddenly, the British were ready to declare war on the Serbs, and the overall sentiment was that it was time to see Serb blood.

As dusk fell over Sarajevo, Akashi, Viktor and US envoy Charles Redman were still huddled around the improvised 'communications centre' in the garden, having intensive discussions with Churkin in Pale. It was a most unusual sight.

By 17 April, it was clear that we were seeing a repeat of Srebrenica. Amid the frantic activity, Karadžić suddenly disappeared, and Churkin had to negotiate with Momčilo Krajišnik, Karadžić's deputy. But the Serbs were about to burn their fingers with the Russians. Krajišnik promised Churkin the shelling of Goražde would stop, that Serb forces would be withdrawn to three kilometres from the town centre and that all UNPROFOR hostages would be freed. They did nothing. Churkin was furious. At a press conference the next day, he commented that he'd heard more broken promises in one weekend than in his entire life. This was strong criticism of the Serbs, and the Goražde crisis was the beginning of the end for them. They alienated both the Russians and Milošević and the Serbs in Yugoslavia, who had no desire to make enemies of the Russians. Milošević washed his hands of the whole affair by saying Karadžić had acted alone, without informing Belgrade.

Throughout the crisis I felt that there was a lack of focus and commitment on the side of the international community. Was this how it worked during war? Did they make things up as they went along? Somehow I'd always thought that political and military leaders had a strategy; that they'd act with greater certainty and resolve under such circumstances. At one stage Akashi threatened to recommend to the Secretary-General that UNPROFOR be withdrawn from Bosnia if the Serbs didn't comply with agreements and release UNPROFOR hostages. I was astonished. How was that supposed to make the Serbs comply? There was nothing they would have liked more than to see UNPROFOR leave, so that they could continue unhindered with their mass murder of Bosnians.

President Izetbegović wrote to Boutros Boutros-Ghali that the so-called safe area of Goražde had become the most unsafe place in the world, and that Boutros-Ghali had done nothing to protect the people of Goražde. Izetbegović wrote that his country was bleeding, and that if Goražde fell, Boutros-Ghali would be morally obliged to resign as UN Secretary-General. Boutros-Ghali requested NATO air power to deter further attacks on Goražde. But NATO was now struggling with its own problems. The clear divisions between Britain and the US had come to a head. The Americans dictated air strikes; the British opposed them. The British said they had put 8 000 soldiers on the ground and the Americans didn't have the courage to do the same. The French and British declared they would withdraw their ground troops if the US continued to push for air strikes. In the meantime, the Serbs continued the all-out offensive on Goražde.

We received regular updates from the UNMOs, UNHCR and MSF personnel in Goražde. They painted a frightful picture. On 18 April, MSF reported deliberate targeted shelling the previous night on the building housing the UNMOs, and that the upper floors had been destroyed. Fortunately the refugees who were living there had sought refuge in the basement.

On 19 April, UNHCR reported that the shelling had continued, and they were preparing for a repetition of the previous day. First light, they said, had revealed 'a scene of desolation', with debris covering the streets and gaping holes in the apartment buildings adjacent to the UNHCR offices. The previous night a shell had exploded within metres of UNHCR's office, causing multiple casualties.

On 20 April the UNMOs reported that the Bosnian defences were holding for the time being, but that the Serbs had targeted the hospital throughout the day with tanks and wire-guided missiles. Staff had to move the patients to the basement, and it was impossible to function in the hospital. Four children were seriously wounded, and casualty figures for the latest spate of attacks stood at 44 dead, including 15 children and 21 women and elderly persons; and 137 injured, including 26 children and 85 women and elderly people. The total casualties were 389 dead and 1 324 wounded.

Later in the day they reported that another eight children had been killed near the hospital, four under five years old. In the same attack, the president of the city council was critically injured. UNHCR said the Serbs seemed poised to level East Goražde house by house in order to gain control of the area.

On 21 April, UNHCR reported that a shell had hit the kitchen of the Red Cross refugee centre, killing one man and injuring nine others, among them the cook, who lost both her hands. The kitchen, used to feed 300 refugees, was destroyed.

On 22 April, the UNMOs reported that the Serbs had accused the authorities in Goražde of holding 1 400 Serb POWs. If they truly believed that, it clearly wasn't deterring them in their efforts to wipe Goražde and everyone in it from the face of the earth. The UNMOs said the claim was ludicrous, since every available inch of space in the town was jammed with refugees; and the Bosnian forces – outnumbered, under-equipped and desperately defending Goražde – were in no position to hold POWs.

The Serbs regularly applied such tactics to waste our time. When allegations were made, we had to inquire and investigate. It was frustrating beyond speech when we knew there was no truth in it. While shells were raining on Goražde, the Serbs made an ultimatum, demanding that all Bosnians leave a specific part of the city. A report from the UNMOs said:

> Regarding the BSA 'ultimatum' of yesterday, demanding that the civilians vacate the right side of the city by 16:00 yesterday. That would have been absolute suicide, because throughout the afternoon the BSA were pounding the bridges and left bank of the river with direct and indirect fire.

The UNMOs visited the hospital under cover of darkness and were met by a horrific scene. The hospital had been the target of repeated attacks by tanks, anti-aircraft missiles and artillery. All the upper floors had been vacated, and every inch of space on the ground floor and dirty cellar was covered with mattresses and wounded people – some soldiers, but mostly civilians. They had improvised an operating theatre below ground level, where doctors were forced to operate under appalling, insanitary conditions.

On 23 April, the UNMOs reported that villages in territory secured by Serb forces were burning, and that they were terrorising the local population. One of the UNMOs added a postscript: 'It warms my heart to hear on BBC that NATO wanted to go for it. Sounds of NATO jets overhead are quite reassuring [to some].'

NATO survived the threat of an internal rift and again issued an ultimatum to the Serbs. They had to comply with three conditions or face air strikes: an immediate ceasefire, withdrawal of troops to three kilometres from the centre of Goražde by the morning of 23 April, and a withdrawal of heavy weapons to twenty kilometres by 26 April. By 23 April there was still no ceasefire, and NATO asked Akashi to authorise air strikes. Akashi refused because, he argued, the Serbs had begun complying with some of the terms of the agreement.

The international community had again, and further, been humiliated by the Serbs.

CHAPTER 22

LIFE IN SARAJEVO

MARCH–JULY 1994

IN FEBRUARY I'D RECEIVED NOTICE from my landlady at the Karamehmedović flat that she wanted to move into the apartment with her family. So when I returned from Italy, I moved into another apartment, which I found with the help of Irma Osim, the other interpreter who worked for the military and shared an office with Jasna. My new landlord was a Serb, Mr Todorović. The flat belonged to his daughter, a doctor who'd left Sarajevo after her husband was killed. Her parents, who had a house near Koševo Hospital, were looking after the place. They were over the moon to find a tenant, which meant no more worries that the flat would be burgled or that refugees would 'move in', and the rent of a few hundred US dollars a month amounted to a princely income. The flat was smaller, with only one bedroom, but more than big enough for me. There was an added bonus: a piano, and I played a little whenever I had time. Also, it was just across the road from Forward, and had the side entrance to the Annex been open, it would have taken me two minutes to reach my office. But even the detour to the main entrance meant I was a mere five-minute walk away. And it was heaven not having the daily climb up 200 frozen steps that resembled a ski slope at the Winter Olympics. The new flat was on the second floor, thirty-two steps up.

Moving out of Forward was an incredible relief. Within weeks of Rose's arrival, it had deteriorated almost beyond recognition. The neat and orderly Annex became overcrowded, noisy and dirty. In no time, none of the toilets had seats; they were almost permanently out of order, and the showers were broken and filthy. Emina and Sabiha, the two cleaning ladies in the Annex, had to cope with three times the number of soldiers, their laundry and the constant mess. Before the war, Emina had been a seamstress and Sabiha a clerk, but they were grateful for the work of cleaning the UNPROFOR HQ in order to stay alive. Even so, there were limits to what they could endure. They were exhausted and complained bitterly.

Life for Sarajevans became somewhat easier as a result of the ceasefire after the market bomb. Since there was no urgent need to move troops and arms through the airport tunnel, food and medical supplies were brought in. The city's electricity supply was restored, albeit initially only for strategic installations. The bakery was up and running and we could buy fresh bread, which was subsidised so that everybody could at least afford this staple. Sarajevo was famous for its delicious bread, and even the war hadn't changed this. Fresh vegetables, meat and other food items Sarajevans had all but forgotten about appeared in the markets, but few people could afford them. Still, thanks to the minor reprieve, life had gone from unspeakably hard to just very difficult. It didn't matter if you went to buy tomatoes and there were no tomatoes; you bought onions, potatoes or spinach instead with a song in your heart, and returned home to cook them. This of course applied only to people with some money, and the majority of people in Sarajevo had none. But many had something to barter, and Sarajevo became much like it must have been hundreds of years earlier. You went to market with a load of potatoes, or you brought books, furniture, or carrots and spinach from the pots on your balcony, and bartered these for eggs and meat. One day Irma came to work with the news that her mother had found a place to buy eggs. We each bought a whole dozen, and I couldn't wait to go home to make an omelette, and pancakes, and a cake. But all the eggs, save three, were bad, and instead of a kitchen wrapped in the wonderful aroma of freshly baked delicacies, it stank of rotten eggs for days.

Except for the situation at Forward, my life improved in every way, and I felt physically restored. Above all, because I no longer needed to climb a thousand stairs a day between home and work and at Radio BH. There was one improvement at Forward: a mobile ablution facility for women. This was necessary because a few female soldiers had been transferred from Kiseljak to Sarajevo. The container with three showers and toilets was kept sparkling clean, and for the first time since I arrived in Sarajevo, I could have a shower in a relaxing environment.

Mipić moved into the flat with me. All her devoted followers had left Forward, and the new group, for the most part, either disliked cats, were allergic or had some other problem with her, so she had to stay at home. She hated the new arrangement. There were no adoring soldiers, no parties in the lounge, no interesting machines, no papers. She sat on the balcony and howled for hours, then curled up despondently in the flower box and gazed longingly at the Annex. I could see her from the office windows and felt like a jailer. Whenever I could I took a tea break at home, gave her a little milk and played with her, tossing her paper ball around the lounge.

Soon after we moved in, I discovered that Mipić had a friend. Early one morning I heard a strange sound, and when I looked through my bedroom window, I saw Mipić lying on her back on the balcony, staring up and making small gurgling, meowing sounds. There was a crow sitting on the ledge above, looking at her and cawing. It was too odd: the crow cawed, Mipić gurgled, the crow 'replied'. It was a strange sight, but I thought nothing of it, till I heard her again a few mornings later. And, yes, there was the crow. It became a regular occurrence. Whenever I heard Mipić 'cooing', the crow would be there. If she was inside when he arrived, he called her, and she'd run up and down, meowing and looking for a place to get out. This strange relationship continued throughout the summer.

At the end of May, I went home to South Africa on leave. It was a joy to be with John and Annéne, and I seriously considered not returning to Sarajevo. I could have kicked myself for not having resigned, but I'd been so caught up in all the issues I was involved in – the Hadžići women and the prisoners, among others – that I just didn't think of leaving them all in the lurch. Still, once I had some distance from it all, I wanted to stay in Johannesburg. I spent the entire three weeks with a dark cloud hanging over me, feeling detached and miserable, crying for hours, trying not to fall apart, and regretting that I couldn't make the most of my time with my children.

When I returned to Sarajevo at the end of June, there was a message from Anja: Seo had suffered a heart attack and was in hospital. I decided I'd call the next day. But I was feeling drained and depressed. Having to leave Annéne and John behind was painful and difficult, and there had again been the inevitable skirmish with the British military in Ancona. I didn't phone back for two days. Then Anja called to say Seo had died. I was filled with reproach. Why hadn't I gritted my teeth and gone to see him in hospital? But I couldn't. The visit to Zdenko Nikolajević's make-shift hospital in Fojnica and one to Koševo Hospital were as much as I could bear. In 1993 I'd accompanied one of my colleagues from Zagreb to visit Koševo Hospital. I decided never again. The sickly sweet odour of death and decaying flesh was heavy in the air and clung to my clothes long after I left. And the sight of horribly wounded men and women, blood and puss from septic wounds seeping through bandages and sheets, and the groans and cries because there weren't enough painkillers to go around haunted me. In the hospitals with which I was familiar, everything was sparkling clean, permeated with the dizzying smell of ether and antiseptics, nurses and doctors marching briskly through the wards, smiling distantly and reassuringly. The staff at Koševo was so exhausted that it was an effort to put one foot in front of the other. Their eyes were empty, their faces drawn and gaunt. For two years they'd been confronted with the Serbs' mutilated victims, working without the most basic medicines, electricity for crucial life-saving equipment, or even adequate water for cleaning. Their souls were weighed down by the awful responsibility that had become the curse of their lives, for they were not only healers, but angels of death. When the Serbs shelled a school or a sports ground, and dozens of maimed children were rushed to hospital, they had to make the soul-destroying decision: who to try to save with the limited means at their disposal, and who to condemn to death because there was a better chance of saving some of the others.

I didn't have the courage to face it at all. That was why I didn't visit Seo; why I hadn't visited Lejzi; and why I hadn't visited Dragana when she was desperately ill.

The supply of electricity was gradually expanded to include domestic use, and during July we started receiving fairly regular supplies of both electricity and water. This was rotated among the suburbs, and we never knew when it would arrive. At first, Irma's mother would phone when it came on, and since Irma was my neighbour, she'd tell me. If I could, I'd drop everything and rush home to fill up the bath, plastic drum and every other suitable container. If there was electricity, I'd quickly vacuum and – always – make tea, because it was a rare treat to make a proper cup: boiling the water, rinsing the pot, brewing it for just the right time and warming the cup. Then we were given a schedule that made life a lot easier:

Tuesday: electricity from 7 a.m. to 2 p.m., water all day
Wednesday: electricity from 3 p.m. to 10 p.m., no water
Thursday: electricity and water from 10 p.m. to 6 a.m.
Friday to Monday: no electricity, no water

I stuck the schedule on the kitchen door and made a copy, which I carried with me. It no longer mattered that there were days without either or both. Just to know that you wouldn't be without water for weeks, or weren't going to run out, and would have electricity at least now and then, was heaven. After some time the schedule was improved, and we had both water and electricity for twelve hours every day, either from seven in the morning until seven at night, or from seven at night until seven in the morning. This meant I could have a hot bath in the comfort and privacy of my home for the first time in more than a year. The simplest chores, things that millions of people the world over took for granted, even complained about, became the epitome of happiness, such as being able to use the automatic washing machine instead of doing laundry in a tub of icy cold water. Even when there was electricity only, I could heat a few pots of water on the stove to have a bath. Those were beautiful days.

In Johannesburg I'd replenished my supplies of tea bags and milk powder, and also bought soup powder and dried vegetables. With the bread and other supplies available at the market, I could keep going without taking meals at the Željezničar restaurant. I could, of course, buy food in Kiseljak, but because of the intermittent electricity supply, nothing that needed refrigeration could be kept for long. Not in summer. In winter one could just leave it out on the balcony. Combined with the inflated prices, hostile shopkeepers and problems at the checkpoints, it wasn't worth it. The Serbs, stopped from firing their heavy guns at Sarajevo, were using every tactic in the book to make the lives of UNPROFOR personnel as difficult as possible. And I was simply too busy to spend hours negotiating my way through the checkpoints.

Things took a miraculous turn for the better when the Danish military in Kiseljak announced they'd be selling food to UNPRO-FOR and UNHCR civilians. The first time I went shopping there, I spent every cent I had on food: meat, two whole Danish blue cheeses, jam, Danish butter, vegetables, fruit, flour, oil, eggs, biscuits and many other things we'd only dreamed of for so long. At home I divided it into more or less equal shares for my friends and their families. It was like paradise. The problem was, though, that you couldn't cook the meat without everybody in your building knowing. People were sensitive, and didn't want to cook delicious meals when their neighbours had none. I didn't buy fresh meat again, only cold meats, ham and salami. For me, Danish blue cheese had always been reserved as a treat. But for weeks my meals consisted of fresh bread from the market with blue cheese.

CHAPTER 23

POLITICAL AND HUMANITARIAN AFFAIRS

MARCH 1994–FEBRUARY 1995

MY OFFICE FOR POLITICAL AND HUMANITARIAN AFFAIRS was like a garage during a jumble sale. UNPROFOR, UNHCR, the military, the Bosnians and the Serbs passed anything and everything to me. My work was a whirl of activity, endless letters and reports, and a maze of meetings. With ICRC about prisoners and detainees. With ministries of the Bosnian government about the repatriation of refugees and displaced persons: the Ministry for Refugees about the repatriation of unaccompanied children; the Ministry of Defence about safe areas and security; the Ministry of Internal Affairs about former prisoners and people evacuated because of a medical emergency. With Minister Muratović about dozens of cases, from nuns who wanted to leave Fojnica to installing a telephone in my flat, which required a formal letter from him. With UNHCR about reuniting families. With the WHO about medical evacuations, and the transfer and exchange of patients between the two sides. With Nenad Dezdarević of the Igman Film company, whose film *L* was shown at the Cannes Film Festival and who wanted to visit Pale. With the cultural organisation FAMA about 300 books they wanted to bring from Zagreb. With the Serbs regarding just about everything. With Special Coordinator John Eagleton's office about curfew regulations, the supply of educational material to schools, the restoration of rail access to Sarajevo and office space for Civil Affairs personnel being kicked out of the Residency. With the War Crimes Tribunal about the discovery of mass graves. With the FAO about seed distribution. With UNICEF about the suspected poisoning of high-protein biscuits for children in Tuzla. With the Sarajevo Women's Organisation about providing them with assistance. With the Halo Trust about mine awareness campaigns. And on and on.

Also with the Ministry of Defence. It had become a permanent battle to keep the local staff at Forward out of the trenches. The army was constantly 'inviting' people to support the war effort. Men not actively engaged in battle were sent to the front lines to dig trenches alongside Serb men in the city who refused to fight for the government. Women were used for back-up support, cooking and cleaning in the barracks and offices. I trod a path to the office of Hasan Muratović, who later became prime minister, armed with letters signed by one UNPROFOR general after another, requesting that the latest call-up order for a staff member at BH Forward be cancelled, since they were working for us. Sometimes it worked, sometimes not. Although they worked at the Residency, they weren't employed by the UN, but were on secondment by their government. But we always managed to keep Gordana, Goran, Izet and a few others, using the implausible excuse that they'd been there so long it would be difficult to replace them without totally disrupting UNPROFOR efficiency.

The Serb Orthodox Church requested UNPROFOR's help to move a very large pile of wood to Greece. If nothing else, the unusual request made me laugh. It was so ordinary and at the same time so ridiculous under the circumstances. The Orthodox Metropolitan of the Dabro-Bosnian Eparchy in Bosnia had donated 98 646 cubic metres of wood for a roof, doors and window-frames to the Hilander Monastery, an ancient thirteenth-century cultural monument in Greece. The material was to be transported from Sokolac in Serb-occupied territory to Greece via what remained of the Federal Republic of Yugoslavia (Serbia and Montenegro) and Bulgaria. However, as a result of UN sanctions against Serbia/Yugoslavia, special written permission was required from the UN Sanctions Committee. It was a matter of the utmost importance to the Orthodox Church, and in view of the influence of the Church over the Bosnian Serbs, it was decided it would be to UNPROFOR's advantage to render the required assistance. We drafted a letter to the UN Sanctions Committee for permission, and wrote to Akashi for support. The Sanctions Committee replied that the matter had to be raised directly by the Greek government with the UN Sanctions Committee in New York. This message was passed on to Pale, and I never heard what happened about the wood for the Hilander Monastery.

The Bosnian Ministry of Internal Affairs asked for help with the deportation of a Kenyan citizen, who was in custody in Sarajevo on criminal charges. The Bosnians had enough to deal with, and obviously didn't need a criminally inclined Kenyan on their hands. When I approached ICRC, they said that they knew about the case, but could do nothing because the prisoner refused to be repatriated to Kenya. He must have been very reluctant indeed to face the authorities at home if he chose to stay in Sarajevo. I asked UNHCR, but they said they could only deal with the matter if they were requested by the Kenyan government to repatriate him. My guess was that the Kenyan government had no idea that he was in Bosnia, and he almost certainly hadn't written home in a while. The prisoner then asked to be expatriated to Turkey, and the matter was referred to the Turkish government. In the meantime, the Bosnians had no choice but to extend their hospitality to the uninvited guest.

The administrator of Koševo Hospital, Faruk Dizdarević, was director of the Fund for Renewal and Development of the Clinical University Centre of Sarajevo. They wanted to start rebuilding the damaged hospital, and asked me to help organise an international congress of surgeons, hosted by Sarajevo. It was a brilliant idea, but bringing delegates from all over the world to Sarajevo was simply not possible. To soften the blow, I suggested that UNPRO-FOR personnel in Sarajevo, starting with me, should have routine medical check-ups done in Sarajevo, rather than in Zagreb. This would generate a little income for the hospital and save us the dangerous return trip. Dizdarević enthusiastically agreed, and after a fairly caustic battle with the administrative personnel in Zagreb, I checked in a few weeks later to have my blood and a few other things tested. Even the outpatient section was harrowing, with hundreds of sick people and children trying to get medical assistance, and no water in the toilets – which one had to brave to provide a specimen for the urine test.

UNESCO requested help with the planning of prefabricated schools, and they also suggested that UNPROFOR allocate forty seats a month on Sarajevo flights for a 'cultural exchange' programme. I told them I'd been doing what I could to support an informal 'cultural exchange' for a year, and since I knew all the political intricacies – and Akashi had ordered it stopped – I suggested it was better to not try to formalise it. They also wanted help organising a rock concert in Sarajevo at which the world famous group U2 would perform, and we had preliminary planning meetings about security and flight arrangements. The concert was eventually held two years later, after the war.

There were also private requests. As when Kasim Begić, Professor of Law at Sarajevo University and a friend of Jamila, needed to transport a few hundred calendars to Sarajevo from Zagreb. Under the guise that the calendars had been printed as Christmas gifts for

UNPROFOR, I asked an old colleague from the UNTAG mission in Namibia, Marie McGehee, to put the calendars on a flight to Sarajevo. And then the undaunted Sarajevans organised a film festival, but they ran out of fuel for the generator. When the organiser, Haris Pašović, told me of this, I gave him the jerrycan of fuel that we all had to have in our cars, told the soldiers at the fuel depot that mine had disappeared, and was given a replacement.

By and large it was the horrors of the war that occupied my time. One of these was ethnic cleansing, the Serb method of realising their dream of an ethnically pure homeland by purging it of Bosnians and Croats. With the growing international outcry against ethnic cleansing and condemnation of their practices, the Serbs were becoming innovative. They rounded up forty-nine Bosnians from the Serb-held town Rogatica, on the front line just outside Sarajevo, and then contacted ICRC to arrange a 'prisoner exchange'. The ICRC head office in Geneva had warned us to be on the outlook for this kind of 'dirty business'. ICRC classified such people as 'war-related prisoners' as opposed to POWs or bona fide detainees, and therefore they couldn't be exchanged. The Serbs said the prisoners couldn't stay at Rogatica, and threatened to send them to prison camps. ICRC pointed out that that would be a human rights violation, and emphatically refused to become involved in the matter except to register the prisoners' names. The Serbs promptly 'released' them into Bosnian territory. They were fortunate. They'd been uprooted and traumatised, but at least they didn't end up in a Serb camp. Or worse. A few days later the Serbs rounded up 100 Bosnians from the Bijeljina area in north-east Bosnia, this time wanting to exchange them for Serbs from Tuzla. ICRC reiterated their position. It had no effect, and the prisoners were again unceremoniously dumped on Bosnian territory. Shortly afterwards, a Serb official, someone I worked with on a regular basis, told ICRC that UNPROFOR had agreed to move 2 500 Bosnians from the area between Rogatica and Goražde. This was totally untrue. But, as before, I was tormented by what might happen to people we were refusing to help, leaving them at the mercy of the Serbs to be starved, beaten, raped and possibly murdered. It was no consolation to them that we were registering their names.

At the end of July, I had my first meeting with members of the War Crimes Tribunal, formally titled 'International Tribunal for the Prosecution of Persons Responsible for Serious Violations of International Humanitarian Law Committed in the Territory of the Former Yugoslavia Since 1991'. The aim of the meeting was to make contact and assist them with information and anything else they might need. They had none of their own logistics, not even transport, and I helped them set up meetings with the government for Justice Richard Goldstone, who would be visiting Sarajevo in September or October. He was a widely respected fellow South African, and I was looking forward to meeting him.

I dealt with the many different, and often maddening, components of my job as best I could. With just about everything being either political or humanitarian, or both, I couldn't refuse a single request or task. If an individual asked for assistance I helped, even if it was just by listening and then referring them to the right place for their particular problem. Similarly, every request by the Bosnian government or the Serbs, ICRC, UNHCR or my military colleagues had to be dealt with. The sheer enormity of the need and my responsibilities was draining and exasperating. It wasn't surprising that I started suffering quite severely from empathy fatigue. I began avoiding people, declined invitations, and went out less and less because there was always someone who wanted me to do something for them. It wasn't that I didn't care or didn't want to help – I'd simply become overwhelmed, and the pile of problems on my desk never got any smaller.

Of course, I should never have stayed in Sarajevo for so long. The UN shouldn't have allowed it. ICRC and UNHCR had strict rotation policies for their staff in stressful and dangerous locations, and exchanged them every three to four months. So did the UNPROFOR military. But not the UN Secretariat. Nobody ever asked me whether I was coping. On the contrary, the UN made no effort whatsoever to make our lives easier. For all of 1994, I received only my 'danger pay' in Sarajevo. For the entire year my salary was never paid, and my financial affairs were in crisis. My numerous requests for the issue to be addressed were simply ignored. One of my colleagues, in a similar predicament, had to return to the US and sell his house. Another irony was our 'danger pay'. There were no banks in Sarajevo, or anywhere in Bosnia, and no shops where one could get change. Yet we were paid in $100 bills. It was impossible to buy anything anywhere with these. Numerous requests to administration officials in Zagreb had no effect. At the end of July, I filled in a travel request to go to Zagreb. As the reason for my visit, I put: 'To get change for the $100 bills I was paid with.' The administrative officer processing my flight request said it wasn't a valid reason and I had to fill in something else. I refused point-blank, and said it was the reason why I was going, and I wasn't going to use another excuse. It took months before Zagreb took notice of the increasing unhappiness about this situation, and they eventually sent us some smaller denominations. I was dangerously close to burn-out. If I'd taken more regular breaks I would have been in better shape, but getting in and out of Sarajevo added to the risk – and I just didn't have the stamina to weather the additional harassment by the British military at Ancona. It took me years to recover from the acute emotional trauma of my time in Sarajevo, and I'll suffer for the rest of my life from the physical effects.

CHAPTER 24

PRISONERS AND THE POPE

JULY–AUGUST 1994

NOT LONG AFTER I took over the Humanitarian office, I met Peter Deck, a protection officer with UNHCR who'd asked for help with a serious refugee issue. The Serbs were bringing Bosnian refugees they'd rounded up for unsuccessful 'prisoner exchanges' to the Bratstvo Jedinstvo [Brotherhood and Unity] Bridge between the city and the Serb-controlled suburb of Grbavica. UNHCR had endless problems obtaining permission for the refugees to enter Sarajevo. The Bosnian authorities were refusing to accept them, because they said it encouraged ethnic cleansing. An even bigger problem was that, once permission had been granted by the Bosnians, the UNPROFOR military often wouldn't allow the refugees into the city. I agreed to accompany UNHCR when there were people on the Serb side who needed to get in. Soon after we'd met, Peter called to ask for assistance with a large group of people who had been brought to the bridge. When I arrived, he and his interpreter, Milica, were already there. This time the problem was with the Bosnian military guarding the bridge on the Sarajevo side. They said they couldn't accept people without agreement from Amor Mašović, the Bosnian official responsible for prisoner and detainee issues. I insisted they call him, and after a fairly lengthy wait, he arrived. We'd met a few times in connection with the Tarčin prisoners. He was a sullen man, but he had a terrible job, one I wouldn't have wanted for all the money in the world. I explained my point of view, which was that we had innocent, traumatised, starved and exhausted civilians who'd lost their homes and spent days, weeks or months in Serb prisons, were lucky indeed to be alive, and now desperately needed to get into Sarajevo. He curtly replied that it would be encouraging ethnic cleansing, and that the government wouldn't allow it. I persevered. As I saw it, I said, the ethnic cleansing was committed when the refugees were forced to leave their homes and became Serb captives. They no longer had homes to which they could return, and I was certain they didn't wish to return to Serb prisons. He wouldn't budge. As a passionate dancer from an early age, I knew a strong partner inspired one to dance better. In Sarajevo I discovered that the tougher my opponents were, the tougher I could be. 'Fine,' I said. 'But I'm going to call the representatives of the world media in Sarajevo – the BBC, CNN, the *New York Times* et al – and then the two of us can explain our points of view to them. I'm sure they'll find it admirable that the Bosnian government feels so strongly about ethnic cleansing that they'd rather return their people to Serb prisons than allow them into Sarajevo.' He just looked at me. I knew the international media would probably turn the tables on me, ignore the Bosnian government and accuse UNPROFOR of promoting ethnic cleansing. I added that the Serbs had informed us they would regularly be releasing people, and asked him to issue standing orders to let them into the city. He turned round and spoke to the soldier in charge. Then he left. With rare exceptions, the Bosnians treated me with warmth and courtesy. The soldier smiled at me and said, 'It's okay. They can come.'

The other battle was with the UNPROFOR military. During July, the Serbs brought another group of Bosnian civilians to the bridge.

Word had got out, and the media arrived in large numbers to report on their arrival in Sarajevo. The reports again accused UNPROFOR of assisting the Serbs with ethnic cleansing, since we were in charge of the bridge. Consequently General Soubirou ordered that no civilians would be allowed to cross if the necessary paperwork hadn't been presented to UNPROFOR. The 'paperwork' consisted of letters from the Serbs listing the names of the people in question and stating they were refugees who had expressed a desire to go to Sarajevo. Yet another group arrived the next day, were refused passage by the French military, and the Serbs returned them to Kula Prison in Butmir. It took more than a month of difficult negotiations before this group finally arrived in Sarajevo. I failed to see how papers would make a difference in how our involvement was perceived, and tried to convince the military that if the Bosnians and the Serbs agreed to something – anything – UNPROFOR had no right to interfere, especially not if it would place civilians in any danger. Soubirou agreed, but on condition that if more than four people were crossing the bridge, a Civil Affairs officer had to be present. The French soldiers on the bridge were informed, and again everything was fine – as long as I was there. But sometimes I couldn't be reached, and sometimes the Serbs didn't inform us and simply arrived with a group of people. I hadn't fought it out with the Bosnian government to be defeated now by my own side. The commanding officer of the French soldiers guarding the bridge was Lieutenant Colonel de Courtivron. He was a courteous, cooperative man, and I set up a meeting with him, explained the terrible predicament the refugees might find themselves in if there were to be an escalation of hostilities, and the moral responsibility we had to see that they found a relatively safe haven, no matter what the international media said. De Courtivron agreed to issue the orders that nobody was to be turned away, and that I was to be contacted if anyone turned up. In turn

I had to confirm in writing that the matter had been cleared with the Bosnian government and that the responsibility, were anything to go wrong, would rest with my office. I didn't have the necessary authority and it should have been passed to Zagreb, but I knew it would then get bogged down in red tape and meetings, and there wouldn't be any decision for months. I bit the bullet, took poetic licence with my powers and responsibilities, and issued the disclaimer. I had long made peace with my conscience. If the UN fired me for breaking the rules because I was afraid women and children and very old people were going to be raped and killed, I could live with it. If God asked me to justify why I'd allowed these women and children and very old people to be raped and killed, I knew it would be very feeble to say because it was the UN's rules and because the media would have accused me of supporting ethnic cleansing.

The crossings at the bridge became a regular feature of my work. It was the saddest job, and I often had to brace myself not to weep. Some people were so overjoyed at the prospect of their tenuous freedom that they embraced us, went down on their knees and kissed our hands, and wept unashamedly as they carried their small bundles of earthly possessions from Serb territory across the Bridge of Brotherhood and Unity, which was now the dividing line between life and death, into the city of dreams, which had become a nightmare. Others showed no emotion, looked neither left nor right, stoically carrying their pain and loss with them into the bleakness of their new life. One day there was a couple in the group. The woman's face was young, but her eyes old and her hair grey. She was well dressed and groomed, and it was obvious that she'd been used to a life of comfort. The man with her was handsome and dressed in an elegant, expensive suit. But his face was empty, and he clearly no longer had a functional mind. He stared straight ahead without making a sound or showing he was in any way aware of his surroundings. I don't think it had been a long-term condition. People who suffer serious mental affliction over a prolonged period look different; their facial muscles react differently. This man's beautiful face was completely blank. The woman held him gently by the elbow and steered him through the sandbagged checkpoint onto the bridge. They were about thirty-five. What had happened to him? Had he been wounded? Captured and tortured? Was she so prematurely grey because of his condition? Had they lost a child, or children? Had he simply caved in under the immense weight of all the tragedy?

Despite all the effort, communication and paperwork, things constantly went wrong. When a new intake of soldiers took over control of the bridge, we were faced with the same problems all over again. One day I'd just returned from the front-line town of Dupovći after a meeting about a very large prisoner exchange we were negotiating, when ICRC called to say there were people on the bridge and the French were refusing to let them pass. Fortunately the Serbs no longer immediately returned refugees to prison when the French refused them passage, and kept them in Grbavica for a few hours, giving us time to try to organise the crossing. I found a middle-aged woman and her fifteen-year-old daughter on the Serb side, dejected and bedraggled. They were originally from Sarajevo, but had been stuck on the Serb side since the beginning of the war. It was wonderful, and painful, to see how happy they were to return home. The next day a large group of people were turned back because the new soldiers still hadn't been informed of the policy, and didn't contact me. Peter was furious, and I rushed to the Serb side to see Dragan Bulajić, the Serb official responsible for prisoner issues. I pleaded with him to bring the group again the next day, and to see that all the paperwork was in order. Then I went to De Courtivron and asked him to set up standing orders that would be passed to every successive group of soldiers who worked on the bridge, so that the constant repetition of these problems could be avoided.

When we arrived at the bridge at the arranged time the following day, the large group was there and crossed into Sarajevo without a hitch. The Bosnian officer in command knew me by then and agreed to let them cross even though there were some problems with the papers. There were often anxious family members waiting for the arriving refugees. How they knew was inexplicable. There were few telephones, no post office. However, when the large group of people arrived that afternoon, there was nobody to meet them and they had nowhere to go. But the soldiers said they'd make a plan.

That group was one I'll always remember. Perhaps because I'd been so afraid we'd lose them. Perhaps because there were so many children and old people, some too old to walk. There was an unwritten rule that UNHCR and UNPROFOR would supervise the crossing, but in no way assist the refugees. The rationale was that we could then deny 'assisting' the Serbs with ethnic cleansing. The rhetoric and word games could drive one crazy. How could we expect drained, exhausted people to carry not only their belongings, but these old people hundreds of metres across the bridge? The side of one old woman's face was swollen and purple. I asked what had happened. She said she'd fallen, but didn't look me in the eye. We were on the Serb side; what else could she say? UNHCR interviewed all the refugees as a matter of course, and Peter said they'd investigate. I made a quick decision. The French on the bridge had an ambulance, which I commandeered to transport people who couldn't walk. Then I ordered the French soldiers to help me load the luggage into my car. I made several trips with the group's luggage. I couldn't care less who saw me, or what they thought or would write. On the Serb side was a brutal, half-drunk soldier who didn't like it at all. He kept saying the people could walk, and a few times tried to push me out of the way. My blood pressure was slowly rising. When he half staggered towards me and tried to shoulder me out of the way, I turned to him, clenched my teeth, counted to ten, then hissed: 'If you touch me again, I am going to kick you in the groin as hard as I can, and then I am going to drive over you.' He didn't understand English, but didn't need to. At that moment I was quite capable of doing him serious harm, and he understood that. The refugees had the smell of people who'd gone without washing for many days. The luggage had the musty smell of prison. One young girl had a dazed, lifeless expression. Inside I was weeping, and was grateful beyond expression that I needn't ask them about their experiences, needn't hear the tales of horror and deprivation that were so clearly etched on their faces. By the time the Serbs brought someone to the Bratstvo Jedinstvo Bridge – or anywhere else – to be 'exchanged', they'd been driven from their homes in terror, robbed of their valuables, beaten, traumatised and detained in Serb prison camps for anything from hours to months.

However, not only Bosnians were suffering indescribable agonies. Many Serbs in Sarajevo suffered an unspeakable pain in silence: the families of soldiers in the Bosnian Serb army. A Serb soldier in Grbavica once asked me to take a parcel to Sarajevo for his mother. I phoned and met her at Radio BH: old, small, sunken. She was touchingly grateful for the parcel and his letter. Her son was living in the land of milk and honey while she was starving in Sarajevo. There was pain in her eyes, and I wished I could ask her what it was really like to be bombarded and under threat every minute of the day by an army for which your son was fighting.

———————————

Sarajevo was the quietest place on earth at one o'clock in the morning – when there was no fighting. It was quiet as the grave as I walked home, breathing in the fresh air. Viktor was away and I was in charge of Civil Affairs at Forward HQ. The days were long and exhausting, having to do my own work and deal with the extra load. I dragged myself up the two flights of stairs, undressed in the dark and fell into bed. As I drifted off into deep sleep, there was a call on my Motorola. It was Stanislav, the Russian officer on duty. There was a crisis, could I please come back to Forward. I pulled on the clothes I'd dropped on the chair only minutes before and plodded back to the ops room. A bus full of Bosnian civilians was stuck at a Serb checkpoint. The Serbs had put mines around the bus and wouldn't let it move. I asked Stanislav to make radio contact with the Canadian UNPROFOR soldier who'd reported the problem so we could learn the details. The soldier explained: There were three Serbs on the bus who wanted to get off at the checkpoint, but the UNPROFOR military escort wouldn't allow it. The Serbs then put mines around the bus and threatened to blow it up if the three weren't allowed to disembark.

'Was that all they wanted?' I asked.

'Yes.'

'What were they doing on the road at this time of night?'

'They'd been there since late afternoon.'

'Good grief! Had UNPROFOR asked the three people in question whether they wanted to get off the bus?'

'Yes, they said they wanted to leave.'

'Ask the Serb soldier in charge whether they'd take away the mines and let the bus pass if their three comrades were allowed off.'

'We can't do that, we're under orders not to let anyone off the bus.'

'You are now taking orders from me,' I snapped, 'and I'll explain it to your superior if there's a problem. Ask the Serbs.'

Stanislav and I waited. After some time the UNPROFOR soldier returned.

'The Serbs promise they'll let the bus pass if the three passengers are allowed off,' he said.

I had no real faith in that promise. I knew the Serbs. But no harm in trying. I told the soldier to stay on the radio, to let the three people off the bus, but not to hand them over to the Serbs until the mines had been moved, and to give us running commentary on what was happening. The three people in the bus disembarked and stayed next to the bus, the mines were moved, the soldier handed over the three Serbs. The bus left.

I dragged myself home, undressed, and got into bed.

As the months went by, the ceasefire became more tenuous by the day. The Serbs again started shelling Sarajevo and the fighting steadily increased. The tunnel under the airport was once more needed for military purposes, and as winter approached, provisions in the market were drying up. One day I passed a stall with nothing but some furniture polish, a used steam iron, a large ball of rope, a tennis ball and a few bars of soap. The hardship and hopelessness had became more noticeable again: a man and woman transporting a very large carpet on a bicycle in Dobrinja; two men trying to manoeuvre a wheelbarrow with a wardrobe tied onto it down the main road; a woman carrying a (sick?) child of about ten on her back; small children dragging containers with water.

Mipić was virtually the only light relief in my life. I'd left her with Jasna when I went on leave, and when I returned, an amused and slightly embarrassed Jasna announced that Mipić had had male company. In August Mipić had five kittens, and suddenly I had six cats. I knew I couldn't keep the kittens, but for six weeks they provided me with hours of pleasure.

Sarajevo was vainly clinging to the eleventh hour of normality and peace. But, alas, as my horoscope in the *Vanity Fair* of September 1994 merrily pointed out: 'You know how it is. Life goes on swimmingly for a while, then – WHOOSH – the Wicked Witch of the West flies by the window cackling gleefully.' I couldn't have said it better myself.

As winter inched closer, the armies realised they would soon be immobilised by the weather: blizzards, sub-zero temperatures and snow. Any attempts to change the military situation had to be made urgently. The Bosnians once again tried to take control of the road to Pale. The Serbs hated that. I thought they probably didn't like envisioning themselves having to dig a tunnel from Lukavica to Pale, as the Bosnians had had to do from Hrasnica to Sarajevo, in order to survive. And usually when the Serbs were irritated, they tried to destroy one or more of the Bosnian enclaves. This time it was Sarajevo. And before we knew it we were again without water and electricity, and ducking Serb shells and bullets.

In mid-August it was announced that the Pope was to visit Sarajevo. Our world went berserk. Urgent letters went to and fro between the Vatican and Boutros Boutros-Ghali, who passed them to Kofi Annan, then Under Secretary-General in charge of peacekeeping. He sent them to Akashi, who sent them to Viktor, who passed them to me. The Pope was expected in Sarajevo on 8 September, and less than a month before the visit, the UN was doing what it did best – its senior officials were writing letters to each other. The visit echoed how everything went in Bosnia: the final responsibility rested with the Catholic Church and the Bosnian government, but all the work had to be done by UNPROFOR, and the visit would happen only if it were sanctioned by the Serbs.

From the word go I said it would be a grave mistake for the pontiff to visit Sarajevo. The thought made me shudder. I was convinced it would increase the danger for the city's residents. We had enough experience and proof to know that the presence of prominent visitors and the accompanying heightened media attention attracted increased attacks by the Serbs. And people would make an effort to see him, making themselves vulnerable. Many people didn't share my view, but that didn't surprise me. For those with political or personal agendas, the Pope was now the king in the Bosnian chess game. Everyone else on the board were pawns, of little or no significance.

In anticipation of the visit, UNPROFOR scheduled daily meetings, starting on 24 August, and set up a committee with a large group of representatives of the Bosnian government, the Catholic Church and the Bosnian police in order to do the necessary planning. I was representing Civil Affairs and thus, indirectly, the Secretary-General. The first agenda item at the committee's first meeting, to deal with 'ground assistance', was deciding where the Pope would conduct Mass in Sarajevo. There was no point in working out detailed security for his arrival without an appropriate place to conduct Mass. The first suggestion was the skating rink at Zetra Stadium. Although badly damaged by Serb shells, it still had a roof and was thought to be big enough to accommodate the 4 000 to 5 000 people expected to attend. As with everything else in Sarajevo, this was liberally tinged with the absurd. The French military, totally unaware of the English connotation of the words, said the roof was unstable, and if thousands of people were singing there, it could bring the roof down. Koševo Stadium wasn't a suitable alternative because it wasn't covered and was supposed to seat 50 000, and with only ten percent occupation it would be virtually empty and look like an insult to the Pope. The covered stadium at the Skenderija sport complex was ruled out because it was virtually on the confrontation line, and it would be impossible for the pontiff in his fragile state of health to climb the hundreds of stairs. The skating rink had several advantages. The small adjoining stadium was used as a helicopter landing pad, and there would be access for the Pope without stairs. However, the Engineering Commission, after a detailed inspection, said that the roof at the skating rink was safe, and would *not* come down if thousands of people were singing.

The cathedral was another option, but Father Tucci said both President Izetbegović and Boutros-Ghali had advised against an uncovered venue, as too many people would have to stand outside and be at risk of snipers. Despite this, he seemed to warm to the idea of having it at the cathedral, and said if it were held there, UNPROFOR would be asked to provide a giant TV screen so everyone outside could see the Pope. That was totally absurd, but I kept a straight face and said I honestly didn't think it would be possible, because the logistics were too daunting and there would be considerable risk not only to the Pope, but to everyone who wanted to see him. A Bosnian representative said if people's desire to see the Pope was greater than fear for their own safety, it was their decision. But eventually common sense and Izetbegović and Boutros-Ghali's advice prevailed, and it was agreed that the cathedral was not a good idea. Someone suggested the tennis courts, but this was an uncovered venue, and one of the Bosnians said access to the tennis courts was restricted to people with tennis shoes. I had great problems suppressing raucous laughter. (In my notebook I made a note in anticipation of the next question: 'Will UNPROFOR provide 4 000 pairs of tennis shoes in different sizes?') Yet I suddenly felt real compassion for the man who, with half of Sarajevo in ruins, was still concerned about preserving the tennis courts. A French officer mentioned that the gate where the Pope would enter was next to the cages for the Bosnian police's dogs, and it would be inappropriate for the Pope to have to pass them. The Church asked whether UNHCR could provide sandwiches and drinks for people attending Mass. I said we couldn't justify this without offering the same to everyone else in the city. It would start a riot.

After this general meeting, we agreed to continue with 'technical meetings', attended by the Bosnian police; Nedim Avdagić, representing the Bosnian government; two Church representatives; Lieutenant Colonel de Courtivron and Lieutenant Colonel de Laforcade for the UNPROFOR military; and me – as 'political advisor'. We met several times a week to thrash out all the intricate details. We had to decide on a route from the airport: via Dobrinja or through the Serb checkpoint at Kasindolska. The Bosnian government favoured Dobrinja, so that the Pope wouldn't set foot on Serb territory. The Church also preferred the Dobrinja route. The police would join the convoy at Dobrinja, provide extra security in the vicinity of the Tito Barracks and the Holiday Inn, see that Bosnian checkpoints were opened, and have a vehicle right in front and behind UN vehicles. What kind of vehicle would the Pope be in? An APC or the Pope Mobile? We had to find out whether he was bringing the latter.

UNPROFOR would try to arrange an overhead aircraft for additional security, and the police would secure the two high buildings overlooking the skating rink. Further security measures were that the police would only take control from Nedžarići and not from the Stup Bridge on the confrontation line, as it was too dangerous to do a switch there; a surveillance camera would be installed in the altar; and explosives teams would check the venue for explosives prior to Mass and then secure the entire area. De Courtivron said we could provide eighty percent security, the other twenty percent had to come from the Holy Spirit. Viktor, reading my report, said it was the other way round. I agreed with him.

Apart from the real possibility of the gathering being shelled, there was the additional danger of a sniper firing into the large crowd, causing a stampede. It was decided that anti-sniper teams would provide protection at Zetra and along the route. The government asked for mixed Bosnian/UNPROFOR anti-sniper teams, probably to be able to verify and witness any needed action. UNPROFOR agreed, and offered to provide a sniper liaison officer. (That had to be a first in world history, a new job description coined in Sarajevo.) In return they asked for a Bosnian sniper liaison officer to expedite communications.

Other problems were that the street in front of the seminary, where the Pope would rest, was in bad condition, and crushed stone and sand would have to be brought from Butmir, but there were mines on the road to the quarry. Nedim undertook to see that the mines were moved.

It was suggested that the Pope should stop at the new graveyard after Mass, and this route had to be checked for safety.

The Church would make all the arrangements for the Mass with the government. They had to come up with a system for security checks. Perhaps entrance would be regulated with a card system, but nobody quite knew how such a system should work.

There would have to be ambulances on standby, as well as a helicopter, and medical personnel at PTT. Three tents would be set up in Zetra Stadium. Extra blood in all the major blood groups had to be arranged.

The UN fire service would provide at least one truck with drinkable water.

Up to a thousand journalists were expected to converge on Sarajevo for the occasion. If the airlift was operating normally, it was expected that up to 500 could be brought in by air. Clearance would have to be arranged, including for some Serb reporters. The Vatican would also send their own media, and requested that all media be confined to the same location and not be allowed to move around.

The military, especially the French military, were not fond of the media, and they were preoccupied with the thought of dealing with a horde of journalists. During a meeting at the airport, about a dozen senior French officers grilled me about media arrangements as though it were my personal project. What about media who couldn't make it onto flights? Were they to be allowed in across

Mount Igman? Further, the Dobrinja and PTT roads were to be closed at 09h00 on the day and also at 18h00 for the return trip, so the media would have to enter and leave through the Serb checkpoint. They were convinced the media horde would block Kasindolska Road, which would cause serious problems if the military needed to get through in case of a crisis. While this meeting was in progress, a report was brought in that a Puma helicopter had been shot at while landing at the airport. The helicopter just managed to land without crashing, and fortunately there were no casualties. It seemed a bad omen.

I was increasingly exasperated. Surely I couldn't be the only person recognising the many potential hazards? I also couldn't shake the feeling that the whole thing was farcical, a circus, and a huge waste of time. In the beginning of August we'd started working on an important prisoner exchange, and now I had to spend hours each day on something that was little more than a glamorous – and unnecessary – PR exercise. The meetings, which took long enough, had to be followed up with individual discussions on the bits each of us had to sort out, further discussions and feedback to Viktor and General Rose, and written reports. And when we received official confirmation on 1 September from the Vatican that the Pope would go ahead with the visit on 8 September, it became a frenzy. I reiterated my reservations to Viktor. He said, put it on paper for the Secretary-General.

The Secretary-General would be in a most unenviable position should some catastrophe befall the pontiff while in the care of the UN in Sarajevo. But, truth be told, I couldn't care less about the Secretary-General's career, and if the Pope chose to expose himself to the dangers of Sarajevo, that was his prerogative. Sarajevo's besieged people had no such choice, and my sole concern was for the safety of the thousands who'd be at risk while lining the streets to greet him. It seemed the pro-visit lobby had forgotten the massacres where groups of people had gathered: the bread queue, the children playing ball in Goražde, the children playing on a sports field in Dobrinja, the market bomb. I thought cynically that none of the major players in the Bosnian tragedy would lose sleep over the death of a few hundred more Sarajevans. But in Sarajevo this was not just newsreel, and as long as I had a voice, I would protest. The dangers were real, the risks ominous. And unless they physically gagged me, I was going to say so in no uncertain terms.

Knowing what I did about the UN, I was certain that the urgent confidential report on the Pope's visit would blaze its way like a heat-seeking missile through the maze of red tape from Zagreb to the UN Secretariat in New York, and right onto the Secretary-General's desk. Therefore, I drafted the report with the utmost care, weighing every word, considering and reconsidering every implication of the six-page document. Whatever happened, those responsible at the UN Secretariat would never be able to say there was anything we in Sarajevo didn't tell them. It was all there, black on white. Sure, it would ruffle some feathers, and I could imagine the dismay of some of my colleagues when they read it. Hardly any of them – those in Kiseljak, in Zagreb, and certainly in New York – had lived through the terror of a Serb attack. But I had, day after day for eighteen months, and nothing could persuade me to ignore a situation that would endanger thousands of people. Inter alia I wrote that Civil Affairs had grave reservations about the prudence of the Pope's visit, given that we didn't know what to expect after the Serbs' rejection of the latest peace proposal. An incident (such as the assassination of the Pope) would result in an escalation of the conflict, and a further setback to the peace process. Although I had no confidence that the latest peace proposals would be successful, the UN seemed to, so I harped on that quite a bit. I also pointed out the obvious: that it was impossible to provide safety guarantees for the Pope and also (although this seemed to be more my concern than anyone else's) that of Sarajevans.

The Vatican had reiterated that the Pope had no concern for his own safety, but did care for that of the people wanting to see him and attending Mass. I emphasised that his presence in Sarajevo would encourage people to disregard the dangers and place themselves at risk. My coup de grâce was that the Vatican and the UN were accepting an awesome responsibility. If nothing else was guaranteed to make senior UN officials sit up and take note, the words *accepting an awesome responsibility* would definitely do the trick. The one thing UN officials in general avoided like the bubonic plague was accepting responsibility. For anything. I attached a fairly detailed summary of our discussions and arrangements, and took the document to the Commcen for urgent dispatch.

The report went to Zagreb, and from there to New York. As I'd expected, it caused near hysteria, because the Vatican had to be informed of any reservations or potential problems. After the report, things happened very fast. The Holy See dispatched a special envoy to Sarajevo, Monsignor Einaudi, the Papal Nuncio to Croatia. A new Civil Affairs officer, Colum Murphy, had just arrived in Sarajevo, and Viktor said Colum should accompany the Nuncio to Pale because Colum was Catholic. But the trip to Pale was an ideal opportunity for me to have an 'off-the-record' discussion with the Nuncio. I told Viktor that if ever I'd heard a lame duck motivation for anything, this was it. Colum had only just arrived and knew nothing about the issue. He was welcome to come along, but this was my project. So, Colum and I both dutifully accompanied the Nuncio and his two assistants to the bishop's office in Sarajevo, and from there to Pale for talks with the Serb leadership. I left no stone unturned in making my view known to the Nuncio. On the way back, he briefed us on his meeting with the Serb leaders. They had told him that as fellow Christians they had no problem with the Pope's visit, but there was absolutely no way they could guarantee his safety. For once I agreed with them. All it would take was a 'rogue element' within Serb ranks, or one demented Bosnian soldier, to create absolute mayhem. The Pope would be dead, and the world would say: *What was the UN thinking?* And then it was also quite possible that a shell or two could be lobbed into the crowd – a second market bomb.

The Nuncio sped back to Rome with the information. We carried on planning for the Pope's visit. There was no knowing whether the decision-makers were crazy enough to go ahead with the ill-conceived plan, so everything had to continue as if it were going ahead.

The day of the Pope's visit, 8 September, was a Thursday. Final arrangements were that UNPROFOR would set up a tactical HQ at Zetra on the Wednesday; that the Bosnian army's First Corps would provide security but under control of the Bosnian police, not the military; that the police would start checking every inch of Zetra Stadium with a dog team at 13h00 on the Wednesday; and that a surveillance camera would then be installed at Zetra. On 29 August, Sector Sarajevo's chief of staff, Colonel Gaussere, issued a hefty document listing all the tasks and responsibilities. It looked like preparations for the final invasion on D-Day, including a map and lists of companies, battalions, air operations, airport and road reconnaissance, ground security, geographical boundaries, a radio net and radio checks, anti-sniping teams and traffic control.

Also, the police had to check each and every gift offered to the Pope. Then, as though to overturn all of this, we were informed that the Pope would drive into the stadium in an open car provided by the government. Since his safety would by then be the Bosnian government's responsibility, we just shrugged. But then the Bosnians and the Church said they wanted people to line the streets in welcome. I was almost hysterical. Had they all lost their senses? Thousands of people standing on the roadside in the most dangerous parts of the city, through Dobrinja and down Snipers' Alley! They were inviting disaster. As if to underline my concerns, the Danish

HQ Company, while setting up camp at Zetra at the site marked for Mass on 8 September, came under sniper fire from the Bosnian side – five days before the Pope's visit. Apparently not everyone in Sarajevo supported the Pope's visit. When UNPROFOR investigated the incident, the liaison officer for the Bosnian army's 105th Corps said the Danish had been fired at because they hadn't received the necessary permission to set up camp at that spot, but that was of course utter nonsense because the government, police and military were involved in all the planning. Both the UNPROFOR military and I were convinced it was about the Pope's visit.

Sarajevo had been turned on its head. The people whom the American media in particular had taken such great pains to label 'Muslims' were printing thousands of posters of the Pope with welcoming messages emblazoned across them. Radio BH approached me with a request for fuel so that they could cover the event. They asked for an exorbitant amount, and I had to solicit the help of UNPROFOR engineers to establish how much fuel they'd really need.

On 6 September we did a complete convoy recce, a kind of dress rehearsal. We started from PTT Building at 15h30, met at the airport and did a whole security rehearsal, and after that a rehearsal of the trip into Sarajevo with the Bosnian police et al so that any potential problems could be ironed out.

The airport dress rehearsal was very impressive, with hundreds of soldiers lining up in different places and with different orders. If nothing else, the Pope would be received with due pomp and ceremony.

When I got back to Forward, I received the news: the visit had been cancelled. I was very relieved. But I was also furious. Weeks of wasted time, effort and energy, which we could ill afford.

CHAPTER 25

WHERE THERE IS A WILL

AUGUST–OCTOBER 1994

OF ALL BOSNIA'S TRAGEDIES, the greatest was the children. Thousands were killed, tens of thousands wounded, hundreds of thousands banished from their homes. They lost parents, brothers and sisters, and friends. They ended up in concentration camps, became refugees and orphans. By the summer of 1993, the WHO found that children in Sarajevo had stopped growing as a result of trauma and starvation. They were small, pale, quiet, their eyes didn't smile, their faces were old. By the end of 1994, parents and teachers were complaining of listlessness, lack of concentration and aggression. Many thousands of children were separated from their parents when people fled the advancing Serb and Croat armies, and many were never reunited – parents or children were killed or simply swallowed up by the chaos. Children too young to articulate memories or information about their parents ended up in orphanages. Almost a decade after the end of the war, between 20 000 and 30 000 Bosnians were still missing – many no doubt buried in the unmarked graves that scatter the Bosnian earth occupied by the Serbs. The suffering and anguish of children who had witnessed their parents or other loved ones killed or wounded, or had themselves been wounded or killed, chilled me to the bone.

The world knew of the toll over two years of war and siege had taken on Sarajevo's children, and many organisations wanted to help those worst affected to escape the city for at least a few weeks. In August an invitation arrived for forty children from Sarajevo to have a holiday in Croatia. The question was: How would we get them there? UNPROFOR couldn't even entertain the possibility of flying them out; it was just too dangerous. The thought of an aeroplane full of children going down in flames was enough to nip that idea in the bud immediately. The only other way was by road. But that was equally dangerous. They would have to cross Mount Igman, where there was heavy fighting between the Bosnian army and the Serbs. I took up the matter with the Serbs, and Dr Nikola Koljević wrote back that they couldn't guarantee the children's safety if they went by air, nor if they took routes that weren't under Serb control. However, if the buses were to take a route through Serb territory, they would guarantee the children's safety. That made sense, and I believed Koljević that the children would be safe. But I knew the Bosnians would never agree, and one couldn't blame them. Would I entrust my children to the Serbs after they'd been wounded by a Serb sniper, watched their home burnt to ashes by the Serbs or witnessed a family member dying after Serb shelling? I simply passed Koljević's letter to the Bosnian authorities, who rejected the proposal outright.

While I was racking my brain to make a plan for forty traumatised children to have a holiday, I received a report from the military that the children had been taken through the airport tunnel.

Despite the hardships, the children, like everyone else, made the most of every moment of normality. Whenever there was a lull in the shelling, small groups of children in my neighbourhood played outside, or gathered around a friend with a guitar, singing and dancing.

They often organised little concerts, to which I was invited, as well as to children's parties, hoping I'd bring sweets and drinks. I tried to go when I could, but often had to disappoint them.

When the Soroš Foundation proposed a pen-pal project, I eagerly agreed to help. It was called Pen Pals for Peace, and would be organised by Timothy Shannon, a young American working for the foundation in Sarajevo. They needed assistance in getting the mail to and from the USA. It was an excellent idea; Sarajevo's children needed every bit of support they could get, and also the distraction. Most of all, they needed the simple therapy of talking about their problems to peers – about the terror, the trauma, the pain of losing family, homes and friends. Schools in Sarajevo were cooperating with the exchange programme, but the Soroš Foundation was having great difficulty getting the letters in and out of Sarajevo. Mail was a sensitive issue. The Serbs wouldn't allow the mail to leave the city, because they claimed the Bosnians would use it to smuggle out military secrets. Military secrets, my eye! There were no Bosnian military secrets – the Serbs knew just about everything. There were a myriad problems: we'd need to formulate an elaborate plan of how the mail would be checked, who would handle it and who'd be responsible for distribution. UNPROFOR personnel were expressly forbidden to carry mail in and out of Sarajevo, but of course we all did. However, it was one thing to do this covertly with a few personal letters. To do it legally and officially with piles of mail would run into a quagmire of UN rules and Serb obstruction. I raised the matter with Civpol, who said they could under no circumstances support it, because it would mean their having to censor each letter that came and went in order to assure the Serbs that military information wasn't being transmitted. I didn't accept that the Serbs were concerned the project would be used to transmit sensitive military information. It was just a way of enforcing the isolation, further undermining the morale of Sarajevans (even the children), and reminding everyone who was holding the sword over their heads.

Because of all the problems, the plan died. It was hard explaining to Timothy that it really wasn't possible. It broke my heart, because I'd read some of the children's letters:

My name is Suada Rasidagić. I was born in Sarajevo and I live there. I'm 10. When the war started I left home with my mother, father and sister. We went at my aunt's place because there was less shooting there. I could play with my cousins and friends there. Near the house I could see our army. I was afraid of them until I was told they want to beat our enemy. I became fond of our young lilies. [The ljiljan, or lily (fleur-de-lis), is the Bosnian emblem.] My father was keeping guard at Faletići – the part of town where I lived. My mother was visiting the house with him. They took me with them only once. My house was already destroyed by shells. When I saw the big hole in the wall I felt pain. I didn't know why they had done that. Inside the house there was a terrible mess. Everything was very strange and sad. I could cry at that moment. My doll was lying on the floor with no legs, the wardrobe didn't exist any more, dishes were broken, my bicycle was destroyed and everything looked like a nightmare. After the house, a new trouble came. My daddy was wounded by a sniper. When I found out about it, I cried my heart out. I didn't enjoy playing with children any more. My only wish was for my daddy to get well. The wound in the leg wasn't dangerous, but the doctors couldn't save his life. He lost a lot of blood. When I was told about his death, I wasn't crying, I was screaming. I was very sad those days. After his death my mother, sister and I moved to a hotel. We had food there. My mother was looking for an apartment. After 5 months she found one. I was happy then, for the first time after my father's death. I would like most in the world for the war to stop and everyone to get back home. I don't want anyone to get killed any more. I hope there is going to be peace again, but life must go on, even in a war. I would like to exchange letters with you. And I would also like to meet you. Please send me your photo.

As an American journalist, Lynn Gourley Karl of the *Patriot News* put it: 'They write of war and pain. They want the killing to stop. They want peace. They want chocolate.'

The plight of Bosnia's children touched the hearts of people everywhere, and many wanted to help and bring them some relief, not understanding that Bosnia wasn't just a country at war, but a country largely under siege. And they simply could not understand why UNPROFOR couldn't assist them with their well-meaning proposals, or allow them to carry out their projects themselves, often at great personal expense.

In October, General Rose passed a letter to me with an offer from an ex-RAF officer, Michael Gillman, who wanted to organise a Christmas party for 'the children of Bosnia'. He proposed sending a vehicle to Split in Croatia on 19 December with 'enough goodies to give the children of Bosnia a Christmas party'. Personally, I'd have given anything for the children of Bosnia to go to this party in Split, on the beautiful Dalmatian coast, and never come back. It was a heart-warming idea. The kind-hearted Gillman didn't quote numbers, so one couldn't be sure whether he meant all the children of Bosnia (tens of thousands) or a representative group from Sarajevo. It didn't really matter. Mr Gillman also asked whether the British Army Catering Corps would bake and decorate a large Christmas cake for the occasion. The British soldiers in Sarajevo were on strict rations, so it would have to be British soldiers somewhere else, which could probably be organised. I hated admitting that things were impossible, but sometimes they just were. Apart from the logistical nightmare, parents certainly wouldn't let their children travel through enemy territory. I told General Rose the only possibility was for the UNPROFOR military to fly in a few loads of gifts and edible treats to Sarajevo, and to ask UNHCR to take it to places like Goražde by road – if we could get it past the Serbs. Either way, we'd have to disappoint Mr Gillman. There simply was no way of taking Bosnia's children to Croatia for a Christmas party.

Ines, my interpreter, had been awarded a scholarship at Durham University, but there was no legitimate way of leaving Sarajevo. So I smuggled her out, after forging papers for her to catch a flight to Zagreb. She had to say goodbye to her parents and boyfriend, not knowing whether she'd ever see them again, and the parting was agonising for them all. When we drove away from her home, her face was tight with pent-up emotion. I told her she'd feel better if she cried. She said: 'No, if I start crying I'll never be able to stop.'

At the airport we had to apply all the cunning we possessed between us to get her six heavy bags past the Civpol officer. Passengers were only allowed what they could carry, and Ines obviously couldn't carry six bags. I told a bunch of lies and we smiled a lot, and he let us through. Then, as usual, disaster struck. The rules had yet again been changed, and we hadn't known Ines now needed a visa for Croatia, where she had to pick up her visa for the UK. We raced back to the Croatian embassy in Sarajevo, rounded the corner on two wheels, and my heart stopped. The scene in front of the embassy was reminiscent of Saigon and Phnom Penh on the day the Americans left Vietnam. UNPROFOR had negotiated with the Serbs to open some roads out of Sarajevo, and since fighting and shelling was again escalating, thousands of Bosnian Croats and others wanting to leave were trying to obtain Croatian visas. There was an ocean of people swimming in front of the enormous wrought-iron gate. Those in front were clinging to the gate and the fence, screaming at the guards to let them in, or to let them see so-and-so with whom they had an appointment. Some were pleading and crying. The guards, like guards all over the world, had faces of stone. They didn't even respond. I was propelled forward by Ines's anxious face. Like a deranged animal, I pushed and shoved and fought my way to the front of the crowd, dragging her after me. Once at the gate, I waved hands and arms and shoved my UNPROFOR ID through the bars of the padlocked gate. The guard didn't even look at me. Both Ines and I shouted: 'United Nations! United Nations!' but he didn't blink.

The only place where anything was working was Forward, so I headed to my office. As fate would have it, a senior official at the British Embassy called as I walked in to ask whether we could provide transport for a British journalist at his office who desperately wanted to leave Sarajevo. In a moment I saw a gap to solve Ines's problem. I was certain there wouldn't be any problems putting her on an UNHCR flight to Italy, and I offered to take the journalist to the airport if the embassy official promised to organise a visa for Ines, which she could collect in Rome. We picked up the journalist and raced back to the airport. At least Ines now had someone to help her carry her bags. We managed to book them both on the next flight to Ancona, and I made the journalist promise that he'd keep an eye on her. I gave Ines a last hug and waved as she boarded the aircraft. Back in my car I slumped over the steering wheel and cried and cried, from sadness that Ines was gone, from relief that Ines was gone.

She sailed through course after course, starting with a degree in International Marketing and Arabic at Durham. In 2004, she completed a doctorate in Bosnian History at Oxford University.

There were plenty of reminders that many Serbs and Croats were as much victims of circumstance as the Bosnians.

Sanja, the young Serb checkpoint guard, was one. As we came to know each other better, she often invited me to have coffee at her house, but since she was on duty and I was always in a hurry, this never materialised. One day I was on my way back from prisoner exchange negotiations at Dupovći, and she was on duty at the checkpoint near Hadžići, which was close to her house. She was about to go off duty, again invited me for coffee, and this time I went. Although we'd known each other for more than a year, we'd never talked for more than a few minutes, and I knew nothing about her. When we arrived at the house, a wholesome meal was cooking on the stove in the kitchen and the aroma filled the lounge. It smelt like home, and I wished I could stay for dinner. The house was like any on the Bosnian side: the same atmosphere and furniture. The difference was the smell of food, coffee, perfume, soap and detergent. Here they had all these things, and in abundance. We settled down over coffee and biscuits, and I stupidly asked whether she'd always lived there. No, she said. She now lived there with her sisters Dragana and Rada, and they were refugees. Before the war, she'd lived in Zenica with her parents.

Sanja had been one of four sisters. The eldest was killed in a Bosnian attack. Sanja and another sister were wounded. Their parents lost their house in Zenica, had to leave everything behind and settle on Serb territory in Brćko, one of the centres of heavy fighting, and she feared for them. 'This is such a terrible tragedy,' she said, and tears started running down her face. Once she started, it was as though the sluice gates had been opened. 'I am twenty-two,' she said, 'and I have no future.' The worst was that she'd never again see the man she'd loved since their schooldays. They'd been inseparable, and as they entered adulthood, had begun planning to turn their dreams of a life together into reality. 'Now,' she said, 'I don't even know where he lives, except that he's in Germany.' He was a Bosnian, and like many young men on both sides, had fled the country rather than fight against people he had loved and lived with all his life. 'I still love him,' she said. 'He was the only man I ever loved, and I will always love him. For us it never mattered that he was a Muslim, that I was a Serb. We never even thought about it before the war. And I loved him so much.'

'I don't hate the Bosnians,' she said, 'I respect them.' Rada came in with some mail. Her eyes were filled with tears. There was a letter and a photograph from their Bosnian neighbour in Zenica. While some of them were killing each other, others were writing letters, sending photos and crying for each other. Sanja said: 'We are all tired of war, but it's politics.' She'd been in a bus that was attacked a few days earlier. A woman in the seat right in front of her was killed and a man seriously wounded. She said she'd been terribly frightened. She took a few sips of coffee, dried her tears. 'Thank you,' she said. 'I can never talk about this with anyone else.' Then she said, again: 'You know, my people don't hate Bosnians and Croats. This thing about Serbs and Croats and Bosnians is nonsense. But we are like brothers and sisters who cannot live in the same house without quarrelling and fighting. We really care for each other, we just need to live apart.'

The Sarajevans were determined not to go through another winter without heating. Two murderous winters had eroded them to such an extent that they couldn't face another. Carlos knew someone who said she'd rather kill herself than go through another winter in Sarajevo. There was an agreement with the Serbs to allow gas into the city, and although nobody knew whether this could be relied on, everyone in the city nevertheless set to work laying and connecting gas pipelines. Enormous gorges appeared in the roads. When the Bosnian military didn't need the tunnel under the airport for bringing in military equipment and soldiers, people were allowed to bring in food, and even things like stoves and fridges. And suddenly it was possible to buy gas. My landlord said he had a contact that could get me a bottle of gas. He mentioned a price, and I paid it. It was expensive but I didn't care, and triumphantly connected the bottle to the stove. Many stoves in Sarajevo had two plates for electricity and two for gas. That turned out to be a blessing, for when there wasn't electricity, I could now use gas. When I told Irma and Jasna, I found out that they, too, had bought gas, but for a quarter of the price. This frequently happened to UNPROFOR officials, since we didn't have our ears close enough to the ground and didn't always have the connections to buy things cheaper.

Once the main pipes were lain, secondary pipes had to be fed into the buildings and then into individual flats, and I also applied for piped gas. It was a catastrophe waiting to happen. There wasn't enough: equipment, piping or fittings. Buildings took on the look of abstract works of art in progress. Any manner of pipes were fixed to the walls or draped down the stairwells. Gas for my flat was fed into the kitchen with a length of green plastic garden hosepipe, from the stairwell through the skylight above the front door, where a valve was installed. From there the hosepipe snaked through the entrance hall and dining room, through the skylight above the kitchen door, and across the floor to the stove, where there was another valve. Gas, like electricity, came and went, and it was critical to close both valves when the stove wasn't in use. If you forgot to close the valve when the gas went off, and it came on while you were away, it would fill the flat with gas. Then, when you struck a match to light a candle or the stove … well, whoosh! I was a nervous wreck. I was terrified of going anywhere near the gas hosepipe, tiptoed around it as though it were a deadly snake, and gingerly turned the valves on and off. I often turned back halfway to Forward, or got up at night, to check whether I had in fact closed the main valve. Yet another hazard to survive. There were many fires in Sarajevo – and no fire brigade or water. Life continued to be hell, one way or another.

CHAPTER 26

FREE AT LAST

SEPTEMBER–OCTOBER 1994

There is nothing quite like the sight of the prisoner desperate to talk and to convey some terrible truth that is so near yet so far, but who dares not. Their stares burn, they speak only with their terrified silence, and eyes inflamed with the articulation of stark, undiluted, desolate fear-without-hope.

ED VULLIAMY, *Seasons in Hell*

ON WEDNESDAY 5 OCTOBER, everything was ready for the large prisoner of war exchange: 351 men were anxiously waiting to be freed after many months of captivity, to be reunited with their families and leave behind long months of uncertainty, fear and torture. The exchange involved 211 Bosnian prisoners held by the Serbs, and 140 Serb prisoners held by the Bosnians.

The preparations had involved over two months of meetings with ICRC, exhaustive negotiations with the government and the Serbs, and meticulous planning. It was a tremendously complicated operation, involving an exchange of bodies of deceased combatants, the return of eight Serbs from Sarajevo to Goražde in exchange for Bosnian civilians from Goražde, the release of a Bosnian prisoner held in Belgrade, a medical evacuation from Goražde – and the exchange of the prisoners on the Bratstvo Jedinstvo Bridge. From the beginning the process was rife with obstacles. The UNPROFOR military wanted the Bosnians to bring Serb prisoners from other locations across Mount Igman to Hrasnica. But there was heavy fighting on Mount Igman, and the only way to bring the prisoners into Sarajevo from Hrasnica was through the airport tunnel. If they weren't in Sarajevo they couldn't be brought to the bridge, and we had a moral obligation to get them to the exchange alive. It was as simple as that. The trip via Igman was too dangerous, and the Bosnians weren't going to take Serb prisoners on a guided tour of the tunnel and then release them. Another really dangerous thing the military had agreed to was transporting the Bosnian prisoners. That meant driving around in UNPROFOR APCs with the Bosnians in Serb-held territory for five to six hours, which was how long it would take to pick them up and take them to the Serb-occupied parts of Sarajevo. I insisted that the Serbs should remain responsible for them until they were at the bridge. What if Serbs in those villages took the prisoners from the UNPROFOR vehicles and killed them? The Serbs had been known to do worse. My military colleagues said UNPROFOR would protect them. Ha! We couldn't protect Hakija Turajlić, the Bosnian deputy prime minister, who was killed inside an UNPROFOR APC in January 1993. And three French APCs and a bunch of soldiers couldn't protect Messrs Andjić and Dejanović in November 1993 when the Serbs at Rajlovac simply forced open the hatches of the APCs with crowbars and dragged them out.

The military, however, often had to focus on other tasks, and it was mostly left to ICRC and me to thrash out the difficulties with the two exchange commissioners, Amor Mašović on the Bosnian side and Dragan Bulajić on the Serb side. The prisoners, including at least ten identified as civilians held by the Serbs, but excluding three who had to be brought from Serbia, were being held at Serb prisons in the towns of Rogatica, Batković, Rudo and Foća, and Kula Prison in Butmir; and at Bosnian prisons in Goražde, Konjić and Sarajevo. At the beginning there'd been 391 prisoners on the list, 206 held by the Serbs and 185 by the Bosnians. But that number was whittled down as both sides withdrew certain names from the lists. As part of the agreement for the exchange, some other things had been thrown in. An UNHCR convoy blocked by the Serbs at the town of Dobrun would be allowed to proceed on 4 October at the latest. Another seven humanitarian convoys would be allowed into Goražde, starting on 3 October. The three Bosnians who were negotiating the release of prisoners held in Goražde would be allowed to travel to Goražde by helicopter at least twenty-four hours before the exchange. Five doctors would be allowed into Goražde, and forty medical evacuations would be allowed.

The Serbs wanted their prisoners, and the Bosnians took full advantage of this. The reason for the Serbs' vulnerability was their misplaced sense of Serb unity and honour. They were totally illogical about prisoners and the loss of any soldiers in action. Since the Bosnians didn't know when they might next have such an opportunity, they had to milk it for every drop. Prior to the exchange of the main group of prisoners, and in addition to the main stipulations, the Bosnians wanted the following: the three negotiators who were returning to Goražde were to be allowed to include in their luggage official gazettes, 60 000 DM in cash, two parcels of medicine, 300 kg of glue (I couldn't find out what for), written education material and 100 kg of stationery. Also, each member of the delegation would be allowed to carry five kilos of coffee, five kilos of tobacco, five boxes of cigarettes, personal effects and several hundred letters for people in Goražde. I realised that many of these things (the medicines, letters, cash) were what the Muratović delegation had hoped to take into Goražde months earlier. It was very sad that the lives of 351 people had been reduced to the equivalent of things such as books, coffee and tobacco.

The Bosnians also asked that ten people in Sarajevo be allowed to return to Goražde. The Serbs drove a hard bargain. In exchange, fifty Serb civilians should be allowed to leave and go to Kopaći, a Serb-held area just outside Goražde. That I could understand, but not the ten Bosnians who wanted to return – it was hell on earth. A chilling stipulation was that twelve prisoners from each side would be held behind, and released only if all the other stipulations of the release had been met by the deadline, 11 October. Hasan Muratović and Momčilo Krajišnik signed the agreements.

At noon I went to the bridge to check with the French soldiers, the Bosnians and the Serbs that everything was in place. I was nervous; I didn't want anything to go wrong. Before I left the Residency, I asked an officer to see that we didn't have a crowd of UNPROFOR military spectators on the bridge. It was understandable that our colleagues wanted to witness a good-news event, but it complicated things if there were dozens of people walking around if they had nothing to contribute. Also, it attracted media attention, and we'd taken pains not to alert the media, as we didn't want the whole thing to turn into a spectacle. I checked everything with the Bosnians, then drove across the bridge to check things with the Serbs. The mines on the bridge had been removed for the occasion. When I got back to the Bosnian side there were a dozen soldiers hanging around, including the officer I'd asked to prevent this. I blew my top, told them all to go back to where they'd come from and threatened that there would be serious consequences if any dared return. We were busy with an extremely serious and delicate operation, not a circus.

It was agreed that we'd start the exchange at 14h00. ICRC
arrived, and so did Mašović and Bulajić. And the buses with the
prisoners, which parked on either side of the bridge. I thought
about those 351 men, finally within sight of freedom, and tears
sprang to my eyes. But if anyone had thought we'd simply arrive,
do a head count, drive the buses onto the bridge and let the men go,
they were sorely mistaken. Every name on every list had to be
checked over and over again. And then the problems started. The
Bosnian prisoner who was supposed to be brought from Belgrade
had suddenly disappeared. Immediately Mašović wanted to call off
the whole operation. We coaxed him into waiting and seeing. Then
we received a report that there were problems in Goražde with the
medevac: reportedly some of the evacuees weren't considered ill
enough to be evacuated, and people who weren't sick at all were
storming the vehicles, trying to get out. Didn't they understand, I
thought sadly: everyone in Goražde was ill. How could people
who'd been starving and freezing for almost three years *not* be ill?
Matters were deteriorating by the minute. The Serbs threatened to
call off the medical evacuation. No medevac, no prisoner exchange,
said the Bosnians. On both sides of the bridge, groups of people had
gathered; they'd been alerted that their husbands, fathers or brothers
were to be freed. There was a feeling of excitement and expectation
in the air. They were all looking happy, talking, laughing.

By the time we'd ironed out the problems and again checked the
lists of names against the miserable men in the buses, it was late
afternoon. The first snow had settled on the mountains, and it was
bitingly cold once the feeble winter sun began to set. With everything apparently in place to start the complex process, Mašović
started grumbling that it was getting too late to complete the
operation before dark, and suggested we stop, return the prisoners
and continue the next day. I refused point-blank. The prisoners had
been through agonies most people couldn't even imagine. They'd

known for some time that they were to be exchanged, and now they were here. Over my dead body would they go back to those hell-holes called prisons. A Bosnian official complained that it was cold, and everyone was tired. I lost my temper. 'Yes, we're all tired,' I snapped at him, 'and we're all cold. I, too, am tired and cold. But those wretched men have been sitting in those uncomfortable buses for hours, hungry and shivering, and urinating through a hole in the side of the bus. As long as they're prepared to wait, we aren't leaving. If you're cold and tired, go and sit in your car and turn on the heater.' He turned around and walked to his car like a chastened schoolboy. I could hardly believe myself; I was behaving like a witch.

We continued. Gradually the people waiting for the prisoners left to meet the curfew. One by one the sticking points were sorted out. One by one, new ones popped up. I was rushing back and forth across the bridge: to the Serb side to negotiate with Dragan Bulajić, then back to try to twist Mašović's arm. I was exhausted. At nine o'clock Deyan arrived with a flask of coffee, laced with whisky. I hadn't had anything to eat or drink since morning, and it restored and warmed me up a little. The exchange was stuck on a minor point, but we couldn't continue if it wasn't resolved. A Serb official in Kopaći was refusing to let the medevac continue because he had a problem – with what it wasn't clear, because by the time the message had been relayed via several UNPROFOR soldiers to Bulajić, it had become unintelligible. I suggested Bulajić talk to him directly to try to resolve the deadlock, but the mountains in the way made direct radio contact with Kopaći impossible. I asked the UNPROFOR military whether something could be done. They brought a signals officer, who suggested setting up relay connections. He explained that a signal would be relayed to one point, then from there to another. I didn't understand at all how it would work, but would settle for anything. However, it would take time. It doesn't matter I said, we'll wait. They started working. Can faith really move mountains? I wondered. If I prayed hard enough, would those mountains move?

At 3 a.m., Sergio de Mello called me on the Motorola and said, 'Look, you've done what you can. Call it a day – you can continue tomorrow morning.' I'd been on the bridge for fourteen hours. My feet were throbbing and I was numb with cold and fatigue. The thought of warmth and a bed almost made me weep. But there were 351 men who had, for over twelve hours, been huddled in the buses within sight of freedom. How could we stop now that we'd come this far, while there was still a chance to succeed, and allow them to go back to prison? From experience I knew that if we stopped we'd probably have to start the whole process all over. By the next day new obstacles would have emerged. And by the time we got here again, if we ever did, it could be months from now. By then some of them might be dead. Or the war could escalate and both sides refuse to release any prisoners. And that after they'd been metres away from freedom. No, we wouldn't stop unless there was absolutely no way of resolving the problem. It was just as well I persisted. A short while later the radio connection with Kopaći was established, and Dragan could talk to the obstreperous officer. He gave him a direct order to let the medical evacuees leave, and finally the convoy was under way.

Just after six o'clock on the morning of 6 October, we received a report that the medical convoy was within sight of Sarajevo. Around seven o'clock it was confirmed that they'd arrived at Koševo Hospital and the patients were being admitted. The prisoners could be released.

The buses were brought onto the bridge and the men disembarked. A new day was breaking, cold, crisp and clear. The first day of freedom for 351 men, some of whom had been subjected to unspeakable horrors. They all had the grey look of mortally exhausted, traumatised and undernourished people. Their shoulders were bent, their faces haggard. Some showed hardly any emotion, others were weeping. Still, they didn't look as bad as I'd expected. Both sides had had more than two months to get them into reasonable shape for release, and nobody wanted to release bruised and battered skeletons, because they expected the media to be there. And they were. Overnight they'd got wind of the operation and some early birds started arriving, but the French soldiers were keeping them behind the containers that had been set up as barricades.

I watched as the men disembarked from the buses, one by one, setting foot on home ground. They were alive and they were home. But there was nobody to welcome them. It was early, and their families, who'd waited until the curfew forced them to leave the previous might, had not yet returned to the bridge. There was no president or prime minister to welcome them home, to thank them for the sacrifices they'd made, to promise them peace. I felt empty.

At the morning briefing I was congratulated on the success of the mission by Sergio and General Rose. After the briefing, Claire, the civilian UNPROFOR spokesperson, asked whether I'd answer the media's questions on the operation at the press briefing later that morning. All I could think of was bed. I'd worked more than twenty-four hours straight without rest and was on the point of collapse. And in a few hours I had to meet Justice Richard Goldstone and accompany him to a meeting with the Bosnian government. Reluctantly, I agreed. She was back in a few minutes, saying ICRC had objected: they felt it was 'their mission' and they should handle the questions. I could only smile wryly. While I'd been running around on the bridge all night in the freezing cold, pleading, arguing, negotiating, planning, the ICRC representatives were sitting in their car with the engine running to keep the heater going. The only support I'd received was from my UNPROFOR colleagues – and now it was ICRC's mission? I couldn't care less, and told Claire so. I had breakfast and a shower, climbed into fresh clothes, wrote notes for my report on the exchange and then went to meet Justice Goldstone. On the way there, I suddenly changed my mind. When I met Goldstone outside the Presidency, an icy cold gale was blowing us almost off our feet. We shook hands, said a few words about South Africa, and then I explained that I'd been up all night, simply couldn't make a rational contribution to the pending meeting, much as I would have wanted to, and asked him please to excuse me. He said he understood and it was fine. I went home and climbed into bed.

While we'd been in the final throes of the frenzy around the Pope's visit, General Rose gave me a letter from the director of the Opera Italiana Cultural Association in Venice, Michele Stochino Weiss. It was a request to help the Sarajevo Philharmonic Orchestra get to Italy where they'd perform, inter alia, at a concert at the ancient Greek Theatre in Taormina. The concert, organised with UNHCR cooperation, was to raise funds for the people of war-torn Rwanda. It would be marvellous to have an orchestra from Sarajevo playing there. If anybody in the world understood the agony of the Rwandans, the Sarajevans did. It would be as important for Sarajevans to lend their support to people in a similar predicament as for the organisers to have the Sarajevans for their publicity campaign. But as usual the logistics were mind-boggling. This wasn't half a dozen people and a few crates as in the case of the 'Witnesses' exhibition. There were forty-three orchestra members and all their instruments. The simplest way would have been to put them on an UNHCR flight to Italy. But even though UNHCR was involved, the countries running the airlift could not be persuaded to fly the orchestra to Italy. The alternative was for the orchestra to fly to Zagreb in an UNPROFOR aircraft. But by now a formal order had been issued prohibiting this kind of thing. Yes, well. I called Sergio, who agreed to help, and he roped in my former colleague Guy de Battista. It was a mammoth task. On the one hand I was battling the UN bureaucracy, and on the other hand I had to provide progress reports to Michele and Messrs Nuhanović and Pajanović of the Sarajevo Philharmonic – when there was no progress to report. The orchestra people understood. Michele didn't. Like other people in the 'normal' world, he couldn't understand why the orchestra couldn't just board one of the dozens of aeroplanes flying in and out of Sarajevo every day. I didn't understand it either, but those were the conditions 'on the ground'.

The concerts in Italy were to be held from 17 to 25 September, and Michele asked if the orchestra could leave on the 7th to allow them some time for rest and rehearsal beforehand. Of course it wouldn't work like this. There were more obstacles than even I could foresee, and from the word go it was impossible to make the 7th their departure date, because we were expecting the Pope on the 8th and all our efforts were concentrated on that. We just had to try our best for the soonest possible date after the 7th. It was a real endurance test, but I'd had enough 'training', and after three weeks of intense bargaining and conniving, everything was ready for them to leave. We'd managed to 'charter' an UNPROFOR aircraft (a Russian Antonov) for the orchestra, but there wasn't one available that could take all forty-three passengers. Thus Mr Pajanović would fly to Zagreb on 22 September on a regular UNPROFOR flight, Mr Nuhanović, and two of the musicians, Messrs Romanić and Simonje, on Friday 23 September, and the remaining thirty-nine passengers on the special flight, also on the Friday. They'd arrive in Italy just in time for their concert, with no time to rest or rehearse. But there was no other way. All forty-three passengers would return to Sarajevo on 30 September.

When I checked with G-3 ops on the Friday morning of the orchestra's scheduled departure, I was told there was heavy fighting around the airport, and that it might have to be closed for all flights. At nine o'clock, when I arrived at the National Theatre where we'd pick up our thirty-nine passengers, they were all there. Some had been there since seven. They hadn't been out of the city in two and a half years, and were as excited as children. My heart sank. How was I going to tell them they might not go? It had to be done. I took a deep breath, and told them. But, I promised, if there was the slightest chance of getting them out, I'd do it. The soldiers loaded the instruments and the musicians clambered aboard the APCs. The next problem, as usual, was at the UNPROFOR airport checkpoint. The French soldiers wouldn't let the APCs full of Bosnian civilians through, and I had to rush around like a maniac to find a French officer who could order them to do so. It drove me insane that I'd spent weeks getting papers filled in, signed and stamped, to be refused entry by some snot-nosed UNPROFOR soldiers who couldn't read. All the while the heavy fighting continued, along with repeated warnings that the airport might be closed. As usual in Sarajevo, everything was balanced on a knife-edge.

Miraculously, the airport was still open. But then another disaster struck. The Antonov, I was told, had arrived – but it had a flat tyre! A flat tyre? Surely they couldn't be serious! I'd never in my life heard of an aircraft with a flat tyre. The members of the orchestra were now even more excited, because they were on the point of leaving. Or so they thought. This trip meant the world to them, and now I had to give them more bad news. I had no idea whether it would be possible to arrange another aircraft at all, let alone on the same day. I tried making calls from the airport, but they were experiencing communications problems, so I had to drive back to Forward where we had satellite communications. After a frenzied trip back to the city through Snipers' Alley, and several frantic phone calls to Zagreb, I finally, thanks to Guy de Battista, had authorisation for the Sarajevo Philharmonic to board UNPRO-FOR's regular afternoon flight to Zagreb. I rushed back with the happy news. The flight wasn't until three, but I suggested the orchestra wait at the airport. It was dangerous, but if I took them back to the city a myriad other things could go wrong – and that was equally dangerous. They readily agreed to stay, even if it meant several more hours of discomfort in the middle of an immense battle, and with nothing to eat or drink. Damn! I hadn't given a second thought to refreshments while I was trying to arrange the flight, and this wasn't the kind of airport where one could buy coffee and sandwiches at a snack bar. For up to half a dozen people, and if one had the right connections, the French military would oblige with at least a cup of hot coffee. But their makeshift logistics couldn't handle forty people without prior notice. Also, because of the heavy fighting, making coffee wasn't a priority for the French soldiers. That meant I had to grit my teeth, try to ignore the raging battle, and make another death-defying dash to the city and back, across the deadly no-man's-land and down Snipers' Alley, to buy drinks and snacks for the musicians who'd been patiently sitting on their bags since sunrise.

An hour later I was safely back with two boxes of Coke, a box of beer, biscuits, chips and chocolates. We sat outside the reception area and, with variations on the 1812 Overture supplied by Serb artillery and gunners, had a picnic. The musicians hadn't seen such a feast of luxuries for more than two years and polished it off in no time. They were in the best of spirits. There was no aircraft in sight, but they'd made it to the airport and had had a picnic, and in Sarajevo that was as good as it got.

At three o'clock they boarded the flight to Zagreb.

On my return to Forward, I called Michele to tell him his orchestra was en route to Zagreb. He was very pleased, and invited me to attend the concert in the old Greek Theatre on the 25th as his guest. The dear man, despite all my explanations of the immense difficulties of life in Sarajevo, couldn't get his head around it. I didn't receive the invitation until the next day. Even if I'd received it the previous day, there was no way I could have made it there in time.

I didn't give the orchestra a second thought from the minute they left. I had to concentrate every bit of energy and effort on the POW exchange. All the arrangements for the orchestra's return on 30 September had been made, and Guy was taking care of that in Zagreb. But a few days after they left, I received a call to ask if they could return on 10 October. I told them to speak to Guy, and he arranged for them to return later.

Then, on 4 October, I received a letter stating that the orchestra had been invited to play for the Pope, and it would mean a lot to him since he hadn't been able to come to Sarajevo. To me it seemed like an opportunity to make amends for my opposition to the Pope's visit and my possible role in having it cancelled. Unfortunately the orchestra had to wait for confirmation of a date from the Vatican, and according to available information it wouldn't be until the end of October, or even early November. I said that was fine, and asked Guy to cancel the arrangements for 10 October. Since I was going home at the end of October and wouldn't be in Sarajevo, I told Michele to organise their return flight directly with Guy. That, as far as I was concerned, was that as regards the Sarajevo Philharmonic Orchestra.

But of course it wasn't. I should have heard the Wicked Witch of the West cackling.

CHAPTER 27

GETTING OUT

OCTOBER–DECEMBER 1994

WINTER WAS FAST APPROACHING. The fact that there might be gas wasn't much in the way of reassurance, and seeing that the Serbs were again stopping humanitarian aid, and not even allowing convoys with supplies for UNPROFOR into the city, people were making whatever plans they could for survival. Some wood was brought into the city, but it was a drop in the ocean and very expensive. Darko, Viktor's interpreter, who'd heard it was possible to buy wood in Hrasnica, went with another Civil Affairs officer and bought wood at a reasonable price, and agreed to take me to place an order. People in Sarajevo were already doing an inventory of what could be burnt in the way of shoes, clothes, books and furniture, but by then there wasn't much left. In the park opposite my flat, a hut-like structure burnt down, and by the next day it had been stripped of every piece of wood. I went to Hrasnica with Darko and placed an order for twenty bags of wood. I'd have to make two trips to fetch it, which was fine – although the route was anything but pleasant. The road was hazardous, in terrible condition and hardly passable, and the Bosnian soldiers at the checkpoints were very hostile. I understood their anger, but it was still unnerving. Their families and friends had not the means to buy nor transport wood to their homes in preparation for winter, and they were angry at outsiders who could make life easier for themselves. They had no way of knowing that almost all the wood I was buying would go to local families. As it turned out, I never used a single piece of the wood myself. On Monday 17 October, I went to fetch the wood I'd ordered. I borrowed bags wherever I could, because part of the deal was that you had to bring your own bags. This time the soldiers were even more unfriendly than when I'd gone with Darko, and I felt vulnerable and insecure. But I gritted my teeth and pressed on. At the home of the man supplying the wood, there was a large pile of timber. Fortunately my leather gloves were in the glove compartment, and I put them on and got stuck in alongside the man and his son, putting wood into the bags. The man said something to his son and wife and smiled at me warmly. His son interpreted in very broken English that his father was pleased with me, because not even the men who'd fetched wood had helped pack it. They thought because they paid they didn't need to, he said. As a child, I was expected to contribute to household chores, and even as an adult I could never sit and watch others work without at least offering to help. It was strenuous work, and then we had to pack the bags in the car. I decided to squeeze in as many bags as I could and leave it at that, because I didn't want to make another nerve-racking trip to Hrasnica. The longer I was in Sarajevo, the less I wanted to travel out of the city. My nerves were frayed, and I didn't want to add any more stress if I could help it. I only went to Kiseljak, Lukavica and Pale, not to mention Zagreb or Italy, when I absolutely had to.

Loading the wood was quite a job, but I'd spent my entire life moving from one place to another, and could squeeze more stuff into a given space than anyone I knew. So I surveyed the space and the wood and then directed the packing like an expert. After much huffing and puffing and rearranging, there were seventeen bags of wood in the car. I explained that I'd take only what we'd loaded, but would pay for the twenty bags I'd ordered, but the good man wouldn't hear of it, and we parted friends. The trip back to Sarajevo was even worse than the one to Hrasnica, and I was very glad I'd decided not to return for more wood. At one place a man on a bicycle got a fright when he suddenly heard the car behind him, swerved, hit the bank on the side of the road and went crashing down. I had of course seen him and would have passed him quite safely, but this happened close to a checkpoint and in full view of the soldiers on guard, all of whom threw looks full of anger and reproach at me. There was no point in even trying to explain that I'd had nothing to do with the man's fall. They didn't speak English and my Bosnian was too poor, and I just said I was very sorry about ten times. They scrutinised my UNPROFOR ID and the car far more thoroughly than was necessary, and when I left I was close to tears from impotence, frustration and general dejection. It was late afternoon by the time I arrived in Sarajevo. I went to Jasna's house, and we carried three bags of wood into her garden shed. Then I went to Mima's flat, and Anja and I wrestled three bags of wood up four flights of stairs to their storeroom. Armin was waiting at his father's flat, my next stop, and he carried five bags up the seven flights of stairs, and after that two bags up another five flights of stairs for him and his flatmate Damir. We carried the last four bags up the two flights of stairs to my flat: two bags for Irma and her mother, and two for me. I was so exhausted from the mental and physical exertion I could hardly breathe, and was just fed up with everything. I very much felt like packing up and leaving. But of course I would never have done that; I had work to do, and that was the credo by which I had been raised and lived: the Calvinist work ethic, to earn your keep by the sweat of your brow. Boy, was I sweating.

Because of the Serb convoy blockade, UNPROFOR was running out of food, and even fuel. There was no fuel for the generator at Forward, the offices were freezing, and I worked dressed like an Eskimo, gloves and all. We only used our vehicles when we absolutely had to. All indications were that winter would be as bad as it could be. The Serbs were again shelling Sarajevo and the snipers were back at their posts. Things were looking grim.

The Bosnian government extended the call-up orders to all men who had until then been doing other war-related tasks, such as working for radio and TV. Within UNPROFOR, documents circulated of an impending thrust by the Bosnian army in a last-ditch attempt to drive back the Serbs. A possibility opened up for Armin to work abroad. The previous time I'd helped him leave Sarajevo, to visit his brother in Italy, he couldn't wait to come back. I might – might – be able to get him out again. It was very difficult for him to leave Sarajevo, because his father, sister and niece were there, but they encouraged him to go. Anja had received a scholarship to study in the US, so she also needed to leave. Since my plans to go home on leave had already been made, I had to entrust the task of getting Armin and Anja out of the city to someone else. The only person I felt I could trust with that was Colum Murphy. Anja's affairs were more or less straightforward. She had the right papers, and all she needed was to get onto a flight from Sarajevo to Zagreb. From there everything had been taken care of. Armin was an altogether different kettle of fish. He was a male of fighting age, and would only be given permission to leave the city under exceptional circumstances. As with Ines, I forged papers and bent all kinds of rules to help him. Colum was in Zagreb and would only return once I'd gone, so I left all the instructions in writing for him to study on his return. Then I set off for South Africa. I called regularly from Johannesburg for progress reports. Armin was to leave Sarajevo on 11 November and Anja at the end of the month. I knew how difficult it had been for Ines to leave. Bosnian families were close, and it was terrible not knowing whether they'd ever see each other again. On the morning of the 11th, I called to wish Armin luck. The plan was that he would go from Zagreb to Umag, a town in northern Croatia, where an old colleague of his was staying. From there he'd go to Italy. As with Ines, there were numerous problems. The soldier who took him to the airport just dropped him off and left him there, and he had to struggle through mud and slush with his heavy bags. He was quite chuffed, though, when he was given a seat on Akashi's jet and his fellow passenger was CNN's attractive Jackie Shumanski. When they arrived in Zagreb, everyone scattered and left him there, with no idea what to do. When he asked where to go he was misdirected, with the result that his entry visa was never stamped. Later this would cause all sorts of other problems.

The last time I spoke to Colum before heading back to Sarajevo, he assured me everything had been sorted out for Anja's departure. This time I'd been in a better frame of mind in South Africa and made the most of my leave, concentrating all my energy on creating a happy atmosphere and helping Annéne through her Matric exams. On 26 November I caught a flight via Vienna to Zagreb. From there I'd return to Sarajevo and be back in the office on Monday the 28th. But while I'd been on leave, the situation in Sarajevo had taken a turn for the worse. When I arrived in Zagreb, I heard that the Serbs had even stopped UNPROFOR flights in and out of Sarajevo. This was bad news, not because I was in any great hurry to return, but because Anja had been scheduled to leave on the very next flight out and was now marooned in Sarajevo. Flights were expected to resume on 2 December, and I booked in at a spa not far from Zagreb, where accommodation was cheaper than in a city hotel. When I returned to Zagreb, it was to find out that there were still no flights, and that road traffic had in the meantime also been stopped. I went back to the spa and called HQ every day to check about flights, but there were none. I'd used up all my leave, and so started going into Zagreb HQ every day to help out, since many people had gone home for the Christmas holidays. Elvira Coakley, whom I'd met on the UNTAG mission in Namibia, offered me the use of her apartment when she went on leave. In the meantime I was worried about Anja, and called Mima as soon as I could to find out what was happening. She said Anja had managed to leave, and was in Zagreb en route to the US. I arranged to meet her, and was deeply shocked when I heard how she'd managed to leave Sarajevo. With no hope of flights any time soon, she'd arranged to leave through the airport tunnel. This didn't surprise me – I knew Anja. But it was a horrific experience. They had to wade through mud and thigh-high, icy water, then travel on the back of a truck and crawl up Mount Igman on their knees while there was heavy fighting close by. She, like Ines, didn't shed a tear while telling me of her farewell to Mima, family and friends, and her harrowing journey to Zagreb. She had the same tight, stoic mask I'd seen on Ines's face when she'd left. And Anja said the same: 'I didn't cry, because if I started crying, I'd never stop.'

One day I received a call from Michele concerning the orchestra. I thought they were by now either back in Sarajevo or settled somewhere else, but discovered that they were all in Zagreb, stranded, and wanted to return to Sarajevo. I started the exhaustive planning and organising necessary for their return.

One of my colleagues, who worked in Akashi's office, told me there was a new position in Zagreb, and a number of my colleagues in Zagreb had proposed me, because they thought I was perfect for the job. So did I. It required briefing visiting dignitaries about the situation and conditions in Sarajevo, and nobody else had spent two years in the city, as I had. Also, my colleagues felt I'd done my bit 'in the field', and I couldn't agree more. Everyone was certain I'd get the job, and I started making plans. I found a flat in the Zagreb suburb Jarun, sparsely but comfortably furnished, with a view from the balcony over a snowy field and a clump of trees. For a while I borrowed the car of a colleague who'd gone home over Christmas, then arranged for the UN transport people to pick me up in the morning and take me home at night. That was better: no problems having to dig a car out of the snow in the mornings as I'd had to do several times. I started settling in. Life was wonderful.

I gave up my flat in Sarajevo, and asked Mima to pack up my things and keep them with her until I could fetch them. I was so certain I wasn't going back, I told her to take all the wood, food, cosmetics, soap and whatever else there was. But the official in charge had decided differently. Someone in his office said they should never have suggested me for the job directly but in a round-about way, because he rejected everything that wasn't his idea. The bottom line was, I had to return to Sarajevo. It was awful. I was drained, stripped to the bone and afraid I might have a total mental collapse. It was very difficult; I'd lost my nerve. The thought of a flight to Sarajevo with the fighting going on sent me into a terrible state. I felt absolutely certain I was going to die. I didn't easily expose my weaknesses to other people, but I was trembling inside and out, and told some of my colleagues. They were furious with the small-minded man who was forcing me to return. So was I. But I was an idiot. I should simply have refused to go back, and they would have had to find me a job in Zagreb; it was as simple as that. I don't know why I didn't do just that. Partly because I was no longer thinking straight. Partly because I was brought up not to make a fuss. Partly because I was too proud. I should have shaken that ridiculous nonsense by the time I was forty, but I hadn't. And so I returned to Sarajevo.

CHAPTER 28

THE LAST STRAW

JANUARY 1995

WHILE I WAS MAROONED IN ZAGREB, I called Claire to let her know what was happening and check about Mipić, who was staying with her. She said Mipić was fine, no need to worry. Claire had decided to leave Sarajevo, and arranged for Mipić to stay at the Annex where Jasna could keep an eye on her. When I finally returned to Sarajevo in mid-January, I immediately went to look for Mipić. As I arrived at the Residency, the Danish guard at the gate said, 'Your cat will be very happy to see you. She was here yesterday, waiting for you.' I went on a search but couldn't find her anywhere. Jasna said not to worry, she was around somewhere; she'd been there all the time. However, she'd caused quite a stir, because Rose had found her sleeping on his bed. He was not amused. I walked around, calling for her. I went to the flat in case she'd gone back there. But she'd disappeared. I had strong suspicions that someone had got rid of her. She'd lived at HQ for a year and a half, knew every inch of the territory and everyone knew her. She wouldn't have left of her own free will. I never saw her again.

Many things had changed when I returned to the Residency after my absence of more than two months. Viktor was leaving. Carlos had left, Deyan and Luuk were getting ready to leave and there were a dozen new Civil Affairs officers. Rose had left and been replaced by another British general, Rupert Smith, and the atmosphere at BH Forward took an immense turn for the better. But the situation in the city was dire. And I was physically, mentally and emotionally overwrought.

Having given up my flat, I was sleeping on a mattress in my office until I could find a new place. The office next to mine had been turned into a Dutch TV room, and off-duty soldiers watched television and videos there until three in the morning. It was -20°C, the pipes had burst and there was no water in the Annex. The women's bathroom in the container halfway between the Annex and the Residency had become rundown and dirty, and I had to climb the icy marble stairs and then brave 100 metres of frozen wasteland to get there and back. Icicles clung to the frozen branches like leftover Christmas decorations and reflected thin rays of shivering light. Civilians were again allowed to eat at Forward, but the food was cold and very unappealing. There was no gas or electricity in the city. My feet were permanently frozen. I wished I had cigarettes – and I didn't smoke.

Colum went on leave and asked if I'd stay in his flat to ensure no one else moved in. It was a godsend. When he left, I took my things to his flat, just after lunch, and went back to the office. It was growing dark by the time I left for home, earlier than usual, because I didn't know my way around and didn't want to arrive in a strange place after dark.

It was too far to walk so I took the car, having been assured by Colum that the police kept an eye on UNPROFOR vehicles in the neighbourhood. I drove a fair distance up the narrow mountain road to find a place to turn the car around, so that I wouldn't have to do it the next morning. On my way down, the wheels struck a patch of lethal black ice, and it was touch and go that I didn't lose control of the car and plummet down the side of the mountain. It was a frightening experience – and totally derailed me. I parked the car and stumbled to the flat through the snow with one thought in my mind: I needed hot tea to steady my nerves. Colum had said his area had gas but there was none, and with tears streaming down my face I searched through the flat for some whisky or brandy, but in vain. By now it was dark, and, sobbing loudly, I wandered aimlessly through the freezing apartment with a spluttering third-grade Sarajevo candle clutched in my shaking hand. In the lounge I collapsed in a chair and cried like a lost child. When I'd calmed down I piled all the blankets in the flat onto the bed, took off my boots and uniform, pulled on two pairs of warm trousers over my thermal underwear, put on two pairs of wool socks, wrapped my large Russian wool scarf around my head and face, and crawled into bed. But I couldn't stop shivering, and kept thinking that I could have been dead, or lying out there in the snow in pitch darkness waiting for an UNPROFOR rescue team. I started crying again.

During a sleepless night I realised the time had come to leave. The evening's experience didn't warrant my vastly exaggerated reaction. Yes, it was unnerving, but I'd experienced far worse. It was clear: I was on the edge. A year, even six months earlier, the incident would have left me a little shaky and thankful to have escaped unharmed, but not on the brink of a total breakdown. I had to pack it in.

The next day I resigned.

The end of February, when I would be leaving the mission and Sarajevo, was fast approaching. These were some of the most difficult weeks of my life. During intense emotional experiences, people become closer to each other than they ordinarily would. And after two years of being so firmly intertwined with the fate of the city and its people, I had to start disentangling myself. I went to Lukavica, to tie up loose ends on things I was working on. There I spoke at length with Brane and Indjić about recent developments. Brane said: 'The situation now is very tense. The Bosnians carry out attacks all around the twenty-kilometre zone and think the Serbs are bound by the NATO ultimatum not to attack Sarajevo.' Neither side had respected the NATO ultimatum for months. Major Indjić was even more angry and bitter than usual. Because I'd been decent and helpful to him, he treated me with a curious kind of ... not respect or affection exactly – perhaps esteem was the word. While we sipped our coffee, he looked at me very seriously and quietly said, 'It is good that you are getting out. Don't change your mind.' This was very unlike his usual ranting about wiping out all the Muslims and the Serb rhetoric of taking back what was rightfully theirs. A shudder ran down my spine. Brane nodded gravely, then said, 'It is going to get very ugly.' I could imagine what that meant. It would be hell in spring, when they resumed fighting in earnest. The worst, fiercest fighting always happened in spring, after the Bosnians were further weakened by another winter. 'They think we will not attack Sarajevo, but we will,' Brane continued. I thought that was a strange choice of words, seeing that they'd been attacking Sarajevo every day for three years. But I knew what he meant and I found it hard to associate Brane with it: the definitive battle, fighting in the streets, going from door to door slitting people's throats and raping women and children as the Serbs had done in every other town and city they'd taken. I didn't think they had the courage to take on Sarajevo again, and I knew that if they did, they'd get a hell of a surprise. But I said nothing.

On 9 February a Japanese delegation visited Sarajevo, and one of my last tasks was to brief them about the situation in Bosnia and accompany them on their high-level meetings, including those at the Presidency. I asked our military assistant Philippe to drive us. I had something in common with the Japanese: Japan and South Africa were among the few countries that hadn't yet recognised Bosnia-Herzegovina as an independent state, and we spent an interesting morning discussing the whys and wherefores of this. I briefed the delegation on some of the political and practical issues in Sarajevo and Bosnia, and also about people's feelings of gloom, despair, frustration and hopelessness. Ambassador Kurasawa said this was to be expected during 'the season of war', and that I obviously spoke for the people of Sarajevo. Then Minister Sato said he'd heard about me, that I'd become too Sarajevan, too attached to the city and too adapted to the way of life here. 'Oh,' I said, and thought, 'Well, you try living here for two years and keeping your distance.' But I said nothing more. When I took them to Prime Minister Silajdžic's office, he came out to meet them, and as always started speaking to me in Bosnian. As usual I answered in English, saying that my Bosnian wasn't good enough for a conversation with him. He apologised and said, 'I thought you were one of us.' I saw the knowing look that passed among the Japanese.

My last tense interaction with the Serbs stemmed from the visit by the Japanese delegation. They'd brought a CD player from Zagreb for one of the new Civil Affairs officers, who was Japanese, but forgot it in the car and discovered it on the way back to the airport. They asked me to give it to her. With the delegation safely at the airport, we used the road past the Serb checkpoint rather than the road through Dobrinja, which we'd used on the way there because it was Bosnian territory and safer. But it was very congested. The Serb soldier on duty asked what was in the box in the back of the car. Philippe said we didn't know, and got out to open the box for the soldier, who asked whether we had papers for the CD player. The minute I saw the expression on the soldier's face, I knew we could expect trouble. While he was explaining that there were regulations against bringing 'strategic equipment' into Sarajevo, I was thinking in highest gear. He rambled on that he'd have to confiscate it, but would give us a receipt. He'd take it to the Ilidža police station and we could fetch it there later. Ha, I knew very well how that worked. Nobody would ever see it again. My story was ready. I simply shrugged and said, 'That's fine, as long as you then take the responsibility to see that Mr Krajišnik gets it, and explain to him why it was you, and not I, delivering it.' He was immediately on his guard. Why, what did I mean? Well, I lied, the Japanese delegation we'd just taken to the airport had brought it as a gift for Mr Krajišnik, but unfortunately we couldn't make it to Pale, and they'd phoned him and said I'd bring it the next day. The soldier was between the devil and the deep blue sea. Then he thought of something: Why, he wanted to know, had Philippe said he didn't know what it was? I was giving an Oscar-winning performance, not my first in Sarajevo. Excuse me, I said, you asked the driver whether he knew what it was, and he said no, because he didn't know, or for whom it was meant. If you'd asked me, I would have told you, as I just did. As a good military man, the soldier could relate to the 'need-to-know' principle, and I could see him crumbling. I kept going. 'If you take it to Ilidža, we won't be able to retrieve it in time to take it to Pale tomorrow morning, but as long as you give me the receipt that's fine – I'll just give that to Mr Krajišnik and tell him his gift is in Ilidža.'

I turned it up a notch. 'Philippe,' I snapped, 'please give him the parcel, I'm late for a meeting.' The soldier was convinced. Nobody handed things over without putting up a fight. No, he said, if you have to take it to Mr Krajišnik, you take it.

The poor soldier was only about twenty. Another soldier approached and asked what was going on. The young guy said, '*Ništa, ništa*' ['nothing, nothing']. We shook hands with him, and drove off. En route to the Bosnian checkpoint I made up another story in case they wanted to confiscate the CD player. I'd say it was a gift from the Japanese ambassador for his old friend and former ambassador, Mr Dervisbegović, whom they couldn't see because he had the flu.

'Wow, you did well there,' Philippe said with grudging admiration.

'Wait until you've been here two years,' I said. 'It comes with the territory.'

'I'm not crazy,' he said, and laughed. 'When my time's up, I'm out of here.'

CHAPTER 29

DON'T FORGET US

FEBRUARY 1995

MY LAST WORKING DAYS WERE FRUSTRATING. It felt strange having to programme myself to become detached, to cut myself loose from things that had come to matter perhaps too much, as Minister Sato had said. There were meetings about yet another prisoner exchange. The UNHCR spokesman said people in Bihać were facing starvation. I didn't know how to behave about matters that were being discussed and planned, but that would only happen after I was gone. I couldn't promise anyone I'd try my best for them, because in a few short weeks I'd have no influence over anything that happened in Sarajevo or elsewhere in Bosnia.

The nights were crisp and cold, and more cold was predicted. The Serbs at the checkpoints were again becoming more belligerent. Definitely a sign of things to come.

Armin's good friend and flatmate Damir and I went to Dobrinja to take a parcel to his family. In terms of agreements that had been negotiated with the Serbs during 1994, some Sarajevans were allowed to leave the city, but only after special application and under stringent conditions. There was a long line of cars in Dobrinja waiting to cross the airport to Butmir and Hrasnica, but they weren't laden with luggage, so these were people who'd be returning. It appeared as though everyone who could had already left Sarajevo. And the people still in Sarajevo were either those with too much to lose if they went, or with nothing to lose. Damir told me that 1 800 young people had left the city in the last three months. How they'd managed to leave I had no idea, but I thought, 'Good for them!' As Damir said, the government was just looking for 'fresh meat' to send to the trenches. Every time this topic came up – the expected major battles in spring – I felt frightened and sad for all the friends I was leaving behind. I wept constantly at the thought that they had to stay and face – who knew what.

Peter Deck and I discussed the situation, and I was grateful I still had a few colleagues to talk to who really knew what it was like. The new military intake and civilians I was working with had yet to learn about the reality of life in Sarajevo and other Bosnian enclaves. Most Bosnians didn't have two Deutschmarks to scrape together for a little food from the market. For them there was no buying fresh meat, cheese, milk, fresh fruit and vegetables, and imported goods at the markets. No meals at the recently reopened restaurants New Concept, Ada's, Bohemie or even Indi's Pizza, all frequented by UN personnel.

It had become the custom to arrange a going-away party for UNPROFOR civilians. We'd sent off Viktor and Claire in that fashion in January. A dinner was arranged at one of the elegant restaurants and money collected for a gift, usually a painting. Such an evening cost each participant a pretty penny. I asked my friends not to buy a gift for me, and for us to have drinks and a snack at the unfashionable cafe where the soldiers had their meals, and for the money to be donated instead to my friend Gertruda's children's charity. At the end of the evening I was handed an envelope with the money for Naša Djeca, and as soon as I got to my room, I ripped it open to count the hundreds of dollars inside. I almost fell to the floor. Inside the envelope was a pathetic $55. This money was for children without food, clothes and, in many cases, parents! I was limp with disappointment. The dinner-and-gift routine would have cost these same people over $500, and they would have spent it willingly. I was still learning the most astonishing things about human nature. I felt like giving the money right back to them, and have often regretted not doing that. I took $500 from my fast dwindling personal funds and put it in the envelope.

I had many friends and had to say my farewells to the people with whom I'd worked and shared so much. This was difficult enough when you were just moving to another city or country. When there was a barbaric war raging and you didn't know whether you'd ever see your friends again, nor even whether they'd still be alive in a few weeks' time, it was heartbreaking. The strain and intensity were sapping me emotionally. First, I went to say goodbye to my friend Lejla, and after that to the Sarajevo Philharmonic Orchestra. Emir Nuhanović, Duška and Mr Romanić who'd all been to Italy, were there. When we were saying our goodbyes, Mr Romanić said, 'Don't forget us.' Lejla had said the same.

Not 'remember us', but 'don't forget us'. Lejla had said the same.

Lejla had been through her own hell for three years, trying to hold onto her family's property in the city. They'd lost their property in Grbavica after the Serb occupation. Her sister was in Italy and her family was urging her to leave, saying that so many other people had lost everything, they at least still had each other, and hanging onto the property wasn't worth her life. But, she said, the three years of hell would have been all for nothing if she left. She simply couldn't. She was painfully thin, her skin had lost its elasticity and there were deep indentations on her cheek where she leant it on her hand. When I hugged her to say goodbye, she felt like a little bird, small and vulnerable. She said, 'We will be in touch, if we survive here in the city.' And then she added, 'Please don't forget us.'

'Remember us' is a nostalgic request. 'Don't forget us' was a plea. It was a plea not to forget these people who, for three years already, had suffered indescribable deprivations and loss – and had been forgotten by the world.

I could never forget. I would always remember Lejla telling me how, during December, she would actually weep when she had to get up and get dressed to go to work (for which she wasn't paid), because she was so cold.

And I would always remember Anja saying, 'I had boiled rice with powdered milk for breakfast and I am hungry. I am always hungry.'

Worse than the hunger and the cold was the isolation, the knowledge that you were trapped, and that if you did find a way out, there was nowhere to go. The Bosnians, like all refugees, were no longer welcome anywhere in the world. No one wanted them. And they were proud: they didn't want to live as refugees on handouts. Even though they were the products of socialism, they'd been allowed to have their own businesses, money, a comfortable life and opportunities to travel. And now they were prisoners. Duška had just seen her mother, who lived twelve kilometres from Sarajevo, for the first time in three years, and she could only stay in Sarajevo for two days. Emir had just returned from Konjić, less than an hour's drive from the city, to see his family for the first time since the beginning of the war.

I went on a drive through the city to bid it farewell. I took the long way round, through Baščaršija, past the market that had resembled a slaughterhouse a year earlier. I looked at the houses halfway up the hill, where all life had been stopped by the guns from above; the fortress at the top, basking in the day's last light;

the cemetery, peaceful and so beautiful, with its leaning tombstones, like diminutive towers of Pisa. And at the dusky narrow streets and the destruction and decay, which I hardly noticed any more. Past the eternal flame (the monument dedicated to Sarajevo's World War II liberators), Kamerni Teatr and the Presidency. Past the mosque on the corner where an old man was urinating behind his coat.

I'd left thousands of my footsteps in those streets when shells were exploding everywhere and snipers added to the macabre drama, refusing to run or hide, just fatalistically 'standing my ground' like so many other Sarajevans. Refusing to be intimidated into a state of paralysis or mere sub-human existence. It was crucial to resist, even if all that was gained was psychological victory. When that was all there was, it became vitally important. There were the many homes I'd visited as a guest, where I'd drunk strong Turkish coffee and eaten war cake made with the most incredible ingenuity, where food was grown on balconies in elegant pots meant for elegant plants. Where the hostesses, using the paper from precious books to boil water for coffee, wore gloves while making the fire to preserve their hands since there were no hand creams. And there were the many thousands I'd come here to help, and couldn't help at all. The children who'd begged '*bombon* please' when we walked or drove through the city. The lean, mean dogs, many limping from old shrapnel or bullet wounds. I'd heard little children cry in terror during attacks; I'd heard the dogs howl in agony on being injured. I'd seen a man wandering aimlessly through the streets in the snow, practically naked and oblivious to the bitter cold, his mind lost through who knew what grief and horror.

I'd been here when the city wept for days after the market bomb massacre. And when there'd been a short reprieve from the fighting, I'd been here to see joy return to people's faces, their childlike eagerness to grab at any straw that would help them improve and continue with their lives.

How could I ever forget?

I went to say goodbye to Gertruda in her flat, full of her precious mementos of a life devoted to music. I recalled a frightening Sunday afternoon when the city was shaking under vicious Serb bombardment and we sat quietly looking at each other over our cups of tea, not knowing what to say; and the lemons I'd smuggled out of the Residency's kitchen so that she could have the Vitamin C so crucial for her voice.

I met Selen and Dragana at the Residency, and we shared a few last, awkward words.

Armed with a small stash of used cosmetics, I went to say goodbye to my dear friend Mima. Never before would I have dreamt of offering someone half a bottle of shampoo or deodorant, leftover moisturiser and hand cream. But in this deprived city, it was a precious gift. This was the hardest goodbye. Mima was alone: Seo had died, Anja was in the US. I took some beers and we sat drinking in virtual silence. What was there to say? We both knew the score. When I stood up to leave, she took my hand and walked to the lounge, knelt down next to the tape player and said, 'Let's listen to my favourite song together.' It was one of the current popular favourites, 'Simpatija', a nostalgic love song by the Croatian group Magazin. We sat on the floor with our arms around each other, listening to the song, sobbing. 'What am I going to do when you are gone?' she cried. I felt terrible. I was always working and never had enough time to spend with her – just a quick coffee or the odd evening here and there.

But I knew it had meant something to her to know that I'd been there. I represented the world outside Sarajevo, hope and a normal life, and in two days' time that would be gone, that link would be severed. The Sarajevans, through the grapevine, already knew what I'd learnt from Major Indjić and Brane. They'd merely confirmed rumours that had started months earlier: that the spring of 1995 would bring a final thrust by the Bosnian army to somehow try to end the war, and that was why they were calling up every able-bodied man in Sarajevo. The Serbs, too, knew it was do or die. Three years of war had brought them no closer to the end result they'd expected to achieve within a few weeks in 1992, and there was increasing international pressure on them – and no longer any sympathy. Even Milošević and their brethren in Serbia had turned their backs on them.

It was terribly painful to say goodbye to Irma and my dear friend Jasna. Irma's father was a famous soccer coach abroad and she, like Gertruda, could have left Sarajevo, but had not. I gave them my magazines, some office supplies and other small things, and for Jasna a book of short stories about South Africa. By now I was virtually beyond tears. A strange, dry, choked sound came from my throat when I tried to talk. I just turned around and walked out, feeling very old and very tired.

Studio 99 asked if I'd do a TV interview to talk about my time in Sarajevo, and I agreed. Adil mentioned that the peaceful transition after the 1994 elections in South Africa had surprised the whole world, and asked me what it could be attributed to. I said to one fact only: that Nelson Mandela, unlike the Serb leaders, wanted peace. Had he talked of retribution and settling old scores, there would no doubt have been war. I hoped Radovan Karadžić and his henchmen were watching, and would take to heart what I was saying. But there'd been more than enough attempts at changing their murderous ways, all met with the same scorn and contempt. Nothing, including Mandela's saintly example, would make an iota's impression on them.

The morning of my departure I went to say my final goodbye to Armin's family, his father Hadžo, sister Nerma and niece Lana. I took them boxes packed with my blankets, sheets, towels, medicine, clothes and other things I was leaving behind. What they didn't need they'd give to others.

It was a relief to stumble down the stairs and into the car where Philippe was waiting. I felt that I just couldn't take any more, that if I had to say one more goodbye I'd just crumble and stay. It was more than anyone should have to endure, and I thought of Ines and Anja's stony young faces when they were leaving. They were so young, but they were stronger than me. That was what the Serbs had done to those two lovely girls and tens of thousands of youths like them. It had robbed them of their innocence, and of allowing themselves the luxury of emotions. They had to be strong for the sake of their parents, and to work, provide money, fight in the trenches, fetch water and queue for food.

In these last moments Philippe showed me real kindness. He used his contacts to get me through the final process as painlessly as possible, explained at the airport why I had more than the regulation number of suitcases, and took care of my boxes of books.

In the UNPROFOR aircraft that took me out of Sarajevo was a large government delegation on their way to some meeting or negotiation. I recognised several people, but mercifully didn't know any of them. I wasn't capable of conversation. Any conversation. I was leaving Sarajevo. It had become dearer to me than the land of my birth or any other place I'd ever been. I had wept for its sons and daughters, sharing graves in cemeteries with shattered grave-stones, scattered flowers and the broken bodies of those who had come to mourn. I'd supported and fought for the courageous peo-ple who clung to life through music and film, art and theatre. I'd tried to cheat death by smuggling a handful of lives out of its icy, unrelenting reach. But I was spent, wrung out; I had nothing more to offer.

When the aeroplane finally took off, I cried loud, choking sobs, wrenched straight from my soul. The noise of the take-off drowned out the sound, but it couldn't mask the fact that I was crying. The men in the aircraft – the Bosnian delegation and a few soldiers –

uncomfortably tried to look in any other direction. It didn't matter to me. When you are really distraught you feel no embarrassment.

————————

During the two years I spent in Sarajevo, thousands of people crossed my path, literally and figuratively, like lost souls in the mist. For a fleeting moment they appeared in my vision and were then enveloped by the thick fog of Bosnia's brutal war, never to be seen again. Some were anonymous faces or soon-forgotten names, others were indelibly etched into my memory. It was simply impossible to keep track of everyone and what had become of them. There were still thousands of unanswered questions. About the fate of the children of Bilalovac, Dr Nikolajić in Fojnica, the mindless well-dressed man led by his attractive companion across the Bratstvo Jedinstvo Bridge, the prisoners in Silos Prison who'd occupied so much of my time, the prisoners I'd helped liberate. And about the murderers, rapists and torturers who had devastated a beautiful country and its valiant people.

————————

I had been part of the terrible black legacy of the Bosnian war.

GLOSSARY

ABBREVIATIONS

APC Armoured Personnel Carrier
BH Bosnia (and) Herzegovina
BSA Bosnian Serb Army
Civpol (UN) Civilian police (as opposed to military police)
Commcen Communications Centre
DCOS Deputy Chief of Staff
HVO Croat Council for Defence
ICRC International Committee for the Red Cross
JNA Jugoslovenska Narodna Armija (Yugoslav People's Army)
MSF Medicines Sans Frontieres
NCO Non Commissioned Officer
POW Prisoner of War
PTT Post and Telegraph Head Office
PX 'Post Exchange': in US military terminology bases are 'posts'
RPG Rocket propelled grenade
SAS (British) Special Air Service
SRNA Serb Radio and News Agency
UN United Nations
UNHCR United Nations High Commissioner for Refugees
UNICEF United Nations Children's Fund
UNMO United Nations Military Observer
UNPROFOR United Nations Protection Force (to the Former
  Yugoslavia)
WHO World Health Organisation
WFP World Food Programme

BOSNIAN WORDS

baklava – cake with nuts and honey

burek – pie with meat, vegetables or cheese

čevapčići – grilled minced meat fingers, served with flatbread and yoghurt

kadaif – cake with syrup or honey, similar to baklava

kandilo – simple oil lamp

ništa – nothing

palaćinci – pancakes

sir – white cheese

šlivovic – plum brandy

uštipci – bread dough fried in oil; Afrikaans 'vetkoek'

NOTES ON PRONUNCIATION

A a is 'a' as in blast

E e is 'e' as in yes

C c is 'ts' as in cats

Č č is 'ch' as in march

Ć ć is 'tj' as in tune

Đ đ substituted as 'dj' as in Djure Džaković

H h is 'ch' as in Scottish loch

J j is 'y' as in you

Lj is 'lli' as in million

O o is 'o' as in more

Š š is 'sh' as in shoot

Ž ž is 'zh' as in measure